Selling: Its Broader Dimensions

Selling:

A Macmillan Marketing Book under the General Editorship of
Schuyler F. Otteson

Its Broader Dimensions

TAYLOR W. MELOAN, D.B.A.
Professor and Chairman
Department of Marketing and
Transportation
School of Business
University of Southern California

JOHN M. RATHMELL, Ph.D.
Associate Professor of Marketing
Graduate School of Business
and Public Administration
Cornell University

NEW YORK — THE MACMILLAN COMPANY

First Printing

Library of Congress catalog card number: 60-9956

The Macmillan Company, New York
Brett-Macmillan Ltd., Galt, Ontario

Printed in the United States of America

Preface

The editors have selected articles for this book of readings which they believe supplement, broaden, and enrich the traditional content of college and industry courses in salesmanship. Hence, the title, *Selling: Its Broader Dimensions*. Because the book covers the selling function *in toto,* the editors envision its use, too, in new courses which focus on promotional strategy—the art and science of appropriately blending advertising, personal selling, and sales promotion to achieve company goals.

Because of the swift evolution of American enterprise, there is a continuing need to introduce current thinking into courses on selling. Texts become dated quickly, and college libraries cannot accommodate floodtides of students with lists of assigned periodical articles. An integrated book of well chosen readings provides a ready means of keeping courses up-to-date.

In making the selections, over 3,000 articles were screened from the business literature, and from journals in the behavioral sciences. All text and trade books in the selling field were reviewed too. Because of the wealth of material at the editors' disposal, choices between equally penetrating papers were often difficult to make.

For the convenience of instructors in making assignments, and in integrating this book with other texts of their choice, the readings are divided into six major heads with sub-topics under each. While many of the articles defy exact classification because of broad coverage, their positioning in the book is indicative of their major contributions. Also included is an outline of the subjects traditionally covered in salesmanship courses and the readings which pertain to each.

The editors are indebted to the authors of the selections, and to the publications in which they appeared, for permission to reprint their work. We appreciate, too, the freedom given us in several instances to edit the articles. Permissions to reprint are individually acknowledged at the bottom of the title page of each article.

We wish to express our appreciation to Schuyler F. Otteson of Indiana University, consulting editor of Marketing for The Macmillan Company, for his continuing counsel concerning the selection and arrangement of the material in this book. Our colleagues, Ralph E. Brownlee and Lawrence X. Tarpey provided invaluable library and proof-reading assistance. While ten secretaries typed part of the manuscript, the bulk of the work was done by Shirley Thompson, Marita Wilkinson, and Sally Comfort. We are indebted to each of them.

TAYLOR W. MELOAN
JOHN M. RATHMELL

Contents

V.   THE SALES PROCESS

Improving Selling Effectiveness

Planning, Organizing and Controlling Selling Effort

VI.   KEYS TO CAREER SUCCESS

Creative Thinking and Speaking

Selling: Its Broader Dimensions

SELLING TRENDS AND PERSPECTIVES

part I

For centuries man was unaware of and ignored or slighted the contribution selling could make to his well being. Early in Part I the negative attitudes of the Greeks, Romans, and medieval peoples toward the promotion of goods and services are reviewed. During the Renaissance and the Industrial Revolution, which bred economies of abundance, references to the need for demand-creation activities appeared. However, it was not until early in the twentieth century that "most of the community accepted the salesman, advertising man, and publicist as useful and necessary members of society." This early history plus the current objectives and results of selling efforts in our complex economy are explained in Part I.

More is known today than ever before about the characteristics and attitudes needed for career success in advertising, sales, and promotion. They are examined along with the challenges and the opportunities in these areas. The future is especially bright for those entering industrial selling and the promotion of business services. Current data about the financial and nonmonetary rewards in selling are presented, and common fallacies about the perquisites and travel requirements of the field are exposed.

There is a growing body of knowledge about the practice and the administration of selling. Formal sales training in college, on-the-job, and in executive development programs is longer and more advanced. Today, most salesmen want to learn new ways to enhance their effectiveness. These trends indicate the advancing professionalization of selling in the 1960's. They are explained in Part I along with the lingering barriers to professional status which still remain to be overcome.

The Development and Changing Role of Selling

1. ECONOMIC PRODUCTION AND SELLING *

by Harold H. Maynard †

What Is Production?

Economic organization exists to serve the wants of consumers. Its complexity is determined by the variety of wants of those it serves and by the degree of separation of the points of production and consumption. In a very simple society some or perhaps most individuals produce just about all they consume and consume about all they produce. In the more complex economy, with division of labor and specialization, there is production of goods and services *for others* and consumption of goods and services *from others*.

Production is sometimes thought of as consisting only of certain manufacturing and extractive processes. Emphasis is placed upon the activities involved in mining and refining minerals, raising crops upon the land, taking fish from the sea, transforming forests into lumber, or changing falling water into electrical energy. Production as an economic process is, however, much broader. The farmer, the fisherman, the miner, and the forester each carry on what might be thought of as the first stage of production. But, in other than the simplest forms of economic organization, secondary processes must take place.

* Reprinted from C.L.U. Study Supplement for Part B. Philadelphia: American College of Life Underwriters, © 1952, pp. 1–2.
† Late of the Ohio State University.

3

The fisherman who cooks his fish almost on the spot where he has caught it, and consumes it at once, profits from the most elementary form of production, just as does the gardener who discovers that a melon is just ready to eat and at once takes out his pocket knife and enjoys the fruit. But only in a primitive society do these simple productive processes satisfy the demands of the consumer. Other processes must take place. Basically they consist of adding certain *utilities* to nature's raw materials. This is done by changing their form, by transporting them to a place removed from the point of production, by permitting a time interval to elapse before consumption takes place and by changing their ownership from one person to another.

Form utility is added by the various extractive and manufacturing processes. *Place utility* is given by transporting the product from the point of production to a place where the product is in greatest demand. *Time utility* is added by storage until it will be of maximum value to the consumer. *Possession utility* is added with each change of ownership of the product. Obviously, these values are greatly interrelated.

For example, in the providing of fish as an item on the menu, we must think of production as including all activities involved in getting the fish from the "briny deep" to the dinner plate. Form utility is provided when the fish is cleaned and later when it is cooked; place utility is provided when the fish is caught and later when it is transported to a convenient market and then to the consumer's dinner plate. Time utility is provided when the fish is canned or refrigerated and when it is stored until eaten. (Thus, the frozen food compartment of a home refrigerator is productive.) Possession utility is being provided each time the ownership of the fish changes hands and until it finally becomes the property of the consumer.

Is Selling Productive?

In the light of this kind of analysis, can it be said that selling is productive? The question can be answered quite positively—and the place of selling in the economic process can be readily fixed—by a brief reflection on the above example. Each time the fish is moved along the production path a sale must be made. In each of these sales the seller must locate the buyer whom he can serve best (i.e., find the buyer willing to pay the best price), and they must agree on terms—quantity, quality, price, method of payment, time of delivery, and risks assumed. Whether these things are done by the company president, by a bookkeeper, by a mechanic, or by some specialist who does nothing but "sell," they all must be classified under the selling function. As long as the individual businessmen who represent the various links in the chain of production are free to choose with whom they deal and on what basis, selling is a necessary phase of production. The only substitute for selling in the economic process is compulsion, and it is not unrealistic to relate the question of the value of the sales function to the arguments for and against a free enterprise system.

Even though we might consider that selling is normally involved only in the creation of time and place utilities, it is not accurate to think in these terms because selling is necessary in every step of the productive process. It has been quite aptly suggested that selling serves as a production catalyst in that it links together the various specialized productive activities. In any event, it must be recognized that selling is a vital factor in a free enterprise system and that those persons performing the selling function are due appropriate recognition both financially and in the esteem of their fellow men.

2. THE DEVELOPMENT OF EARLY THOUGHT IN MARKETING AND PROMOTION *

by William T. Kelley †

Greek Views

When we go back into early history, we find that the trader was not well regarded by society. All value was thought to come from the land, and agriculture and keeping of sheep and cattle were considered noble occupations, worthy of the virtuous man. Manufacturing, such as it was, was not ill-regarded by the philosophers, although it ranked well below agricultural pursuits. The trader, however, was considered a rather immoral person by nature and his status was low indeed, as is shown in the following quotation from Plato's *The Republic:*

Suppose, now, that a husbandman, or an artisan, brings some production to market, and he comes at a time when there is no one to exchange with him— is he to leave his calling and sit idle in the market place?

Not at all; he will find people there who, seeing the want, undertake the office of salesman. In well-ordered States, they are commonly those who are the weakest in bodily strength, and therefore of little use for any other purpose; their duty is to be in the market, and to give money in exchange for goods to those who desire to sell and to take money from those who desire to buy.

This want, then, creates a class of retail-traders in our States.[1]

* Reprinted from *The Journal of Marketing,* © July 1956, pp. 62–7.
† University of Pennsylvania.
[1] Plato, *The Republic,* Book II, Tr. Charles M. Bakewell (New York: Scribner's, 1928), p. 67.

In another work (Laws XI), Plato would seem to recognize the value of the exchange function, but he fears the power to monopolize and make inordinate gains, which a trader with poor ethical standards might have. He takes a dim view of the ethical motivations of merchants, as is shown by this quotation:

Retail trade in a city is not by nature intended to do any harm, but quite the contrary; for is not he a benefactor who reduces the inequalities and incommensurabilities of goods to equality and common measure? And this is what the power of money accomplishes and the merchant may be said to be appointed for this purpose . . . they seek to satisfy our needs and equalize our possessions. Let us endeavor to see what has brought retail trade into illodor, and wherein lies the dishonor and unseemliness of it. . . .

Cle. What do you mean?

Ath. Dear Cleinias, the class of men is small—they must have been rarely gifted by nature and trained by education—who, when assailed by wants and desires, are able to hold out and observe moderation, and when they might make a great deal of money are sober in their wishes, and prefer a moderate to a large gain. But the mass of mankind are the very opposite: their desires are unbounded and when they might gain in moderation, they prefer gains without limit; wherefore, all that relates to retail trade, and merchandise, and the keeping of taverns is denounced and numbered among dishonorable things.[2]

If the best men were made to follow the retail trade, the latter would be an honored occupation. However, the contrary appears to be true from the following: "They must have as few retail traders as possible; in the second place, they must assign the occupation to that class of men whose corruption will do the least injury to the state; and, in the third place, they must devise some way whereby the followers of these occupations themselves will not readily fall into habits of unbridled shamelessness and meanness." [3]

Since retail traders will monopolize trade where they can and take what Plato viewed as excessive profits, the best plan, he thought, was to deny the right to be a merchant to the citizens of Athens—the latter were too valuable to be corrupted. Rather, trade was to be left to "metics" or strangers. Corruption of the moral fabric of the stranger would do less harm to the state! The latter was to come into the picture through strict regulatory powers; the guardians of the law were to determine the rate of profit and fix "a moderate gain to the retail trader" very stringently.

Little is said about sales promotion per se by the ancient philosophers. However, it is obvious that they felt strongly against it. They believed that the seller should be passive in his business relations—that he should sell

[2] *Dialogues of Plato,* Laws XI, 917–20, Tr. B. Jowett (New York: Random House, 1937), Vol. II, pp. 658–9.
[3] *Ibid.*

his goods without the exercise of persuasion in any form. "Puffery" or "praising the goods" was ranked as a crime of lesser magnitude but in the same class as adulteration of products, as is shown by the following:

He who sells anything in the agora (market) shall not ask two prices for that which he sells, but he shall ask one price . . . and there shall be no praising of any goods, or oath taken about them. If a person disobey this command, any citizen who is present, not being less than thirty years of age, may with impunity chastize and beat the swearer.

He who is proved to have sold any adulterated goods, in addition to losing the goods themselves, shall be beaten with stripes—a stripe for a drachema . . . and the herald shall proclaim in the agora the offense for which he is going to be beaten.[4]

Thus, a merchant who "flattered his goods" or gave a guarantee with them (swore an oath) was in danger of being beaten by the nearest customer. Of course, there *were* merchants in ancient Athens, and many were probably *not* beaten; it must be remembered that Plato's "Laws" proposed regulations by which the ideal state was to be governed. However, it is very revealing of the state of mind of the educated person in ancient Greece toward trading, and what we would today designate as selling one's goods.

Aristotle, it would seem, also took a rather dim view of trading. In his *Politics* we find the following observation:

Of the two sorts of money-making, as I have just said, one is a part of household management, the other is retail trade: the former is necessary and honorable, the latter a kind of exchange which is justly censured; for it is unnatural, and a mode by which men gain from one another.[5]

This statement is important, for it reveals an attitude that prevailed right through the medieval period of history. The philosophers could not conceive of a mutuality of benefit from a mere exchange of goods, that is, that the buyer benefits because he gets something which is at the moment of greater utility to him than anything else on which he could spend the money and that the seller benefits from the margin out of which he derives his living. To the ancients, someone had to come off the worse in any transaction. Unfair tactics were presumed (perhaps with some justification, as ethical standards of trade might well have been low in those days), as is shown in the following quotation from Cicero:

Those who buy to sell again as soon as they can are to be accounted as vulgar; for they can make no profit except by a certain amount of falsehood, and nothing is meaner than falsehood.[6]

[4] *Ibid.*
[5] Aristotle, *Politics*, Tr. Benjamin Jowett (London: Oxford, 1905), Book I, No. 10, p. 45.
[6] Cited in Lewis H. Haney, *History of Economic Thought* (New York: Macmillan, 1936), p. 79.

Early Medieval Attitudes Toward Promotion

The fall of Rome in the sixth century A.D. all but destroyed the considerable trade and division of labor that had developed within the Roman Empire. The many small warring states or robber barons into which the Empire disintegrated caused trade to shrink to very low levels. The manor became the prevailing economic unit; the village with its mile of surrounding countryside had necessarily to become self-sufficient in just about all requirements. The simple division of labor possible meant that the man produced no surplus beyond his own needs. It was indeed an economy of scarcity. The simple crafts of the village produced just enough for the village inhabitants themselves, with enough left over to trade for the scanty food surpluses of the surrounding farms, thereby feeding the village. Each producer marketed his own goods. There was no need to sell them since every customer was close by and knew intimately what was available.

The power of the Church over the conduct of life and its moral and ethical standards was supreme. We must look, then, to official Church attitudes to determine how promotion was viewed at this time.

As in Greek and Roman times, agriculture was still considered the basic industry of any economy, and it was praised. Manufacturing did not displease God; but trade could not be pleasing to the Deity. Material wealth was dangerous to spiritual welfare.

Church philosophers had the idea of the "just price" or *justum pretium*. Value of a good was conceived to be an objective thing, roughly measured by the amount of labor that went into the article in question. If trading involved selling goods above this "just price," it was sinful. However, St. Thomas Aquinas, that repository of medieval thought, said that a man might charge more than he had paid for a good "either because he has improved the article in some respect, or because the price of the article has been changed on account of difference in time or place, or on account of the danger to which he exposes himself in transferring the article from place to place, or in causing it to be transferred." [7]

Thus, there was some recognition of the marketing functions of transportation, storage, and risk, a significant fact sometimes overlooked. However, the medieval philosophers would give no recognition to the demand-creation function, nor would they sanction the taking of profit any more than they would sanction charging interest on money.[8]

---

[7] *Quaestio,* lxxvii, Art. iv, Opera XIX, p. 181.

[8] Aristotle had declared, "money is sterile, therefore money cannot breed money." This view was incorporated into the ethics of the early Church: no Christian could charge interest for the use of money without being put in jeopardy of his immortal soul.

Later Medieval and Renaissance Period

Under the stimulus of the Crusades and reopening of commerce with the East, a revival of learning took place in Europe. Men renewed their interest in the world about them. The relative self-sufficiency of the individual manor sooner or later gave way to exchange relationships with the town. Before towns came into existence, all manufacture had been for use, not for sale. Goods were still in the handicraft production stage, made by hand. But division of labor took place, which greatly increased the output of the artisans of the town. Goods were now made for sale rather than for use. The towns set themselves up as local market centers, cutting right across the old grouping of manors.[9] As soon as goods began to be produced in anticipation of demand rather than on order, a need arose for specialized people to perform the marketing functions. Several varieties of middlemen evolved, but there is still some doubt as to whether there were out-and-out middlemen at this time.[10] Most middlemen, it seems, had not yet divorced themselves from a certain amount of manufacturing or even agricultural production.

The lines of demarcation between types of merchants in the Middle Ages were social as well as economic. The chapman or peddler was the first door-to-door salesman. He gathered up surplus local produce from the farmers and sold it to the townspeople and, in turn, bought stocks of goods manufactured in a town and carried them to the country areas in a pack for sale.[11] Above the peddler was the shopkeeper of the town. Next in line was the merchant, who is the lineal ancestor of the wholesaler and foreign trader. He not only retailed goods from his store but kept a warehouse from which he supplied other retailers. The merchant often did business over large areas, trading in goods from other countries as well as in domestic products. Professor Hess gives the picture of Vicko Von Geldersen, a draper of Hamburg, who imported wholesale cloth and sold it both wholesale and retail. "He made use of his connections with Bruges, which was the great cloth market, to send there for sale iron, honey, meat, butter and to get in return oil, spices, and figs, which were then sold to the smaller dealers in many cities in Germany. It was through the merchant class that modern partnership association and later corporations arose." [12]

One of the characteristics of later medieval life was the guild. The guild

[9] C.G. Crump and E.F. Jacob, *The Legacy of the Middle Ages* (Oxford: Clarendon, 1926), p. 435.
[10] *Ibid.*, p. 440.
[11] Ray B. Westerfield, *Middlemen in English Business* (New Haven: Yale University Press, 1915), p. 334.
[12] Herbert W. Hess, *Creative Salesmanship* (Philadelphia: Lippincott, 1929), p. 19.

was an association of artisans or merchants in a given line who united for purposes of maintaining standards, keeping up prices and keeping down competition between members. Guilds prided themselves on giving an official guarantee of the quality of goods to their customers. Hence, they made and enforced complicated regulations for the prevention of bad work. Renard gives a specific description of this close regulation as applied by several guilds. "Hence the minute instructions prescribing the number of vats into which the Florentine dyer was to dip his materials and the quantity and quality of the coloring matters he was to employ; the size of the meshes in the nets which the Roman fisherman was to cast into the Tiber; the length of the pieces of linen to be woven by the Parisian spinner, regulated by that of the tablecloths—which covered the table of 'Good King Philip'; of the color and size of the garments which the silk makers of Constantinople were to make." [13] All that deceived the buyer was also forbidden.[14]

This aspect of guild regulation was most laudable. But certain other facets were not. Invariably, the guilds united competitors, with the natural result that competition was severely regulated and prices were fixed. Often, a town or county was reserved exclusively for the members and trade by strangers was prohibited.[15] Lambert shows a typical regulation: "No merchant who is not of the liberty of the city shall sell by retail any wine or other merchandise within the city or the suburbs." [16] No member might cut prices below what the guild officials deemed "fair," that is, fair to the members, not to the public.

Of great interest to the student of promotion is the attitude of the typical guild, whether artisan or merchant guild, toward promotion. The guild member was to sit passively by and wait for customers, for active promotion was considered to be unfair competition tantamount to "stealing" the other members' livelihood. Renard spells this out:

Again, it was forbidden to monopolize customers, to invite into your shop the people who had stopped before a neighbor's display of goods, to call in passers-by, or send a piece of cloth on approbation to a customer's house. All individual advertisement was looked on as tending to the detriment of others. The Florentine innkeeper, who gave wine or food to a stranger with the object of attracting him to his hostelry was liable to a fine. Equally open to punishment was the merchant who obtained possession of another man's shop by offering the landlord a higher rent. Any bonus offered a buyer was considered an unlawful and dishonest bait.[17]

[13] Georges Renard, *Guilds in the Middle Ages,* Tr. C.D.H. Cole (London: Bell, 1919), p. 32.
[14] *Ibid.,* p. 34.
[15] J. Malet Lambert, *Two Thousand Years of Guild Life* (London: Brown, 1891), p. 94.
[16] *Ibid.,* p. 87.
[17] Renard, *op. cit.,* p. 42.

The Renaissance and the Industrial Revolution

With the coming of the Renaissance, it is obvious that the guild system was doomed to extinction, although the decline was fairly slow over the sixteenth and seventeenth centuries. The city economy was gradually replaced by the national economy. International trade became increasingly important; foreign products began to compete with those of domestic manufacture. Rising standards of living caused consumers to demand a wider range of products than could be satisfied by the local artisans and traders. The freeing of men's minds gave rise to invention, which in turn made machine technology feasible. The outpouring of products initiated by the industrial revolution made it necessary to tap distant markets. This, in turn, emphasized the importance of the marketing process and broke down the sanctions against freer trade and, significantly, against advertising and selling the goods. Capitalism, which had hitherto been confined to a few towns, received an impetus and developed with unexpected vigor. Renard points out that "great" commerce, which spread over a great area, created exchange and banks and great financial institutions for the circulation of capital. "It formed great companies which undertook to exploit the resources of new countries, it accelerated transport and built up in the press a valuable instrument for the spread of information and for advertisement." [18]

With the decline of the guild system, however, the influence of the businessman and merchant did not decline; rather, it was enhanced, for the newer trading classes rapidly acquired money and the influence that goes with money. In most western European countries, the power of the central state was increasing. The respective monarchs found useful allies in the businessmen in consolidating and centralizing their power at the expense of the old fuedal landholding aristocracy. Increased privileges resulted for the trading classes. At the same time, many of the old ways of looking at things were changing. Sales promotion processes were no longer considered immoral or, at best, unfair competition. No longer was the trader considered, as he had been since ancient days, as the least important member of society—one who was the weakest in the community and who could do nothing more useful such as growing crops, tending flocks, or making things. Rather, he gradually gained power and status until, by the seventeenth and eighteenth centuries, his class could constitute a threat to the monarchical system itself.

As capitalism spread and grew throughout the Western world, the function of selling was enhanced, for how can you continue to produce more and more goods without finding those who will buy them? The necessity for promotion became apparent to all and with it came a reappraisal of

[18] *Ibid.,* p. 77.

the position of the salesman and the advertiser. The mid-Victorian gentle-woman would still look down her nose at those who made their money in trade. But times were changing, especially in the new world where a new order of society was emerging. There was still much criticism of the promotion process; economists particularly leveled withering criticism against it. Many old-time manufacturers still felt it beneath their dignity to proclaim the merits of their products in the marketplace. But by the early part of the twentieth century, most of the community accepted the salesman, advertising man, and publicist as useful and necessary members of society.

3. OBJECTIVES OF SELLING *

by Harry R. Tosdal †

The objectives of selling may at first thought appear to be very simple. Some individual or business firm is endeavoring to influence other people or firms to make purchases for the selfish benefit of the seller. But there is much more to the function of selling than this. The objectives ascribed to selling and to those engaged in selling are too often based upon limited experience, observation, and contact. True, the immediate objective of selling is to make sales and to develop buying action on the part of pro-spective or potential buyers; but most sellers are also under heavy economic pressure to deal with buyers or those who influence buying in such a manner that future transactions will be facilitated. Most sellers are looking forward to making repeat sales, that is, to inducing future purchases by the same customers, because the bulk of business transactions takes place between buyers and sellers who have had previous buying and selling relationships. The seller must, therefore, direct his effort so that the buyers will want to repeat the experience. Where freedom of choice prevails in our competi-tive economy, that repetition will not occur unless the buyer is "well satis-fied" to use the words of the Supreme Court. Thus, "enlightened selfish-ness" tends to influence the seller to establish himself as a good source of supply and to avoid methods and practices which would harm the buyer.

Any careful examination of the objectives of selling, however, must go beyond such enlightened selfishness to reach a basic understanding. It is the failure to penetrate more deeply into objectives and results that has

* Reprinted from *Selling in Our Economy* (Chicago: Richard D. Irwin, © 1957), pp. 79–90.
† Harvard University.

contributed to the misunderstanding of selling. As is so often the case in studying social phenomena, it is easy to fail to see the forest for the trees.

It is helpful in the process of the study of objectives to distinguish between individual and group objectives and to separate the purpose of the individual and the private firm from the general social objectives and goals of the total selling process. That selling has as its ultimate purpose a social goal is not quickly apparent because we do not attempt to look at the overall purposes and results. There is need, therefore, to outline the scope of these objectives and to relate the conclusions derived from limited observation and embodied in common opinion to the broader facts of the selling situations and their significance. The objectives of selling to be discussed will be grouped therefore under four major headings:

1. The objectives of selling effort carried on by individuals, directly engaged in selling activity whatever the form

2. The objectives of selling effort on the part of the firms and corporations in relation to those doing the selling work in those firms and in relation to the owners of the selling enterprise

3. The objectives of selling effort in relation to our economic structure and its functioning

4. The objectives of selling effort in relation to our society as a whole.

Objectives of Individuals Engaged in Selling Work

The objective of selling activities generally is obviously to secure buying action, to cause purchase of goods and services by buyers. This leads eventually to higher consumption by many people, although higher consumption may or may not be the objective of a particular seller. Any careful examination of the objectives of selling must lead to the conclusion that the objectives of individuals who are engaged in the practice of selling may differ widely in type and emphasis. Among these objectives are the following:

1. To make a living. From the standpoint of the individual salesman whose income and success depends on his efforts to cause people to buy, it is evident that selling constitutes a gainful occupation at the practice of which he hopes to make a living. His ambition may extend to achieving advancement into executive ranks. This ambition may in turn be motivated by desire to secure the ownership of business that will give him the income desired for the benefit of himself and his family, the enjoyment of luxuries, or the acquisition of power.

It is certainly not assured under the usual plans of compensation that salesmen will make a living, much less go beyond that. Many a young man who has started out to sell aluminum utensils, magazines, or hosiery from house to house, has found out in a very short time that he could not make a living and has given up in despair. He has learned that selling is not easy and that earnings are not automatic, particularly in normal buyers' markets. A substantial proportion of those who try selling fail for want of aptitude, industry, or basic interest in and respect for their work. Some fail also because what they are trying to sell is not wanted.

Those who work in the field of advertising or display, or who perform many other supplementary and staff duties, find that ultimate success in their jobs depends on the estimated contribution that their work makes to selling. They have the same ambitions, the same desires as those who are directly in contact with the prospective buyers. But the difficulty of measuring their contribution to selling results is a handicap to some, perhaps an advantage to others.

We cannot, offhand, condemn the motivation of the individual in trying to make a living and improve his lot in life as purely selfish and antisocial. On the contrary, one's first economic responsibility is usually to himself and family; and unless he meets this responsibility, he cannot ordinarily serve society well. But serving society may be the best way of serving himself. A possible conflict between his obligation to society and private interest may exist; but in selling it need not and usually does not. The salesman who persuades a manufacturer to install a new machine to make a better product or to cut costs is contributing to a higher standard of living, in spite of the fact that the motivation of the salesman may be to increase his own standard of living and that of the manufacturer who, in installing the machine, increases profits and avoids loss. Eventually his purchase will contribute to lower costs and higher scales of living for the people. The salesman who sells an electric washing machine to the housewife is generally raising the family's level of living.

Because selling involves a form of leadership, because it requires those practicing selling to influence other people, selling has frequently furnished a training ground for other positions in business. Selling leadership is persuasive leadership, a type of leadership that is both appreciated and greatly needed in democratic societies.

2. A second objective of those who perform selling work is likewise understandable. It is the desire to secure satisfaction from the work itself. Salesmen who believe in their products and in the benefits those products will convey to buyers feel satisfaction when they make sales, entirely apart from the contribution that such sales make to their personal welfare. In fact, success as a salesman is usually predicated on a firm belief in the merits of the product sold in terms of the satisfactions to be obtained by the buyers. There is no evidence that salesmen, any more than any other group, wish to make a living without regard to the service performed in return.

3. Again, there are special satisfactions from successful sales work which attract and hold a good many workers in the selling field. That is the desire to secure the excitement and thrills from successfully influencing people to take the desired action. Obviously, to the salesman who is ethical in his conduct, such thrills and satisfactions must be the result of selling that is mutually beneficial.

The ease of selling during periods of shortages brought about by global war has for many years obscured the fact that selling in a competitive economy is a difficult task requiring intelligent, often exhausting, effort. In a competitive economy with high standards of living, with many products both old and new, the difficulty of making particular sales at a particular time will furnish a challenge to the keenest brain, a challenge that is paralleled only in other areas of human activity where democratic liberty prevails and freedom of choice obtains. The intense satisfactions which men have often reported at the successful conclusion of a selling project need to be experienced in order to be fully appreciated.

4. Serving buyers and customers. Since most selling is done on a repeat basis, sellers get to know buyers and become friendly with them. Particularly in the sales of technical and complex products, the salesman develops friendships that cause him to serve his buyers and customers to a point substantially beyond the length required by cold and calculating type of enlightened selfishness. The salesman who furnishes selling or merchandising services to customers is adding to the satisfactions that both his firm and the customer feel as the result of the purchasing transactions. But he also derives personal pleasure and satisfactions from the relationship with customers.

5. Lastly, except in the general desire to be engaged in useful work so that the earning of a living or the accumulation of capital for personal or family improvement is accomplished in an honorable manner, one does not expect that many salesmen will engage in such work with vague altruistic ideas of serving society. The man who believes in his product and acts honorably in bringing about a sale that leads to mutual satisfaction is actually serving society, whether the goal he seeks to reach is explicitly service to society or the same goals as characterize other vocations; to make a living, to develop security, to furnish the means for cultural or other development, to attain power, or any of the other objectives that men may hope to reach, directly or indirectly, through a chosen field of effort.

The motivation of the individual may differ from that of his firm. Sometimes the differences in that motivation are not important in the performance of a useful function for society. Sometimes they are. The behavior of the salesman who engages in sharp practice or even the use of illegal means of influence may go beyond anything either permitted or encouraged by the firm itself. In other cases, the standard of the salesman may be merely a more concrete reflection of the carelessness or low standards on the part of the executives of the selling firm itself. It is unlikely that the sales organization in its contact with the public will rise above the character of the top management, but it is also possible that top management with a large and scattered field sales organization may not be able in all areas to control the behavior of those who are exercising influence at the point of contact with the public. The parallel in political leadership is quickly apparent; it need not be spelled out. One may only mention the contrast between some top political leaders and the ward bosses of certain cities. Fortunately, checks upon "bad behavior" and unworthy motivation, inherent in selling in our economy, seem to be more quickly operative than in the political field.

Selling Objectives in Relation to Business Enterprises and Owners and Managers

The business enterprise which is devoted to the production of goods or services, or both, sells for various reasons, some of which are obvious and some not so apparent:

1. In the opinions of a good many businessmen, selling is fully justified if one can show that selling is essential to the survival of an enterprise in competition. In our economy distinguished by large-scale production for national or even international markets, the cessation of selling effort would, except under war shortages or monopoly of necessities, mean more or less rapid failure. If one will examine the balance sheets of many firms, he will find that if the income from sales were cut off, the firm operating at its previous level would consume its capital in a very short time, even where heavy capital investment was involved. Obviously the cessation of selling effort would not cut off all sales, because some buying would take place based in part on connections and past selling, and in part upon need for the sellers' products. Generally, however, the decline in the volume of goods disposed of in the absence of selling effort would be disastrous. For that decline in most industries is likely to be much more than proportionate to the possible decline in costs, thus quickly bringing losses because of the insufficiency of income from sales to cover costs.

To the experienced businessman, it is quite evident that production does not create demand. Sales do not come automatically and purchases are not made automatically despite implications in some economics texts. Basically, survival of the firm is the condition of continuing private profit, but it is also the condition of continuing service to society. Just as in politics the most competent man with the best motives may be forced to pay attention to his survival in office if he is to be able to carry out his program, so the businessman will look to profitable sales as a condition of real and outstanding accomplishment and growth.

It is obvious that for most business enterprises sales transactions constitute the sole source of income. Sales provide the income out of which wages and salaries can be paid and the requirements met for goods, machinery, supplies, and taxes. Without sales income, firms cannot long continue to make these payments without dissipating assets, endangering chances of restoration to economic health, and suffering eventual failure.

2. Businessmen sell in order to secure return on investment. The business executives who are responsible to a board of directors and to stockholders may aim through selling to provide the income necessary for return on investment. They realize that only an adequate volume of sales, made at a profitable price, can provide the dividends, allowance for depreciation, and reserves necessary for continuously satisfactory operation. If return is not earned for a considerable period of time, the difficulty of securing further capital is increased and becomes eventually impossible.

3. Businesses and business executives sell in order to have the satisfaction of achievement. Business executives and leaders take pride in the building of enterprises and look upon the work of building a going concern as a worthwhile economic and social objective.[1] They know that the building of large enterprises is seldom a one-man job. The planning necessary for successful sales operations, the execution of sales plans, and the overcoming of obstacles, thereby contributing vitally to bringing into full operation an enterprise that produces useful goods and services, is an ac-

[1] This attitude and objective is described by Franklin J. Lunding in an address delivered at the National Business Conference at the Harvard Business School, June 7, 1952:

"It can be said without qualification that the typical business manager of America today is not working primarily to get rich. In the first place, it's virtually impossible, at least in the formerly accepted sense of the word, and he knows it. No matter how high his salary goes he is not going to become an immensely wealthy man under present tax laws. Furthermore, he would be likely to find great wealth embarrassing, even if he could acquire it. The opulence which characterized the great business leaders of bygone years is out of place today.

"The chief motivation of today's business manager is a desire to build a sound, healthy organism, financially strong, competitively alert, able to progress steadily and to weather whatever storms might lie ahead. His objective is a smoothly running, tightly knit, cooperative organization to which everyone from the president to the floor sweeper contributes his enthusiastic best and from which each draws his due share of material reward and spiritual satisfaction.

"Such an organization, he is convinced, operates more profitably and offers the best prospects for steady jobs at good pay, for the growth and development of the business and of each individual in it, and for the pursuit of happiness and life's satisfactions for all concerned. The business manager wants all these things for the people who work in the business as much as they want them for themselves. His primary job is to get people to do things cooperatively so those goals may be achieved."

complishment worthy of credit. In the United States more than in some other parts of the world, such men think of businesses not only, or even primarily, as a means of deriving purely personal and family benefit. They often regard these businesses as living organisms which bring benefits to workers, users, and owners as well as to the managing groups. These benefits are realized, developed, and expanded by selling.

4. /Public benefit is the ultimate goal of most selling.\ The objective of serving the consumer public, whether the consumers be ultimate consumers or firms or institutions, constitutes a rarely expressed but implicit objective even beyond the necessity of selling in order to make a profit. Many a businessman who disclaims altruism in his business conduct actually performs a greater social service by what he does in his own business than he could possibly perform in participating in community affairs or in his gifts to educational or charitable institutions.

The obvious connection between selling and employment constitutes a working objective that is a powerful incentive to many businessmen. Selling requires production; production requires employment. Or, to reverse the statement: Employment results in production that must be disposed of for money or other goods. Disposing of goods for money requires selling effort. "Sales means jobs" because without the continual flow of buying and selling transactions, the entire basis for attaining high and rising standards of living and for maintaining those standards which have been achieved quickly disappears.

5. Both owners and executives will, of course, share the range of objectives relating to family and personal ambitions and to standing in the community, in the industry, or in the general economic structure of the nation. The interests of the individuals in management selling and ownership may, therefore, be parallel to those of the enterprise; but at times and in varying degrees they may be divergent. The evidence is that most successful executives identify their own interest with that of the firm with which they are connected. Nevertheless, when the motivation for selling is power or is unworthy, the possibilities of abuse exist and may result in injury and harm to the buying public until correctives are applied. But in this respect as in so many others, selling leadership does not differ from leadership in other fields.

Ultimate Objectives of Selling

One must constantly keep in mind that the basic objective of decent selling effort is to sell goods and services, to influence people to purchase and consume the food, clothing, shelter, the machines and materials—all the millions of items—required for an industrial civilization intended to furnish high levels of living for all the people. In other words, selling effort in all its manifold forms has as its immediate objective buying action taken by people as individuals or as part of a business or other organization. Such action represents the buying of those material goods and immaterial services that make up the economic level of our living. The amount of household production tends to grow less as living standards rise. Only in the early agrarian, pastoral, or hunting stages of economic development could family production satisfy more than a small portion of its needs. Most of the wants of an advanced industrial society such as ours must be satisfied through purchase, because the productive efforts of the family are specialized and may produce directly nothing that the family uses or desires. But only by such employment can workers be productive enough to have their work yield a high standard of living. The fact that selling effort is directed toward all people, not just toward a few privileged persons, needs special emphasis. It aims to sell automobiles not only to the wealthy but to the workman in the factory, to the farmer, or to the teacher. Selling is not the only influence, but it is the most powerful influence to take the type of resultful and productive action that will bring automobiles to the people. It has been a major influence in bringing into operation over 56 million automobiles for 178 million people. It has placed electric refrigerators in more than 90 per cent of wired homes—and one might cite many other instances, to support the fact that it is the many, not the few, who have obtained the increasingly high levels of living.

Successful selling effort obviously implies that people have been led to buy, both for consumptive and productive purposes, those goods and services needed for the continuance of high and rising levels of living. The performance of individuals and firms in persuading many people to buy thus achieves the objective of raising actual levels and standards of living if the persuasion to buy causes people to produce desired goods and services. Therefore, it does no violence to the facts to assert that the *aggregate objective of selling effort, taken as a whole, is to raise* living levels and standards of living. It is the objective of selling not only to bring about high and rising levels of living but also to raise the goals toward which people strive so that when relatively high income levels are attained by the majority of people, there will still be a gap between levels attained and levels desired. Standards are established in a dynamic economy that are a spur to the people to attain still higher levels.

The achieved levels of living in the United States are high for the population in general, higher than anywhere else in the world. They are unique in the history of the world, even though a small portion of our population still endures substandard levels. More production is needed to bring these people up to standard. Higher standards would require even greater productivity and production.

On the other hand, it is to be remarked that the attainment of these higher levels in the United States has not been accomplished by longer or more exacting labor. Rather the reverse. High levels requiring high production do not necessarily increase the amount of time and effort involved. If it were true that high levels could only be secured by longer hours and more exacting work, the question would soon arise as to whether those levels warranted the additional effort. For high levels of living, a balance is required between the work necessary to turn out large amounts of goods and services and the requirements for health and social and spiritual growth, all of which are and should be a part of broadly conceived high levels of living. The reconciling factor, which gives greater production but shorter hours and less exacting labor, is the development and application of technological and management skills and equipment to bring about greater productivity. That this has been done is clear from the record, which will be cited below. That it will continue to enable the reconciliation to be made between greater quantities of goods and services and the burdens of labor is possible but not automatic. Automation is intended eventually to reduce the human burden of producing goods and distributing goods. Nevertheless, although much has been accomplished along this line, it must be stressed that increasing social adjustment in other than economic fields to our high material standards is required before the highest levels of living can be attained.

Logicians will quickly point out that concomitant variation is not a proof of causal relationship; that high living standards in the United States may be due primarily to other causes rather than selling, or may even have occurred in spite of it. Some economists have implied that the high standards of living come first and enable us to bear the "waste" of much selling effort.[2] But it can and will be shown that there is a definite causal connection between high levels of living and selling, which becomes clear from a realistic study of the behavior of buyers and sellers, of businessmen, executives, and the buying public.

4. LEVELS OF SELLING *

by Harold H. Maynard †

Meeting or Filling Demand—Low Level Selling

Two distinct levels of selling are recognizable. One involves filling an existing demand and may be referred to as *low level selling*. The other,

* Reprinted from C.L.U. Study Supplement for Part B. (Philadelphia: American College of Life Underwriters, © 1952), pp. 5–7.
† Late of The Ohio State University.
[2] Cf. John K. Galbraith, *American Capitalism* (Boston: Houghton Mifflin, 1952).

known as *high level selling,* involves creating demand for a product or a service. It may be said that high level salesmanship is creative because previous to the various stages of the sales process the prospect did not recognize his need for the product or service.

It should be clearly understood that use of the terms "low level" and "high level" when applied to the work of sales people does not imply that one form of selling is of any greater economic value than is the other. Both are necessary in modern economic organization. Each type of sales person makes a contribution to the well-being of society.

Low level selling is well illustrated by the work of the "sales persons" employed in the typical variety store whose primary duties are those of change making and bundle wrapping. At intervals some of the more aggressive individuals may perform high level selling by giving an inquiring customer some information about a product which may stimulate a latent interest in it or even sometimes create a sale. It should be emphasized, however, that in low level selling the initiative almost always comes from the customer rather than from the clerk.

Low level selling consists primarily of giving a minimum of assistance in meeting an already existing demand. Little if any aggressive sales effort is required. Very often it is nonpersonal in that a sale takes place because attention has been attracted by an interesting display which either creates a buying urge by showing the virtues of the product displayed, or perhaps merely serves as a reminder to fill a recognized want. Often a sale takes place merely because the vendor is at the most convenient location, as, for example, a sudden recognition of the need for a loaf of bread and the dispatch of a lad to "the nearest grocery store."

In all such cases the customer generates or recognizes his need for the product at a particular moment. Decision to buy a loaf of bread may seem to be casual indeed but it reflects a long process of social and industrial development which substituted wheat cereals for fish or game in a diet and still later took the baking of bread from the home to the factory. Often seemingly simple sales are in reality the fruit of a long period of creating interest and perhaps breaking down resistance to a product by advertising presentations or by personal sales efforts. Often a purchaser could not say with certainty just why he purchased a certain item because the germ of an idea may have been planted weeks or even months before by an advertisement, by a display, or by the seemingly unsuccessful effort of a salesman.

The sale of many services is on a low level basis. The barber or the beautician sells his service because of a convenient location more often than he does because of superior service or any ability to create additional business for himself or other members of his craft. Many products and services are, however, practically never sold on a low level sales basis.

Illustrative are heavy machinery, encyclopedias, most securities, many forms of property and casualty insurance protection and, certainly, almost all life insurance.

Just as water is said to seek its level, salesmen tend to find employment in the kind of selling for which their education, personality and general over-all ability best fit them. It would normally be impossible for the salesman of men's haberdashery to exchange jobs with a representative of an industrial scale manufacturer, or an underwriter who specializes in group insurance. Education and training are clearly related to the type of selling which is carried on and there seems reason to believe that the somewhat intangible factors which make one person a good high level salesman and another a failure in this type of selling are not present to a marked degree in those who generally sell products which can be moved by low level selling procedures.[1]

Active Demand Creation—High Level Selling

Although the primary test of the level of selling which is involved is not always that of the source of initiative, high level sales operations normally involve much more than merely waiting for a customer to appear, or selling primarily by display or because of a convenient location. Willingness to assume the burden of going to a customer, after an analysis of a market has identified logical customers, and the ability to analyze particular needs in such a way as to arouse a buying desire and to direct interest to the particular product are all involved in high level selling. The salesman of a lubricant who is so trained as to make it possible for him to analyze the needs of a factory, the representative of "punched card" office equipment, and the salesman of industrial pumps, serve their customers because they are able to analyze their needs and to recommend the particular product which will best serve these needs. Often the substitution of an improved product is involved. At other times the sale is definitely creative in that the customer is shown that a product which he has not hitherto used, as for example acoustical materials for his office walls, would be a wise purchase.

Many wholesalers' representatives are today much more than low level order takers. They have passed into the higher classification because of the recognition by management that they can help their merchant customers to sell more merchandise. This involves advice on such diverse matters as store layout, display fixtures, pricing, clerk education, the ar-

[1] There are of course many exceptions. Every large department store has a few salesmen of appliances, floor coverings, and even men's clothing whose annual income is in "five figures." Some "door-to-door" men may approach that income. Interesting possibilities in the field of retailing in particular have been opened up by "suggestive selling" techniques.

rangement of window displays, and basic inventory and buying policies. In doing this they are helping the merchant to create sales as well as to attract to his store demand which has been generated by manufacturer advertising. Their sales work is definitely high level in character. Furthermore, their activities enable the retailers' sales personnel to function more successfully even though they sell on a low level.

Salesmen of services are in general entitled to be classed among those who render creative high level selling services. The telephone service salesman who studies the needs of an industrial plant or a large office for telephone service and makes proper recommendations is an example. Companies selling electrical power train their salesmen to analyze needs for lighting in a store building and to make proper recommendations. Furthermore, their work often demands the ability to show a prospective user of electrical power why it might well be substituted for steam, or possibly purchased from the utility rather than manufactured by the company itself. Those who represent intercity trucking companies have a definitely high level creative selling task when they show a shipper why he should use trucks rather than rails for his shipments. These examples of service selling are usually performed by so-called "sales engineers."

Salesmen of intangible services have an even greater challenge in that they normally create a demand for a service which may be latent or nonexistent until the salesman analyzes the need of a prospective client. Assume a casual contact or an answer to a direct mail solicitation which permits a salesman for an advertising agency to discuss the advertising methods and policies of a manufacturer. His task is that of determining whether or not his agency can well serve the particular advertiser and then to demonstrate why an agency should be used or why the account should be transferred to his agency from the one which is now serving it. The same general sales task is carried on by representatives of management consulting organizations. The majority of insurance sales involve both the ability to identify logical prospects and to create sales by showing how the protection recommended is suited to the needs of the customer.

Salesmen who carry on high level solicitations have two problems common to almost all situations which they face. They must present their goods or services in such a way as (1) to overcome prejudices, and (2) to generate interest by giving facts either not known or not properly considered by the prospect up to the time of the sales call. Inadequate knowledge of facts or even worse, misinformation, must be offset by the salesman by relating the facts of his proposal to the needs of the client. If the prospect has a real need for the product or service, and if the facts are properly presented, interest should result. The sales task is then that of building interest into desire and of overcoming objections or excuses as they arise.

An important part of a creative sale is that of studying the situation of the prospect and then recommending the proper solution to the problem identified. This may involve a choice among several alternatives. Which telephone switchboard should be selected? What paint should be used on factory walls? Which of several types of roofing should be the best buy in the long run? Under what conditions is an electric typewriter profitable? Which of the many common stocks or bonds in the portfolio of the securities salesman is best adapted for the investment needs of the particular client? Which type of insurance should be selected and in what quantities? These and thousands of similar questions which come to those engaged in high level selling every day can only be correctly answered if proper initial training is followed by continued education and if the salesman has the imagination necessary to relate his various offerings to the specific needs of the prospect. Salesmen who are entitled to this classification must also be ready to refuse to make a sale, to reduce the total involved, or to shift the order to goods of lesser value than those suggested by the buyer when the judgment of the seller indicates that this would constitute the best service.

The person who is stimulated by the demands of a high level selling job, who realizes that each day gives new opportunities, who is willing to pay the price of constant training, and who enjoys nothing more than facing a difficult sales situation and mastering it, will find his greatest opportunity in such a selling assignment. Naturally enough, income is determined by one's degree of success in high level selling. That is not true in other sales positions for sales result from many factors other than the sales ability of the salesman and that fact is known by employers when compensation scales are set.

Special Problems in the Sale of Services

Emphasis throughout this monograph has been given to the economic basis of demand creation. The important function of creative selling has been explained as have the levels of sales activity. Reference has been made to the sale of services as distinguished from the marketing of tangible products. It now becomes useful to inquire as to whether the sale of services generally presents problems which are not found when commodities are placed on the market. A number of distinct differences do seem to prevail.

The intangible nature of many services presents unique selling problems. It is often difficult to demonstrate to the prospective purchaser the full gain to be experienced if the service is taken. A proposal from a landscape architect is illustrative as is the suggestion that the services of a specialist on pension plans be sought.

A second characteristic of the market for services is that the need is often not generally recognized. Those which are concrete, such as the services of a dry cleaner, a beautician, or a civil engineer are sold under conditions which normally resemble those existing when commodities are marketed. When, however, it is necessary to create a desire for the service because the prospect does not realize his need, definitely high level creative selling is involved. This is often true because it is necessary to present certain facts in order to demonstrate a need, and for many prospects, these facts are not easily understood.

Teaching ability is involved to a marked degree because the teacher-pupil relationship is involved, in that one of relatively great understanding is presenting facts to one of lesser understanding. Often the ability to present an argument by use of an analogy is highly useful in selling a service, because the principles of explaining the unknown by using a comparison between the present situation and a familiar one which exists in the analogy is a help in clarifying the issue. In these and other ways the successful salesman of a service must attempt to make his intangible offerings clear, concrete, graphic, and thoroughly understandable.

Selling as a Career

5. SALESMANSHIP AS A PROFESSION *

by R.S. Wilson †

What Is a Professional?

The earliest use of the word "profession" recorded by the Oxford English Dictionary dates from 1541. There is no corresponding term in any language of the ancient world.

In Greece the lawyer was not specially trained, but usually the litigant's friend.

In the Roman Empire, the physician was generally a slave attached to a rich man's household.

The universities of medieval Europe were training schools for work of a kind that we now classify as professional.

The professions, like the universities, were at first co-extensive with the Church. All medieval university students were ecclesiastic (at least in name); some specialized in medicine, some in law, others in an ecclesiastical career or teaching.

So long as the Church maintained its predominance, the various professions for which the Universities trained members did not become clearly distinct, since all professional men were ecclesiastics. As the culture of the Middle Ages slowly shed its religious character, the professions formerly within the Church emerged from it. As they did so, they became organized. Thus, the Royal College of Physicians of London was founded in 1518.

---

* Reprinted from the Charles Coolidge Parlin Memorial Lecture of the Philadelphia Chapter, American Marketing Association, 1947, pp. 12–27. Copyright 1947, Philadelphia Chapter, American Marketing Association.
† The Goodyear Tire and Rubber Company.

26

By the eighteenth century, law, medicine and divinity—the learned professions—had attained an independent status and organization.

The 1940 census lists twenty-two classes of what they call professional workers. Many of these classifications, however, are really subdivisions of other classifications. Grouping them broadly, there are just nine: clergymen, physicians, lawyers, educators, engineers, writers, actors, artists, and musicians.

There are a number of very interesting definitions of a profession, but *Webster's Dictionary* gives as good a one as I have found:

> Profession—a calling in which one professes to have acquired some special knowledge used by way either of instructing, guiding or advising others or of serving them in some art.

President James Bryant Conant of Harvard University offers this illuminating criterion for judging the professional:

> The difference between a trade and a profession is that the trader frankly carries on his business primarily for the sake of pecuniary gain while the members of a profession profess an art, their skill in which they place at the public service for a remuneration, adequate or inadequate, but which is truly an end in itself. The professional man finds his highest rewards in his sense of mastery of his subject, in the absorbing interest of the pursuit of knowledge for its own sake, and in the contributions which, by reason of his attainments, he can make to the promotion of the general welfare.

In this discussion of what is a professional, I wish to emphasize the difference between "a member of a profession" and the true professional. Merely being a member of a profession does not in itself guarantee that a man will remain a professional. You and I can think of physicians who have never advanced their knowledge beyond what they learned in medical school. You and I can think of lawyers who are not so sharp today as they were the day they passed their Bar examinations.

The true distinguishing mark of a professional is the constant aspiring toward perfection.

In talking to the people within our own organization from time to time I have defined a professional as one who studies and practices, studies and practices constantly until he approaches perfection in his chosen calling.

And so we come to the delineation of a professional salesman. Here we cannot be confined to the strict limitation of a definition. We must rather accept the broader outlines of a word sketch.

The professional salesman is a man who, first of all, has made selling his chosen calling—his life work. In this he is unique, because most men who have the title of "salesman" did not *choose* to be salesmen—they just *happen* to be salesmen. Selling is not a calling with them. It's just a job.

The professional salesman is the man to whom true service is of paramount importance. To quote Henry S. Dennison:

A professional combines science and common sense into an art accompanied with a motive of *service* greater than that motive of *service to self* and also having a loyalty to a code of ethics.

The professional salesman is a man who is constantly studying to improve his proficiency. I am thinking of a surgeon whom I know well who personifies to me the professional attitude. I met him at lunch one day not long ago and he told me he was leaving by plane that afternoon for Dallas. Why? He had read in one of the medical journals of a surgeon in Dallas who had performed a delicate cheek bone operation in a manner that was new to him. He immediately called the Dallas surgeon on the telephone— found he was to perform such an operation the next day, so he dropped everything and left by plane to watch the operation and learn a new technique. This friend of mine was fifty-six years old when this incident occurred and to the end of his career he will go on studying and practicing to improve his proficiency. He is a true professional.

The professional salesman is a man who recognizes there is no substitute for hard work. Charles Kettering puts it this way: "I think this 'know-how' we talk about is eternal *practice, practice, practice.*" Dr. Paul Ivey says, "If you want success in any profession you have to *pay the price* for it; that means *work.*"

The professional salesman is a man who above all else maintains his own self-respect, integrity, independence. In the final analysis, this matter of integrity is the *sine qua non* of the true professional. I know of no man to whom I would give the title "professional" in any line who would sacrifice his own self-respect either through coercion or for the hope of gain.

In this connection I recently made an interesting study. It occurred to me that the man best qualified to describe a professional salesman would be the purchasing agent himself. So I commissioned the R.L. Polk Company to send a simple postcard questionnaire to 500 leading purchasing agents. The postcard asked this one question:

Think specifically of the best salesman representing any company who calls on you and tell us briefly why you consider him the best.

That the purchasing agents were interested in the subject was evident from the fact that over 30 per cent replied—a very satisfactory return. I purposely made the question broad so that the purchasing agents could use their own words.

It wasn't hard to classify the answers in broad categories, and here is the significant thing: Over 50 per cent of the reasons given as to why the best salesman was "Best" centered on the man himself. Not knowledge of the product—not personal service—not entertainment—but the man.

Such adjectives abounded as "dependable," "sincere," "honest," "friendly," "considerate," "intelligent," "loves-his-job." To anyone who has lived selling for any period of time, these answers are no surprise. But as I leaf through these revealing replies, I wonder again at all the fol-de-rol that used to be taught on salesmanship. Remember the catch phrases about "Creating the buying attitude," "Controlling the prospect's mind," and "Forcing action?"

Finally, the professional salesman is a man who puts true value on his services. While monetary reward is entirely secondary to service in his consideration, his own inherent self-respect, his insistence on his own personal independence requires of him that he build up first a reserve and then an estate that will keep him free from the coercions of necessity.

Qualifications of the Professional Salesman

Professional salesmen can be divided broadly into two classifications —those who sell to users and those who sell to resellers. Each of these two classifications has a separate set of qualifications.

I shall list but not attempt to elaborate the qualifications of each classification. These qualifications are well known and much has been written about them. My main comments will be on the *attitude* requisite in each classification and I wish to emphasize that it is *attitude* more than formal training that distinguishes the professional salesman from the peddler, the drummer, the *caveat emptor*.

Salesman Who Sells to the User

Here the requisites are:

1. Knowledge of product
2. Knowledge of how it should be used
3. Knowledge of needs of the user
4. Knowledge of the market
5. Knowledge of competition—strong and weak points
6. Knowledge of the company he represents—financial, historical, etc.
7. Knowledge of the concern or person to whom he is selling—financial, capacity for growth, etc.

These things are fundamental—just as knowledge of physiology and anatomy is fundamental to the physician.

Practically all sellers to users are specialists—hence their knowledge is specialized—and should be.

But the professional salesman in this classification must be activated by a *true* spirit of service and a *militant* spirit of service. He must be imbued with a burning zeal for his product or his service. To use the phrase that appeared so often on the postcard replies from the purchasing agents, "He loves his work."

Of this type, the professional life insurance salesman is a good example. His spirit is the spirit of true service. He wants to help his customer create an insurance estate; he wants to avoid the possibility of overburdening a client, particularly a younger man, with too great an insurance load; but, on the other hand, his belief in the essentiality of life insurance for every man is so militant that he will not allow his client to close his mind to his duty to his family or brush aside his responsibility. A service salesman above all else, but no namby-pamby, he.

An outstanding example in my personal experience of the professional salesman is a salesman of conveyor belt for underground coal mines. He was originally a coal mining engineer. He saw the waste of man hours and hence of money in the old, inefficient mine car and mine pony. Then he saw the results of later day installations of modern rubber belt conveyors in coal mines where accurate track was kept of costs. He concluded that the mine owner who stuck to the old ways was inevitably going to be forced out of business by high costs. Day in, day out—week in, week out, he dons rubber boots, miner's helmet, miner's lamp, and crawls through the coal mines in the Kentucky fields, Virginia fields, Illinois fields, and all over the United States where coal is mined. I don't think he has ever written up an order. But he has sold more mine conveyor belt than any man of my knowledge. His greatest satisfaction is going back to the mines which have followed his advice and figuring how well his installations have paid out.

Great tribute must be paid to the professional salesman of this type for what he has done to raise the standard of living, to reduce the costs of production, to increase employment. At the same time, in all honesty acknowledgement must be made that many salesmen of the unprofessional type made many mistakes in this process of raising the American standard of living—mistakes that were costly and painful to the buyer. But the over-all record is a record of contribution that entitles this calling to rank as a profession and these men to rank as professionals.

The Salesman Who Sells to the Reseller

Here the requisites are:
1. Knowledge of product
2. Knowledge of how it is used
3. Knowledge of the market
4. Knowledge of competition—strong and weak points
5. Knowledge of the company he represents—financial, historical, etc.
6. Knowledge of the concern to whom he is selling—financial, possibilities of growth, etc.

7. Knowledge of the fundamentals of retailing—
   a. Market analysis
   b. Location
   c. Building design and identification
   d. Interior layout and display
   e. Personnel—hiring and training
   f. Advertising
   g. Budget making and expense control
   h. Accounting

Here again, these knowledges are fundamental. Just like knowledge of common law—how to make out deeds, write wills—is fundamental to a lawyer.

But among salesmen who sell to resellers, the professional attitude is far less common and not so well advanced as in the case of the salesman who sells to the user. It is in this class of salesman that we often find the peddler and the drummer—the peddler who leafs through the catalog and looks over the "want list"; the drummer with his glad-hand and the latest story.

Actually, however, the salesman who sells to the reseller has a more difficult job and requires greater ability than he who sells only to the user.

In this class of salesmen, the professional attitude—and remember, it is attitude that is most important of all—is the attitude of the great teacher.

This type of salesman does not make the final sale himself—he succeeds only as the goods move off the shelves of those to whom he sells. Therefore, his success, his satisfaction, must come from the training of others. He is like a football coach or the manager of a professional baseball team —he gets his results not directly but by his ability to train others.

It is said the human body replaces itself every seven years. Similarly, in the average salesman's territory there is a normal but constant turnover of dealers.

So the professional salesman to resellers must do as the wise, foreseeing coach does—he must grow his own.

The former dominance of the Yankees and Cardinals in baseball was attributed to the fact that they first saw the need of growing their own— established the Farm Clubs in the Minor Leagues. Thus when they needed a new player, they could always reach down into one of their Farm Clubs and bring up the right boy.

So the professional salesman to resellers is constantly on the lookout for new, young material, material that he can train in his own way, mold in his own fashion. He gets and holds their confidence. He builds not for to-day, but for next year—he rejoices in the romance of the success of his pupils.

In my experience in selling over the past thirty-five years nothing has given me more satisfaction than watching the growth mentally, spiritually and financially of men whom I have in some way aided to start business from humble, hard-working beginnings. To see them reach full stature of business manhood is one of the best rewards in business life.

Why Are There Not More Professional Salesmen Today?

For three reasons, I believe.

First, because the truly professional attitude is comparatively rare among us human beings, even in the recognized professions. Second, because the need for the professional attitude in selling has not yet been defined and clearly recognized by business. As I pointed out earlier, the salesman originally was considered of a rather low order. He was classified with the peddler, the drummer, the hawker. Many early salesmen perverted their natural talents—hence phrases like, "He was such a salesman he could talk the shirt right off your back," or "He could talk a bird out of a tree." All these phrases associated with the word "salesman" implied benefit to the salesman, but detriment to the buyer.

In some organizations the salesman was and in some cases still is considered a necessary evil—a charge against the business—instead of the indispensable partner of production and finance.

Third, because standards have not been set up. Courses of study have not been outlined. Recognized state-controlled examinations have not been organized. In short, the protective walls have not been thrown around the profession of selling that have been thrown around the professions of medicine, law and the ministry.

But all of this is gradually changing. A new profession is emerging. A new salesman is developing—the professional salesman.

And it's none too soon—for business, for free enterprise, for America.

Big Business is here to stay because of its efficiency and economy and with Big Business, probably Big Labor is here to stay.

Big Business and Big Labor by their very bigness bring with them a certain degree of sacrifice of freedom of the individual. And again let me emphasize that the greatness of our American Republic stems from the freedom of the individual—freedom from coercion; freedom from class or bloc compulsion; freedom from dominance of church, state, or powerful overlords.

That freedom of the individual still finds its untrammeled expression in the farmer, the independent retailer, and in the professions.

The building of a strong profession of salesmanship will contribute to the maintenance of the freedom of the individual in three ways. First, by adding another large and influential group to the professions, we will add substantially to the number of community leaders. Second, by vastly improving the human relations between business and the customers of business. Third, by helping to maintain a strong, independent retail distribution system—its strength resting not on the crutch of legislation, but on the virile two legs of low cost and high value.

6. "I DIDN'T RAISE MY BOY TO BE A SALESMAN!" *

by J. Donald Staunton †

America needs a million new salesmen, according to informed estimates. In a poll of its membership, The National Sales Executives reported last year that its member companies alone were seeking 405,000 men for their sales forces. With virtually no ceiling on the ability of U.S. industry to produce, it begins to look as though a major bottleneck in the way of our expanding economy is the increasingly acute shortage of sales manpower.

Where are the trained salesmen of tomorrow to come from? Certainly we would expect one major source to be the colleges and universities, where an encouraging growth of interest in training for sales careers is already noticeable. Yet, as Milton Mandell noted in a recent issue of *Dun's Review,* "many young men who are influenced in their choice of a career by what their family, friends, and neighbors think still stay away from sales work." This results from the fact that many parents still look askance at selling as an occupation.

Mr. Mandell's observation is confirmed by the findings of a survey recently conducted by *The American Salesman.* (Complete survey results also appear in the February 1958 issue of that publication.) Made to determine the attitudes of students (and, by reflection, of the public) toward selling, the survey covered more than 3,000 undergraduates in 31 U.S. colleges and universities.

The findings of this survey make it clear that American industry has its own selling job to do—a job of public relations that will "sell selling" to the public and make it easier to recruit the additional salesmen so urgently needed. In addition, by revealing the factors that now motivate students in choosing or rejecting a sales career, the survey provides information that can be utilized immediately to enable campus recruiters to slant their own sales talks to the expressed interests and attitudes of the undergraduates they will be interviewing.

* Reprinted from *The Management Review,* © March 1958, pp. 9–13 ff.
† National Starch Products, Inc.

Salesmen: Fact *vs.* Fiction

Although the questions were asked of students, the feelings they expressed quite obviously have deep-rooted origins, going back to their families and teachers. Most have seen salesmen largely through consumer eyes. So their basic attitudes and conceptions indicate much about the general public's understanding of salesmen's jobs and selling.

What does the salesman do? He brings personality, organizational skills, product knowledge, and market knowledge to bear on the problems of moving goods. He works for several people: his customers, his firm, and himself. Today, as industry becomes more complex, the demands on the salesman are greater and he needs to have more technical knowledge, more control over his own personality, and more organizational and selling skill to do his job.

The Free-Association Question

The first question in the survey asked the students to list five words that they associated with the word "salesman." Their answers (question 1) indicate several prevalent misconceptions about the salesman's job. First, they show that, as a hangover from the earlier day of the drummer, aided perhaps by the impact of literature on social attitudes, people tend to think of the salesman in terms of the old cliches—as a slippery, here-today-gone-tomorrow fellow, living by his wits, ready to make a buck by any means and never staying around long because of the amount of traveling he must do. In general, they show a lack of knowledge of salesmen and consequently a lack of confidence in them.

Second, the answers indicate that the students planning on sales careers themselves have a surprisingly poor picture of what their jobs will be like. It is a more accurate image than the one the other students have, but it is still startlingly out of adjustment. In the case of only one institution (Mississippi Southern College) did the students' lists show a real understanding of selling as a career. In many colleges, apparently, salesmanship is a step-child subject that doesn't get the respect it requires.

Third, the returns suggest that even sales-minded students approach the job of selling from a self-centered point of view instead of from one which, more professionally, is customer centered.

One of the most interesting misconceptions involves the word "travel." This was by all odds the most common one found on the word list, appearing roughly twice as often as "money," which came in far ahead of the next. But, as salesmen know, the majority of them are not travelers; few go more than 100 miles from home base or spend many nights on the road.

QUESTION 1

Write Down the First 5 Words that Come into Your Mind in Connection with the Word "Salesman."

Order	All Students (Mentions)	Sales Students	Nonsales Students
1	Travel (1,003)	Money	Fast Talker
2	Money (561)	Appearance	High-Pressure
3	Personality (511)	Personality	Door-to-Door
4	Sales, Sell, Selling (484)	Work (Hard)	Car (Auto)
5	Fast Talker (476)	People	Pressure (Work)
6	Commission (445)	Service	Buy
7	Appearance (409)	Knowledge	Speech
8	Products (399)	Professional	Hours
9	High-Pressure (328)	Help, Helpful	Extrovert
10	Aggressive (246)	Customer	Insurance

Lists are in order of the frequency of mention. Words ranking about the same with both sales and nonsales students were eliminated in the sales and non-sales lists to point up the differences between those two groups.

Attitudes of Professionals

Some working salesmen were asked to make the same word association, and their lists show a striking contrast to that of the sales students. "Knowledge" and "hard work," which appear at the bottom of the students' lists, came near the top for the pros. "Time," "integrity," and "ingenuity," which appear nowhere on the students' list, were prominent on the salesmen's. In general, the professionals were customer-service and business minded instead of preoccupied primarily with the financial returns from the job.

This suggests that salesmen need to modify their sales approach to re-assure prospects who may unconsciously resent or distrust all salesmen, regardless of company or experience. It also indicates that industry has a job to do in getting educators to emphasize more effectively just what pro-fessional selling is and why the successful salesman is the one who is pre-dominantly a consultant to his customer.

One of the most respected professions in America today is medicine.

Doctors have worked hard to gain this respect; they have a stringent code of ethics, which they enforce more strictly than the public enforcement of laws regulating their actions. Such a code of ethics, plus an industry-wide effort to enforce it, suggests itself as one way to let the public know that salesmen as a group are honorable and are not fast-talking, catch-as-catch-can operators.

QUESTION 2

If Someone Asked You What Advantages You Felt There Were in Being A Salesman, What Factors Would You List?

Order	All Students	Sales Students	Nonsales Students
1	High Income	High Income	High Income
2	Meeting People	Own Boss	Meeting People
3	Own Boss	Meeting People Tied with Opportunities for Advancement	Own Boss
4	Opportunities for Advancement	Interesting Work	Travel
5	Interesting Work	Psychic Income *	Opportunities for Advancement
6	Travel	Travel	Interesting Work
7	Psychic Income *	Need for Salesmen	Psychic Income *
8	Need for Salesmen	Recognition and Prestige	Need for Salesmen
9	Recognition and Prestige	Service to Others	"There Are No Advantages"

* Psychic Income is a category into which were grouped such similar items as satisfaction, feeling of accomplishment, challenge, chance for self-expression, creativity, etc.

Advantages of Selling

The answers to question 2, about the advantages of sales work, indicate again considerable misinformation about what salesmen do. For example, time studies of sales work show that salesmen are working alone (preparing for or going to their calls, or doing paper work) most of the day. Generally, about a quarter of their working time is spent meeting people, a smaller proportion than for many other jobs. Nevertheless, almost all the students mentioned "meeting people" prominently as an advantage of a selling career. One significant difference between the sales students and those who are heading for other types of work was in their feeling about the opportunities for advancement. The sales students correctly mentioned this as a major advantage of sales jobs, realizing that a salesman's income, more than that of most other workers, is tied directly to his production. It may be that persons attracted to selling jobs have a tendency to be more adventurous than average. By both sales and other students, "recognition" and "prestige" were rarely mentioned—another reminder of the unconscious attitude of the public toward salesmen.

7. WHAT TRAITS AND WORK HABITS CHARACTERIZE SUCCESSFUL SALESMEN? *

by Eugene J. Benge †

Are you recruiting salesmen?
If so, you might do well to look for men . . .
. . . who have a strong measure of self-confidence;
. . . who have the ability to do intelligent planning;
. . . who are by nature and habit industrious in their work habits;
. . . who rate high in persuasiveness.

These are the qualities, over all others, which distinguish superior salesmen from poor salesmen. And these are perhaps the most significant of all facts developed in a new study, covering 564 salesmen in widely different types of industry. The objective of the study was to determine what factors, what personality elements, attitudes and work habits—make for success in a salesman.

The method—in its broadest terms—was to ask a group of sales managers to rate salesmen (some excellent, some poor) on each of 50 "traits." The word "trait" is used, in the interests of language simplification, to apply to a personality element, an attitude, or a work habit. These "traits," in turn, were assembled into logical groups to be referred to here as "attributes."

* Reprinted from *Sales Management,* © July 15, 1956, pp. 54–6.
† Management Engineer.

The 50 traits checked for each salesman are listed below. Note that some are stated positively, some negatively. The rating form included spaces for information on age, education, marital status, and kind and amount of experience. Its design made it possible to classify results according to the kind of selling: wholesale, industrial, etc.

Our first objective was to look at total scores for the excellent salesmen as a group, and for the poor salesmen as a group, to see whether this set of factors would provide the measure of differentiation we sought. The excellent salesmen averaged 82.1; poor salesmen, 55.6. Hence, we felt that in our analytic rating scale we had a device useful in making helpful and meaningful comparisons on individual items and groups of items.

After grouping the 50 rating items into 10 "attributes," we set up the comparative figures to reveal the differences between the excellent and the poor men. The results are shown graphically in Chart 1. The significant figures are those which show the percentage by which the excellent men exceeded the poor men on each attribute. The attributes are arranged in descending order: the biggest differential (75 per cent on self-confidence) appears as No. 1, and percentage differentiations decrease as we go down the list.

Analysis of 10 Attributes

There are some surprises. The much vaunted attribute of social development, for example, does not seem to differentiate as much as generally thought. In our scale it consists of these "traits":

Item	Percentage Excellent Men Exceed Poor Men
6—Likes People	16
16—Argues with His Customers	18
26—Everyone Seems to Like Him	33
36—Doesn't Mix with Others	25
46—Is Very Tactful	59
Attribute—Social Development	26

Bear in mind, with negatively stated items, that excellent men are superior. On the second factor listed above, they argue *less* with customers.

Later, we shall show that all salesmen, excellent or poor, tend to possess relatively high social development.

Nor does health seem to be a differentiating factor to the extent generally supposed. It here consists of:

Item	Percentage Excellent Men Exceed Poor Men
1—Enjoys Excellent Health	26
11—Has Many Ailments	19
21—Has Abundant Energy	65
31—Has a Physical Handicap	7
41—Seems Tireless	76
Attribute—Health	30

We have here a strong vote for abounding energy, with little differentiation as to health, or ailments. Salesmen as a group are healthy.

The results on "ambition" are puzzling. The five items are:

Item	Percentage Excellent Men Exceed Poor Men
8—Is Resigned to His Lot	51
18—Craves a Higher Job	28
28—Lacks Ambition	42
38—Wants Higher Responsibility	46
48—No Development Ahead of Him	26
Attribute—Ambition	38

These results suggest what many a sales manager has discovered: his men are for the most part content with selling, do not want more responsibility. Even the excellent salesmen are not markedly different in this respect from the poor men.

Our next effort was to determine the value of technical knowledge. The five items are:

Item	Percentage Excellent Men Exceed Poor Men
4—Doesn't Know His Line	34
14—Well-Informed in His Field	70
24—Tries to Bluff His Way	35
34—Is Good Technically	75
44—Doesn't Know Customers' Problems	38
Attribute—Technical Knowledge	44

In our research of individual items we were especially interested in those which showed a 75 per cent or higher differentiation. The only one which meets this standard is No. 34, "Is good technically." The other items re-

lated to technical knowledge do not differentiate excellent men from poor
men as sharply as this one. Other evidence suggests that both excellent
and poor men are somewhat deficient in this attribute.

Interest had revealed the same percentage differentiation (44 per cent)
as technical knowledge; both were below the general average differentiation of 48 per cent. However, both excellent and poor men have high interest in selling. The items are:

Item	Percentage Excellent Men Exceed Poor Men
10—Enjoys His Work	38
20—Lacks Interest in His Job	31
30—Gets a Bang from Selling	55
40—Too Many Outside Interests	24
50—Shows Consistent Enthusiasm	99
Attribute—Interest	44

Obviously, Item 50 offers sharp differentiation. Whatever the devices
which bring about enthusiasm in a salesman for his job, they are well worth
cultivating. Excellent salesmen are much more enthusiastic than poor salesmen. In fact, if we rated this trait alone on a scale of 1 to 100, with 50 being
midpoint, we would find that excellent salesmen score 87.5 and poor salesmen score 44.0 points.

Range of Intelligence

Intelligence yielded a 48 per cent differentiation which is just the average
of the entire scale. The five items are:

Item	Percentage Excellent Men Exceed Poor Men
3—Not Very Intelligent	30
13—Has Excellent Judgment	121
23—Slow to Comprehend	51
33—Is a Keen Thinker	93
43—Poor Education	17
Attribute—Intelligence	48

These figures almost speak for themselves. Judgment in a salesman is
a useful trait, as distinguished from brilliance or wide education. The intelligence level needed for sales work is not exceptionally high; other attributes are more important.

We shall now consider a group of four attributes which showed fairly
sharp differentiations of excellent over poor men. These traits are persuasiveness, industriousness, self-confidence, and planning.

The five factors we classed as persuasiveness are:

Item	Percentage Excellent Men Exceed Poor Men
5—Is Fluent	48
15—Is Too Blunt	25
25—Is Persuasive	92
35—Hesitant in Speech	30
45—Is Convincing	102
Attribute—Persuasiveness	52

These figures suggest that the ability to persuade, to convince, is important to success. Yet most sales training programs seem to concentrate on giving a salesman information about the product or service rather than helping him to develop these vital abilities.

Sales managers know that if a salesman is industrious, makes a stipulated number of calls per day consistently, he will turn in a good record. This belief seems to be substantiated by the results on industriousness. The five items are:

Item	Percentage Excellent Men Exceed Poor Men
9—Is Very Persistent	80
19—Is Readily Discouraged	56
29—Keeps Hammering Away	81
39—Is Lazy	37
49—Repeatedly Asks for the Order	77
Attribute—Industriousness	60

These results are fairly consistent and suggest that perseverance pays off.

We come now to an attribute which sales managers hammer away at consistently, and one which sales training programs probably should stress more. It is planning. The five items are:

Item	Percentage Excellent Men Exceed Poor Men
2—Plans His Presentation	109
12—Is Always Behind Schedule	45
22—Plans His Time Well	128
32—Is a Time Waster	67
42—Gets Information on Prospects	76
Attribute—Planning	74

Here again we see a fairly clear-cut outline of an excellent salesman as far as planning is concerned. He plans his presentation, maintains his schedule, plans his time, avoids wasting time, and gets advance information on prospects.

We often hear it said that self-confidence in a salesman is a useful trait and the figures here seem to confirm this belief. The five items are:

Item	Percentage Excellent Men Exceed Poor Men
7—Is Undecisive	94
17—Is Quite Aggressive	81
27—Is Apologetic	47
37—Takes the Lead in a Sale	91
47—Lacks Confidence in Self	64
Attribute—Self-Confidence	75

We see here a clear picture: The excellent salesman is decisive, aggressive, not apologetic, takes the lead, and has self-confidence.

We have now contrasted excellent and poor salesmen as to ten major attributes. We have shown that the big differentiations occur in self-confidence, in the ability to plan, in industriousness, and in persuasiveness. Of less value, but still important, are the differentiations of intelligence, interest, and technical knowledge.

Finally, excellent salesmen are differentiated from poor salesmen to less degree by the factors of ambition, health, and social development.

CHART 1

Excellent Salesmen versus Poor Salesmen: How They Compare in Ten Attributes

Attributes	Excellent Men Scored:	Poor Men Scored:	Per Cent by which Excellent Men Exceeded Poor Men:
1. Self Confidence	84	48	75
2. Planning Ability	82	47	74
3. Industriousness	83	52	60
4. Persuasiveness	85	56	52
5. Intelligence	77	52	48
6. Technical Knowledge	79	55	44
7. Interest	89	62	44
8. Ambition	77	56	38
9. Health	83	64	30
10. Social Development	82	65	26
Average Score, All Ten Factors	82.1	55.6	48

The Fifty Points on Which the Sales Group Was Rated

(Note that statements are both positive and negative. On No. 7, for example, the majority of the sales executives denied this quality as applied to excellent salesmen.)

1. Enjoys excellent health
2. Plans his presentations *
3. Not very intelligent
4. Doesn't know his line
5. Is fluent
6. Likes people
7. Is indecisive *
8. Is resigned to his lot
9. Is very persistent *
10. Enjoys his work
11. Has many ailments
12. Is always behind schedule
13. Has excellent judgment *
14. Well-informed in his field
15. Is too blunt
16. Argues with his customers
17. Is quite aggressive *
18. Craves a higher job
19. Is readily discouraged
20. Lacks interest in his job
21. Has abundant energy
22. Plans his time well *
23. Slow to comprehend
24. Tries to bluff his way
25. Is persuasive *
26. Everyone seems to like him
27. Is apologetic
28. Lacks ambition
29. Keeps hammering away *
30. Gets a bang from selling
31. Has a physical handicap
32. Is a time waster
33. Is a keen thinker *
34. Is good technically *
35. Hesitant in speech
36. Doesn't mix with others
37. Takes the lead in a sale *
38. Wants higher responsibility
39. Is lazy
40. Too many outside interests
41. Seems tireless *
42. Gets information about prospects *
43. Poor education
44. Doesn't know customer problems
45. Is convincing *
46. Is very tactful
47. Lacks confidence in self
48. No development ahead of him
49. Repeatedly asks for the order *
50. Shows consistent enthusiasm *

* Starred items were those which proved to be outstanding in differentiating excellent salesmen from poor salesmen.

The Rewards of Selling

8. NEW LIGHT ON SALESMEN'S COMPENSATION *

by Berthold B. Baer †

Today, wage and salary administration programs covering nonexempt employees have become standard practice in most companies, and much attention is being given to executive compensation plans. But even in companies with the most advanced wage and salary programs, salesmen's compensation has remained a comparatively uncharted territory.

The reason for this situation is not difficult to find: A necessary first step in the establishment of any sound wage and salary administration program is the development of a basis for comparison with the pay practices of industry in general—and of competition in particular. In the case of salesmen's compensation, however, the absence of any systematic method of classifying salesmen in terms of responsibility and job content has been a major obstacle to the development of a body of data that would give company managements a logical basis for evaluating their practices.

Now, however, the results of a year-long study just completed by AMA's Executive Compensation Service indicate that salesmen can be classified and their pay plans compared for the purpose of establishing realistic and generally acceptable standards of compensation. The survey covered over 17,000 sales personnel in almost 200 companies.

How the Data Were Classified

In order to arrange the information gathered by the survey in usable form, some practical method of classification had to be devised. The first

* Reprinted from *The Management Review,* © September 1956, pp. 804–8.
† American Management Association.

step was to find common denominators in terms of markets served. Does the salesman sell to jobbers, distributors, wholesalers, retailers, or industrial users of his products? Is the product subject to consistent reorders, or is it a capital item? Is it durable, perishable, or subject to early obsolescence? Is technical knowledge required? Are products used as is, or in the manufacture of other products? Are products made to order, or are they stock items? These and other similar considerations comprised the basis for differentiating between various classifications of selling jobs. Applied to the returns in the survey, these factors produced six major marketing categories, among which there were significant differences in compensation practices. The six categories are:

The Food Industry

Consumer Products—Nondurable Goods (other than food)

Consumer Products—Durable Goods

Industrial Products—Raw Materials and Components

Industrial Products—Accessory Materials and Equipment

Industrial Products—Capital Goods

The wide range in compensation of salesmen among companies with similar sales problems—and, frequently, even within the same company— indicates that there is more than one level of salesmen. (Although some companies show only one level, with pay ranges as broad as $5,000 to $15,000, experience in wage and salary administration makes it clear that $5,000 salesmen are not in the same class as those earning $15,000.)

The Three Levels of Salesmen

Upon closer analysis, including personal interviews with many executives responsible for salesmen's compensation in their companies, it developed that, for compensation purposes, there were at least three clearly discernible levels of salesmen. These levels were designated Grades I, II, and III.

The Grade I salesman, usually a beginner, has a limited territory and minor accounts, and his daily activities are subject to a substantial amount of supervision. Except for routine matters and cases where he is specifically delegated the authority, he must follow the established price and delivery policies of the company without deviation. About 60 per cent of the salesmen are in this category.

The Grade II salesman is one level above the beginning salesman by virtue of his training, experience, or both. In companies where inexperienced salesmen are not hired, this is the entering level. The salesman at this level is often technically trained and has a special knowledge of the field in which he operates, although his direct sales experience might not be significant. Approximately 30 per cent of the salesmen are in this class.

Grade III is the highest level of selling at which a man can maintain his identity as a salesman. Operating with only general supervision, the Grade III salesman handles key accounts or a large territory. Depending on his experience or knowledge, he may deal in technical sales at an advanced level. About 10 per cent of the salesmen are at this level.

Other positions identified by the survey are the Sales Trainee, who is just below the Grade I salesman; the Sales Supervisor, who is immediately above the Grade III salesman; and District and Regional Sales Managers. These six classifications, which are somewhat generalized, are composites of the organizational levels revealed by a detailed study of the sales organizations of participating companies. They were *not* chosen to show a model sales organization; rather, they were developed from the report as a logical structure on which to base salesmen's compensation.

Range of Average Total Compensation

Combining all six marketing categories (which are analyzed separately in the report), average compensation ranges for the three levels of salesmen are as follows:

Grade I	$5,000 to $ 7,500
Grade II	$6,000 to $10,000
Grade III	$8,500 to $15,000

The above ranges include more than 80 per cent of the field sales personnel covered in the survey. The ranges of the Grade II and III salesmen are wider than would be established under most formal job evaluation plans, but they result here because the various marketing categories have been combined, plus the fact that bonus and commission payments have been included.

Future surveys may narrow these ranges by the addition of further breakdowns in the marketing categories, and further refinement of these data will make the information more specifically applicable to the particular situations of individual companies.

Methods of Compensation

There are three basic methods of paying salesmen: salary alone, salary plus bonus or commission, and commission alone. Approximately 10 per cent of the companies pay their salesmen straight commissions, and about 23 per cent pay salaries only. The remaining companies pay their salesmen some combination of salary plus incentive, such as bonus or commission.

The most popular method of paying salesmen, found in over 36 per cent of the companies, is the salary-plus-bonus arrangement.[1]

Incentive plans often have different objectives, and, in evaluating a particular plan, the specific purpose for which it was designed must be kept in mind. In some cases, such plans are used to achieve other goals than increased sales; one company, for example, provides incentives with an eye toward keeping sales-volume level throughout the year, so that constant production rates may be maintained. Other plans, designed to reduce selling costs, provide bonuses when sales expenses are reduced.

Most companies do not have any specific limits on salesmen's expense accounts, including travel allowances, as long as the total involved is "reasonable." The definition of "reasonable" varies from company to company, of course, but most companies prefer to keep the limits flexible to meet special situations as well as constant changes in the costs of traveling.

As far as other forms of extra compensation are concerned, salesmen today seem to do as well as other employees. All the companies in the survey provide group life insurance and group hospitalization for the salesmen, and 90 per cent have pension plans under which their salesmen are covered. Other group insurance benefits are provided for salesmen to about the same extent as they are for other employees.

9. INCENTIVE COMPENSATION AND

THE INDUSTRIAL SALESMAN *

Introduction

In the expanding economy of the United States, effective manpower is our scarcest resource. Therefore, selecting, training, motivating, and supervising manpower resources is one of the most important tasks of the marketing executive. The purpose of this article is to present an approach to increasing the effectiveness of the industrial sales force, a resource that

* Reprinted from *Cost and Profit Outlook,* © November 1956.
[1] Of interest to many companies will be the survey report's data on the frequency, type, and amount of general increases that have been granted salesmen since the end of World War II, and a discussion of the effect that compensation has on turnover. The report also discusses and analyzes the provisions of incentive plans currently in use and includes, whenever possible, the actual dollar amounts paid to various levels of salesmen, in order to enable the executive concerned with salesmen's compensation to evaluate the effectiveness of these plans and to determine whether the use of a particular bonus or commission plan in his company would produce results that would justify its costs.

is especially critical since the time required for the development of a good man is not measured in months, but rather in years.

During a period when competition for technically trained personnel who are at the same time possessed of competence, intelligence, and drive is at an all-time high, no producer of industrial products can afford to pass up the remotest possibility that a tailor-made incentive compensation plan can be constructed which is compatible with his marketing program. While it is true that in many industrial marketing situations the stubborn simplicity or extreme complexity of the sales situation to be confronted defies the development of workable plans, this should not lead to the conclusion that incentive compensation is a management tool available only to the sellers of consumer goods.

The efficiency and effectiveness of the industrial salesman is a continuing area of interest for sales management. The degree to which performance can be improved through the use of incentive compensation plans is a topic of lively discussion with successful managements which are both pro and con in their opinions on the question. It is generally agreed that in the field of consumer goods selling, the installation of an incentive plan that is equitable, understandable, and easy to administer is far more simple than in the selling of industrial products. However, the more standardized industrial products moving through established channels of distribution such as mill supply houses, or industrial distributors, are quite similar to consumer goods in relation to the construction of incentive plans.

Industrial Application

This article is pointed toward the larger, old-line industrial corporations where, traditionally, basic salary has been all or almost all of a salesman's financial reward. Many of these companies have adopted the organizational theory of decentralization or creating semiautonomous divisions. The differences in problems that led to the creation of these separate and clearly delineated visions may also be the basis for requiring a different type of incentive plan in tune with the problems and requirements of each individual division within a company.

The complexities of industrial marketing immediately raise many problems which on first examination appear insurmountable with respect to the installation of an effective incentive plan. However, many of these difficulties melt away under hard scrutiny. The position taken in this article is positive and the number of apparent roadblocks examined should not be allowed to create a negative impression.

In its simplest form, the most common type of incentive compensation plan is designed to reward a salesman for producing more-than-anticipated sales, especially sales which add marginal volume with a greater-than-average contribution to profits. Hence, the company is willing to share in-cremental profits with the salesman on the basis of a formal plan which prescribes the reward. Since a plan is directed at extra effectiveness, not necessarily extra effort, it must be based on a clear understanding of normal effectiveness and anticipated normal sales results. This analysis is the thorny part of the problem since industrial selling is complex and subject to severe variations. Industrial selling can range from "reason why" specifi-cation engineering selling to commodity tank-car type selling oriented to service customer maintenance and development. These variations may exist not only within a company, but even in the case of the selling task assigned to one salesman in the company, depending on whether the sales-men are deployed by geographic territories, by product lines, or in some other way.

A crucial initial decision is whether to reward solely hard sales dollars with the result of disregarding effort to a large degree, or whether to reward excellent effort even if, for some good reason, extra sales dollars are not forthcoming as a related result. In other words, does sales management reward *cause,* or *result?* They may not be directly connected because of the effect of selling variables. In highly centralized companies there is a tendency to emphasize effort as the criterion since this insures the carrying out of the sales plan, and in highly decentralized companies paying off is based only on impersonal numerical results.

Problems and Solutions

Other important market situations which may tend to confuse the issue and make it difficult to evaluate the actual contribution of the salesman are the following:

1. A few major customers may account for a large proportion of sales, with the result that these key accounts are cultivated by sales executives, district managers, technical specialists, and others, making it difficult to isolate the contribution of the regular salesman. There is no easy solution to this problem. Some companies remove such accounts from the incentive plan, classify them as "house accounts," and consider the motivation of salary level and promotion as adequate to require the salesman to service the customers. Others leave the accounts in the plan considering the sales-man as the quarterback, calling the signals on the use of executive and specialist selling, and thus justify reward for the salesman.

2. An important problem arises when a company is both a large cus-tomer and a major supplier. Here, sales results may be determined more by the total relationship than by any possible activity on the part of a salesman. This type of relationship may be handled either by the house account method or by a reduced percentage reward for such customers. In

any event, the salesman is still expected to provide a satisfactory level of service.

3. Windfalls can seriously affect the results of even the most carefully constructed incentive plan. The opening of a new plant in a new territory, an unforeseen shortage of supply, an epidemic situation, technical developments, market shifts, and other unforecasted favorable developments can result in rewarding a salesman for developments beyond his control (instances of nonrecurring demand). Protection against these contigencies can be secured either by specific clauses in the plan or by a simple percentage ceiling on total incentive reward. Unexpected decreases should be handled by a review board, perhaps with alteration of the compensation base as an adjustment.

4. Another constant problem results from "headquarters purchasing" with deliveries of materials to geographically decentralized plants in other sales territories which require service calls. The cold-blooded application of a split credit arrangement in the plan is the arbitrary solution which simply grants that some inequities will probably result, but with the realization that nothing in life is perfect.

5. The migration of plants from one sales territory to another creates problems of constant adjustment, for each territory, of the expected normal sales volume which is the base for the computation of the incentive reward. This variable can be handled through the mechanism of a review and adjustment committee or board. Such a vehicle should exist in order to provide necessary administration for an incentive plan.

6. In the case of industrial products, geographical patterns of concentrated use occur, and a company's marketing or product development emphasis may inequitably affect a salesman of, for example, base chemicals for pesticides versus a more fortunate salesman of plasticizers, in another territory where consumption is concentrated and current use is high. In other words, at any given time, the opportunities in a product line may differ by territory, with unfortunate results to any salesman. Unfortunately, about the only answer to this possibility is that such results will tend to even out over time between the opportunities of different territories.

7. Some fears exist that new product introduction may be affected if the salesman's interest is directed at the more profitable incentive aspects of established products. However, an incentive plan cannot be a substitute for or interfere with the function of good sales management and unflinching control over activities of the sales force.

8. Another situation which may plague a plan is found when the plant or factory produces, for an extended period of time, certain inferior products which are difficult to sell in competition. If this can be established as the fact of the matter and lasts long enough substantially to affect the results of the plan on an annual basis, the review board can remove the prod-

uct or products involved from the calculation of the incentive as set forth in the plan. If unattainable goals are allowed to exist, the confidence of the sales force in sales management is damaged.

9. One danger in any plan is that it will reward only sales increases in relation to an established opportunity, and will fail to reward the salesman with an already high share of market—who is doing an excellent job by simply maintaining high performance against the onslaughts of competition. Both situations are hard to take into account in one incentive plan and prove the point that an incentive plan is no substitute for good salary administration and promotion rewards for the superior salesman in either case.

10. Negotiating concessions (price, service, etc.) that management may make available to one salesman for one important sale, but which are not available to all the sales force, can affect results of the incentive in terms of consistency of reward between salesmen with the same gross opportunity. These inequities cannot be adjusted readily but may even out over time.

These situations are illustrative of market conditions, largely beyond the control of the salesman, which can influence the results of an incentive plan.

It is apparent that this list of variables can, and does in some cases, create substantial inequities in the case of some salesmen in any given time period. Most industrial sales executives feel that an incentive plan, to be effective, must come close to mathematical precision in establishing a relationship between reward and sales effectiveness, or it will do more harm than good. However, many industrial salesmen are willing to live with the possible inequities of an incentive plan in order to obtain its benefits. As a group, industrial salesmen are generally well educated, especially in the sciences, and therefore can understand the mathematical pattern of an incentive formula and the effects of variables on the end result. Frequently the recognition accorded a high score in a competitive situation is as important to salesmen as the monetary reward. In addition, salesmen usually have faith in their supervisors' fairness in presenting inequities to the review board where problems are resolved.

The point of the preceding paragraphs is that the admitted existence of selling conditions or circumstances which are largely beyond the control of a salesman should not automatically bar consideration of the value of a sales incentive plan to a company. Our income tax rulings frequently seem arbitrary or capricious, but the law is generally effective.

Effects on Administration and Control

Sales management, in turn, generally has some reservations concerning the effects of an incentive plan on sales administration and control.

Common concerns are:

1. Will too high an incentive lead to short-term, unsound selling practices, rather than long-range, investment type selling? Will too small an incentive be ineffective and be considered by the sales force an inferior substitute for good salary administration?

2. Will cultivation of new, small accounts or introduction of new products be hampered?

3. Will the transfer of salesmen from one territory to another be affected, depending upon the structure of the plan?

4. How can technical service and development personnel be rewarded for their assistance which is frequently vital in specification selling?

5. If an incentive plan fails to work, can it be dropped after two or three years without adding incentives to regular salary base as the price of elimination?

6. Some men are already turning in a superlative performance. An incentive plan could not exert greater effect on these men. Therefore, will the plan only reward the mediocre performer?

7. Will the management and administration of the plan be time consuming and difficult for home office sales executives?

8. Will freedom to move certain products over to industrial distributors be complicated?

9. If sales management decides not to meet lowest competitive prices on a short-run basis, will ill feeling arise among the salesmen on the basis of lost volume?

10. Will reassigning of accounts or realigning territories be resisted? Currently, many companies are more intensively cultivating smaller territories.

These objections by sales management to the possible adverse influences of an incentive plan tend to melt away, if it is made unmistakably clear to the salesman that his long-run career development rests primarily on salary administration and promotion, used as the principal tools of sales administration and control, rather than on the moderate benefit of an annual incentive plan. With this understood by all concerned, a good climate of cooperation can be established readily.

Other Considerations

Many times companies fear that the installation of a sales incentive plan will arouse the resentment and envy of other departments within the company for whom no such special reward is available. This unfortunate condition will only exist if the company has failed to presell the basic requirements for a sales incentive plan.

First, it is important to point out to the other departments that, generally speaking, direct supervision and leadership is available to them on a daily basis which insures maximum effectiveness, and personal observation by immediate superiors to set the standards for salary increases and promotions. Opposed to this situation is the life of a salesman, frequently out of sight and out of mind and suffering from lack of direct, continuous, and personal supervision by his immediate superiors. While salesmen may consider an incentive plan a reward, sales management should consider a plan as another tool of indirect supervision rather than a financial reward to subordinates.

Second, a salesman's life requires protracted absences from home, arduous travel schedules and irregular working hours. In most instances, personnel of other departments would not exchange jobs for the addition of a modest incentive reward. Experience indicates this feeling is stronger than would be expected.

If the above factors are carefully presold to personnel of other departments, we have found little or no evidence of jealousy of the salesmen receiving a moderate incentive.

For industrial salesmen an important factor is the high degree of cooperation which must exist between salesmen within a district and between districts. Industrial selling requires a high degree of team play. Therefore, in many instances it is best to allow the incentive reward to reach each district as a group incentive, and either to prorate the fund in relation to percentage of each man's salary to total district salaries or, if such a method would be too arbitrary, to place considerable discretion in the district sales manager's judgment as to how the pool should be allocated. While it is agreed that group incentives tend to dull individual motivation, a combined group and individual plan is probably the best method to reward both team and individual effort.

It is of crucial importance that statistics be available for measuring performance as an impartial offset to the exercise of subjective judgment or the simple use of last year's sales as a standard by sales management. However, if product statistics are not available in all cases, sometimes forecasts based on the customer's industry may be used instead, particularly if they are put through a dry run for the past few years in order to evaluate any important and pertinent special circumstances which may exist.

One of the dilemmas of installing an incentive plan is that the simpler the plan is to understand, the greater may be the inequities which creep in, and the more equitable the plan, the more complex and difficult it is to understand. Some moderate compromise must be reached.

Company Objectives and the Compensation Plan

An industrial sales incentive plan must be specifically tailored to the specific problems of the individual company and its place in its industry. Adopted plans are too frequently unsuccessful. Management must clearly set forth in the first instance the objectives of its sales policy which will materially control the type of plan. For example, a plan may be devised to maintain a current high share of the market. A plan may be devised with its major objective being control of sales expenses. A plan may be devised directed at simply fast volume growth, or a plan may be devised to increase share of market in relation to opportunity methodically.

This decision is especially important when the salesman makes a number of decisions himself. If he must decide how often to visit and how much time and effort to devote to each customer and potential customer, the salesman in effect operates like an independent business enterprise. He has his own reward and cost relationships which will be taken into account by him in allocating his time and effort. Here the sales incentive plan must serve to coordinate the objectives of the firm with those of the individual salesman. They must literally assure the salesman that: "What is good for the company is good for you."

It is at this point that sales incentive plans can go wrong by employing indirection. For example, an executive whose company's main objective is long-run profit may decide against basing sales incentive compensation on the profitability of the item sold, perhaps because some of the profitable items are in high demand, and he does not want to reward the salesman for doing something which requires little effort. The effect of a decision to reward effort by offering a higher incentive for sales of hard-to-push items can only be detrimental to the company. Such a compensation scheme seeks to induce a salesman to direct his time to items which sell infrequently and bring in low profits when they do sell.

Another related fallacy in incentive planning is the so-called fallacy of "suboptimisation"—the promotion of a proximate objective instead of a final goal. A large sales volume can add to profits, but not if sales consist largely of loss leaders or other less profitable items. It can be desirable to promote items whose manufacturing cost is low, but not if their market price is too high. In other words, it is desirable to base rewards in an incentive plan on sales volume only if the company's objective is share of market *for its own sake,* and this is not an intermediate objective adopted as a substitute for profit criterion as the standard of a plan.

Sometimes it may not be possible to devise a practical incentive plan which directly rewards contribution to profit or to whatever ultimate objectives the firm has adopted. This may occur, for example, because the relevant data are unavailable, or the resulting plan may be too complex for salesmen to follow. In such a case some substitute criteria will have to be employed, but these criteria must always be measured by the fidelity with which they approximate the ultimate objectives of the company.

Conclusion

In conclusion, in constructing a sales incentive program (and space here does not permit dealing with all pertinent factors) *first,* sales management must understand the detailed character of the specific selling job and the part which extra effectiveness with a reward can play. *Second,* there must exist some type of index for impartially measuring performance, and while this may appear impossible at the outset, many ingenious methods have been devised. In the case of consumer goods, such statistics are generally available from published sources, special services, or market studies. *Third,* full account must be taken of all major selling variables even if this requires arbitrary methods; most salesmen have a basic confidence in the fairness of management. *Fourth,* incentive compensation plans can only be superimposed on an already good salary administration and careful sales management controls, they are not a substitute for these. *Fifth,* it must be remembered that it is at the salesman-purchasing agent meeting that products are exchanged for money, the basis of our economy, and any tool which will strengthen the motivation of the salesman in this relationship is the starting point of profits.

Currently some companies seem to feel that an incentive plan reduces their control of the daily activities of a salesman, while others feel that a carefully devised plan is an excellent method of improving control since a plan can be a means of indirect supervision. This again indicates how personal to the individual company's character and problems is the need or lack of need for such a tool. However, if reward, recognition, and security are the three basic motivating factors in job satisfaction leading to superior performance, incentive plans can strengthen the impact of the first two.

10. MORE AND MORE "BENEFIT" FACTORS COMING INTO SALESMEN'S PAY PLANS *

"Firms eager to hire the best qualified young men as salesmen are likely to find from now on that they have no appeal for these candidates unless they are in a position to offer certain benefits over and above immediate monthly compensation."

This view is expressed by William Hardy, sales manager, West Coast

* Reprinted from *Sales Management,* © September 7, 1956, pp. 92–9.

Life Insurance Company, San Francisco. The benefits he refers to include retirement plans, various kinds of health insurance, paid vacations, and a long list of other adjuncts to salary and commission now coming into more general use in a wide variety of industries.

Some of these benefits have been in effect for years among the more enlightened companies. But elsewhere they have been adopted as a result of labor unions' shifting emphasis on concessions beyond wages and hours.

Forgotten Men?

Even in the face of today's tight situation in sales manpower, it is easy to find many companies where salesmen are not offered any of the benefits enjoyed by factory workers. The salesmen, as one executive put it, "are left out in the cold with only their rugged individualism wrapped around them."

Under the aegis of the San Francisco Sales Executives' Association, Hardy recently was co-chairman of a round table discussion on the subject of fringe benefits for salesmen.

During the meeting a questionnaire was passed out and filled in by 33 members, anonymously. The questionnaire asked for fringe benefits offered by firms the participants represented. It was pointed out that in the years ahead "more and more salesmen under consideration for employment will be asking more about your fringe benefits than about the job itself." It was suggested that regardless of how management felt about this attitude on the part of job candidates, companies would do well to forget some of their old policies and prejudices and adjust their sights to the realities of the situation.

(Some months ago *Sales Management* pointed out that these "realities" are based on simple economics. Under today's tax structure it is almost impossible for a man to save enough money to provide retirement income unless he is the fortunate possessor of inherited equities. This situation preys on the minds of salesmen as it does on the minds of workers in any other trade or profession and it, more than anything else, is responsible for the pressure to gain retirement and insurance benefits.)

The Union Issue

Discussion during the San Francisco round table brought out the opinion that programs of fringe benefits for salesmen are effective in heading off unionization of sales forces. Sales managers expressed the belief that "since the merger of the Congress of Industrial Organizations and the American Federation of Labor there is a strong possibility that further pressure will be exerted for unionization and sales forces may well be a target."

The San Francisco and East Bay Areas are among the most intensively unionized areas of the country, hence the concern of the management men about the relationship between fringe benefits and unionization. On the coast, unionization has extended into just about all of the businesses that employ driver-salesmen—wholesale and retail bakeries, dairies, groceries, beverages, and similar fields. Sales staffs of many automobile dealers are unionized, and some insurance personnel.

The executives participating in the round table were somewhat startled at the range of benefits now being given to their sales forces. Here is the breakdown covering the 33 firms:

Hospital, surgical, medical, for self and dependents: 19

Group life insurance, self and dependents: 17

Accidental death: 11

Retirement plans, contributory: 4

Retirement plans, noncontributory: 8

Paid vacations and holidays: 21

Company-owned automobiles: 10

Pay roll deduction services and personal purchase privileges: 16. (These cover instances where companies do the bookkeeping for employees who wish to have a specified amount taken out of salary for such a purpose as the purchase of U.S. bonds. Or instances where deductions are made to cover additional insurance, or different kinds of insurance, not provided in the over-all insurance plan. "Personal purchase privileges" refer to sale, at a discount, of company products to employees, or to plans the company sets up with outside suppliers through which the employee can buy at a discount with bills paid through pay roll deductions.)

Recreation sponsorship (bowling teams, softball, etc.): 10

Salary continuance after illness or accident: 17

Subsidized lunches: 11

Guaranteed annual wage: 4

Medical consultation: 4

Social functions paid for by the company: 11

Several of the reporting companies give an extra vacation after a specified number of years of employment. Several others reported a company stock purchase plan. The sales executives pointed out that in cases where companies offered benefits to home office employees but not to salesmen, the salesmen could be expected to ask for these same benefits.

"Off the Record"

Although admitting off the record that fringe benefits for salesmen will be increasingly indicated if further unionization of sales forces is to be staved off, many sales executives interviewed by *Sales Management* felt the issue to be so full of dynamite that they talked only with the understanding they would not be quoted by name.

"If we except the men usually described as driver-salesmen, I do not believe salesmen generally are receptive to the idea of unionization unless they are working under conditions where the pay arrangement is obviously unfair and where they are more or less continuously harassed by worries over ups and downs of income," says one sales manager. "In such a case the company is asking for unionization, and is likely to get it."

Here's the kind of situation he has in mind:

It involves approximately 550 car salesmen employed by 46 franchised new-car dealers in Minneapolis. Some of these men contended that a union was needed to protect them from sharp practices of the dealers as car sales volume and profits of the dealers declined.

One salesman said he earned $780 in May 1955. On the same volume of sales, he said, he would have earned $375 in May 1956 under the new plan of commissions and guarantees the men were asked to accept. Actually his sales were down in May of this year, and his check amounted to $260. This same man earned more than $1,000 a month in four months of 1955.

Another salesman was working on a "20 per cent washout" commission basis. (The salesman gets 20 per cent of the dealer's net profit on a sale, but if there is no profit, the salesman is "washed out.") This man sold an air-conditioned new car for $4,000. When he presented the proposed trade-in-and-new-car deal to the sales manager, the salesman was told he could close the sale only if he agreed to pay half the cost of the new-car license. The salesman did close the deal. The new-car price had been discounted $600 to move the expensive model off the showroom floor. That was subtracted from the dealer's net profit. Then the dealer figured in $100 for servicing the trade-in car, and $150 for servicing and going over the new car. These amounts also were subtracted from the dealer's net profit.

When the figuring was over, the salesman had a commission of $7.00 for selling a $4,000 car. He paid $13.00 for his half of the new-car license, and ended up with a net loss of $6.00.

While shopping around for a union, the auto salesmen at one time considered the International Brotherhood of Teamsters as bargaining agent. The teamsters union represents garage mechanics. The salesmen knew that in the event of a strike, the dealers presumably could operate without salesmen but they couldn't get along without mechanics.

At the time, however, the teamsters were involved in labor dynamiting incidents in Minneapolis and St. Paul (two teamster officials were convicted in Minneapolis but found not guilty in St. Paul in two identical cases). There was also an unsavory case in which four union officials were convicted of accepting a $10,000 pay-off from an industrial company.

The auto salesmen voted to join the Retail Clerks International Association, a powerful union in some parts of the East and on the West Coast. The retail clerks began negotiations for an initial contract for the auto salesmen, demanding a monthly guarantee of $400, increased commissions, and other additional demands which the dealers considered "outlandish."

The auto dealers sent an industrial relations consultant to a few meetings with union negotiators, to remain within the law, but it was apparent from the outset that the union wasn't going to get anywhere. On May 10, the auto salesmen went on strike. The teamster mechanics went through the picket lines to report for work.

(Teamsters traditionally recognize picket lines of almost any union. When asked whether they ignored the retail clerks picket lines because they did not recognize the retail clerks as a union, one teamster official said, "Hell, we don't even recognize the clerks as human beings.")

Why Salesmen Quit

The ill-fated strike continued three weeks, with about a dozen of the 46 garages picketed. Windows in two display rooms were smashed and one striker was arrested.

When the strike was about to fall on its face, the salesmen returned to work under an "agreement" in which the dealers promised to "sit down and discuss the issues, just as we've always been willing to sit down and discuss the issues." There wasn't much question as to how the discussions would come out, if, indeed, they are ever held.

Old hands among car salesmen are frankly puzzled by what the dealers have in mind. One said, "It has been reasonably clear for a long time that if you want to get any work out of a horse, you have to give it some oats once in awhile. We haven't been getting even hay for the last six months."

One of the largest new-car dealers has had three sales managers since the first of the year. One left after three weeks. Another lasted two and one-half months.

The salesman who has had top new-car sales volume in seven of the last ten years in Minneapolis left shortly after the strike for California. He is setting up a business in which he will sell to retail souvenir shops inexpensive jewelry and art objects turned out in the Portuguese settlements around Los Angeles. He says he's through with car selling.

This perhaps is an extreme case, but it provides a revealing contrast to situations where companies enjoy happy and productive sales forces and minimum turnover rates. The majority of sales executives who were asked for both practices and opinions on fringe benefits as factors in salesmen's compensation said they had observed that generous fringe benefit programs were usually in operation among companies where the percentage of turnover on the sales force is very low. But turnover dogs certain kinds of selling even when extra benefits are in force.

One of these fields is specialty selling direct to the consumer. One natural gas utility, with a force selling gas-using appliances, offers hospitalization (at $1 a month cost to the salesman), life insurance (no cost to the salesman), paid vacations, Christmas bonuses, and a retirement program in which the company pays two-thirds of the cost. Yet, says one of its executives, "we still have a heavy rate of turnover."

One type of fringe benefit in operation in many industrial companies requiring salesmen with engineering backgrounds is extended education partly paid for by the company—a plan which seems to have wide appeal to ambitious engineering graduates. Line Material Company, Milwaukee, for example, has a scholarship program under which a sales engineer may take advanced training in any phase of business that he and his supervisor consider beneficial. The company pays two-thirds of the fee every semester.

Benefits and Turnover

In this firm the sales engineers enjoy the same benefits as other employees, including life insurance, comprehensive medical coverage, a bonus plan, and a retirement fund. Thomas C. Hughes, manager, sales services, believes that this program contributes materially to a low turnover rate: Line Material has lost less than 1 per cent of its sales engineers so far in 1956.

Another plus—awards of company stock—is popular with district fountain men (contacting jobbers, theater concessionnaires, cup vendor operators) who sell fountain syrup, and zone managers for Dr. Pepper Company, Dallas. The top district fountain man, and top zone manager each year get 25 shares of Dr. Pepper stock. A company spokesman says: "They prefer the stock to money because, for one thing, they know they won't go out and spend it. Salesmen who win stock very rarely sell it. We like to award stock because once an employee becomes a shareholder, he is more solidly tied to the company. Often he'll buy more stock to add to what he has won. Though our cash bonuses and other incentive awards all are effective, nothing quite equals the appeal of stock."

Dr. Pepper's program of "extras" includes vacations; medical, surgical and hospital coverage at a slightly lower rate than an individual could get for himself; group insurance (company pays 50 per cent); vacations (longer on a seniority basis); a credit union in which employees save money and from which they can borrow for emergency needs at a very low interest rate; cash bonuses (a man can earn as much as $6,000 a year in bonuses) and incentive awards to bottlers' salesmen (and most bottlers have their own incentive programs).

Dr. Pepper lives in two worlds so far as unionization goes. Some of the driver-salesmen are unionized; in St. Louis, Dr. Pepper's company-owned bottling plant is unionized.

Why Executives Are Cagey

The reticence of sales executives to talk freely on the relationship between fringe benefit programs and the union issue is traceable to a number of factors:

1. The shock some of them experienced on being confronted with the fact of unionization when they had ridden along for years on the assumption that "it couldn't happen to us." Now they must find ways to work harmoniously with unions. Company lawyers and personnel "brass" have gagged everybody on unionization.

2. Some sales executives are in the process of attempting to sell top management on the desirability of installing a program of fringe benefits and in cases where they have been unable to do so—at the same time acutely sensing the need for such a program—have a sense of frustration. Diplomatically, they cannot come out and say they're at odds with a board or an executive committee over policy.

3. Some prefer to sit tight on a no-extra-benefits policy until circumstances force action. From the standpoint of employee relations, they cannot put themselves on record.

4. Hundreds of companies are operating with nonunion sales forces, but with unionized factory and service people. Any opinion an operating sales manager might express about disadvantages he sees in unionized salesmen would almost surely be picked up by production and service unions and used in or out of context, justifiably or unjustifiably, as evidence of prejudice and lack of good faith in any union bargaining session.

Subject to the limitations encountered in all attempts at generalization, the most thoughtful opinion in the field simmers down to something like this:

Benefits to Spread

Without any consideration of the possibility of more extensively unionized sales forces, fringe benefits of all kinds are here to stay. They *are* important factors in attracting good sales talent, in holding down turnover, in maintaining morale. A man who may have years of savings cleaned out through one serious family illness is almost sure to be a less effective worker for a long, long time. And a man who continuously worries over the prospect of arriving at retirement age without adequate savings, cannot attack the daily job of selling with the bouyancy and affirmative attitudes selling requires.

The economies brought about by a drop of even a few percentage points in sales force turnover may pay for a good program of fringe benefits.

The obvious values in a stabilized sales force, where experience is accumulated and used to progressively better advantage, are hard to express in terms of dollars and cents, but they are undeniably substantial.

And just as obvious: The trend is all in the direction of providing salesmen with fringe benefit programs. Companies that are slow in doing so not only put themselves at a disadvantage in the labor market but open themselves to adverse criticism, both from within the company and from without, for unenlightened employee relations.

Finally, there *is* unionization to consider. If a company does not want to be forced into the position of dealing with a salesman's union, the best possible insurance against such a development is a pay-benefits-and-good-working-conditions program. Here is the answer for a union organizer in the words of a salesman with a progressive company where salesmen are recognized as the motive power of the business and are treated accordingly: "What can you get for us that we haven't already got?"

11. THERE'S MORE TO MOTIVATING
SALESMEN THAN MONEY *
by William L. Burton †

Assume that you have just announced a new compensation plan, a plan as fine as any offered in your industry.

What should you expect from it?

I hope you are not expecting wonders, for this is what will actually happen: Your salesmen will be appreciative and you will hear fewer complaints for they, as well as you, will realize that the plan is more equitable and the salesmen producing the most profitable business will be the big earners.

Your big producers, as in your previous compensation plan, will continue to be your big producers; your average producers will stay average, and your low producers will continue to be low producers. Each of your salesmen will be motivated by your new compensation plan only to the degree that he is motivated by his desire for personal gain—no more, no less.

Your compensation plan and your other job inducements are simply the terms you offer your salesmen. If your motivation stops with such terms, then I submit that there is no cause to complain about the degree of effort and interest that is forthcoming from your salesmen. . . .

* Reprinted from *Sales Management,* © July 3, 1959, pp. 38–40.
† Maritz Sales Builders.

Every move, every decision your salesmen make is actuated by some motive. In building your motivational program, I suggest that it be built around the eight basic motives that stimulate salesmen to expend greater effort:

1. Personal gain (money, power, prestige)
2. Desire for praise and recognition
3. Avoidance of monotony and boredom
4. Pride (job satisfaction)
5. Fear and worry
6. Desire to be needed
7. Love of family
8. Conscience (obligation to others).

Now I lay no claim to being a psychologist so I'll confess here and now that this list of motives has been approved by five psychologists. It should be obvious from this confession that I am not at all averse to using the same sources our brethren in the advertising field use in getting scientific information for motivating the consumer.

These motives provide the desire and the "want to" that develops the action that brings success. They are the motives that bring your compensation plan to life. They are the motives that offer the challenges that will keep your sales organization reaching for every goal you establish. They are the guide posts for your motivational program and the tools for your sales management team for personal inspirational leadership.

Before discussing them briefly, let me point out that they, similar to so many other things in life, present mixed blessings. While all of these motives may be used effectively in your motivational program, do not overlook the fact that these same motives are, at the same time, providing tremendous competition for your salesmen's time and effort in off-the-job activities.

Desire for Personal Gain

When it is the dominant motive, it should keep approximately 25 per cent of your sales organization working well above your average performers. These are the salesmen who will take full advantage of your compensation plan and who will receive additional stimulation from the awards offered in your motivational program. These same money-hungry fellows are also stimulated by other motives, but to a lesser degree.

Desire for Recognition and Honor

At one of my ports of call I have for years been stopping at what could be termed a second-rate hotel, simply because every time I pick up the telephone in my room a telephone operator will ask, "What can I do for you Mr. Burton?" Being over a thousand miles from home, how good it sounds to hear your own name. Whose name looks best to you in print?

When looking at a group picture, whose mug do you look for first? Recognition . . . my, my, how we all love it! For praise and recognition the ladies in our lives keep our homes attractive, feed us well, and wear those perfectly ridiculous hats. For praise and recognition men get themselves beaten into a pulp playing a game called football . . . run a mile in less than four minutes . . . pole vault over 15 feet . . . high jump 7 feet . . . scale the highest mountains.

This motive, if used freely in your motivational program, will keep your sales organization reaching for new highs to obtain your objectives.

Avoidance of Monotony and Boredom

There has to be a reason for the average and below-average salesman to be such an authority on all forms of entertainment, hobbies and pastimes. I suspect that all of these diversions were invented to enable salesmen to escape the boredom they find in their work.

With an exciting, challenging, stimulating motivational program you can channel a high percentage of the time, energy, and enthusiasm now being dissipated in off-the-job activities to attainment of your objectives.

Pride of Job Satisfaction

Salesmen who take pride in their work always can be depended on to turn in a satisfactory sales performance. A well-planned motivational program should provide additional opportunities for this type of salesman to take pride in his accomplishments. In everything we do this pride motive is the motive that stimulates us to try to do it better.

Fear and Worry

If this were not such a powerful motive, I would have deleted it from this list because of its essentially negative nature. Fear can be a deadly gnawing thing that completely saps a man's vitality. I think it safe, however, to assume that in the case of our low producers fear may well be their dominant motive: fear of losing their jobs, fear of bill collectors, fear of criticism. A motivational program should give you a splendid opportunity to build confidence in these low salesmen and alleviate their fears.

Desire to Be Needed

Have you ever experienced that empty feeling of being alone in a big city? Were you ever left out of the party or dropped from the team? If so, then you understand the tremendous motivational force tied up with this desire to be needed.

Quoting Dr. Karl Menninger: "Closely related to good leadership as a key to high morale and good mental health is adequate motivation. Unless we help a man to understand what his job is and give him a picture of what his part on the team is, he never can really be a member of the team, never can really identify his own interests and aspirations with those of the larger group."

Let your salesmen know in your motivational program how much they are needed and their response will be heart-warming. Team spirit is the perfect answer for this desire to be needed, and need I remind you that team spirit wins ball games, made Knute Rockne immortal, and in the case of our Marines produced the finest fighting force in the world.

Very very few salesmen will ever let you down if you let them know how much you, their team, and your company need them.

Love of Family

If this motive were taken out of salesmen's lives, this nation would have a business decline that would far exceed the depression of 1929. About 85 per cent of the salesman's earnings are spent in satisfying the needs and wants of his family. Less than 15 per cent of the prizes won in the incentive programs we handle are for the salesmen who won them. The balance are for the wives, the children and the homes. The lower the salesman is on the sales totem pole, the more things his family needs and wants.

Include the salesmen's families in your motivational planning and you will gain an ally capable of exerting more pressure than you would ever dare exert.

Conscience

Psychologists claim that the desire to live is the strongest motive of all. We get an indication of the power of conscience when we remember the cases of people taking their own lives in an attempt to get away from a guilty conscience. You have this powerful conscience motive working full time for you if you utilize the two previous motives: desire to be needed and love of family.

Make sure your motivational programs pinpoint not only your sales objectives but pinpoint as well the obligations your salesmen owe to their families, to their teams, and to their company.

Covered all too briefly, I feel sure, there you have the tools for personal inspirational leadership and the format for your motivational program.

These eight motives provide the keys to opening the door to limitless potential inherent in your sales organization.

Why then should top management, in so many cases, be content to use only one motive to stimulate their sales organizations while these same companies, in their advertising programs, are utilizing every conceivable appeal to motivate the consumer?

Depending solely on a compensation plan to motivate salesmen is comparable to restricting all advertising to featuring only price.

OUR EXPANDING
FRONTIERS

part II

We are in the midst of an explosive increase in population combined with high and rising incomes. Advancing educational levels, plus increasing leisure are two other illustrative variables which influence the strength and variety of consumer demand for goods and services. Men and women in selling need to be aware of these trends and their probable direction if they are to maximize effectively the profit and service objectives of their firms.

The articles in Part II delineate the important structural changes in markets in recent years, and, in several instances, project them into the future. Broadly speaking, the section on "Selling in Today's World" covers the quantitative, observable modifications in markets such as changes in the number, age, income, and location of consumers. "Market Segmentation" deals with the more elusive, qualitative differences in key divisions of our population. Evidence of heterogeneity within a market that is more homogeneous *in toto* is presented. The promotional strategies of firms selling to Negroes, juveniles, women, and older buyers are examples of this section's coverage.

To meet active customer wants or to arouse those that are latent demands continuous analysis of ultimate consumer markets. While this is obvious in the case of manufacturers of consumer goods, it is equally true of producers of industrial equipment, parts, and supplies whose sales depend upon derived demand. The latter are giving increased thought to shifts in markets, new products, packaging developments, and changes in consumer taste in order to better serve their own accounts and thereby withstand competition. Thus, the trends revealed by the articles in Part II are of paramount importance to those at all levels of selling.

Selling in
Tomorrow's World

12. THE CHALLENGE OF TOMORROW'S MARKETS *

by Philip M. Hauser †

Markets are people with purchasing power. And to appraise and to prepare for tomorrow's markets, it is necessary to foresee tomorrow's population and tomorrow's income.

National Population

The population of the United States is one of the two key elements which make up the American market. The 1950 Census reported a total population of about 151 million people.

The U.S. population doubled five times between 1790 and 1950. The first three doublings each took place in twenty-five years, the fourth doubling in the thirty-five years from 1865 to 1900, and the fifth doubling in the half century from 1900 to 1950.

Two basic trends are discernible: first, very rapid growth; second, a declining rate of growth, as indicated by the increased period for doubling.

Before World War II, it was generally accepted that the maximum population of the United States would be about 165 million persons—a figure that would be reached by the end of the century. Futhermore, it was believed that the population would decline from such a maximum after the turn of the century. As a result of postwar marriages and the baby boom, however, we passed the 165 million mark by 1955, and are a nation of over 175 million people today.

* Reprinted from *The Journal of Marketing,* © July 1959, pp. 1–7.
† University of Chicago.

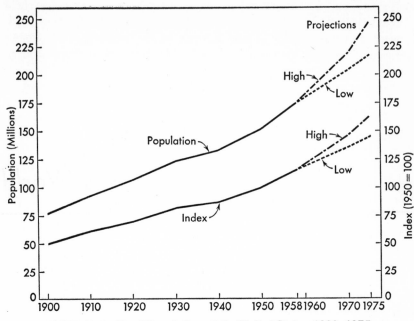

FIGURE 1. Total Population of the United States: 1900–1975.

The Bureau of the Census projections of national population growth indicate a total population of 216 or 244 million persons by 1975. (See Figure 1.) These figures mean that, in the twenty-five years between 1950 and 1975, the United States stands to increase by from 65 to 95 million persons. This at the lower limit is greater than the present entire population of the United Kingdom and Canada combined; and at the upper limit is greater than the present entire population of Japan.

Households

For many marketing purposes, interest attaches to the number of households as the basic consumer unit, rather than the number of persons. Certainly the household remains the primary buying unit for many commodities.

But the rate of growth of households does not necessarily parallel that of total population; and the number of U.S. households has grown more rapidly than total U.S. population. In the first half of this century, for example, while the population doubled, the number of households almost tripled. In the decade since the close of the war we experienced an increase of 11 million household units, more than twice as many as ever previously added in a single decade.

Yet, despite the rapid growth of households after World War II and the continued rapid rate of total population growth, the rate of new-household formation is declining and is likely to continue to decline until about 1965. Between 1947 and 1950, annual increase in the number of households averaged 1.5 million. Between 1950 and 1955, however, it dropped to an average of 833 thousand.

The lower average increase in number of households is largely the result of decreases in the number of persons reaching marriageable age, reflecting the low birth rate of the depression thirties. The Bureau of the Census has projected further decline in the average annual increase in households to a possible low annual average of 643 thousand between 1960 and 1965.

As children born during the postwar baby boom reach marriageable age, the average annual increase in number of households may increase to at least 850 thousand between 1965 and 1970, and to about a million between 1970 and 1975. By 1975, the number of marriages may again reach a level of over 2 million, as in 1946, and net increase in households, a level of over a million.

Between 1950 and 1975, the number of households in the United States is likely to increase by from 20 to 25 million to a total of 64 to 69 million. Marketing aimed primarily at households rather than persons, however, must take into account the cycle in the rate of household formation described.

The difference between the rate of growth of households and of total population is, of course, accounted for by the decrease in the size of households. As a result of the shift from the large-family to the small-family system—the process by which parents and in-laws have been separated in residence from the nuclear family—and the long-time decrease in the birth rate, the number of persons per household has gone down in every Census report since 1790.

At the first Census, there were some 5.8 persons per household; by 1950, there were only 3.5 persons per household. As a result of the postwar boom in the birth rate, this trend toward smaller number of persons per household may be reversed in future censuses. It is also possible, however, that households will continue to decrease in size, because the rate of "undoubling" (the shift from the large-family system to the nuclear family) may offset the increased number of children per family. In any case, between now and 1975, changes in number of persons per household are not likely to be very great or to have special marketing significance.

Income

The gross national product of the United States—the total value of goods and services produced has been between 1880 and 1955, in constant dollars, almost doubled every twenty years, and has increased twelve times. In the same seventy-five years, population increased about three times.

National product per person, in constant dollars, therefore, has increased about four times.

Taxes have also greatly increased since 1880. Disposable income per person, however, has nevertheless just about tripled, increased from $530 to $1,510 in 1956 (expressed in 1956 prices). Family disposable income has increased from $2,200 to $5,300; and the larger amount is available for a smaller number of persons per family.

These figures are based on an analysis by the Committee on Economic Development. Assuming the continuation of the 3 per cent increase in real gross nation product per year, the CED projects a gross national product of $725 billion in 1975 (at 1956 prices). Such a gross national product would provide the average U.S. family with a disposable income of $7,100, as compared with a disposable income of $5,300 in 1956.

McGraw-Hill's Department of Economics has also projected gross national product to 1975. In 1957, U.S. GNP totaled $434 billion. It was produced by a labor force of 65 million persons working an average of 39 hours per week (for 52 weeks), with an output of $3.29 per man hour. The McGraw-Hill projection indicates a GNP of $835 billion by 1975 (in 1957 dollars). This amount of goods and services would be produced by a labor force of 88 million workers, working a 35½ hour week, with an output averaging $5.14 per man hour.

According to the McGraw-Hill projections, consumer expenditures would, between 1957 and 1975, increase from a level of $295 billion to $585 billion. Income per person after taxes would increase from $1,760 (in 1957) to $2,497.

Thus, continuation of past trends indicates by 1975, whether the CED or McGraw-Hill projections are used, a doubling of gross national product and of aggregate consumer expenditures, and an increase of about two-fifths in average personal income after taxes.

Metropolitan Population Growth

The increasing concentration of the population of the United States in a relatively small number of standard metropolitan areas has the greatest marketing significance. So does the trend toward increasing decentralization of population within standard metropolitan areas.

At the beginning of the century, about one-third of the people in this nation lived in areas which today would qualify as standard metropolitan areas. Between 1900 and 1950, while the population of the country as a whole doubled, that in the standard metropolitan areas almost tripled; and the nonmetropolitan area population increased by less than 50 per cent. In consequence, by 1950, over 85 million people (57 per cent of the population) lived in some 168 standard metropolitan areas.

The trend toward concentration of population in standard metropolitan areas is an accelerating one. For example, in the half century between 1900 and 1950, the standard metropolitan areas absorbed 73 per cent of the total population increase of the nation.

In the last decade of this period, that is, between 1940 and 1950, they absorbed 81 per cent of the total population increase. In the first half of the present decade (that is, between 1950 and 1955) standard metropolitan areas have absorbed over 97 per cent of the total population increase of the United States!

Also, population within each area has become increasingly decentralized. That is, within each standard metropolitan area, there has been a tendency for larger and larger proportions of the population to be resident in the "rings" or suburban part, rather than in the central city of the area. In 1920, for example, less than 35 per cent of the population of the standard metropolitan areas were resident in the rings; by 1950, this percentage had increased to 42 per cent; and by 1956, it was close to 47 per cent.

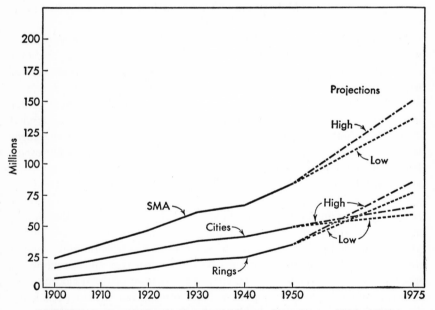

FIGURE 2. Population in Standard Metropolitan Areas: 1900–1975.

From 1900 to 1950, the rings, in relation to the central cities grew at a rate of about 1⅓ to 1; between 1940 and 1950, at a ratio of about 2½ to 1; and, in the first half of the present decade (1950–1955), at a ratio of 7 to 1, 28 per cent, as compared with 4 per cent.

If these trends continue, then by 1975 about two-thirds of the market of the United States, as measured by population, will be resident in approximately 200 standard metropolitan areas. It is possible that by 1975 these metropolitan areas will have a population of over 150 million inhabitants—as many as in the entire nation in 1950. (See Figure 2.)

This would represent an increase of some 65 million persons in metropolitan areas in twenty-five years. If this increase were distributed in the same manner as the population increase between 1950 and 1956, then, of the 65 million persons added to metropolitan area populations, 12 million would be added to central cities and 53 million to the suburban rings. Of the 53 million added to suburbia, 32 million would be resident in what is now largely unincorporated open country area in suburbia.

In 1950, of the 85 million inhabitants of standard metropolitan areas, 49 million, or 58 per cent, lived in central cities. By 1975, of the 150 million persons in standard metropolitan areas, 62 million would be resident in the central cities; and 88 million, or about 60 per cent, would be living in suburbia.

Metropolitan Area Structure

Accompanying the population changes are important structural changes in metropolitan areas which will vitally affect distribution practices. Our urban and metropolitan areas have developed from one or more centers of origin representing their original economic base. As both the economic base and population grew, residential areas expanded from the original center or centers of origin. The newer and more desirable residential areas tended always to be located toward the periphery of the expanding urban aggregation. The older and less desirable residential areas tended to be closest to the center of origin of the city.

As a result, the population of our metropolitan areas tended to be stratified in space in accordance with social and economic status. The lower socioeconomic population groups tended to be domiciled in the older, inner, and decayed zones of our metropolitan areas. The higher socioeconomic groupings tended to be located in the outlying and peripheral zones of the area. In consequence, our urban areas have grown through a continuous process in which newcomers to the city, at the bottom of the socioeconomic ladder, have tended to be located in its inner zones; whereas, older residents, climbing the socioeconomic ladder, have tended to move from inner to outer zones in keeping with their improved ability to compete for the more desirable residential locations.

This process of urban growth has been, then, one of continuous displacement of older residents by newcomers entering the center of the city. The present tendency toward "suburbanization" is merely a continuation of this process. Rings or suburbs are now growing more rapidly than central cities for the simple reason that our central cities are mostly filled up, both with population and economic enterprises.

An additional trend with respect to the physical structure of our urban areas should also be noted. This is the very rapid growth, and paralleling it the very rapid decay and obsolescence, of the inner zones of our urban areas. Our cities grew, not structure by structure, but by subdivision, neighborhood, and community. And our cities have also decayed, not structure by structure, but by neighborhood and community.

While the inner decayed zones of our central cities are being rebuilt, outlying suburbia is subject to the rapid growth experienced by our central cities during the nineteenth century. It is possible that the slums of the future will be located in the suburban rather than the central-city portions of our standard metropolitan areas.

The previously observed patterns of population stratification, described above, are likely to break down in the next stage of metropolitan area development. It is almost certain that the future metropolis will be much more heterogeneous in structure than that of the past or present. That is, the future metropolis will probably contain both "good" and "bad" areas in suburbia as well as in the central cities. This will mean that various agencies and institutions, including business, will have to deal with much more heterogeneous population groupings than is now the case.

Finally, there is an increasing tendency for a number of our standard metropolitan areas to merge into linear bands along our great lanes of communication. One such emergent "megalopolis," the greatest, is that which stretches from Boston to Washington, D.C., on the East Coast. Another is that in the Midwest, from Milwaukee to Chicago to South Bend.

On the West Coast an emergent megalopolis reaches from San Francisco and Sacramento to Los Angeles and San Diego. In the Gulf Area, there is evidence of the merger of standard metropolitan areas from Galveston to Dallas and Fort Worth and down to San Antonio. Other such potential metropolitan mergers may be anticipated, and by 1975 the gaps in the ones mentioned may be expected to fill in considerably.

Other Characteristics

Birth Rates and Death Rates

Great changes may also be anticipated in the age structure of the population. This is due to rapid changes in the birth rate, and continued decline in the death rate. Between 1950 and 1975, for example, depending on the course of the birth rate, youngsters of elementary school age, from five to fourteen years, may increase from 51 to 113 per cent; and youngsters of high-school age, fifteen to nineteen years, by from 91 to 108 per cent.

Simultaneously, the population will continue to age. Our senior citizens, sixty-five years of age and over, will increase by about 77 per cent during the same twenty-five year period.

Labor Force

The labor force will continue to contain increasing proportions of women. By 1975, it is possible that two-fifths of our females fourteen years of age and over will be in the labor force and constitute about 36 per cent of all workers. By 1975, more than half of our women thirty-five to forty-four may be working.

Ethnic Composition

Important changes in nativity and "race" composition of our population are also in store. By 1975, our foreign born may decrease to make up only 2 to 3 per cent of the population. The generation thereafter will be the first generation of Americans to have a common nativity.

While the foreign born disappear as an important element in the American market, however, Negroes will become an increasingly important part of the market and especially of the urban market. As recently as 1910, 89 per cent of the American Negroes lived in the South. But Negroes are migrating to the North and West, and by 1975, there may be as many Negroes in the North and West as in the South. In many of our large metropolitan areas, Negroes will constitute from a third to half of central city markets.

The Challenge

Tomorrow's market constitutes one of the greatest challenges, and opportunities, ever to confront the American business community. Total national population growth alone constitutes a major challenge. For it is necessary for the American economy to expand sufficiently, within a period of twenty-five years, to provide goods and services for an additional 65 to 95 million Americans consuming at the American level of living.

This population increase, together with increasing productivity, will make possible a doubling of gross national product by 1975 (in constant dollars), even while the average hours of work per week decrease. Consumer expenditures will double between 1957 and 1975, as average income per person after taxes increases by 40 per cent. The increase in family income between now and 1975 will be greater than present family expenditures for food and clothing combined.

In brief, what we shall add to our gross national product by 1975 will be greater than the gross national product of any nation on earth, other than that of the United States itself!

For many purposes the anticipated increase in population will be reached through the household as the purchasing and consumer unit. Business will be confronted with an increase of from 45 to 55 per cent in household units by 1975.

The American market will be increasingly concentrated in the great standard metropolitan areas. It may be possible to reach two-thirds of the population in 200 metropolitan areas. Within these metropolitan areas the major part of the market will have shifted from central cities to suburbs which by 1975 may contain three-fifths of the entire metropolitan population.

In addition to facing the challenge of increasing and more concentrated markets, the American businessman will also be confronted with the problem of changing metropolitan-area structure. The tendency toward much greater heterogeneity in the community composition of a metropolitan area, on the one hand, and the coalescence of metropolitan areas into megaloposes, on the other, will undoubtedly call for major changes in distribution practices.

Finally, production and distribution of commodities consumed by specific population groupings (age, ethnic, educational, labor force, and the like) will be even more profoundly affected than indicated by total population changes. For example, whereas the total population may increase by from 40 to 60 per cent, persons of high-school age may double . . . persons sixty-five and over will increase by over three-fourths . . . the foreign born will virtually disappear . . . and Negroes will become a much more important part of the urban market.

The basic challenge to American business will continue to be the challenge afforded by the opportunity to continue to serve the American people, and to contribute to the continued rise in the American level of living—the highest ever achieved in the history of man.

13. OUR CHANGING CONSUMER MARKET °

by Robert Ferber †

Had anyone predicted ten years ago that the mainstay of postwar prosperity was to be consumer spending, he would have been ridiculed. Traditionally, business investment in plant and equipment and in inventories had been the spark plug, as well as the foretoken, of business conditions; it helped determine consumer income, which then led to a more or less predetermined level of consumer expenditures.

* Reprinted from *Business Horizons,* © Spring 1958, pp. 49–66.
† University of Illinois.

The experience of the last decade has shown, to almost everybody's surprise, that the process can also work the other way around. In 1948–49, and then again in 1953–54, it was consumer spending that remained high and paved the way for further prosperity, while activity faltered in other sectors of the economy.

These developments have been among the most spectacular and widely publicized characteristics of consumer spending in the postwar years. Yet, they reflect in large measure more basic changes that have been taking place over many years, and particularly during the past two decades. These include changes in the characteristics as well as the number of consumers, changes in consumer income and assets, and changes in consumer wants and preferences—all of which add up to a strikingly different present-day market structure for consumer goods, and which presage additional changes yet to come.

The slowing down of the postwar boom and the concomitant availability of a major new set of data on consumer expenditures make this a convenient time to take stock of these changes and to evaluate their effects in relation to possible future trends in business conditions. These new data were obtained in the course of a nationwide survey of consumer income and expenditures completed in 1957 under the sponsorship of *Life* magazine. They represent the most extensive private study of this market ever undertaken to date, and rival in scope the mammoth 1950 consumer expenditures study of the U.S. Bureau of Labor Statistics. Comparable in many respects with these earlier government studies, the *Life* data enable us to bring up to date the broad developments that have been taking place in the consumer market and to examine the current state of affairs.

Money, Money, Money

Consumer income after taxes has more than quadrupled during the past two decades, from 1936 to 1956 (Figure 1). In 1957, disposable income after taxes appears to have hit a new peak of almost $300 billion, or an average of well over $5,000 for each of the 50 million families in the country. (Some of this $300 billion is not earned by families, but by trusts, individuals in institutions, and so forth.)

Almost half of this increase has been brought about by rising prices—about 40 per cent during the first of these decades, and about 60 per cent in the postwar decade. Another portion of this increase can be attributed to our growing population, particularly during the postwar decade when the number of people in the country rose almost 20 per cent—almost twice the rate of the preceding decade. However, even after allowance is made for these increases in prices and population, the fact remains that consumers' purchasing power has undergone a rather hefty increase; in 1956,

FIGURE 1

Much of the Rise in Incomes after Taxes

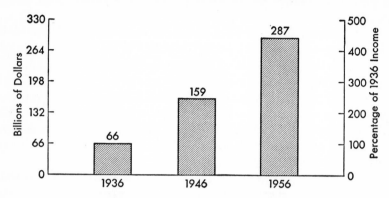

Is Attributable to Higher Prices and a Larger Population. Nevertheless, Purchasing Power Has Risen Substantially Too.

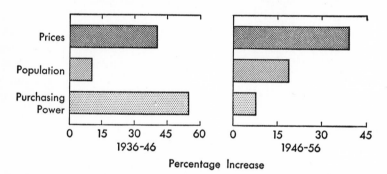

(Computed from U.S. Department of Commerce: "Survey of Current Business" and various supplements; U.S. Bureau of the Census, "Census of the United States" and various supplements.)

the real income of the average consumer was 71 per cent more after taxes than it was in 1936. Most of this increase came during the war years; the increase in purchasing power since 1946 has been less than 10 per cent.

The rise in consumer spending that has taken place during the past two decades has paralleled the rise in incomes. More important, it has varied markedly with different types of goods and services. Homes, cars, and household durables are among goods that have experienced the main increases, partly because of their unavailability during the war and partly because of rapid technological advances in their design and operation.

Among the services, education and foreign travel have registered the largest gains, reflecting the newly found discretionary spending of millions of families and the growing popularity of overseas vacations. Consumer spending has risen much less than average for rental housing and for purchased local and intercity transportation, which have suffered because of the shift to home and car ownership; for clothing, which has lost for the time being much of its former glamor; and for domestic service, which has declined as a result of the widespread labor shortage, enabling workers in this field to make more money elsewhere.

Of course, much of this rise in expenditures—approximately 60 per cent of it—is due to increases in price and population. However, much the same pattern of consumer spending emerges when allowance is made for the effects of price and population changes. This is supported by a comparison of household expenditures in 1936 with the corresponding *Life* magazine data for 1956 (Figure 2).

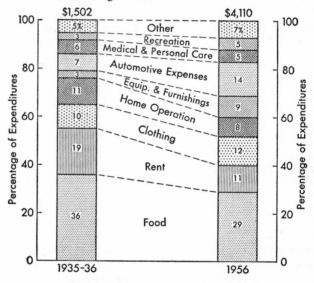

FIGURE 2. The Effect of Prosperity on the Consumer Budget. (Percentages for 1935–36 are derived from National Resources Committee, "Consumer Expenditures in the United States, Estimated for 1935–1936"; and supplementary reports by the Department of Labor, Bureau of Labor Statistics. Percentages for 1956 are derived from "Life Study of Consumer Expenditures," copyright 1957 by TIME, Inc.)

Such a comparison shows that gadgetry, particularly in the form of durable goods, and pleasure have been occupying an increasingly important position in the American family budget. The average urban household in

1956 went in relatively more for home furnishings and equipment (including appliances), recreation, and automobiles, and related expenses (much of which in turn can be charged to recreation), and less for clothing, rent, and household operation.

In fact, symptomatic of the great postwar prosperity has been the decline in the proportion of the family budget devoted to the traditional necessities of life—food, clothing, and shelter. American families roughly doubled their outlays on food, clothing, and shelter between 1936 and 1956, but during the same period their over-all expenditures on other items of family living nearly quadrupled. As a result, the importance of food, clothing, and shelter in the family budget fell from nearly two-thirds of the total in 1935–36 to just a little over half in 1956—and this is without allowance for the sharp increase in purchases of such luxury items as fancy foods and air conditioning.

When we get down to individual products, differences between family outlays then and now become much more pronounced. For some products, such as fresh fruit, potatoes, railroad travel, and domestic service, expenditures have risen hardly at all in dollar terms, and have actually declined, once price increases are taken into account. However, purchases of such items as new homes, washing machines, and margarine have risen in some cases almost fourfold (Figure 3). Perhaps the most striking indication of the changes that have taken place in consumer markets is the growing proportion of the family budget going to new products that had no counterparts in 1936—air conditioning, television, clothes dryers, and frozen foods.

The Story Behind the Story

Essential to an understanding of the nature of these changes and what they portend for the future is a consideration of the factors responsible for the changes. In general, among such factors there seem to be four principal ones (Figure 4): (1) income; (2) population; (3) assets; (4) credit.

Income

The tremendous rise in the level of consumer incomes alone would have been sufficient to bring about pronounced changes in consumer spending. This rise has been reinforced by the decline in the concentration of incomes. There has been in particular an increase in the proportion of middle-income families brought about by the needs of a full-employment economy. Higher wages, especially for unskilled labor, serve to increase the earnings of those already employed and, at the same time, induce more family members to enter the labor force.

These developments have produced a more equal distribution of incomes. Thus, in 1935–36 the 10 per cent of families with the highest in-

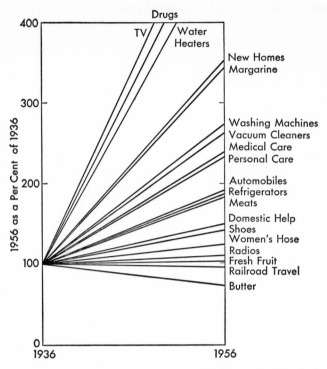

FIGURE 3. Trends in Purchases of Selected Goods and Services. (Percentages for 1936 are computed from U.S. Department of Commerce, "National Income," 1954 Edition: "A Supplement to the Survey of Current Business." Percentages for 1956 are computed from U.S. Department of Commerce, "Survey of Current Business," July, 1957.)

comes accounted for 36 per cent of total family income in that year, whereas in 1956, according to the *Life* data, the same highest 10 per cent of families accounted for only 24 per cent of total incomes. More families were above what would be defined as a subsistence income in 1956 too—about 44 per cent in 1956 as against 24 per cent in 1935–36 (taking $4,500 and $1,750 as the corresponding respective subsistence levels). The result has been not only higher levels of spending but the creation of mass markets for goods previously in the luxury category.

Population

That more people need more goods is axiomatic. However, when characteristics of the population that are closely related to spending patterns change markedly, shifts in consumer markets are an almost inevitable consequence. The changes in the present instance are indeed pronounced. Dur-

FIGURE 4

Contributing to the Changing Consumer Market Have Been:

**Rising Family Incomes, Particularly
at the Lower Income Levels**

A Changing Population Structure

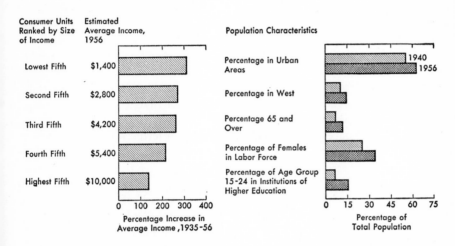

**A Tremendous Increase in Financial
Assets, While Liabliities Rose Much
More Slowly**

**And a Concomitant Expansion of Consumer Credit, Particularly for Auto
Purchases**

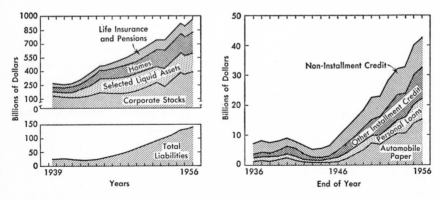

(Computed from various issues of U.S. Department of Commerce, "Survey of
Current Business" and supplements; U.S. Department of Labor, Bureau of Labor
Statistics, "Monthly Labor Review"; and Board of Governors of the Federal Reserve System, "Federal Reserve Bulletin.")

ing the past two decades, our population has become more educated; more white collar and professional in class; more suburban; older, yet, paradoxically, with more children and larger families.

These changes, interacting with the growth and redistribution of incomes, have led to a growing sophistication in tastes and preferences (or at least so people like to believe), as well as to substantial expansion in markets for various products. The current boom in hi-fi sets, in foreign foods, in sports cars, in white shirts (as against colored shirts), and in wines and brandies is largely a manifestation of these changes. When a family moves into a different income or population group, its spending patterns invariably tend to conform to those of the new group, albeit with some lag.

The growth of suburban living has led especially to pronounced shifts in consumer purchases; producing, among other things, a booming market for home improvement and do-it-yourself materials, a not unrelated surging market for bandages and medical supplies, and a fertile new field for novelists in search of material.

Assets

When a person has money in the bank, he is more likely to spend liberally out of current income than when his pocket is holding his last dollar. If, in addition, his holdings have risen well above customary levels because of a scarcity of goods and pressure to accumulate government bonds, he is likely to spend very well indeed once the emergency lets up; and this is what appears to have happened in the postwar years.

The high proportion of aggregate consumption expenditures to personal disposable income during this period—nearly 94 per cent—would hardly have been reached had most consumers not had a cushion to fall back on in case of sudden reversals. This cushion not only has been a comfortable one but, what may not be widely realized, has been increasing throughout the postwar period. Thus, savings (time) deposits of individuals rose from $232 per capita at the end of 1936 to $771 per capita in 1946 and then further still to $1,077 per capita at the end of 1956. At the same time, there is some evidence that liquid asset holdings (savings and checking accounts and U.S. government bonds) have become more concentrated during the past decade. Ten per cent of American households were reported to have $5,000 or more of liquid assets in early 1956 as against 6 per cent in 1946. At the same time, the proportion of households without any assets rose slightly, to one-fourth of the total.

Credit

To a large extent, the expansion of consumer credit can be alleged to be an outgrowth of these other changes. After all, really poor people are not able to borrow! The most frequent users of credit in recent years have been households in the middle-income brackets, earning between $4,000 and $7,000 per year. Many of these households have liquid assets as well but prefer to borrow anyway, treating repayment of the loan as a form of disciplined saving. The cost of this borrowing seems to be of little consequence to the consumer as long as his income is sufficient to cover the payments.

On the whole, there is little doubt that credit expansion has served as a major stimulus to consumer spending, bringing about many purchases which would not otherwise have been made—especially of cars, homes, and other durable goods. In effect, this credit expansion can be interpreted as a reflection of the growing importance of capital goods in family living, spurred in part by the sharp decline in the availability of competent household help at reasonable prices. As in business operations, outright purchase of consumer capital goods is often too costly. The consumer therefore follows the alternative of purchasing these goods on credit, thereby obtaining for himself the services and pleasures provided by these capital goods well before the time he can actually afford to own them. Whether one likes it or not, paying in the future for present enjoyment is becoming an increasingly popular way of life.

Other Factors

Diverse price movements could to some extent be labeled a fifth factor accounting for the present structure of our consumer market. It is not so considered here because during a period of rapidly rising incomes such as have characterized the last two decades, price considerations become of secondary importance in most purchase decisions. There have been notable exceptions, however, when the price of a product went completely out of line with that of competing products. This invariably has had disastrous results—as in the case of butter.

Many other factors have also contributed in one way or another to the present state of our consumer market. Most notable of these is perhaps technology, which has spurred demand for new or improved products, often at the expense of other, more prosaic products. Advertising, changing styles, and mass communications (especially the homogenizing influence of mass media) have also contributed in one way or another. Competitive pressures for mass production and standardization are also not to be ignored. Indeed, some maintain that these are the principal factors impelling consumers to "be alike and live alike."

A Telescopic View

The present consumer market can be eulogized in terms of a tremendous variety of adjectives. It is bigger, better, broader than at any time in our history. There are more different goods and services for sale, more of most items available, more people and more money bidding for the goods—and, of course, more advertising exhorting us to buy still more goods.

Huge as this present market may be, all indications are that it will be dwarfed by consumer markets of the future. Estimates of the size of these markets can be obtained by extrapolating past aggregate growth trends, a favorite parlor exercise of business analysts. Such an approach may yield a rough idea of the general size of these markets, but it tells us little about their characteristics—how expenditures will be distributed among different types of consumers, how expenditure patterns will be adjusted to different economic circumstances, how competition will affect expenditure patterns, and many other questions. These questions can only be answered by studying current expenditure patterns of a cross section of the population and using this as a springboard for insights into the future. Such data, if current enough, can also throw considerable light on the structure of the present consumer market and thereby serve as a basis for gauging short-run market potentials, guiding the use of promotional efforts, constructing more effective sales territories, and determining investment plans.

In a rapidly moving economy such as ours, expenditure patterns can change substantially within a few years, and it is therefore of particular importance to have data recent enough to yield an up-to-date cross section of the consumer market. It is in this sense that consumer expenditure studies, such as the recent *Life* survey, come in so handy. Changes in early postwar consumer expenditure patterns have already been pinpointed by the 1950 Consumer Expenditures Study of the U.S. Bureau of Labor Statistics and the University of Pennsylvania, and this new study indicates the extent to which further changes have taken place.

Diminishing Influence of Income

One of the striking characteristics of the present consumer market brought out by this study is its apparent homogeneity. This is true, on the whole, even with regard to income; for within a few percentage points, high-income households distribute their expenditures in much the same way as do low-income households. The only exception of any consequence is the tendency for the higher-income households to spend less on food and more on automobiles, homes, furnishings, and appliances.

The principal effect of income on the household budget seems to lie in determining how large a proportion goes for food; the allocation of the budget among other types of expenditures is determined by the homogenizing influence of mass tastes and preferences, modified by specific social and demographic factors affecting particular households.

Of course, this is a very general tendency, and numerous exceptions will be found when data for individual households are examined. In addition, we have to consider that although households in different economic and social circumstances may allocate their expenditures among different categories in the same manner, this does not mean that the same products are bought. Not only may altogether different products be bought, for example, steak and lobster as against hamburger and smelt, but the quality of product may differ substantially: The high-income family may purchase a Cadillac or an Imperial while the low-income family goes in for a Ford or a Studebaker. It may well be these quality differentials that constitute the main difference between household expenditures at different levels of income; for preliminary examination of the distribution of household budgets among individual products shows, on the whole, surprisingly small differences.

Further evidence of the declining role of income is provided by the large number of expenditures that seem to be relatively insensitive, or *inelastic,* to income changes. As incomes move up, manufacturers and distributors of goods possessing high income elasticities are in a favored position, since a given rise in income produces proportionately more outlays on these goods than on others. This approach has also provided a basis for sales forecasting and gauging market potentials, by estimating the income elasticity of demand for a good from consumer expenditure surveys and then applying it to alternative projections of future income levels and distributions.

In 1956, however, only a few of the 65 groups of goods and services used in the *Life* study exhibited elastic demand:

Categories with Elastic Demand

Between Low- (0–$2,000) and Middle- ($4–5,000) Income Levels	*Between Middle- and High- ($7,000 up) Income Levels*
Miscellaneous home improvements	Wines, brandies, liquors
Small appliances	Miscellaneous home improvements
Furniture	Floor coverings
Automobiles	Photographic equipment
Photographic equipment	Sport goods
Games and toys	
Sport goods	

If finer classifications were used and individual products treated separately, this list would become many times longer. It is nevertheless apparent from the above and from what has been said before (Figure 3) that the importance of income, although still great, is diminishing and will continue to do so as incomes rise further.

This is not to say that income effects can be ignored. Clearly, without income there could be no purchases, and even at present levels of income, substantial variations in purchases exist among different income levels. This is particularly true when quality considerations are taken into account.

Then, too, income effects interact at times with other characteristics, so that the direction of change in consumer expenditures shifts as the level of income is varied. Thus, expenditures for infants' clothing are higher among low- and middle-income families whose heads have more education, but the reverse is true among high-income families.

Concentration of Markets

The present-day consumer market is highly concentrated. This has been brought about on the one hand by the steady migration of the population to urban centers, particularly to metropolitan areas and their environs, and, on the other hand, to the not unrelated fact that incomes are highest in these areas. Nearly six out of every ten American households resided in metropolitan areas in 1956. These families earned on the average over $5,000 apiece in that year (in the suburbs of the large cities nearly $6,000), while household incomes in other parts of the country were averaging not much over $4,000.

This huge metropolitan market of nearly 30 million households accounted for two-thirds of the total purchases of goods and services by American households in 1956. More than three-fourths of household expenditures for beer, liquor, housing, and floor coverings took place in this area. As one would expect, there are substantial variations in the market shares of various goods and services between the central cities and the suburbs of metropolitan areas. Central city households accounted for disproportionately large shares (in relation to their number) of expenditures on liquor, women's and girls' clothing and footwear, accessories and clothing care, housing, spectator fees, and writing equipment; while expenditures in the suburbs were disproportionately high for nearly all housing items, appliances, and house furnishings; as well as for liquor (those exurbanites again!), automotive items, sporting goods, and pet foods—all reflecting the emphasis in the suburbs on comfortable living.

The consumer market is also highly concentrated in various other ways. Thus, households with children spent considerably more than other households, particularly on most food items (not to mention baby food!), clothes, decorating material, and writing equipment.

Concentration by income is also pronounced: The one-third of households with the highest incomes accounted for nearly half of the total household expenditures for goods and services. However, this percentage was actually greater when incomes were lower and more unequally distributed. Geographic concentration is a much more recent development.

Despite this concentration, the fact remains that the consumer market has become so large that even the smaller segments comprise substantial markets in themselves. A commodity that appealed to only 1 per cent of this market would still have a sales potential of half a million units, representing a population exceeding that of all but four of our cities. It is largely for this reason that markets for such specialty goods as custom-made furniture, motor scooters, and such canned "delicacies" as maggots and rattlesnakes have been able to do so well alongside the development of the homogenizing mass market.

Emergence of Other Forces

Occupation, education, family size, and other social forces have always influenced consumer expenditures to some extent. Now, however, with income gradually losing its traditional role as the principal, almost sole, determinant of the types of goods and services a household will buy, these social and demographic factors are assuming positions of new importance. Differences in expenditure patterns already appear to lie about as much between households of different social characteristics, different age levels, different educational attainments and sources of livelihood, and different geographical locations, as between households of different income levels.

Many of these differences become especially pronounced when comparisons are made of expenditure patterns of households possessing different social and demographic characteristics but at the same levels of income. Thus, whether a household is earning less than $3,000 a year or over $10,000 a year, we find that the one headed by a college graduate spends relatively less on food, clothing, and medical and personal care, but spends more on the home and automotive expenses. Again irrespective of income, families headed by younger people spend proportionately less than older families on food and medical and personal care but spend more on clothing and automotive supplies.

Region and marketing location seem to exert special influences of their own on the allocation of household expenditures. Households in the Northeast devote more of their expenditures to food than households in the South or West. At the same time, as the size of the community increases, more of the household budget goes to food, shelter, education, and recreation expenses and less to automobile expenses.

The Consumer in the Bright New World

There is little doubt that the consumer market of the future will, with occasional setbacks, be still bigger and more grandiose than anything yet seen. Rising incomes and standards of living will take care of that. The implications of these trends are many, but perhaps the principal ones are the following:

1. *Consumers are becoming increasingly able to act differently from each other, yet in practice they seem to act more like one another.* This paradoxical behavior of the consumer may well be such as to give market

analysts and psychologists alike a completely new set of frustrations. For as incomes rise and consumers obtain more leeway in allocating expenditures, the former emphasis on subsistence gradually fades into the background. Already, probably not much more than half of the average household income goes for subsistence expenditures, and this proportion will undoubtedly decline further. Thus, consumers will have at their command an ever increasing latitude in allocating expenditures, so that consumer budgets might be expected to differ increasingly from each other.

But what has been happening? Despite the growing potential for increasing heterogeneity between consumer budgets, the trend seems to be in the other direction. Consumer budgets on the whole are very similar to one another, even when comparisons are made by income levels; the main differences appear to lie in the qualities of the goods and services that are bought rather than in what is bought. Whether it is due to mass communications, to a pervading desire for conspicuous consumption, to pressures from manufacturers, or to some other forces, consumers appear to be becoming more homogeneous in an era when they are being endowed increasingly with the capacity to behave differently.

To be sure, individual exceptions are numerous, as is only to be expected in an economy containing 50 million households. Hardly ever are we likely to reach a stage when the behavior of all individual consumers conforms to the average. In the present situation, dispersion about the average is yet to be determined, but indications are that the same tendency toward uniformity will be found to exist.

2. *New concepts of market analysis are needed.* The growing impact on consumer expenditures of a host of factors other than income means that the past practice of predicting sales by deriving a simple relationship between income and expenditures will yield increasingly inferior results as time goes on. Accurate forecasts will entail the use of methods that take into account the effects on expenditures of a number of different factors simultaneously. This is not the place to go into such methodological issues, but it might be mentioned that some "multivariate" techniques already exist for handling such problems and other techniques are in developmental stages.

3. *The role of the consumer as a purely passive agent in business fluctuations is a relic of the past.* With incomes well above subsistence levels and with enormous reserves of unneeded spending power in the form of durable assets and unused credit, consumers are much more free to spend as they please. Concomitantly, consumer expenditures are less likely than before to vary with moderate fluctuations in income. A substantial portion of the national income is brought about by sales at the consumer level. If incomes in other sectors of the economy dip but consumers keep on spending, the net effect can be a considerable boost to these other sectors and

renewed prosperity. Postwar experience, particularly in 1949 and 1954, has demonstrated conclusively how effectively consumer spending can support the economy and mitigate the effects of recessions.

To be sure, consumer spending can work the other way, and precipitate a recession when one might not otherwise have occurred. Then, again, consumer spending may at times assume a passive role while more traditional forces, such as business investment or government spending, call the turn. The point is that the consumer has become, with these other forces, a potential catalyst in business fluctuations. His influence cannot be ignored. Whether he will choose to take the initiative at a particular time may well be the $64 billion question of the future!

14. INTERURBIA IS HERE TO STAY *

by John M. Willem †

What will be the role of American business in 1980? What part will the businessman play? Prognostication now is important because a sizable flow of investment, and new techniques of production and methods of doing business will be involved. None of these can be altered overnight. Market research studies recently have revealed important reasons why businessmen must look to tomorrow today. There is obviously a change coming over America—a change more rapid than any transformation the world has ever seen.

What Is Interurbia?

This changing face of America is to be seen in the merging of larger cities into long, so-called strip cities that should challenge the imagination of business executives when it comes to future planning. Essentially, the role of the businessman now should parallel that of the missile researcher who is engaged in a program of awareness and preparedness. He not only is responsible for military defense, but also seeks answers for the problematical methods of peaceful space travel. The indications are that future success in business will be attained only to the extent that the executive understands the velocity and extent of growth of this new strip city—a city that may stretch for hundreds of miles, gobbling up former metropolitan areas to make one lengthy Interurbia.

* Reprinted from *Business Horizons*, © Spring 1958, pp. 25–32.
† J. Walter Thompson Company.

The J. Walter Thompson Company has devoted the last several years to a detailed study of certain aspects of urban growth and decentralization in the United States. Our research has unveiled the dramatic story of an economic and social transformation in this country, the speed with which that change is taking place, and the significance it has for all of us in our daily lives and our ways of doing business.

Interurbia, by our definition, has these characteristics: It is an area comprising at least two adjacent cities—two with not less than 100,000 population each, or one with 100,000 and three with 25,000 population each. The area connecting the cities must have a population density exceeding 100 persons per square mile and no more than 25 per cent farm population. The phenomenon of interurbia appears to be evolving from the now-familiar plan of suburbia. The forces shaping this pattern of strip growth are: (1) the increase in our population; (2) our road-building program; (3) the increase in automobiles; (4) the unprecedented development of our industry; (5) the suburbs that grow up almost overnight; (6) the quick expansion of our cities.

Preparation Needed Now

Perhaps all of this seems too obvious. Yet, we, as a nation, have failed to anticipate the pace of our growth. We did not predict the rate at which our population would grow. In 1946, the U.S. Bureau of the Census forecast a population total of 150 million in the United States by 1955. However, by that year there were nearly 167 million people in the United States—a forecasting error of 17 million people. The auto boom was not predicted either. In 1946, automotive economists forecast 36 million cars on the highways by 1955. A total of 52 million cars were registered in 1955. The nation failed to anticipate many factors that affect housing. By the late forties playground areas were overlooked for city apartments designed for young families. Just as we failed to foresee the number of cars people were to buy, so we failed to anticipate the demand for television sets, automatic washing machines, and air conditioners. Hence, many new buildings were electrically obsolete while they were still new.

Few provisions were made for the space needed to rear children. So when young families faced the lack of bedrooms and playrooms, the trek to the suburbs started. However, conditions in most suburbs were much the same. The little homes lacked adequate bedroom space and had no garages or carports. The young home owners then were forced to invest more dollars to expand their dwellings—if the lot area permitted—or move on again.

The automobile has been the answer to many problems, carrying people beyond the suburbs to more open space. The most graphic demonstration of this spread is in New York City. There, as elsewhere, it is no longer realistic to speak of a city and its suburbs. The New York metropolitan area has long been a conglomeration of many cities and suburbs. This is also true of Greater Boston, Philadelphia, Baltimore, and Washington. The former East Coast metropolitan islands are now virtually one 600-mile city, stretching from Maine to Virginia. Actually, there are only two stretches in this 600-mile city—one of 2 miles and the other of 17 miles—that are not part of metropolitan areas. This "world's longest city" contains not 2 per cent of the nation's land area, but it represents over one-fifth of its population and almost one-fourth of its retail sales. And it probably hasn't stopped growing yet. It may well grow toward the Piedmont. One feeler, now moving up the Hudson, will in all probability follow the New York Thruway to Buffalo and link with Cleveland, Detroit, and Chicago, and then stretch downward through Illinois to St. Louis.

That would be an interurbia about twice the length of the Atlantic strip —a city more than 1,200 miles long.

Where Will They Be?

Although the Atlantic strip is the largest of the new urban strips, it is by no means the only one. Other strips are rapidly forming. The steel belt, from the mines to the Great Lakes, is now an almost continuous urban area joining Pittsburgh, Youngstown, Canton, Akron, and Cleveland. Another urban strip comprising Lansing, Pontiac, Flint, Detroit, and Toledo has also emerged and could be linked with Cleveland via Sandusky and Lorain. Lake Michigan has an industrial strip that sweeps across northern Indiana and may soon connect with Detroit. The cities linked along that lake shore are Milwaukee, Racine, Kenosha, Waukegan, Chicago, Hammond, Gary, and South Bend. An interurbia strip has emerged along Puget Sound, including Seattle, Tacoma, Portland, and Salem. Another is moving from San Francisco inland toward Oakland, Sacramento, and Fresno. Los Angeles now joins with Riverside and Long Beach and reaches toward San Diego. Two other interurbias are developing in the Southwest. The Dallas and Fort Worth development could conceivably extend itself in one direction toward Waco, Austin, and San Antonio and in another direction toward Houston and Galveston. The St. Louis area presents another interurbia. While it may move westward to join with Kansas City, the St. Louis area could also move in a northeasterly direction to touch the Milwaukee–Chicago strip. Still other interurbia areas could spring up along the Florida coastlines; in the Atlanta–Birmingham–Chattanooga–Knoxville section of the Deep South; in the Minneapolis–St. Paul–Duluth region of Minnesota; the Denver–Pueblo area of Colorado; and the Salt Lake City region of Utah. People will, as in the past, settle close to a waterway, whether it be ocean, lake, river, or canal. But there will be other motivations, too, such as the climate, the need for land, and the desire for better living.

Cause and Effects

Mobility

Now what has caused our cities to merge? The explanation is simply that homes and jobs, at one time closely tied to each other and firmly fixed in their places, both have been made movable—at the end of increasingly long ropes. The central characteristic that distinguishes interurbia from suburbia is that, in interurbia, the labor force does not move in a single direction, but rather in a series of crossing lines. From Westport, Connecticut, for instance, the majority of commuters go southwest to New York City, but many go northeast to Bridgeport and New Haven. Westport itself gets its labor force from lower Connecticut and from New York. Thus the interchangeable day and night populations that used to be so exclusively a feature of the central city are now typical of interurbia's satellite cities as well.

Factories in the Open

The emergence of interurbia from the now outdated concept of city, suburb, and country has been stimulated more by the growth of satellite cities than it has from the big central city. Industry must have large tracts of land for the new more sprawling factories. While spending billions of dollars on plant expansion, industry has found it cheaper to vault directly from cities into the country, skipping the suburbs. New highways and superhighways are practical avenues of transportation for the worker to his job from places even 40 miles away. The superhighways also make the factories more accessible to trucks.

The future growth of strip cities will probably extend from the large centers of population down the "limited access" highways and expressways projected in the federal government's 50 billion dollar road construction program, and fill the sprawling areas between population centers.

Big Cities

The growth of the strip cities may not stop the growth of the large central cities. The big cities are growing at unprecedented rates and probably will continue to grow. In Chicago, for instance, many new office buildings are under construction in the Loop or in adjacent downtown business districts. A group of city planners also have drawn plans for redeveloping the Near North Side area which is separated from the business district by the Chicago River. It is estimated that the population of the Chicago metropolitan area will increase by one million from 1955 to 1960. Similar urban renewal is taking place in other big cities. But the really spectacular growth will be in interurbia.

Farm Land

Naturally, the question arises: "Will this development of interurbia cause a shortage of farm land?" There seems little reason for worry on this score. In some areas, of course, the farm may have to move out of the path of interurbia; but contrary to popular belief, most of our wide-open spaces are not crop land. According to the 1950 Census of Agriculture, only about 20 per cent of our land is in crops, another 30 per cent in pasture. The rest is grazing land, forest, mountain, desert, suburb, and city. And, as farm technology makes the land increasingly productive, still fewer acres will feed more and more people. So as we look to the future, we can with some confidence predict that the day is not too far distant when most of our people—and most of our sales—will be encompassed within interurbia.

Population Density

For business and industrial leaders the view of the nation's future holds answers to questions they have been asking about the markets of tomorrow. These evolving interurbias are forerunners of areas where there will be twelve times as many people per square mile as there are in the average square mile in the country as a whole. Correspondingly, it is predicted that, within the next 25 years, market areas inside interurbia will claim 70 per cent of the country's retail sales. The markets should reach this high plateau because the mobility of homes and jobs that has brought it to its present stage will become intensified.

Fragmentation

As interurbia develops, we are likely to see more fragmentation in living conditions. Beneath the shell of uniform mass housing there probably will be a series of communities, each catering to different age and income groups. The trend toward uniformity is creating a counter desire to be different. The reason is mobility. More and more people are leaving their old home towns in a series of moves from home town to college, from college to a great organization. The old home town may look much the same. Yet if we check the leadership in the traditional town, we will find that the sons of the pioneer families have more often than not left to join the transient life. But there is another more familiar kind of mobility—the great exodus from the city to the country. This mobility breeds more mobility. Once a person has learned to change environment, it becomes easier to adapt to another. The good transient is quite professional about this. He has learned how to keep his bags packed mentally.

Upgrading

One aspect of this mobility is the tremendous upgrading urge it produces. It is remarkable how frequently this upgrading urge has been under-estimated. One of the most characteristic complaints you will find in the new villages of interurbia is about the kind of goods they have in the stores. The complaint usually takes the line "Who do they think we are, anyway?" Perhaps the most interesting thing about this upgrading urge is how very much it is conditioned by the immediate group in which a couple finds itself. It seems to be the group in interurbia that determines when a luxury becomes a necessity. When only a few housewives in a block have auto-matic dryers, for instance, other housewives can take them or leave them. As more and more housewives follow suit, it soon becomes an almost un-social act not to own one.

Individuality

At first, anyone looking down on a mass housing development in inter-urbia might say the people living there are all living the same life. In reality, they are not. They are sensitive to even minor differences in living, and they will continue to seek those minor differences as they move about. It is important to note that the role of the businessman in interurbia will be affected by how much he knows about the individual people living there. If he knows the psychological needs of an individual, the businessman will be in a better position to influence that individual.

The Interurbian

The J. Walter Thompson Company studied several thousand people and projected the principal drives of these people into an interurbian situation. The results showed the interurbian man to be significantly above the na-tional average in his expressed desires to produce, to do his best, to get prestige and acclaim. He has a strong desire to rival and surpass others. He has an equally pronounced need to dominate other people, to be a leader and influence others. He is more willing to talk about sex and less strict in his attitudes than his predecessors were. Our interurbian man likes to be the center of attention and to make an impression on others. It appears that vanity and self-dramatization motivate him more than the man living else-where in the land. The interurbian man doesn't mind change. In fact, he likes to do new and different things, to change his daily routine. He likes variety and novelty. Possibly this is one reason why he accepts the need for mobility with such calm. Our interurbian woman also is an interesting creature. Her attitudes toward sex differ, too, from those of the rest of the country. She is more willing to talk about the subject. She immensely enjoys

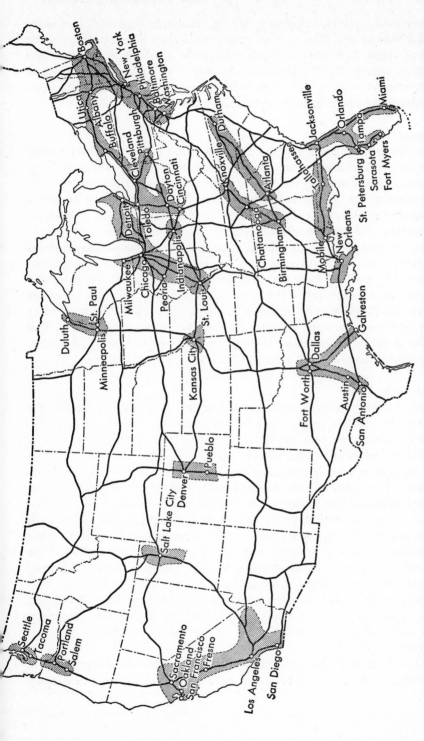

Interurbia by 1980, Connected by the Projected System of Interstate Highways, 1965. (Adapted from the author's map and from Bureau of Public Roads, U.S. Department of Commerce, "General Location of National System of Interstate Highways," Washington, D.C., U.S. Government Printing Office, n.d., p.v.

97

understanding others, examining motives, analyzing behavior. The inter-urbian woman also likes to have others notice her. She, too, has a great deal of vanity. It is of great significance in the development of future advertising appeals that the characteristics which are most highly developed in the men and women of interurbia will be those on which so many successful advertising campaigns have been built and will be built.

Changes in Economy

Let us consider for a moment the economic significance of interurbia. Interurbia will push us toward an economy that will be bigger and probably more stable. The stability will be due to the changing pattern of ownership and consumption interurbia imposes. Except for a little furniture and a closetful of clothes, most city apartment dwellers have no real possessions. By contrast, the interurbanite who has left the big city is forced to become a man of property. His ownership of a house creates a hunger for hard goods that inevitably drives him to work harder than the metropolitan dweller. Our national labor force has been swelled by family members who urgently need money, not to eke out a comfortable livelihood but to pay for the extras. The stabilizing influence of interurbia on the economy is being seen in a huge spending program on the part of business, utilities, and public authorities. Interurbia requires new highways, schools, hospitals, waterworks, factories, and stores.

Changes in Labor

Still another stabilizing influence lies in the increased opportunity for workers to maintain employment by being more mobile. Unemployed industrial workers are now mobile enough to go to another factory. In the eastern Connecticut woolen district, for example, the town of Danielson was hit hard by closing mills. But now many of the workers of Danielson drive some 60 miles to East Hartford and collect the higher wages paid by United Aircraft. The expansion of interurbia may include some built-in relief for the shortage of manpower. As homes and factories follow each other into the countryside we may be able to recruit—or keep in the labor force—people whose training and experience might not otherwise be utilized. These may include married women who could work part-time; people who have reached the retirement age but have no desire to stop working; individuals who must work within minutes of home if they are to work at all; and the physically handicapped. All of these and more may find increased opportunities to add to the family income in the new interurbia.

As a result of the greatly increased competition for good employees in interurbia, companies will be forced to take more initiative in developing benefit programs. Every activity that can conceivably be used to knit an organization together will be exploited. Employers will find it necessary to develop new methods of integrating new employees into their new communities. Companies will have to expand the coverage of their community-relations activities as their workers tend more and more to spring from outlying communities. Increased automobile ownership by employees has already broadened the labor pool of most plants to 30 miles or more and improved highways will lengthen the practical commuting distance.

Changes in Markets

The marketing problems created by interurbia will be no less complex. With 31 million changes of residence every year, the retailer, worrying about new locations, may have to know more about his customers and where they come from. The friendly neighborhood dealer may lose some of his old sales punch. The manufacturer may find that the focus of marketing is no longer the central city in interurbia, but somewhere in between. Test marketing may no longer be exclusively confined to individual market entities, but more to interurbian strips. The same may be true for product research.

As more and more people cluster together in the nation's interurbias, manufacturers' sales organizations may grow smaller as they concentrate on retail service. The 2,000-man sales force may become a thing of the past. New stores, service stations, and discount houses will expose customers to brands they've never seen before. As New York and Boston push toward each other in the nation's largest interurbia, they'll carry with them certain brands that New London, Connecticut, has never heard of. The same may apply to prices. Someone may roll down the interurbian highway and introduce some price cuts hitherto unknown to various communities along the way. And the mobility of the interurbian woman will simplify this new task of price cutting. Miles will mean nothing for the interurbian woman looking for a bargain!

As we change from the old concept of a metropolitan marketing area to a new interurbian marketing area, probably we should re-examine the methods by which we separate and study our markets. Perhaps it may not be too early for market research firms to break down their findings on the basis of interurbia versus non-interurbia. Perhaps instead of viewing the United States as a total market, we might see what these fourteen interurbias might represent as a total sales opportunity. Perhaps a manufacturer might consider his time well spent if he anticipated this inevitable move toward greater interurbia and isolated even one of these fourteen areas— studied it from every conceivable marketing angle, developing one interurbia well before being lured to greener pastures.

Changes in Communications

Our look at the interurban business picture would not be complete without some consideration of advertising and media. The development of interurbia may completely revolutionize the attitude we take toward markets. It seems inevitable that as populations tend to merge and come together in bigger groups, the political or corporate boundaries as we now know them will lose their identity and their significance. Concentration of population has virtually always meant lower advertising costs. The bigger the mass of circulation an advertiser buys, the lower the relative cost he pays for it.

Interurbian man will continue to have two major appetites for news: one, national and international; the other, regional and local. How will this dual appetite be satisfied? The metropolitan daily may seek to satisfy both with more zoned editions, as some large dailies already are doing. Or it may sign over the depth of local news to the smaller daily and weekly and concentrate more on national and international news. The metropolitan daily may become less and less identified with the central city of interurbia and more with interurbia as a whole. The smaller daily and weekly may stand to benefit from the interurbian development, because they are in the happy position of having their market come to them. If the smaller newspapers can meet this opportunity, theirs is indeed a bright future.

Interurbia also suggests that more regional publications could lead a profitable existence. Or perhaps Sunday supplements of the future will concentrate their coverage on interurbian clusters. Magazine sales also could follow a different trend in interurbia. Already some magazines are selling their circulations sectionally—usually in the traditional Eastern, Middlewestern, and Pacific sections. This would lead to an adjustment of both circulation and editorial content.

Radio and television inside interurbia also face changes. Both electronic media could become more efficient. Ownership of television sets throughout interurbia will increase to something close to the 90 per cent that is now usual in metropolitan areas. Then radio will become more restricted to the less expensive news and music programing. Concentrations of population will make it possible for a few television stations to reach larger numbers of families. Today up to thirteen television stations are needed to cover the interurbian area developing along the Northeast coast of the United States. Electronic progress probably will reduce the number of stations needed for saturation to as few as five.

The big, unanswered question about television in interurbia is the speed with which the magic of electronic journalism will focus on community life and paint it possibly with more intimacy than is now true of the printing press. Until that day comes, it seems reasonable to suggest that newspapers and radio will continue to perform a rather specific editorial function in interurbia, while magazines and television do a broader job.

The Shape of Things to Come

We are now at the foothills of a way of life that will require a higher degree of research than we have ever employed before to know people's motivations and desires, to know how they live and why they live as they do, and to know it all before it is too late. How soon and how fast this process of interurbanization will take place must remain in the realm of speculation. Of one thing we are certain: interurbia will produce fundamental changes. And as it does, probably no one of us will be able to do business as we have been doing. With interurbia will come problems and also opportunities. No one will find paradise there. Paradise always will be just around the corner. And that, for all of us, may be our greatest opportunity.

Market Segmentation

15. U.S. NEGRO MARKET—GROWING TARGET
FOR ADVERTISERS *
by Victor J. Dallaire †

Do you feel the urge for more sales volume coming on? Then take a look at America's Negro market—it might be just what you have been looking for.

It will be just as well at the outset to discard any conceptions you may have of the Negro market that are based on conditions of ten or even five years ago.

The Negro market is changing day by day, so fast indeed that in this midway-between-Census year a good deal of conjecture and guesswork must be substituted for facts. But you can bet your bottom budget dollar the Negro market is:

—big and getting bigger
—rich and getting richer
—easy to reach and getting easier
—highly brand-conscious and getting more so every day.

It's Big

One in every ten Americans is a Negro, a proportion that would give us a total of more than 16,000,000 Negro consumers now, assuming that the Census Bureau's estimate of total U.S. population of 162,500,000 is correct.

* Reprinted from *Printers' Ink*, © September 16, 1955, pp. 52–8.
† Printers' Ink.

102

According to the 1950 Census, the Negro population stood at 15,042,286, roughly 10 per cent of the total at the time. The Census Bureau estimated that in July 1954 the total nonwhite population in the country stood at 17,410,000. Since only a small number of these are other races—Chinese, Japanese, Indian, etc.—16,000,000 would seem to be a conservative estimate for the present Negro population.

Actually, the Negro population in the United States is increasing at a faster rate than the white population. Studies of birth rate and school enrollment indicate that before long Negroes will make up 11 per cent or 12 per cent of the total population. But it ought to suffice for the present that the Negro market in the United States is larger than the entire Canadian market.

It's Rich

On the basis of 1950 Census figures, each million Negroes earned $1,000,000,000 a year, a grand total of $15,000,000,000, a billion more than the total income of Canada and half again as much as the value of U.S. sales beyond its borders. There's no reason to believe that America's 16,000,000 Negroes aren't maintaining at least the same volume of income, so a most conservative estimate of income this year for the Negro market would be $16,000,000,000.

It's probably more than that because since 1940 there has been an increasingly large flow of Negroes from low-pay farm jobs to industry where earnings are a good deal higher. The 1950 Census, for example, showed that Negro family income increased 192 per cent during the previous ten years as compared to an increase of 146 per cent for white families.

Another factor contributing to the rise is the advance in the educational status of Negroes in the past fifteen years. College enrollment of Negroes now is larger than the total of all colleges and universities in the British Isles. Negro college enrollment rose more than 2,500 per cent between 1930 and 1950. A good deal of the jump came during and after World War II.

This rise in educational standards, getting stronger every year, has helped to build Negroes to a stable group of people who are striving for better standards of living. They are better equipped than ever before in the nation's history to demand and get higher-income jobs.

Another factor contributing to higher Negro income is the large proportion of women who work. There are no figures for the present available, but Bureau of Census report No. 29, issued May 20, 1951, showed that 37 per cent of all married Negro women were employed as compared to approximately 23.7 per cent of white married woman. This, of course, has somewhat increased the combined family income for Negroes, a most important consideration for makers and sellers of products for family use.

It's Easy to Reach

Right about here you can junk any notions about most Negroes living in rural areas. The move of Negroes away from the farm has been so heavy in recent years that more than 60 per cent of the Negro population now live in urban areas.

Just to show you how fast this trek to the city has taken place, let's take a look at Census reports for 1940 and 1950. In 1940, more than half of all Negroes in the U.S. lived down on the farm; by 1950, the Negro population had become predominantly urban, living in well-defined urban areas which are virtually cities within cities.

Why did they move? The increased urban population is due largely to a shift in residence of younger people with fewer ties to their former homes than older, more settled people. Also, after World War II, many Negro veterans, confronted with lack of employment opportunities in farming areas and small towns, chose to remain near larger urban areas. These men,

NEGRO POPULATION, SELECTED METRO AREAS *

	Negro Population		% of Total Population	
	1950	1959	1950	1959
New York—n.e. New Jersey	1,013,616	1,447,338	7.9	10.0
Los Angeles—Long Beach	218,954	457,798	5.0	7.1
Chicago	586,663	1,013,323	11.3	15.8
Philadelphia	480,134	677,464	13.1	15.4
Detroit	357,857	547,860	11.9	14.0
San Francisco—Oakland	147,361	195,231	6.6	7.1
Pittsburgh	82,453	108,399	3.7	4.5
St. Louis	153,766	212,391	9.0	10.3
Washington, D.C.	337,757	490,242	23.1	25.1
Cleveland	147,847	251,116	10.1	14.3
Baltimore	265,415	370,616	18.9	22.8
Buffalo	36,645	78,192	3.4	5.8
Houston	124,761	210,874	15.5	17.3
Milwaukee	22,129	60,892	2.3	5.2
Cincinnati	112,828	170,730	12.5	15.9
Kansas City	55,682	88,313	6.8	8.5
Dallas	56,958	101,601	7.7	9.9
Seattle	16,753	25,845	2.0	2.5
San Diego	16,999	29,084	3.1	3.1
Atlanta	165,591	214,539	22.8	23.2
Miami	40,262	76,544	8.1	8.8
New Orleans	181,775	165,809	26.5	19.1

* Copyright by *Sales Management*, March 4, 1960, pp. 36–44.

because of their travels, had developed a desire for a higher standard of living.

Don't get the idea, either, that Negroes living in cities are scattered throughout them on a 10 to 1 basis. They are concentrated heavily in the large industrial cities, the biggest markets for consumer goods. Roughly 30 per cent of the entire Negro population is found in 29 major industrial cities. Negro populations in those cities range from 10 per cent of the total in New York to 35 per cent in Washington, D.C.

This heavy concentration of higher-income Negroes means two things to makers and sellers of goods: (1) because Negroes are located in major markets, most manufacturers already are set up to handle any increased volume they may win from Negro consumers; (2) because Negroes tend to concentrate in large cities and within the cities themselves, it is relatively easy to reach them with special advertising and promotional campaigns.

They're Highly Brand-Conscious

The Negro's desire to improve his lot, his increasing income, and the fact that he's been burned so badly and so often in the past with shoddy merchandise makes him a highly brand-conscious consumer. Dr. Joseph T.

NEGRO MIGRATION TRENDS *

The rate of migration out of the South has been in excess of past trends. In the six "Deep South" states of Alabama, Florida, Georgia, Louisiana, Mississippi, and South Carolina the Negro percentage of total population has declined from an average of 32.8% in 1950 to 28.5% in 1959. Rural southern areas have been the chief losers, for some southern metro areas actually increased their Negro proportions.

Negro migrants have continued to flow toward the major northern urban concentrations of New York, Chicago, Philadelphia, and Detroit, all of which have gained 50% or more in Negro population since 1950. Perhaps more surprising has been the even greater percentage gains in Los Angeles, San Francisco, San Diego, Seattle, other western areas.

These trends suggest that Negro population in the future will be more and more evenly spread, although even at the rapid rates indicated here, two more decades would be required to reduce the Negro population of the Deep South to 20% or so of the total. It is significant that in 1950 the state which had the highest Negro proportion was Mississippi, with 45.3% of its population Negro. Today, Washington, D.C., proper with 52.3% of its population Negro has the highest Negro concentration in the nation.

Johnson of Lincoln University summed up the most important of these buying factors in these words:

In an effort to show its status generally, the urban Negro market tends to be exceptionally brand conscious.

A recent survey by Daniel Starch and Staff of readers of a leading Negro family publication (Ebony) shows that: 25.9 per cent wear Stetson hats (men); 31.6 per cent wear Florsheim shoes (men); 42.5 per cent use Pillsbury Cake Mix (women); 49.7 per cent use Calumet baking powder (women); 64.2 per cent use Kellogg's dry cereals; 47.5 per cent use Colgate toothpaste; 19.4 per cent own General Electric refrigerators; 24.9 per cent own Hoover vacuum cleaners.

Part of Total Market, But Specialized Too

Obviously, a good part of this demand for well-known brands was inspired by general advertising. In a larger sense, there's no such thing as a Negro market—it's just a part of the U.S. market as a whole. But many astute advertisers, who don't pinch pennies when it comes to building up general recognition for their products, put a measure of extra effort into cultivating the Negro market. It must be sound business practice. The difficulty, of course, is pinning down the results of this extra advertising effort. You can't separate Negro volume from total volume on a general-use product; you'll just have to be satisfied with a decent share of the Negro business.

Leaders among advertisers gunning for a bigger share of the Negro market are the liquor, tobacco, petroleum, and food and drug companies, just as they are the leaders in soliciting the market as a whole. Some of these companies employ Negroes for contact work; some don't. But, in both cases, the advertiser makes every effort to understand the Negro consumer and reach him with advertising specifically directed to Negroes.

16. TEEN-AGE CONSUMERS *

One particular group of consumers—the teenagers—has been coming in for special attention from advertisers in the past few years. Since the teen-agers themselves offer a substantial market and since the patterns now being established will affect their behavior as adult consumers in the future,

* Reprinted from *Consumer Reports*, © March 1957, pp. 139–41.

CU's economic consultants have been looking into the views of those who are trying to mold this market.

"Teenagers offer the advertiser a market that grows larger in size and purchasing power every day," says the Bureau of Advertising of the American Newspaper Publishers Association in an advertising promotional pamphlet called *"Tell It to the Teens."* Some of the biggest names in the national advertising roster have been sponsoring special campaigns for the teens for some time. There was a time not so long ago, according to the newspaper advertising lineage sellers, when this was considered primarily a market for kid stuff—"bikes and soda pop." Those days are over. Today's teens, they calculate, will pocket some nine billion dollars a year in allowances, gifts, and incomes from jobs. About 800,000 teens have steady full-time jobs. Nearly five million have part-time jobs after school or on Saturday—working in local shops, supermarkets and filling stations, at baby sitting, gardening, odd jobs around homes, etc. And in the summertime the teenage working force swells to close to ten million.

Economic Emancipation

In short, one of the by-products of fifteen years of full employment is the teenage part-time wage earner; or, as one used-car dealer put it: "This is the age of the economic emancipation of the juvenile."

The nine billion dollars in teenage hands are only the first reason why advertisers are directing sales pressure to this group. The second reason is that a rapidly increasing number of teens become brides and grooms before twenty. And the third reason is that a teenager has, in this day and age, a considerable emotional lever with which to influence family spending.

It is no secret that parents across the land are uneasy about how to handle the teenager. And what the teenager does with his own money is not the least of the parents' problems. The press evidences the uncertainty about the teenager in an avalanche of articles of advice, reports of research, news of civic committees, etc. Movies, stage plays, novels, pocket books on how-to, scientific publications, and local and Federal governmental agencies add their own flood of comment on how to handle the problems of living with teenagers. In a hard-living, fast-driving, urbanized community, where adult privileges often desired by the young include alcohol, tobacco, and late hours, the parent has to say "No" much too frequently; hence he is looking for places to say "Yes" graciously and easily. A high-school principal expressed it this way: "Parents, today, feel a need to prove to their teenage children that they are 'Good Joes.'" Acceding to pressure from the youngster on the spending of his own money, as well as on the choice of the new family car, the purchase of a family TV set, where to take a vacation, what movies to see, what brand to choose, what clothes to buy for both adult and child, is one way to say "Yes."

The magazine *Business Week* (June 1, 1956) characterized the teen influence on family spending as "a pressure which ranks with that of the most powerfully organized lobby." The automobile is one of the chief concerns of this lobby: better than half the teens expect to influence the choice of the family's automobile, according to some surveys; and somewhere in the neighborhood of 25 per cent of the boys from sixteen through nineteen years of age are estimated to own or be part owners of cars. Today, the first objective of most of the boys earning money is a jalopy.

You can define a jalopy as a used car that would probably be junked if it were not for the teenage demand. To be sure, jalopies take a great deal of tinkering to keep them in running order, but machine shop courses and how-to magazines are there to guide the young car-tinkerer, some of whom now make up the breed known as Hot Rodders. Keeping an old car running is apt to be expensive under any circumstances; from the point of view of the parts supplier, the hot rodder is an especially good consumer. His remodeling expenditures may run as high as $1,500 to $3,000 when enthusiasm is keen and wherewithal available.

Costly "Junk"

Standard parts for car repairs are quite expensive, as any adult car owner knows, but the youngsters go beyond these to buy specialty parts from some 2,000 speed shops across the country which sell custom-made parts for souped-up engines at prices double and triple the cost of standard parts. An estimated 100 manufacturers are in the business of designing and supplying these particular items. Along with the mechanical products they also supply an assortment of gimmicks, called "junk" in the trade, chrome gingerbread, giant dice, wolf whistles, special headlights, crash helmets, etc. And around the activity of making a speed car out of a jalopy have sprung up a number of Hot Rod Clubs—these also soak up a portion of the teenage earnings and allowances in outlays for special jackets and particular club emblems. Together the club plaque and jacket can come to a total as high as from $35 to $50.

Merchants report that their teenage customers are not price conscious. "If they want it and have the money, they buy it," is the impression of most retailers. They seldom shop around. When it comes to records, jewelry, table radios, clothes, and cosmetics, price comparisons are reported as rare.

Tell It to the Teens reports that 57 per cent of the youngsters who spend their own money buy records, and record shops report that most of the sales are rhythm and blues music, progressive jazz and, of course, Elvis

Presley. The popularity of this singer, especially with the girls, has already produced a list of more than 50 items with the Elvis Presley imprint: sofa pillows, shoes, jeans, shirts, sox, record players, plaster of Paris busts, bracelets, and even a line of Elvis Presley furniture and lamps. In cosmetics there are available lipsticks in Hound Dog Orange, Heartbreak Hotel Pink, and Tutti Frutti Red (from Presley record titles). For obvious reasons, none of the published teenage-market surveys mention beer as a product of importance to this group. The teens are, so far as the public attitude has it, soft drink consumers. That they do consume soft drinks, and in oceanic volume, is certainly a fact. But juvenile police officers and high-school authorities report that many teens drink beer and often liquor at their social get-togethers.

Another product purchased by the teens that receives no mention in the published surveys of their buying habits is cigarettes. No one with eyes to see can escape the knowledge that these youngsters, both boys and girls, do smoke. How important they are as a market is evidenced by the attention they received from the largest tobacco manufacturer. In a story titled "Teenage Customers," the *Wall Street Journal* (December 6, 1956) comments:

One of the most delicate problems of appealing to teenagers was faced by American Tobacco Co., maker of Lucky Strike cigarettes and sponsor of the Hit Parade, long a teenage radio and TV favorite. Many a teenager smokes, of course, but no cigarette company would risk the opprobrium that probably would attach to a direct sales appeal to teenagers. American Tobacco, however, conducted a careful study of teen musical tastes to guide its Hit Parade show.

Recently the American Tobacco Co. introduced a new brand of cigarettes and named it Hit Parade, obviously to further capitalize on the popularity of its radio and TV program.

Socially Acceptable Bids

In the list of products that are socially acceptable bidders for teenage custom, sports equipment is high for boys and lipstick for girls. Lipstick and hand lotion are far and away the favorite cosmetic products, although variety chains report that cosmetics for eyes (eyebrow pencil, mascara and eye shadow) are now chalking up the greatest percentage gains in sales to the high school and college market. For both boys and girls deodorants are a big item, and in the later teens, shaving cream is bought by the boys. Jewelry appeals to both sexes. In some communities the credit jewelers, whose goods are typically grossly overpriced, deluge each high-school graduating class with direct mail offers in spite of the fact that a juvenile signature on a credit contract renders the contract invalid. (Since neither parents nor children are apt to know the details of sales law and since the collection tactics of most credit jewelers are rough and tough, the risk to the seller is not great.)

When it comes to buying clothes, the teenager is an easy customer to handle, according to shop owners. Both boys and girls are more influenced by style and color than by materials or workmanship and they are not contributors to what the merchants call "the returned-goods problem." When a teenager does bring back a purchase it is usually because his parents refused to let him keep it.

As a general rule, teenage consumers not only fail to exercise their right to demand replacement when goods are faulty but their pressure is also against their parents' return of goods. There seems to be a greater urge to spend money than to get good value for what they spend. As the newspaper publishers point out: "Dollars . . . acquired by the teens are not tied up in rent, electric bills or other expenses of household overhead, as so many of Pop's dollars are."

The result is that foolish expenditures fail to produce the same awareness of waste and even deprivation experienced by an adult with economic responsibilities. To put it another way, the spending habits and consumer attitudes fostered by most teenage buying these days cannot be expected to result in good consumer education; clearly, informed guidance by adults is badly needed.

Advertisers seem to expect the guidance to flow the other way, however. Eugene Gilbert, who runs a recently organized marketing service for advertisers called Gilbert Youth Research, and who calls himself "the George Gallup of the teenagers" says, as quoted in the press:

An advertiser who touches a responsive chord in youth can generally count on the parent to finally succumb to the purchase of the product. Since youth is graced with unparalleled resiliency and buoyancy, parents generally have little resistance or protection against youth's bombardments. Thus, with parents rendered helpless, it becomes evident that youth is in the market.

Another research into youth as a consumer was quoted in the *Wall Street Journal* as saying:

What the adult considers a luxury, the young people consider a necessity to keep pace with today's living; furniture, a new piano, a hi-fi set, and an automobile fall into this classification.

The desire of advertisers to appeal to the youngster has set in motion a number of specially designed advertising efforts. For example:

• The Ford Motor Company is taking space in teenage magazines to advise youngsters on "how to safety check a car in two minutes" and will launch a campaign this spring on how to buy a used car.

- The General Electric Company marketed a table radio designed to appeal to teenagers in shape and color.

- Kraft Foods is promoting Velveeta cheese to teenagers via a jingle contest featuring prizes of a year's free personal telephone service.

- The Fragrance Foundation, a cooperative perfume manufacturers' venture, is planning a campaign to convince the teenager that "perfume is for wearing every day . . . every hour of the day."

- Four advertisers—Schrank Dreamwear, Canada Dry Ginger Ale, Coty, and RCA Victor—have joined hands to spend a million dollars this spring promoting pajama parties for teens, the idea being that a fad for such parties would sell all four products: pajamas, ginger ale, perfume, and records.

- Mars Candy Company is preparing to launch a "Candy bar indoctrination" scheme.

And so it goes. What's more, straws in the wind indicate that there will be much more teenage market exploitation in the future than there is today. By 1965, promise the newspaper publishers, the size of the teenage market will have swollen to 24 million and the free-wheeling pocket money in that year will bulge to 14 billion dollars.

Business Week has issued a warning to advertisers, however, that this oncoming avalanche of teens can be a threat as well as an opportunity. "They can be won by enterprising merchandising techniques; but they can be swiftly lost if the advertiser allows his outlook to be colored by complacency," says that journal. Hence, it continues, advertisers "must continue to know what young people are doing . . . what standards are shifting, and in what direction the flow of youthful enthusiasm is flowing" productwise.

Consumer Reports would like to add that perhaps a paraphrase of that warning is in order for parents and high-school teachers. If the nation's advertisers mean what they are saying these days, if the aggressive pressure of the hard sell is to be turned full force onto the teenage consumer, adults had better forearm themselves with an arsenal of consumer information and market know-how and also with the backbone required to give buying guidance to their teenagers. There are already indications that the lure of possessions is too strong among the youngsters. Without exception, merchants report that shoplifting by teenagers has become a major headache. Both high-school principals and police on the juvenile detail add that eagerness to spend on recreation and operation of jalopies is a source of delinquency. Training by both parents and the schools in buying and in understanding the responsibilities of the consumer in the market place might help counteract some of the bad effects of increasing sales pressures.

17. SPENDING PATTERNS OF OLDER PERSONS *

by Zoe Campbell †

The importance of changes in consumption patterns as one grows older is underscored by the relative aging of the population that has already occurred in the United States. The proportion of the population sixty-five years and over has doubled in the last fifty years. Even further growth for this group is expected in the future.

Growth in numbers is not the only factor which has made the older population an increasingly large and important consumer market. Although estimates of aggregate income for any age group are very uncertain, they do give some guide as to the economic strength of a group.

The Joint Committee on Problems of the Aging of the New York State Legislature in its 1956 report, "New Channels for the Golden Years," estimated the total income after taxes of persons sixty-five and over to be 20 billion (dollars) in 1954 and predicted a rise to 32 billion by 1965. By size alone, then, this group warrants examination. More than that, it is a group with distinct needs and desires which is growing faster than the rest of the population.

One way to determine these needs and desires, of course, is by an examination of past spending patterns. What appeals to the older group now presumably will be indicated by how they behaved in the past.

Family Spending Patterns of Two Age Groups

The importance of an individual's economic position is largely dependent on his family status rather than on the size of his income alone.[1] Approximately 70 per cent of men and women sixty-five years and over live in their own households. Furthermore, 88.5 per cent of the older men are family heads. (One drawback in examining spending patterns of families by age groups is that in most surveys, the title of "head" is often given to the senior family member as a matter of courtesy rather than as an indication of the actual financial head.)

Families whose "head" is sixty-five or over, on the average, spend less than younger families. This is perhaps no more than one would expect,

* Reprinted from *Management Record,* © March 1959, pp. 85–7 ff.
† Division of Consumer Economics, National Industrial Conference Board.
[1] For a fuller discussion of this point, see The Conference Board's *Studies in Business Economics,* No. 52, "Income and Resources of Older People," pp. 21–2.

even without an examination of family budgets. But the extent of the difference between the amount of spending by younger and older families can only be appreciated by contrasting a few figures. The 1956 survey of consumer expenditures conducted in urban communities by Alfred Politz Research, Incorporated for *Life* [2] (the most recent major study containing pertinent data) shows that families headed by persons sixty-five and over spent $2,405, whereas families whose head was less than sixty-five spent $4,430 for consumer goods and services. However, when put on a per capita basis, the difference is much less, although it still exists—$1,146 for the older family as against $1,230 for the younger.

Age Not the Only Answer

The difference in expenditures between the two groups is not entirely due to the difference in age. Further, not all members of the older family will be sixty-five or over; nor will all members of the younger family be under sixty-five, although there is an expectation that the age of the household head can be taken as an indication of the age ranking of its members.

The older families differ from the younger in several important characteristics, all of which can be expected to have an influence on consumption patterns. First of all, differences exist in the income levels of the two groups. Over *40 per cent* of families headed by older persons received *less* than $2,000 in money income, according to the *Life* survey. By contrast, slightly over *10 per cent* of younger families received *less* than $2,000. The median income of urban families headed by older persons was $3,000 in 1957. This compares with a median income of $5,359 for all urban families.

Second, the differences in spending level, and more particularly the composition of spending, are also influenced by the size of the family. In 1956, the older family in the *Life* survey was composed of 2.1 persons, whereas the younger family was composed of 3.6 persons. There is some indication that the older family is decreasing in size, while the younger family is increasing. Census reports show that the older husband-and-wife family is now composed of 2.0 persons and that all husband-and-wife families are composed of 3.7 persons.

Another factor that can be expected to have an influence on consumption patterns is the amount of liquid assets held by the two family groups. According to the Federal Reserve Board's 1958 "Survey of Consumer Finances," 20 per cent of spending units [3] whose head was sixty-five or over

---

[2] "*Life* Study of Consumer Expenditures," Volume I, 1957.

[3] A spending unit as defined by the survey consists of all related persons living together who pool their incomes. Other related persons in the household are separate spending units if they earn more than $15 a week and do not pool their incomes. This is different from the Census definition of a family, which includes all related persons residing together.

had holdings of $5,000 or more in early 1958. This compares with 9 per cent of all families who had liquid assets of $5,000 or more. However, 27 per cent of the older spending units had no holdings, while 26 per cent of all spending units had no holdings. Even so, the amount of liquid asset holdings tends to increase with age; and, also, older people in the lower-income levels have larger holdings than the younger people at the same levels.

A fourth factor that influences consumption patterns is the geographical location of the family; this is important because of differences in climate, local habits, and price levels.

Data, unfortunately, are not available to disentangle all of these factors on the spending patterns of older and younger families. Anaylsis is possible, however, of the spending patterns of the two families at identical levels of income, after adjustment is made for differing family size. However, it was not possible to assess the role of liquid asset holdings, nor the influence of geographic location.

For a multidimensional analysis, resort must be made to the 1950 study of consumer expenditures conducted by the Bureau of Labor Statistics.[4] The analysis was carried out separately for nine categories, as follows:

Food (including alcoholic beverages and tobacco)

Housing (shelter and home repairs and replacements)

Fuel, light, and refrigeration

Household operations (includes such items involved in running a home as laundry service, telephone service, domestic help, etc.)

Furniture (including home furnishings and equipment)

Clothing

Transportation

Medical care

Miscellaneous items (which include personal care, recreation, reading, and education as well as the items assigned to the miscellaneous group because they did not easily fit into any other groups).

Family-Size Adjustment

An adjustment had to be made to eliminate the effect of family size in examining the expenditures of the two age groups. In the first place, the average size of the older family is smaller than the average size of the younger family at all income levels; and second, the average family size increases as income increases in both instances. Of course, an adjustment factor would not be needed if the data in the bureau's study for a particular size family had been used. However, a clearer picture emerges—because

[4] "Study of Consumer Expenditures, Income, and Savings," Wharton School of Finance, University of Pennsylvania, 1957.

of the greater reliability of the larger sample—when the total data are used.

Although any size family could have been selected, the two family groups were standardized at 2.2 persons, in order to correspond closely to the average size of the older family. The adjustment factor was determined by finding the average relationship between family size and expenditures.[5]

Total Expenditures at Different Income Levels

Even after making the adjustments for family size, older families tend to spend less for consumer items than younger families. At the very low-income levels, where both families spend more than they receive in income, younger families spend in greater excess of their income than the older.[6]

The older family, which no longer receives an income from earnings or has a limited number of years to receive earnings, cannot afford to deplete its savings. The older family, also, has difficulty obtaining loans. Therefore, because of its limited sources of income and little prospect of rising to higher-income levels, the older family has to budget its expenditures closely. Younger families, on the other hand, can be more confident in anticipating larger earnings, or, at least, a sustained income from earnings over a longer period of time.

In the $2,000–$4,000 income range, aggregate expenditures of both families are very nearly the same. The older urban family's median income just falls within the $3,000–$4,000 income level. And their consumption level compares favorably with other urban families in the same income bracket. Even if the older family's median income slid below $3,000, into

[5] Factors for adjusting data for family size were derived from a multiple regression analysis for each category of expenditure. Where least squares methods yielded unreasonable results, graphic correlation methods were substituted. In each case, expenditures were related to income and family size, using the logarithms of all variables. The regression coefficient of the family-size variable was then used to adjust expenditures to those of a 2.2 size family.

For example, the complete equation for housing expenditures in the sixty-five-and-over age group was: $.35 \log x + .53 \log w + 1.154 = \log z$, where x represents income, in dollars per year, w, family size, and z, annual housing expenditures. The coefficient of the family-size variable, .53, is then used to scale housing expenditures for a family of any size in the sixty-five-and-over group to the average family size of 2.2 members. A specific example will illustrate how this was done. At an average annual income of $4,787 in 1950, the average family size was three persons, with annual housing expenditures coming to $448. The logarithm of 448 is 2.6513; the logarithm of 3 is .4771, and of 2.2, .3424. Expenditures for housing are then adjusted to the 2.2 family size by the following computation: $2.6513 - .53$ $(.4771 - .3424) = 2.5799$, which is the antilogarithm of 380. On this basis, outlays for housing totaling $448 for a three-person family are equivalent to an expenditure of $380 for a 2.2-person family.

[6] Family income refers to money income before taxes, which includes money income from all sources, less occupational expenses, but before deduction of net personal taxes.

the $2,000–$3,000 income level, their total spending would be comparable to the spending of other families on the same level.

From this point on, however, younger families spend increasingly more than the older families. Therefore, at income levels where the older family could best afford to spend a larger share on goods and services it does not. For example, the older family at the $5,000–$6,000 income level spends 11.1 per cent less than the younger family. The median income of younger families falls within this bracket (the median incomes for the two groups fall in two different income levels), and the actual differences in expenditures are considerable. And when the expenditures of the older family at the $3,000–$4,000 level are compared with those of the younger family at the $5,000–$6,000 level, the older spends 32.3 per cent less than the younger family.

At a $7,500–$10,000 income level, the older family spends 14.8 per cent less than the younger family. At today's higher prices, expenditures at these income levels would, of course, be larger than at the time of the BLS survey, but the spread between the outlays of the two age groups would probably be about the same. And, although the estimated adjustment for family size

CHART 1

Spending Pattern of Older and Younger Families with 2.2 Persons at Different Income Levels. (Bureau of Labor Statistics; The Conference Board.)

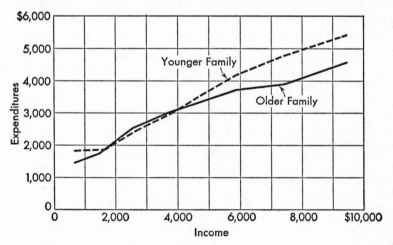

may have reduced the total expenditures below the real level of spending for a 2.2 size family, the younger family would still spend a larger portion of its income than the older family.

Response of Total Expenditures to Increased Income

On the basis of estimates made on the relationship between income and expenditures for a 2.2 person family,[7] it was found that, generally, for every 1 per cent increase in income, older people increase their expenditures by half this amount (0.5 per cent), while younger families increase their expenditures by 0.6 per cent. Although the difference appears small, the spread between the two groups increases as income increases.

This generalization applies particularly to the middle-income classes ($3,000–$7,500). As family income rises in the very low-income brackets, the increase in expenditures is very small; and at high-income levels, as already stated, the spending of older families tends to slope off.

Importance of Items to the Older Family

One of the reasons for the aged's seeming disinterest in consumer goods and services may be that until only recently almost this entire market has been slanted toward the younger consumer. Since many goods and services did not fit the needs of older people, they did not spend their money.

Yet, some items are relatively more important to the older than the younger. In the past, older families, at all income levels, have consistently spent a larger portion of their total expenditures on housing. The United States Federal Council on Aging in 1958 reported that 68 per cent of the families headed by older people owned their own homes and that 80 per cent of these were mortgage free. However, many of these homes are physical and financial burdens to older people, because of their size and the cost of upkeep. Older people would, therefore, be likely to spend more if their incomes increased or were at higher levels for homes or apartments that suited their needs. Or, the "younger" and healthier older couples might be induced to vacation at lodgings which catered to their age group.

From the $5,000–$6,000 income class upward, transportation is also a relatively more important item for older families than for the younger group. Since the older generally have more time to travel, travel agencies which give special attention to the older person could perhaps find a new group of customers for transport facilities. Automobile advertisements have been appealing to the older age group, with illustrations showing that "grandfather" enjoys his car as well as the younger family. The trailer industry, also, has found a new market for its products.

Food is the most important item for both family groups. At the low-income level, food expenditures comprise a slightly larger percentage of the

[7] See footnote 1 on page 115.

total expenditures in the older family's budget than in the younger family's. Even at this level, though, the older family's outlay for food is 3.3 per cent less than the younger family's. In other words, the older family spends less than the younger for food items, but it spends a larger share of its budget.

Older people also spend less than younger families for food as income rises. In the $7,500–$10,000 income class, older families spend 30.7 per cent less than the younger families for food. However, a new market in this area has been discovered, as specially prepared foods, which appeal to the older age group, are now being sold.

Older people spend less than the younger for clothing at all levels of income. Their spending pattern follows somewhat the same one as total expenditures, except that in the $2,000–$4,000 income range, their clothing

CHART 2

Major Consumption Expenditures of the Older Family as a Percentage of Expenditures of the Younger Famliy at Four Income Levels.
(Bureau of Labor Statistics: The Conference Board.)

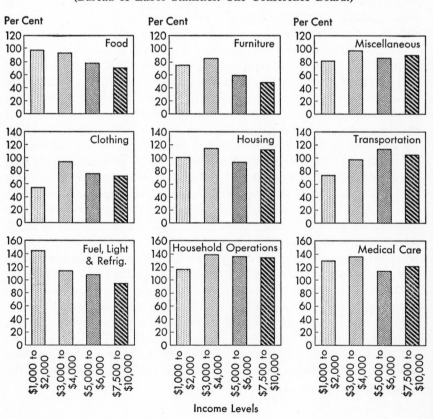

Income Levels

expenditures do not reach the level of the younger group's. Furniture is also a less important item to the older family at all income levels. At higher incomes, older families spend considerably less than the younger. Little difference exists in furniture spending between an older family having a $3,000 income and one with a $10,000 income. Most older families very likely made all the major purchases for furniture in their younger years.

Although older people spend less than the younger for miscellaneous items at all income levels, it becomes slightly more important in their total budget in the high-income class. Since older people usually have the time to develop hobbies that would give them an outlet for their creative abilities, it would seem that many items could be marketed to appeal to the older group. A growing number of communities that have recognized this need have recreational centers primarily for older people who cannot afford to spend much of their money on recreation because of their limited incomes.

Household operation expenditures of the aged are more important in their budget than in the younger family's at all income levels. The basic necessities of fuel and medical care also take up a larger share of the older family's budget.

Response to Rise in Income

From 1954 to 1965, the older population is expected to rise 28.4 per cent —from 13,735,000 to 17,638,000 persons. In order for the aggregate income to reach $32 billion by 1965, median income would have to rise at a rate of 2 per cent a year. However, if the aggregate income of older persons rises only in proportion to the projected rise in population, it is unlikely that the spending patterns of older families will change appreciably. Aggregate income of persons sixty-five and over would thus reach $25.7 billion by 1965, assuming that their aggregate income was $20 billion in 1954.

If the median income rises at 1.5 per cent a year (or half the rate of increase between 1947 and 1957), there could be a shift in spending patterns by 1965. The aggregate income, in this instance, would be $30.3 billion. This would mean an increase of 51.5 per cent in aggregate income and an increase of 18.0 per cent in per capita income. With such a rise, a larger portion of the older family's income would go toward clothing, transportation, household operations, housefurnishings and appliances, and miscellaneous goods and services. On the other hand, the older family of 2.2 persons would spend proportionally less for food, housing, fuel, and medical care than it had in the past. This is assuming that the consumer price level remains stable. A rise of 1.0 per cent a year in prices would greatly reduce the amount of additional purchases that the older family would be able to afford.

A spread between the expenditures of the two family groups will, in all

Consumption Expenditures of Older Families with 2.2 Persons as a Percentage of Expenditures of Younger Families of the Same Size at Four Income Levels

Income Levels	All Items	Food	Housing	Fuel, Light, Refrigeration	Household Operations	Furniture	Clothing	Transportation	Medical Care	Miscellaneous
$1,000–2,000	93.2	96.7	100.4	142.7	115.2	72.9	54.7	74.1	130.0	80.0
$3,000–4,000	100.6	91.5	113.6	112.3	139.5	86.2	94.0	99.7	137.4	98.4
$5,000–6,000	88.9	79.1	94.0	107.8	137.1	58.2	76.3	115.7	112.6	84.8
$7,500–10,000	85.2	69.3	113.2	94.2	133.5	45.6	71.4	106.3	120.2	90.2

Sources: Bureau of Labor Statistics; The Conference Board.

probability, continue to exist regardless of a rise in the older family's income —unless their income rises at a faster rate than that of the younger family, and this is a development which seems very unlikely.

However, this study has shown that older families do spend more than younger families of the same size at the same income level for some goods and services. At all levels, more is spent for medical care and household operations, and at most levels, more is spent for fuel. More was spent by the older group in the past for housing, except in the $5,000–$6,000 income level. However, with the boom in housing, younger people have in recent years undoubtedly been spending more than the older people, and this is true even at the lower-income levels.

Between $4,000 and $5,000 income, older people begin to spend more for transportation. Also, older people would spend more if their incomes rose, but not to the extent that the younger families would. With the development of new items designed especially for the older person, however, their spending patterns could very well change.

18. WHAT MAKES WOMEN BUY? *

by Gilbert Burck †

The intrepid marketing men of American business, charging in where poets, philosophers, and sociologists have often made fools of themselves, are striving assiduously to measure the economic power of women. They propose to find out how much the American woman buys for herself and how much she spends as a purchasing agent for others, indeed to discover exactly how much she has to do with all buying decisions, and even how she makes up her own mind. And to do this they propose to expose thoughts that are hidden even to her, to lift up the skirts of her very psyche.

American business, to be sure, has always pursued the female consumer ardently, but it is now accelerating its efforts, both in force and in sophistication. Not only the women's wear and soap industries but a host of others —the appliance, auto, glass, and even men's wear industries—are enlisting the research talents of advertising agencies, marketing counselors, economists, and sociologists; and together they are laying siege to that enigmatic and glittering prize, the female consumer. Even the Broom Manufacturers Association recently issued a copy publicity release confessing its suspicion

* Reprinted from the August 1956 issue of *Fortune Magazine* by Special Permission. © 1956 by Time Inc.
† Board of Editors, *Fortune.*

that housewives bear a negative attitude toward brooms, and announcing its intention, "in a mood of nothing ventured, nothing gained, (to) delve into the hidden corners of milady's mind to find out her attitude on brooms."

The most obvious reason for this intensified assault on the mind of the American woman is that she exerts an enormous power over the nation's consumer expenditures, which last year came to a colossal $252 billion. More specifically, her expanding role as wage earner, as expounded in *Fortune* last month, is augmenting greatly both her direct buying power and her influence on all spending. Furthermore, the rising pace and cost of introducing new products like Orlon clothing and frozen foods is compelling manufacturers to find out all they can about how women will react to the products before they are actually put on the market. And the truth is that business, like man himself, does not know a fraction as much as it would like to know about woman.

One of the most persistent myths in American business, said to have been concocted years ago by a Butterick Company advertising salesman, is that women control 85 cents of every dollar spent by American families. This, of course, is an arrant exaggeration. Even if a woman buys all her husband's shirts, the actual choice of brand, style, color could easily be his. The 85 per cent myth, like the admonition "Never underestimate the power of a woman," has an authoritative ring, but it is a myth nevertheless, and it has been refuted several times. Back in 1949, for example, Paul D. Converse, professor of marketing at the University of Illinois, in a study of female buying estimated that the American woman does 55 per cent of the family buying and a little more of the deciding; since then many other researchers, including those working for the men's magazines, have essayed to "deflate" female purchasing power.

The Softly Sprung Ride

Well, what does American business know about the American woman as consumer? It has spent hundreds of millions of dollars on market research, much of it designed to make the female buyer a surer and easier target for advertisers and sellers. It has not learned nearly so much as it wanted to, but it has acquired some pretty good ideas about the influence and vulnerabilities of women as buyers, and in a wide range of situations.

Business has learned, for example, that women have a lot to do with the purchase of the family car. Although surveys have shown that men overwhelmingly dominate the actual purchase of the family car, the American automobile has always been designed with at least one eye on the American woman. It is a cliché among motorcar *aficionados* the world over that American cars are sprung softly because American women want a "boulevard" ride, and that in America it is the woman who decides what the man gets.

And auto manufacturers have recently stepped up their appeals to the female. (In doing so, they have splattered their colors around so riotously that a reaction has set in—a minor stampede back to black.) Men claim to be primarily interested in a car's power, economy, and acceleration, but surveys made by Alfred Politz for Chrysler show that when men are caught off guard—e.g., when they are asked what they think their *neighbors* buy cars for—they esteem color and looks as much as their wives do. So color and style, now that horsepower claims are losing their selling power, will probably continue to dominate motorcar changes—at least until somebody discovers that women, in their heart of hearts, are interested in something else—economy, say or mechanical simplicity.

The Urge for Approval

There is no industry that cherishes and ponders the female consumer more deeply than the food industry. Food manufacturers and processors have been leaders in market research, and they have done a shrewder job of selling women than most other industries. Indeed, it was the food industry's salesmanship that broke the venerable generalization known as Engel's Law, which held that the percentage of income spent on food must decline as income rises.

Food, soap, and cigarette manufacturers have led in the use of Motivation Research, which (as *Fortune* related in June) claims to get at the "real" and often hidden reasons why people behave as they do, not by mass sample surveys but by "unstructured" or rambling "depth" interviews of relatively few people, who are probed with such "projective" devices as thematic apperception tests (a respondent is shown a picture of a situation, and his reaction is calculated to reveal his hidden attitude). Many if not most Motivation Research studies of women confirm the age-old belief that women yearn to be told they have done a good job. From this stems a basic principle: to sell the housewife anything from soap to prepared pudding, do not lecture her on how wonderful your product is, or how it will eliminate her drudgery; tell her—or imply—that using it will not merely make life easier but will surely bring her recognition and approval.

At the retail-store level, however, the food business has relied as much upon intuition, experience, novel ideas, and trial and error as on any scientific analyses of women and their buying habits. A&P, for instance, does not generally make surveys. "We've been in business so long," says a spokesman, "we just *know*."

The success of the Grand Union chain under Lansing Shield is based on Mr. Shield's conviction—conditioned, however, by surveys and consumer panels—that women today can afford to and want to buy luxuries and new things, and that they do *not* regard shopping as sheer recreation—therefore they must be lured by attractive stores and the opportunity to clean up a long shopping list in one big sweep through one store. Thus Grand Union is capitalizing more than most chains on unusual and exotic foods, is constantly experimenting with new store arrangements and color schemes, and seems bent on converting food stores into department stores. The company's newest supermarket in Keansburg, New Jersey, stocks 20,000 items, of which only 5,000 are food products. The other 15,000 encompass everything from toothpaste to dresses.

"Like Conservative Trustees"

One of the harshest canards of our time, if eminent merchandisers are to be believed, is the common assumption that women are impulsive buyers, with an almost neurotic compulsion to squander their household money on any bauble that chances to catch their fancy. "Women," says Earl Puckett, chairman of the Allied chain of department stores, "spend money like conservative trustees in charge of someone else's money. . . . Men's participation in shopping is growing, for which we are duly thankful. It's been demonstrated over and over again that sales checks go up when papa goes along."

Sol Polk, chairman, owner, and operator of Chicago's aggressive Polk City emporium, is equally emphatic about the American woman. "She's become very sharp," he says, "very efficient in shopping for appliances and other big-ticket items; never forget that she's the one who has made us retailers more efficient. But when it comes to buying her clothes, maybe it's a different matter . . ." Women also tend to adhere closely to their shopping lists, according to a survey made by Alderson & Sessions, Philadelphia marketing consultant; although they are inclined to pick up bargains, the bargains usually fit into the family needs. A survey recently made by the Film Department of du Pont indicates that 70 per cent of all supermarket purchases are "store decisions," but any such figure must be qualified by the fact, now commonly accepted among marketers, that women use the systematic displays of supermarkets as a kind of substitute for a shopping list.

Most merchandisers, however, depend on the old observation, which in turn is substantiated by modern psychology, that women as a rule are more intuitive than men. "And they are more swayed by emotion," says Gordon Metcalf, manager of Sears' Chicago stores. But it seems that their emotional approach does not affect their ability to make sound judgments. "This business," says one chain-store operator, "is founded on the proposition that women don't think, they feel. By which I mean that they think in a different way."

Many merchandisers, including Puckett, believe that women are more venturesome buyers than men, at least in the sense that they are more sure of themselves and hence are not so worried about someone else's stamp of approval. One reason they may be more self-assured is that women, as both surveys and observation testify, are usually better informed than men on brand differences because they are more experienced, and because they have usually gone to more trouble to read up on the differences and to talk them over with friends, relatives, and neighbors. Taking everything together, women as buyers are behaving more and more as only men were supposed to behave not so long ago.

The Latest Emancipation

Businessmen have also discovered that women have more to do with handling family finances, either by themselves or with their husbands, than ever before. A survey just completed by the Survey Research Center at the University of Michigan for the U.S. Treasury shows that the wife handles the money and bills in 38 per cent of all U.S. families, the husband in 30 per cent, and the husband and wife together in 31 per cent. In the great and growing middle-income groups, wives tend to assume more than average fiscal responsibility.

Nothing could be more natural, indeed more inevitable. What has happened, during the past ten years, is that the changing American economy has produced a new kind of emancipated woman. She is very different not only from the home-tied woman of fifty years ago but also from the self-consciously "liberated" woman of the roaring twenties and the bitter thirties. The postwar evolution of woman has been documented in *Fortune*'s studies of The Changing American Market and in its reports on the new suburbias like Park Forest: the rise of the great "mass class" market, with a uniformly high standard of living; the renewed desire for children, expressing itself in an astonishing rise in the birth rate; the relative decline in apartment living and the great migration to the suburbs; the rebirth of family life, indeed even the birth of a filiarchy; the suburban way of life, which has put family happiness at the head of the shopping list.

In achieving this new normality, however, the American woman has not returned to a restricted world of childbearing and household drudgery. She is more active than her counterpart of thirty years ago in politics, schools, churches, and other organized community activities. And, as *Fortune* demonstrated last month, she is also successful as a working woman. The 21 million women in the U.S. labor force today comprise a third of all women above fourteen, and 30 per cent of all married women. The importance of their earnings is indicated by the fact that in 1954 the median income of families in which wives were working was 32 per cent higher than the median income of families in which wives were not.

This emancipation, in turn, has resulted in a new division of family labor —not along fixed lines, with the husband responsible for mowing the lawn, washing the car, and changing screens, and the wife for cleaning and cooking and minding the kids. Just as economic circumstances have sent many a husband into the kitchen, the laundry, and to the chain stores, so many a wife monkeys with machinery, takes care of the books, negotiates with the mortgagor, supervises the servicing of the car.

Who's in Charge Here?

George Katona, program director of the Survey Research Center at the University of Michigan, who has been surveying American consumer behavior for fifteen years, says that husbands and wives are amazingly alike in their financial and economic expectations and opinions. He also observes that there is probably more "intercommunication" between husband and wife in America than in any other country. It is not that America has abolished the ancient institution known as the War between the Sexes—i.e., the urge of each sex to dominate the other. So long as man arrogantly insists on regarding *his* differences as superiorities, woman finds herself forced to compensate, as all who are discriminated against compensate, by developing superior artifice and guile. Even when the initial idea of buying something is hers, she often allows, indeed encourages, her spouse to believe that it was his.

All this helps merge the buying roles of husband and wife. They not only buy for each other and with each other; they influence each other as buyers in countless ways, blunt and subtle. And so they make it harder than ever for the marketer to gauge the power of the woman accurately and to approach her effectively.

Socks and Stoves

It is not surprising that a great many contradictory (and partisan) figures are in circulation. For fair samples of the confusion, consider the "statistics" on a thoroughly masculine line of products—men's clothes—and on a seemingly feminine line—kitchen equipment.

A poll of a group of stores by the *Ladies' Home Journal* showed that in 91 per cent of the stores women bought more than 75 per cent of all the men's "dress" (business) shirts sold. But surveys by Cluett, Peabody and others indicate that she buys less than 50 per cent. It is an axiom in the trade that women buy 70 per cent of all men's socks, but a Fawcett Publications survey has suggested they buy only 52 per cent, and a survey by the National Association of Hosiery Manufacturers a year ago indicated that even 50 per cent may be a high figure and that women who buy men's socks often have definite restrictions as to color, price, etc. And although a *Ladies' Home Journal* poll has indicated that women buy most men's underwear, other surveys again have reached the opposite conclusion.

The results of surveys to determine the influence of women on the purchase of kitchen appliances have not been very consistent either. A Fawcett survey has credited husbands with making 30 per cent of the brand decisions, wives with 21 per cent, and both jointly with as much as 44 per cent. Other surveys have turned up figures crediting the wife with making the buying decision as much as 57 per cent of the time. A recent Survey Research Center study showed that the wife had most say 37 per cent of the time, the husband 9 per cent of the time, and that they decided jointly 54 per cent of the time. Most surveys tend to agree that the husband and wife jointly account for around half the kitchen-appliance decisions, and many advertisers and sellers are basing their sales pitch on this fact. General Electric, for example, alludes to its "dual" audience, and therefore runs a great deal of its advertising in general magazines like *Life* and the *Saturday Evening Post*.

Four Roles

The very inconsistencies of consumer surveys, which have generated a large body of analysis and argument, have made more and more businessmen realize that research that simply counts female noses or the number of shirts or socks bought by women, or asks who does what buying in the family, is not sufficient to gauge the American woman as consumer and describe her accurately as a prospect. Women, after all, may be said to function in the market place in at least four different ways:

1. as purchasers for themselves;
2. as nonpurchasers who influence the buying decisions of their families, friends, neighbors, relatives;
3. as purchasing agents who make some or all of the buying decisions;
4. as purchasing agents who make no decision but merely perform an errand.

Plainly, a wife who follows her husband's explicit directions in buying his shirts, socks, and shorts is not so important to the seller as a wife who buys nothing but influences the buying decisions of people in her orbit. And neither is so important as a wife who makes both the purchases and the decisions. Obviously, too, the actual purchase, whether by man or woman, is usually the last step in a long and complicated series of decisions and actions that are influenced by advertising, news, children, neighbors, relatives, friends—to say nothing of spouses. For marketers, the problem is to break down this decision-making process into its essentials, and then to formulate some useful principles about woman's buying role. And today the job is being tackled with considerable imagination.

The Survey Research Center, for example, is not only beginning to make special studies of male and female buying influence but is also trying to measure the amount and type of "deliberation" that goes into a purchase.

Columbia University's Bureau of Applied Social Research is analyzing the role of personal influence in marketing. A recent book, *Personal Influence,* written by Elihu Katz in collaboration with the bureau's Professor Paul Lazarsfeld, finds that woman's word-of-mouth influence on woman is one of the major forces in marketing, and plays a larger role in some female buying habits than even mass-media advertising. What most disposes a woman in a supermarket to pick this cake mix or that frozen food, in other words, is what her sister-in-law told her about it yesterday, or what she learned at the kaffee-klatsch the day before yesterday.

A Significant Pattern?

One of the most ambitious attempts to describe and measure the American family's buying habits was begun in 1953 by the Advertising Research Foundation, which is supported by advertisers, agencies, and media. After working two years with National Analysts of Philadelphia, A.R.F. claims to have developed nothing less than a technique that will reveal, for any product studies, such information as how people regard it (e.g., whether as a necessity or a luxury); the factors that made people think of buying it; the exact extent of collaboration among husband, wife, and other family members; factors influencing decisions to buy a particular brand; who in the family first thought of buying it; who made the final decision; and who made the actual purchase.

The technique consists, in the main, of a series of carefully contrived subjective and objective questions. A respondent is asked to evaluate a list of products by several standards; next to choose from a printed list things she would take into consideration if she were buying those products; next, to answer questions designed to get at family relationships, and so on through scores of tests and questions.

So far, A.R.F. has made only small experimental studies with this method. One of the studies, however, suggests that in the purchase of an expensive appliance the wife tends to think of buying first and to carry her idea to the decision stage, but then to have relatively little say about price, brand, store, and the purchase itself. Here, it may turn out, is a significant pattern. Although wives appear to be shrewder buyers than their husbands, it is a truism among marketing men that wives, if only because they are exposed to more pressures to buy, generally want more for themselves and their families than husbands do. "When we show our new electronic kitchens," says a G.E. man, "the husband looks at them in wonderment but the woman looks at them and wants them."

But a smart wife, when she wants something, does not hit her husband over the head with the idea. On the contrary, she suggests it a little at a time, maybe in terms of the kids' needs, and if possible so that the husband comes to think of the idea as his own. Once he does that, woman achieves another victory in the War between the Sexes. But when the survey man comes around to find out who was responsible for the purchase, the husband, of course, gets the credit.

The New Creativity

Hundreds of woman-minded businesses are turning to Motivation Research to expose the attitudes of women, because women's real attitudes are often understood not even by themselves. Dr. Ernest Dichter, the Austrian-born psychologist who runs the Institute for Motivational Research Incorporated at Croton-on-Hudson, New York, thinks that today the characteristic American woman is a happy compromise between the hard-working housewife and the career woman who regards household chores as beneath her. Although Dr. Dichter used to stress the notion that woman was obsessed by feelings of guilt about using shortcuts in her work, he now thinks of her as an independent, often individualistic, creature, driven by a creative urge that manifests itself even in the imaginative way she uses ready-to-serve foods, considering herself knowledgeable and mature, rejoicing in the fact that she is harder to fool, preferring "to save happiness rather than dollars," and disposed to buy the better and more expensive item if she can afford it.

More and more marketers, even when they spurn Motivation Research because it does not produce data that lends itself to statistical analysis, are using some of M.R.'s "projective" techniques to supplement and enrich the statistical findings of mass surveys. Other marketing specialists, like the Survey Research Center at the University of Michigan and the Marketing Department at the University of Illinois, aiming to find out what makes consumers make up and change their minds and just how they convert buying intentions into actual purchases, are studying representative "panels" of consumers over weeks and even many months.

The Buying Game

A noteworthy combination of several such approaches is the experimental "behavior research" method developed by Wroe Alderson, partner in

Alderson & Sessions of Philadelphia. The large sample interview, Mr. Alderson argues, suffers from the respondents' lack of candor (they characteristically give answers calculated to bolster their prestige in the eyes of the interviewer), and the fact that most people, because the thoughts behind their reactions are often on a subconscious level, don't really know how they'll act in a situation until they're in it. And the rambling "depth" interviews of M.R., according to Mr. Alderson, don't actually last long enough to justify the diagnoses based on them and usually produce data too diverse for statistical analysis.

So Alderson not only interviews a homogeneous panel of housewives in "depth" but brings the panel into the "consumer clinic" conference room. Here he duplicates the "market situation" as closely as possible by asking the panel to participate in buying games. Recently, for example, Alderson decided to test housewives' reactions to stores with various ranges of merchandise, and their propensity to "shop around" before buying. From the Philadelphia metropolitan area, he drew a panel containing 61 typical housewives whose average age was thirty-six, who had one or two children, whose family income was about $5,000 a year. Every other week for ten weeks these women were interviewed at home; on the alternate weeks they attended the "clinic," where they played buying games.

Women behaved in the games just as they did in actual shopping. They preferred stores that were either very diversified or very specialized, either in price or in merchandise, and were least attracted to the in-between stores. And in their shopping, the interviews disclosed, 87 per cent of the housewives bought "routine" or inexpensive items in the first store they visited, and 50 per cent even bought "major" or expensive items in the first store without any further shopping around.

At first glance this might seem like irrational impulse buying. But interpreted in the light of other experiments, says Mr. Alderson, it is not. It is rather evidence that the housewife has used previous experience, education, advertising, or discussion to make up her mind. Alderson's studies incline him to the belief, which many consultants share, not only that shoppers tend to rely on a single store, and shop at other stores only as an occasional check on their basic choice, but that shopping is an expression of a woman's personality, and the store she prefers is the one that "reflects a view of contemporary life consistent with her own . . . one that offers merchandise that fits in with her home or her vision of what she wants her home to be."

The trend in appraising the woman as consumer is thus fairly clear: increasingly subtle and complex interviews of panels of women, exploring one by one the circumstances that go to make up women's buying decisions. Before long, marketers may well agree on certain general principles, now largely hypothetical, such as that it is almost always the woman who dreams up and promotes the idea of buying an expensive item in the first place;

that women habitually underestimate their role as buyers when talking to interviewers; or that women can be approached most successfully by appealing to their shrewdness. Meanwhile marketing men hew their way through the underbrush of conflicting ideas, occasionally working themselves into dead ends of unproductive techniques. But more and more often, they think they are hitting trails that will lead them over the very redoubts of female sales resistance.

19. $41 BILLION FOR FUN: WHO SELLS MOST TO LEISURE MARKET—AND WHY *

"Increased means and increased leisure are the two civilizers of man." Though most modern Americans are probably unfamiliar with that view expressed decades ago by Benjamin Disraeli, they are nonetheless following the dictum of the famed nineteenth-century British statesman to the hilt this summer.

For as the season for recreation and leisure reaches its height now, the nation's population is happily spending at least an estimated 41 billion dollars of their increased means on their increased leisure.

Moreover, manufacturers of the array of products that they buy for this purpose, overjoyed with the way sales are going now, get positively ecstatic over the future potential for sales. Most of them conservatively look for a steady 5 to 10 per cent annual increase in the various segments that make up the vast market for leisure-oriented products, barring a major war or recession.

Its Scope

There is as yet no universally accepted definition or statistical yardstick for the scope of the leisure market. For this study of it, *Printers' Ink* took the broad view of what constitutes a leisure-time product. There are, however, some specific major components. The sums spent on them would stagger our forefathers. For example:

- $2.1 billion on boating
- $2.1 billion on photography
- $300,000,000 on power lawn mowers
- $600,000,000 on swimming pools

* Reprinted from *Printers' Ink*, © July 10, 1959, pp. 25–31.

- $500,000,000 on musical instruments
- $300,000,000 on the components that make up high-fidelity and stereo systems
- $2.3 billion on overseas travel
- $5 billion over-all on radios, television sets, phonographs, tape recorders and repairs, not counting records
- $3.5 billion on gardening equipment
- $16.8 billion over-all on recreation and domestic travel.

And so it goes, from playing cards to summer and outdoor furniture ($70,000,000 annually).

Certainly no other era in history has seen so many people spending so much money on fun.

Fun apparently is its own salesman—with an assist from astute marketing and changes that have occurred in the country in the past decade. Just six years ago, for instance, the leisure market was estimated at 30 billion dollars annually. Its growth since then, which has outrun the 9 billion increase predicted then, has paralleled the spectaculor boom in the nation's over-all wealth.

Talk to a marketer of leisure products, and that's the first factor he cites. The second is the increase in leisure time available.

Market Mainspring

There's certainly no disputing either of these. But the truly significant factor in the nation's increased wealth—now around 467 billion dollars annually in the gross national product—is the widespread sharing of it. More than 30,000,000 American families now have after-tax incomes above $4,000, a gain of 18,000,000 families just since 1950 alone. So rapid has population growth and rise of income levels been that by next year there will be some 36,000,000 families in this group. Significantly, they control something like 60 per cent of the nation's 135 billion dollars in discretionary income—the money left over after taxes, food, clothing, shelter, and other necessities.

Moreover, the income levels are still rising. Predictions are that by 1970 there will be about 25,000,000 families with after-tax incomes over $7,500. They will constitute 40 per cent of the population and control 85 per cent of the discretionary spending. Put another way: They will be the dominant factor in marketing. For leisure products, they make an increasingly alluring sales target.

And their leisure time will probably rise too. In the past ten years the total weeks of vacation enjoyed by Americans have doubled to 70,000,000.

But time away from work is only one dimension. Labor-saving devices around the home, faster transportation to and from work, and the nature of labor itself have all contributed as much to the boom in leisure-oriented products as available time has.

The latter is a significant though often overlooked factor. Take the way people earn the money they now spend on leisure. At the turn of the century, only 15 per cent of the nation's work force was classified as "white collar." Today it is more than double that and in the next eleven years will rise to 40 per cent. Skilled and semiskilled workers now are as numerous as white-collar workers and will constitute another 40 per cent of the population by 1970. The important factor, however, is that in both groups exhausting labor is a thing of the past. Technology has devised machines to take the back-breaking strain out of labor in factories and the monotonous drudgery out of most white-collar jobs.

These changes in the nature of work have expanded *the capacity to enjoy* leisure beyond measure. Perhaps this has played a role in Americans' more active participation in leisure time activities now.

For instance, in 1934, the National Recreation Association made a survey of what people then *actually did* with their leisure time and what they *would like to do*. Heading the list of things they did then were such passive pastimes as reading, listening to the radio and going to the movies. In contrast, they said they would like to play tennis, swim, and go boating— all very active pastimes. The survey very accurately forecast the change in Americans' approach to leisure in the decade of the fifties when the population did have the money to do the things its forebears wanted to do twenty years earlier.

In addition, the mass migration to the suburbs in the postwar era has given impetus to the boom in leisure-oriented products. Freed from what sociologist C. Wright Mills calls the "nagging frustrations" and "chaos" of the city, some 40 per cent of the nation's population now enjoys life in the suburbs. If past growth is an accurate guide, the trend is likely to continue. For instance, the suburbs have grown by 29.3 per cent since 1950 while the central cities themselves have grown only 4.7 per cent.

Today, nearly as many people live in suburbs—around 50,000,000—as live in central cities. In the decade ahead, when 17 per cent of the present population reaches marriageable age and a rapid rise in new family formations begins, suburban growth will doubtlessly surge again.

More, at the Middle

At the same time, the blue-collar workers' steady upward migration into the middle-income group, and the over-all expansion of this group, has wrought a revolution in tastes. Exposed to the standards enjoyed by the

over-$7,500 group, which has always been the pace-setter, the middle-
incomers have gradually adopted them, too. As Dr. George Brown, marketing research manager for the Ford division of the Ford Motor Company,
points out, spending habits of the middle-income group, far from changing
radically, are still following traditional patterns. There are just more of
them today.

And the things they buy to fill their leisure hours often serve as signs
loudly proclaiming that they have arrived in the middle income group, or
moved up another notch in it; in other words—status symbols. For instance,
a motivational research study conducted for a power lawn-mower company
that *Printers' Ink* was permitted to read shows that owners of such equipment tend to look down on the few remaining owners of old reel-type lawn
mowers. They didn't, of course, express it so bluntly. Rather, it was said
that the power mowers did a "more professional" job of trimming their
lawns; ergo, reflecting a superior type of home.

Dr. Ernest Dichter, president of the Institute of Motivation Research,
has maintained that the boat and the swimming pool have replaced the
automobile as a status symbol. (Ford's Dr. Brown doesn't agree with him.)
Marketing-minded men in these fields do feel that status plays a role in
the sale of leisure-time products. As Norman Owen, sales vice-president of
the McCulloch Corporation, put it: "The kind of a boat and motor a fellow is able to park in his driveway (on a trailer) has the same kind of snob
appeal as a second car."

Swimming pools are another case in point. With growing acceptance
among the middle-income group, they are now being installed even in
$7,000 homes. Jerome Y. Rudolph, president of the United States Pool
Corporation, says motivational research has shown that status is a big
factor. Just as a bigger car, or a small foreign car, is an indication that one
is coming up in the world, so, too, is the swimming pool. And it's no more
expensive than a new car. (Average price: $4,417.)

Buy Now, Pay Later

In their quest for the good life, Americans apparently are unwilling to
wait. This is evidenced by the soaring spiral of consumer credit now outstanding at the 34.5 billion dollar level. Indeed, why should they in this
era of "buy now, pay later?" The trend is certain to increase.

Boating, perhaps, offers the best example. Fifteen years ago a man who
asked for a loan to buy a boat would have been thrown out of a bank
bodily. Today, banks are courting boat buyers and boat manufacturers with
ardor.

They get the willing cooperation of manufacturers. For instance, Howard
Larson, sales vice-president of the Outboard Marine Corporation, thinks
far too many boats are bought for cash—more than 50 per cent. To rectify

that, the manufacturers did some research and found boat purchasers are more scrupulous about making payments on their boats than on cars or houses. The banks were persuaded. Now at most major boat shows throughout the country, bankers are on hand seeking dealer lists and potential purchasers. Boat manufacturers, for their part, have taken to putting on displays at banking association meetings.

Selling Fun

Though there is a natural inclination toward spending on fun, it also gets a skillful assist from astute marketers in the field. Let's take boating, amateur photography, and hi-fi sales as examples.

Of the three, boating has probably undergone the most drastic revolution.

It has progressed from the "rich man's sport" of yesteryear to one in which 37,000,000 Americans now participate. The greatest growth has been in outboards, of which there are now some 3,620,000 craft expressly designed for this type of power.

Not too many years ago an outboard engine was something you put on a flat-bottomed rowboat to go fishing. Skillful marketing changed all that, so that today fishing ranks at the bottom of the scale of usage.

Improved technology quieted the motors. Industrial designers were called in to design attractive cowls. A range of color was provided—each manufacturer previously offered only his "house" color—to attract and influence women. Advertising efforts were greatly stepped up. But they sell more than a boat. As Outboard Marine's Howard Larson explains the marketing strategy: "We try to sell boating as a tool to more family fun. You can justify the expenditure because the whole family benefits."

In practice, that means boating becomes an adjunct to picnicking, fishing, sight-seeing, swimming, and just plain lazing in the sun out on the water. There's something there for everybody in the family.

"I'm convinced that this is the right approach," says Larson. "People don't want to own a boat anymore—they want what the boat will do for them."

As evidence of this, he cites the popularity now of aluminum and fiber glass as materials for boating construction. Their big appeal is ease of maintenance. But the old-time yachtsman got as much fun out of scraping and caulking his boat before it was in the water and puttering around with it during the boating season as he did from actually sailing.

"People don't want that anymore," says Larson. "They want what the car does for them; you pour in gas and go."

The boating manufacturers gave it to them, and it has paid off. Now boating requires no special skill, no strength, no special coordination.

In the process, the once lowly outboard, looked down on by the skilled sailor, has gained social acceptance. A study of occupations of outboard-boat owners shows that the semiskilled and skilled worker classes (45.9 per cent) is almost evenly matched by professional men, owner-managers, and other white-collared workers (42.6 per cent). Larson notes that the Milwaukee Yacht Club, which ten years ago was "strictly for sailors," now includes many outboard owners among its members, ranging from company vice-presidents to skilled factory workers. Selling them outboard boating rigs, he says, has been something like selling life insurance.

"We have to sell a family the idea that it is more fun to own a boat than it is to stay home and buy a swimming pool, gardening equipment, or a second car. Once you convince them that a boat will provide more, the product is relatively easy to sell."

A big factor in selling that idea has been advertising. Once confined to a few boating publications, marine manufacturers are spending an estimated $125,000,000 this year in all media, according to W.B. Hanft, advertising manager for the C.A. Woolsey Paint and Color Company, a marine paint firm. Hanft, who keeps track of marine advertising expenditures, notes that this sum is $20,000,000 greater than the amount spent in 1958, quite an increase for a one-year period. The marine manufacturers are using major national magazines, radio, and television. Boating sales have climbed from $660,000,000 in 1949 to 2.1 billion dollars this year. "We never would have made it without the advertising techniques of today," says Owen.

A Higher Income Means More Spent on Leisure

One part of *Life* magazine's exhaustive study of consumer expenditures delved into income groups' average expenditures on recreation and recreation equipment. It gives this sharp picture of how rising income affects expenditures on recreation, which is applicable to leisure, though in broader terms.

	$2000– $2900	$4000– $4999	$5000– $6999	$7000– $9999	$10,000 up	All Households
Games, toys	$11	$27	$23	$28	$45	$19
Photo equipment	$6	$10	$12	$27	$30	$11
Radio, TV, phonos	$39	$44	$47	$45	$61	$42
Spectator fees	$19	$33	$31	$41	$65	$28
Sports goods	$5	$18	$16	$37	$74	$16
Others	$55	$94	$118	$133	$221	$92
Total	$138	$233	$256	$322	$513	$215

Specialized Magazines

Enthusiasm for boating and any number of other leisure activities, ranging from skiing to hi-fi, has not only been spurred on by advertising, but the ad potential present in these fields has led to the rise of a host of specialized magazines. Here the leisure-product advertiser has a solid-interest audience that generally considers the activity occupying their leisure more than just a pastime, and who spend more than the average on it. The publications are growing with the fields they serve.

The combined circulation of leading boating magazines, with a new publication debuting almost every year since 1955, has risen from 134,000 in 1946 to almost 700,000 last year. The three leading photography magazines have boosted their circulations from just over 650,000 in 1946 to about 900,000 this year. The newer field of hi-fi has picked up five special-interest magazines since 1951. Their combined circulation last year reached 300,000. It was only 13,000 in 1951.

The ad expenditure of manufacturers serving any one leisure field is rarely disclosed. For the most part, they find themselves in young, growing, highly competitive markets. Tipping of the competition on ad budgets just isn't done. For this reason, a combined industry ad-spending figure is often a matter of guesswork, even by industry association; and measuring all media for cost is difficult.

It can be generally stated that ad spending in the leisure markets has been on a steady upswing since the end of World War II, although last year the recession scare nosed it down somewhat. But as sales have risen, ad budgets have followed.

Travel, by all estimates a prime postwar boom area, has seen a tremendous increase in advertising over the last four years. Travel, hotel, and resort spending in magazines and TV alone rose to more than $27,000,000 last year. In 1954 it was just over $19,500,000.

Advertisers in the broad classification of sporting goods and toys invested $9,712,039 in magazines and TV in 1954. Last year they spent $13,516,215 in those media. The same classifications' 1957 spot-TV expenditure was $1,915,000. In 1958 it had risen to $3,045,000.

Magazine and TV advertising for radio, TV sets, phonographs, and musical instruments was $22,041,029 in 1954. Last year it was $24,174,-850. Market by market, similar increases in spending appear, some more marked than others, but all generally rising. Advertising for hi-fi equipment, another boom area, is estimated this year as reaching $11,000,000, 10 per cent more than was spent in 1958. And ad spending for these "younger" leisure industries shows no sign of leveling off.

Amateur home movies, which have enjoyed a similarly spectacular boom, have soared from $60,000,000 in 1948 to $143,000,000 last year, a gain of 140 per cent or twice the over-all percentage gain in recreational expenditures. One of the leading firms in the field, Bell & Howell Company, saw its own sales surge up from $17,000,000 to $59,000,000 in that period, a 300 per cent increase. Carl G. Schreyer, Bell & Howell's vice-president in charge of marketing, notes that there are several factors that have played a part in this growth: the baby boom, rising incomes, migration to the suburbs, increased leisure, and easy-to-use features that have been built into cameras.

"Those 4,000,000 babies born annually ever since 1948 have had a tremendous influence," says Schreyer, noting that babies rank as the fourth most popular subject for photos.

As in boating, the improvements that have made cameras easier to use have played a major role. As Schreyer explains it: "Our research has shown us that the biggest reason for not owning a camera was that you had to be an MIT graduate to operate it. We've fixed it so you don't have to be. With a movie camera now, you look through a viewer and press a button and—bang—you get the picture thanks to the electric eye which sets it automatically." The emphasis on family life in the postwar era has also helped the movie-camera makers.

Advertising has pushed the home movie boom along—principally by dramatizing the new ease-of-operation features. Bell & Howell, Schreyer says, has found television a particularly good medium for that.

The high-fidelity component industry is one of the newest segments of the leisure market. In nine years it has grown from a $12,000,000 industry to an estimated $300,000,000, according to Joseph Benjamin, president of the Institute of High Fidelity Manufacturers.

What accounts for its growth? Benjamin, who is also president of the Bogen division of the Siegler Corporation, thinks these factors are involved:

• The American habit of keeping up with the Joneses by having everything that is new and latest.

• A desire to inject an aura of culture into the home.

• A desire for good music, and the range available on records and tape from Broadway musicals to the classics.

In this field, too, technological improvements have helped sales growth. Where tonal quality once attracted the species who became known as the audiophile, new ease-of-operation features are appealing to people who just want to listen.

Why the Leisure Market Has Exceeded All Forecasts

The boom in the leisure-time market has surpassed all previous expectations. Just five years ago, spending in this broad area was estimated at $30 billion with predictions that it would go to $39 billion by 1959. It's well above that now, probably in the neighborhood of at least $41 billion, conservatively. There are several factors behind this boom. They include:

The rapid expansion of the $4,000 to $7,500 middle-income group during the fifties.

The 36 per cent increase in the number of people who moved to the suburbs, with its attendant opportunities for increased leisure.

A basic change in American attitudes toward the use of credit, particularly for pleasure.

More leisure itself, through a doubling of the number of weeks of paid vacations, labor-saving devices in the home, faster transportation.

Increased emphasis on family life and the skill of marketers of leisure products in capitalizing on this.

Technological improvements in leisure products that have made once-complicated recreational equipment easy for anyone to operate.

How Much Greater?

Over-all growth for the leisure market has rising population and income levels most strongly in its favor. In the decade ahead, the nation's population will grow to at least 207,000,000, and the nation's over-all wealth will pass the 700 billion dollar mark. By 1970, around 45 per cent of American families will have after-tax incomes of $7,500 or more. The middle income group ($4,000–$7,500) will constitute another 39 per cent of the population. Altogether, they will control an estimated 255 billion dollars of the nation's disposable income, the bulk of which will be discretionary.

But this population and economic growth does not automatically assure across-the-board growth for all leisure products. Manufacturers have already learned that, as witness the television industry. When it entered the market in 1947, 137,000 television sets were sold. Within two years sales were up to the 2,600,000 level and in another five years had topped 7,300,000 sets. As market saturation approached, sales declined to 5,200,000 sets a year. Now industry spokesmen say they can look forward to a steady level of sales for replacements and second sets of between 5,500,000 and 6,000,000 sets a year—until widespread acceptance of color TV gives the market another spurt.

Though market saturation has been achieved for TV sets, there is still much room for growth in the use of electronic products in leisure-time. Take high-fidelity components, for example. The institute's Joseph Benjamin views stereo as a technological extension of hi-fi. He notes that the hi-fi boom didn't really begin until the TV market was saturated. Now the people who already have hi-fi equipment will gradually upgrade to stereo. Little wonder then that he expects the hi-fi and stereo components industry to enjoy a two or three times increase to a level between $600,000,000 and $900,000,000 in the next ten years.

New-Product Impetus

Moreover, Benjamin looks for further technological developments to keep sales in his industry soaring upward. For instance, he predicts that in ten years video-tape will be an important factor in home entertainment. Actually, it is merely a blending of TV's sight and hi-fi's sound, which is already in commercial broadcast use. Price, of course, is the barrier now. The video-tape sets used in TV stations commercially cost upwards of $50,000. But as the "state of the art" advances, costs are bound to come down. When it gets within the $2,000 to $2,500 range, Benjamin foresees the day when many American homes will have a rack full of Broadway shows, operas, or movies on hand from which to choose an evening's entertainment.

"The only question is 'when?' " he says.

Other segments of the leisure market, however, are far from being saturated.

H.B. Atwater, president of the marine products division of the McCulloch Corp., predicts that the number of boats in use in ten years will double to around 15,000,000, with about 74,000,000 Americans enjoying the water—twice the number of participants today.

At least four out of every ten American homes will have their own swimming pools, according to U.S. Pool's Jerome Rudolph. This is a field where the number of residential pools have soared from 2,500 in 1948 to 124,900 at the start of this year.

And Bell & Howell's Carl Schreyer says the home movie industry hasn't yet scratched the surface of its full potential. "We have another 90 per cent to go," he says.

There seems little doubt that the only place for the leisure-time market to go is still up. Precisely how much is difficult to say. Five years ago it was confidently predicted that boating would cross the one billion dollar level by 1959. It not only did, it doubled that. Conservatively, then, it's not too much to expect the over-all leisure market to hit at least 50 billion dollars in the next decade, barring a major war or recession. For, as industrial designer Montgomery Ferar of Sundberg-Ferar Incorporated, reads the mood of the times: "The Puritan ethic has vanished. Americans are out to have fun. It's not only morally right to spend money on it, it has become patriotic to do so."

CONSUMER PREDICTION
AND MOTIVATION

part III

Selling effort is directed toward ultimate and industrial consumers who have relative freedom of choice in their purchase decisions. Salesmen who make an effort to understand buyers' behavior and motivations can improve their performance and serve their customers more effectively.

Until recent years, advertising and selling literature contained little about consumer wants and desires other than lists of rational and emotional product and patronage motives. Following a review of this early literature in Part III, there is a synthesis of the recent contributions of psychologists and sociologists to our understanding of the conscious and subliminal influences on consumer buying habits and attitudes. Selected case histories on the use of motivational research conclusions in formulating advertising policy and promotional strategy are included. This section sheds light on the spending patterns of various social classes, on buyers' views about price, on consumers' images of selected stores, and on the symbolism attached to well-known products.

Such knowledge can be used effectively in personal selling as well as in advertising. Sales messages which appeal to basic human drives and needs have the best opportunity of striking responsive chords in consumers. Also, products and services which reinforce buyers' self-images provide them with psychic satisfaction as well as with material value. To consummate maximum sales requires skill in the art and science of sensing consumer desires and appealing appropriately to them.

Past and Present Theories and Practices

20. MARKETING'S THINKING ABOUT
BUYING AND CONSUMPTION *

by Joseph W. Newman †

Why is it that marketing often has been unable to explain satisfactorily why people buy what they do?—why they have marked brand preferences even when product offerings appear to be about the same?; why they frequently resist product innovations and improvements?; why they have gone in so heavily for such things as the do-it-yourself movement and longer and more powerful automobiles?

For a better understanding of the shortcomings in existing knowledge and what might be done about them, let us take a look at how marketing typically has thought about buying behavior. What has the marketing executive to go on in making the judgments about human wants and probable consumer response which underlie so many of his important decisions?

Measures of Consumer Response

A primary source of information, of course, is sales results. If a product or promotional offering actually has been tried out in the open market or

---

* Reprinted by permission from *Motivation Research and Marketing Management* (Boston: Harvard University, Graduate School of Business Administration, Division of Research, 1957), pp. 12–26.

† Stanford University.

143

in a well-executed market test, the executive may be in a favorable position to predict future response. In the absence of direct data, he may turn to other evidence such as sales figures for what appear to be similar offers made in comparable circumstances or statements of consumer reaction and intention to buy, perhaps solicited in connection with product tests.

Measures of response, however, are not themselves explanations of why the response occurred. When marked innovations are involved, the main reasons for a striking result may be fairly easy to identify. In some situations, such as exist in the mail order business, there may be an unusual opportunity to keep records on offers and response and to experiment. This, of course, provides an improved basis for thinking about the reasons for what happened.

Typically, however, inferences are much more difficult to make. The sales result is an over-all measure of response to the entire product-offer and sales promotional program achieved over a period of time and under certain conditions. The number of influential variables is large, and it is no easy matter to discern cause and effect even under the best of circumstances. The drawing of incorrect conclusions from sales is commonplace. This is due not only to the difficulties already cited, but also to the tendency of businessmen to weave rational explanations for what they observe, even when such are inappropriate.

These are serious limitations. While it is essential to know what happened, it also is important to know why because the opportunity for constructive thinking is directly related to the extent to which there is understanding.

In attempting to interpret measures of consumer response, the marketing executive must reason the best he can just as he must in making judgments and predictions in the absence of such evidence. In doing this, he draws upon his background of impressions gained from both training and experience over the years. Whether he fully recognizes it or not, they have given him individual operating assumptions as to what people are like and what they will accept in the market place. Let us examine some of the main influences, other than sales results, which may have shaped his way of thinking.

Economic Theory

Economists' concepts have had a marked impact on business thinking about the nature of buying behavior. Perhaps the most important has been that of the "economic man" which represents both what many economists have said, at least in part, and what many business people think economists have said. Stated in the extreme, the picture which has emerged is something like this: a consumer is a rational purchasing agent for himself and his family who carefully weighs the utility or want-satisfying properties of all available products, then allocates his limited income among them to get the greatest possible satisfactions for his (or his family's) wants.

The great emphasis placed on economy and rationality is due in part to the fact that this concept represented a direct application in the consumer area of the thinking used by economists to explain the behavior of the business firm. The firm theoretically used its resources to produce goods in order to maximize profits, and the consumer was seen as a small business firm, using his resources (income) to buy goods in order to maximize want satisfaction.

In addition to the over-all idea that people are essentially rational in their buying, several other assumptions are involved in the "economic man" concept: that the consumer knows what his wants are and maintains something like an inventory of them in his mind to guide his purchasing; that he knows of all available products and services which might meet his needs; and that he can discern the want-satisfying content of each product or service, at least in relative terms, so that he can decide which items to buy in order to get the most satisfaction for his money.

The above assumptions may make the consumer sound much more like a computing machine than a human being engaged in everyday living. Nevertheless, this picture reflects both the great emphasis our culture has placed on rationality and the fact that economists generally have not regarded it as their function to investigate the nature of man's wants. Instead, they have been concerned with explaining how man went (or should go) about spending his limited income in order to maximize satisfaction of his wants, whatever their character. Essentially, they have said: given a person's wants and given a number of products with known capacities for satisfying these wants, we can tell you how that person should go about deciding on his purchases if he is to achieve maximum want satisfaction. What is missing here is the very information which would be of most help to the marketing man who must decide what products should be in the first place and how to talk effectively about them to prospective customers: what are these wants and what are the satisfactions a given product provides?

While the "economic man" is an exaggerated and incomplete picture of the consumer, the ideas it represents can be useful if handled with caution. Most people do have incomes too limited to satisfy all of their wants and many appear to exercise at least some care in their spending. On the other hand, the concept can be misleading as businessmen often know from their own observations.

Traditional economic assumptions are being challenged more and more by results of research. A number of interesting findings of this kind have come from the University of Michigan's Survey Research Center which is engaged in studying economic behavior in terms of psychological as well as other variables. A study of purchase decisions for durable goods (TV sets, refrigerators, washing machines, and stoves), for example, provided evidence that people are not always careful buyers, that some are downright careless, and that there are wide differences in buying which cannot be explained in conventional economic terms.[1]

The same study indicated that people with the lower incomes and presumably the greatest economic need for information to guide them in their purchases are the least likely to look for it. Sam Barton, President of the Market Research Corporation of America which conducts a national consumer panel, reports a number of instances of lower-income families buying the higher, rather than the lower priced brands within categories where products would appear to be roughly similar in physical properties.

A number of experiences have served to question the reliability of the common economic assumption of the negatively sloped demand curve which states that more units of a product can be sold at a lower rather than a higher price. One company in the writing instrument field, for example, found in market tests that it could sell about as many units of a new product at $2.95 as at $1.95.

While economic thought has served to emphasize rationality and material wants, a number of economists have been careful not to impose this limitation. Kenneth Boulding has been among those who have stressed that things do not have an intrinsic worth. He has reminded us that:

. . . "worth" . . . is not a physical property of an object like weight or volume, but is simply "how we feel about it." Things are "valuable" because somebody thinks they are and for no other reason whatever.[2]

The apparent inadequacies of the "economic man" concept of the consumer point to the need for learning more about how people make buying decisions and why they select one product or brand rather than another. Boulding's words suggest that this be approached by finding out how people feel about shopping and the things they buy.

Lists of Buying Motives

Emotional aspects of buying have received considerably more attention in the various lists of buying motives which have appeared in marketing literature.[3] Some represent the work of psychologists while others have been compiled by marketers themselves.

[1] George Katona and Eva Mueller, "A Study of Purchase Decisions," *Consumer Behavior* (New York: New York University Press, 1954), p. 53.

[2] Kenneth E. Boulding, *Economic Analysis*, rev. ed. (New York: Harper, 1948), p. 24.

[3] A summary of nine such lists appears in Malcolm P. McNair and Harry L. Hansen, *Readings in Marketing* (New York: McGraw-Hill, 1949), pp. 58–61.

Copeland's Early Work

One of the earliest of these was by Melvin T. Copeland. It appeared in 1924 in his *Principles of Merchandising*,[4] a pioneering work which has had a marked influence on marketing writings since that time. The book was notable in several respects. It emphasized that knowledge of buying motives and habits was the necessary starting point for thinking and planning in marketing. It enumerated buying motives for both consumer and industrial goods, and distinguished among "convenience," "shopping," and "specialty" goods on the basis of consumer buying habits.

The basic classification used by Copeland in presenting his list of 33 consumer buying motives was "emotional" and "rational." He saw emotional motives as those which "have their origin in human instincts and emotions and represent impulsive or unreasoning promptings to action," and rational motives as "those which are aroused by appeals to reason . . . When influenced by a rational motive, a consumer carefully weighs the advantages and disadvantages of the purchase before acting." [5] He stated that a majority of buyers' motives for consumers' goods were "instinctive and emotional." [6]

Copeland's list of consumers' buying motives follows: [7]

Emotional Buying Motives

1. Distinctiveness
2. Emulation
3. Economical emulation
4. Pride of personal appearance
5. Pride in appearance of property
6. Social achievement
7. Proficiency
8. Expression of artistic taste
9. Happy selection of gifts
10. Ambition
11. Romantic instinct
12. Maintaining and preserving health
13. Cleanliness
14. Proper care of children
15. Satisfaction of the appetite
16. Pleasing the sense of taste
17. Securing personal comfort
18. Alleviation of laborious tasks
19. Security from danger
20. Pleasure of recreation
21. Entertainment
22. Obtaining opportunity for greater leisure
23. Securing home comfort

[4] Melvin T. Copeland, *Principles of Merchandising* (Chicago and New York: Shaw, 1924).
[5] *Ibid.*, p. 162.
[6] *Ibid.*, p. 207.
[7] *Ibid.*, p. 160.

Rational Buying Motives

24. Handiness

25. Efficiency in operation or use

26. Dependability in use

27. Dependability in quality

28. Reliability of auxiliary service

29. Durability

30. Enhancement of earnings

31. Enhancing productivity of property

32. Economy in use

33. Economy in purchase

Copeland also differentiated between "primary" and "selective" motives. "A primary motive is one which imparts to consumers the major, initial impulse to purchase the kind of article offered for sale," he wrote, while a selective motive "is one in which the aim is to divert the consumer's expenditure away from other brands of the same article." [8] Another distinction made was that between a buying motive which "induces a customer to buy a particular commodity or type of article," and a patronage motive "which induces a customer to trade with a particular firm." [9]

Copeland insisted that "analysis of buying motives be based on actual conditions, not upon *a priori* reasoning." [10] His approach was to examine 936 advertisements in then current general magazines, women's magazines, national weeklies, and farm papers. He decided to do this because the material was economically at hand. In addition, he believed that a field survey "would not have yielded equally dependable results, because a majority of the buying motives of consumers are not rational motives, and in many instances dependable answers could not have been secured from consumers." [11] He pointed out that his findings could not be regarded as final, but that they appeared to represent the collective experience of a large number of advertisers.

Copeland made a similar study of 756 advertisements in business journals, recognizing the possibility that there might be many buying motives which were appealed to in personal salesmanship, but which might not appear in advertising. He noted that all of his buying motives for industrial goods were "rational" which he considered logical "because an industrial firm makes its purchases for business reasons, not for the personal gratification of individual executives." [12] At the same time, however, he indicated that he was not completely at ease with this assumption by noting that "ex-

[8] Melvin T. Copeland, *Principles of Merchandising* (Chicago and New York: Shaw, 1924).

[9] *Ibid.*, p. 190.

[10] *Ibid.*, p. 158.

[11] *Ibid.*, p. 159.

[12] *Ibid.*, p. 207.

perience with the methods used by salesmen in the solicitation of orders for industrial goods has shown . . . that in personal interviews appeals frequently are made to the emotional motives of the buyers." [13]

Copeland's list of buying motives for industrial goods follows: [14]

(Product or Commodity) Buying Motives

1. Economy in use
2. Protection against loss
3. Enhancing productivity of plant
4. Dependability in use
5. Dependability in quality
6. Durability
7. Flexibility in operation or use
8. Simplicity in operation
9. Handiness
10. Facility of installation
11. Facility in making repairs
12. Enhancing salability of product
13. Facility in executive control
14. Aiding sales promotion
15. Safeguarding welfare and morale of employees
16. Sanitation of plant
17. Economy in purchase

Patronage Motives

1. Reliability of seller
2. Punctuality of delivery
3. Promptness in delivery
4. Securing exact fulfillment of specifications
5. Variety for selection
6. Engineering and designing service
7. Dependable repair service

Many years passed after the publication of Copeland's work in which little further progress was made toward understanding buying behavior. Until relatively recent times, marketing writers generally have failed both to share Copeland's interest in this area and to heed his warning against relying on *a priori* reasoning.

Hattwick's "Basic Wants"

An example of a more recent list of buying motives, which reflects a somewhat different approach, is that of Melvin S. Hattwick, a psychologist. [15]

---

[13] *Ibid.*
[14] *Ibid.*, pp. 190–215.
[15] Melvin S. Hattwick, *How to Use Psychology for Better Advertising* (New York: Prentice-Hall, 1950), pp. 18–21.

He listed "eight basic wants in life," which, he said, were common to all inventories of people's wants and desires which had been made by psychologists. They were represented as being those things which people desire most often and with the greatest intensity. Here they are:

1. Food and drink
2. Comfort
3. To attract the opposite sex
4. Welfare of loved ones
5. Freedom from fear and danger
6. To be superior
7. Social approval
8. To live longer

The basic wants were so named because they were believed to be based on "fundamental drives." It has been the opinion of some psychologists, which Hattwick shared, that people are born with the same fundamental drives or wants and satisfy them in about the same ways. According to this view, drives easily are aroused by appealing to the "basic wants," and once a drive is set in motion, the person wants to satisfy it almost immediately. Hattwick also identified the following nine "secondary wants" learned by people through experience: [16]

1. Bargains
2. Information
3. Cleanliness
4. Efficiency
5. Convenience
6. Dependability, quality
7. Style, beauty
8. Economy, profit
9. Curiosity

Duncan's Study of Industrial Buying

Prevalent thinking about industrial buying is reflected in Delbert J. Duncan's study of the motivation of purchasing agents. He compiled a tentative list of motives on the basis of personal interviews in which executives were encouraged to talk freely of their purchasing experiences. The list later was submitted to members of the National Association of Purchasing Agents who were requested to indicate which motives were the more important ones for heavy machinery, raw materials, and supplies. The results follow:[17]

[16] Melvin S. Hattwick, *How to Use Psychology for Better Advertising* (New York: Prentice-Hall, 1950), pp. 23–25.
[17] Delbert J. Duncan, "What Motivates Business Buyers," *Harvard Business Review*, Vol. XVIII, No. 4 (Summer 1940), pp. 448–54.

Heavy Machinery

Product Motives

1. Economy
2. Productivity
3. Dependability
4. Time or labor saving
5. Durability

Patronage Motives

1. Reliability of seller
2. Cooperation
3. Low prices
4. Quick repair service
5. Past services rendered; satisfactory relationships

Raw Materials

Product Motives

1. Right quality
2. Uniformity
3. Dependability
4. Purity
5. Ability to increase salability of user's product

Patronage Motives

1. Reliability of seller
2. Continuous supply under all conditions
3. Accessibility of seller
4. Low prices
5. Quick and reliable delivery of product

Supplies

Product Motives

1. Right quality
2. Dependability
3. Uniformity
4. Economy
5. Durability

Patronage Motives

1. Reliability of seller
2. Continuous supply under all conditions
3. Accessibility of seller
4. Low prices
5. Quick and reliable delivery of product

Duncan concluded that while both rational and emotional influences entered into the purchasing, the rational motives predominated and were, by and large, the governing factors. In commenting on his personal interviews, however, he observed that many purchases were made on a rational basis as a matter of habit or in accordance with past custom. He noted some cases where executives had difficulty in naming rational considerations which influenced their decisions.

Comments on the Lists of Motives

The lists of motives focus attention on the consideration of buyer wants and benefits and suggest factors which might be investigated in specific business situations.

At the same time, however, they have important limitations as bases for explaining and predicting behavior. One is their questionable accuracy and completeness as generalized statements of what people want when they buy. Copeland, for example, had to make the doubtful assumption in his study that advertisers knew from experience what appeals were most effective and that their ads reflected this knowledge. The marked tendency of people to rationalize is a major problem in studies like Duncan's which ask respondents directly for explanations of their actions. While Duncan took steps to minimize distortion, his final product still consisted of the traditional factors every good, rational purchasing agent should take into account, according to all conventional treatises on the subject. While these factors are of importance, they probably represent only a partial explanation. It is interesting to note that the purchasing agents did not report being greatly influenced by the fact that they liked a salesman or by a policy of reciprocity in buying.

The inadequacy of the list-of-motives approach has been noted by a few writers from time to time over the years. Arthur W. Kornhauser advocated its abandonment more than 30 years ago.[18] This viewpoint was largely ignored in marketing circles until relatively recent times when other writers and researchers began to reflect the more modern thinking on personality and motivation in which the motive concept has given way to other ideas. Sharing some of the opinions of Kornhauser, Douglas McGregor contributed another significant statement of the limitations of "motives" for marketing, writing in 1940.[19] Steuart Henderson Britt in 1950 wrote an article in a somewhat similar vein which has been widely quoted.[20] One of his main

[18] Arthur W. Kornhauser, "The Motives-in-Industry Problem," *Annals of the American Academy of Political and Social Science,* September 1923, pp. 105–16.
[19] Douglas McGregor, " 'Motives' As a Tool of Market Research," *Harvard Business Review,* Vol. XIX, No. 1 (Autumn 1940), pp. 42–51.
[20] Steuart Henderson Britt, "The Strategy of Consumer Motivation," *Journal of Marketing,* April 1950, pp. 666–74.

points was that there is no such thing as a universal set of explanatory motives.

McGregor pointed out, as had Kornhauser, that motives are terms of classification of observed behavior rather than forces which constitute explanations of behavior. By way of illustration, he wrote as follows:

We arrive at the concept of motive by a process of observing, classifying, and naming abstracted similarities among different behaviors. For example, we observe that a variety of patterns of behavior tend to maintain and increase the individual's value in the eyes of his fellows. Then we name this class of behavioral patterns in terms of the abstracted common quality. We call it, perhaps "the desire for social approval," or "the desire for popularity." Then, when we are asked why people behave in these ways, we answer glibly: "because they have a motive to obtain social approval," or "because they have a desire for popularity." Obviously, the process of classifying a variety of observed phenomena under a common name does no explaining! . . . Yet this process of naming, and then attributing causal significance to names, has been the basis for practically all the theories of motivation which have been proposed until recently.[21]

McGregor also pointed out that knowledge of a "motive" did not make prediction of behavior possible because a number of different forms of behavior were lumped together under each term or "motive" in the process of classification. More detailed knowledge of the individual concerned and the environment in which he behaves is necessary for explanations and predictions. As McGregor noted, this is why our most accurate predictions are made in connection with those persons we know best.

The thinking outlined above leads to a recommendation that consumer wants and reasons for buying be studied by investigating the factors in the total makeup of the individual and his environmental situation. McGregor expressed it by means of a formula: $R = f(S, I)$. He explained that "any given reaction (R) is a function of a complex pattern of relationships between factors making up the environmental situation (S) and the individual (I) as they exist at the moment of reaction."[22] An understanding of R must come from an analysis of both S and I. McGregor noted that the concept of motives was not needed in the point of view he expressed. Instead of explaining behavior in terms of motives as forces or drives which could be listed as entities, he saw reasons for action as consisting of "complex patterns of factors including such things as capacities, skills, habits, attitudes, knowledge, physiological state and personality traits."[23]

McGregor cited the need for developing research techniques which would

[21] Douglas McGregor, *op. cit.*, p. 44.
[22] *Ibid.*, p. 45.
[23] *Ibid.*

get behind outwardly deceptive behavior or opinion. Britt emphasized the "tremendous importance of unconscious motivation" and advocated the use of the qualitative interview or the clinical approach to interviewing.[24]

The lists of motives are of interest to us here because they have been prominent on the marketing scene and therefore represent an influence on the way marketers have thought about buying behavior. The implied concept of the consumer is that of a person driven by a number of universal forces which can be enumerated. According to this view, understanding behavior is simply a matter of consulting "the" list of motives. This kind of thinking, which has been prevalent in marketing for some time, now is being increasingly recognized as an oversimplified theory of motivation. Whether or not such lists actually include the things strongly desired by most people, they provide no ready answers as to what satisfactions people get from the purchase and use of any given product or why they choose one brand over another. The lists cannot state what appeals would be most effective in a given situation.

21. WHAT ARE THE *REAL* REASONS PEOPLE BUY TODAY? *

by Ernest A. Dichter †

What man who sells—or manages the activities of salesmen—hasn't said, "If I could only get inside my customer's brain and find out what *really* makes him buy, my troubles would be over."

Sometimes, listening to the talk that spins round about the new science of motivation research, you get the feeling that the answer to this seemingly impossible miracle has been discovered.

For the last two decades, motivational research has been my day, night, week-end, and even holiday activity. Today, when The Institute has opened a new research center on a ten-acre estate overlooking the Hudson, and when we have begun to see the international implications of our work with the undertaking of a study for the Japan Air Lines Company, Limited, I still cannot say that we've gotten anywhere near the goal of final solution to the No. 1 problem of everyone who sells. Still, there has been progress in the search to learn why buyers tick. It is appropriate that, at this confluence of circumstances, we take stock. We can at least say this: If you

* Reprinted from *Sales Management*, February 1, 1955, pp. 37–8 ff.
† President, Institute for Motivational Research, Inc., Croton-on-Hudson, New York.

and your firm are not taking advantage of the new psychological insight into consumer behavior now available, you may be missing one of the most important selling tools.

Many people in selling still regard motivational studies as pure bunk or just interesting experiments, O.K. for someone else but far removed from their businesses. On the other hand, an increasing number of successful firms, large and small, are using the findings of social scientists.

As Robert Whitney, president, National Sales Executives, Incorporated, explains, there are two major reasons: "First, the probers often come up with answers which, when tried, have worked. Second, even if recommendations haven't panned out exactly as hoped, they have lifted managements out of mental ruts. And re-examining worn-out approaches has caused many concerns to come up with fresh ideas."

Last year, it is estimated, U.S. businesses spent approximately 9 million dollars for such studies. Expenditures for 1955 should be at least a third higher. Most believe they're getting their money's worth.

Some businessmen insist that seeking out customers' motivations and giving them new names and rationales is simply Freudian mumbo-jumbo. "Human nature," they insist, "remains pretty much the same over the years. The only way to sell is by appealing to four fundamentals: the desire for sustenance, recognition, sex, and security."

There's no doubt that whatever terms you use, these are the four horsemen of buying motivation and behavior patterns. But you can't ignore the fact that the relative importance of each in the lives of most of your customers has changed since World War II. And the speed of events is altering attitudes accordingly.

Just think what has happened in three months, any three months, of the postwar years. Recollect the headlines and ask yourself: "Can all this occur without an impact on my customers? Will they remain the same?"

The answer, we believe, is no. What moves people today is not necessarily what made them reach for checkbooks last year. Customer attitudes and states of mind influence your sales, as much as need or logic. More Americans today buy discretionary items not when required, but when they're in the mood. That mood can be natural or created through stimulation. Psychological factors, rather than need, are the motivations of almost 60 per cent of our yearly purchases.

Since successful use of the right appeals at the right time and place so often determine your sale, it is wise to ask: What is the psychological climate influencing American customers today? What are the top-ranking appeals and the best ways to use them?

We have conducted some 500 major research studies, and compiled over 100,000 individual consumer case histories, for such blue-chip firms as the American Broadcasting Co., Ralston Purina Co., Brown & Williamson

Tobacco Corp., Equitable Life Assurance Society of the U.S., General Electric Co., General Foods Corp., Jewel Tea Co., Inc., Endicott-Johnson Corp., Goodyear Tire & Rubber Co., Inc., General Mills, Inc., Lever Brothers Co., The Andrew Jergens Co., Miles Laboratories, Inc., and Associated Merchandising Corp. Over 300 psychologically trained interviewers in 55 major markets funnel information to our analytical staff.

These studies show the four principal factors affecting today's sales climate, why they have become important and are likely to become more so in the immediate future. They also demonstrate how some firms and associations—our own and others—have taken the vital step in using this research, switching old appeals to new ones geared to the thinking of today's customer.

Our method is to study the firm and product personality. Then, rather than check questionnaires alone, we have trained researchers make hundreds of interviews in depth so that hidden motives may be dredged out and analyzed according to psychological knowledge. From this procedure come facts that you, the businessman client, can use to reorient or improve your sales appeals.

But down to cases. These are typical. You may not agree with all of them or even with the terminology, for motivational research is still far from an exact science. But they will certainly give you challenging ideas to mull over—and to act on in your own business.

Major Shifts in Our Thinking

Since World War II, there have been four major shifts in our thinking, strongly affecting buying attitudes:

1. *Puritanism is on its way out.* More and more Americans have adopted the attitude that it's not wrong or sinful to get as much pleasure out of life as possible; that it's not necessary to pay in pain for each pleasure. And they're purchasing accordingly.

2. *Why-shouldn't-I?* We are increasingly willing to give vent to our whims and desires, to say: "Why shouldn't I have this or that?" We also realize that often an emotional, irrational basis lies behind many of our actions. But we are more willing to let our instincts and emotions determine "I'll take it," particularly if the seller knows how to follow up emotional appeals with convincing evidences of benefits that make us believe our purchase wise and indicative of our good judgment.

3. *We are more mature.* Since we are increasingly giving in to our whims, this may sound like a paradox. Yet the constant series of crises and fears under which we live have forced us to think ahead in long-range terms— and buy that way.

4. *We would be more individual.* We admire America's mass-production, assembly-line products. But there's a reaction, a desire for expression of

individuality and for recognition, manifesting itself in countless activities—and purchases.

Perhaps you are already aware of these fundamental changes and are using some of the new appeals developed from them. But unless you are employing all to the fullest, you may be missing your best untapped sales opportunities. As many astute businessmen have discovered, one added appeal for your product or service, properly employed, can mean the difference between success and failure, profit and loss.

The real selling secret, we have found, is not concentrating on one appeal in your product or service as applicable to everyone. It's discovering how many different, directly personal appeals, based on major consumer thinking changes, you can send out, like a series of radar beams, seeking potential customers. Some must be used head-on, others obliquely. For while all basic human motivation boils down to the desire to stay alive as happily as possible, there are infinite ways to appeal to this desire—and to make your sale.

Factor One: Puritanism Is on Its Way Out

What psychologists call the "Puritan complex" in our national mentality is a result of our total history and culture. For generations most Americans believed that it was somehow sinful to get too much pleasure out of life. Self-denial and thrift were key virtues. Worldly goods, beyond certain requirements, were considered the prerogative of spendthrifts and millionaires. Since the Puritans and those who followed them had to conquer virgin territory and lead lives of hardship, they made a virtue of their frugality. But as we became more secure, settled, and prosperous, modern technology provided more products for more people at lower prices. With income rising —and in part, because of it—advertising to encourage consumption of more products and distribution to make them more available, helped to dissipate the Puritan heritage. Both these factors also broadened every kind of communication: greater interchange, national and international, has brought people new, direct personalized impressions, made the forbidden familiar and not only desirable but available. World War II made moral standards more lax, self-denial less restrictive on our purchasing moods.

What New Appeals Has This Put Forward?

Saleswise, the lessening of Puritanism has pushed forward three major sales appeals: (1) the desire for *comfort*. This doesn't mean Americans are getting lazy, but rather that they realize that unnecessary work is something to be legitimately avoided, and the time thus gained spent for other things; (2) the desire for *luxury,* to enjoy sensual pleasures that go beyond mere comfort, to enjoy new sensations, to permit secret dreams to find realization; (3) the desire for *prestige* and improved social status reflected primarily in the desire for products and services which not only connote *quality* and improved, upgraded social position to the individual, but which the customer can use to show others where he now stands.

Firms That Have Switched to the Comfort Appeal

The appeal for comfort works everywhere, not only with products obviously sold for that purpose. Today even a tractor can be sold more readily when comfort is stressed. Not long ago a major producer, finding sales of heavy equipment below quota, called us; asked what motivations we could research out that might be helpful. Customarily the firm sold on the basis of engineered performance, adaptability for many jobs, and related factors —all important. Studies revealed one overlooked aspect, fully as vital: what the man who ran the machine and who had a major voice in its selection, had in the back of his mind—even if unwilling to express it openly before the boss—was comfort on the job. Motivation studies showed he wanted such passenger car comforts as automatic gear shifts, upholstered seats, heaters, arm rests, and glove compartments. All were installed. And to win the boss, stress was put on the fact that the comfortable man does a better, safer job. The comfort approach, based on sound psychological proof, has not only raised sales for this major tractor manufacturing company, but other leading equipment makers have also successfully employed it.

No Need to Sweat

Power tools long sold primarily on the basis of increased efficiency. Now, as the result of seeking out real purchaser motivations, more and more manufacturers appeal to the growing belief that there's no need to sweat. An example of smart exploitation of this appeal is Hiller Engineering's Yard Hand. A brightly colored little power vehicle, its psychologically perfect extra is a seat enabling you to ride astride while doing lawn chores or even snow plowing. That rider seat offering comfort, pleasure, and family sport not only sells Pop and the kids on Yard Hand, it has made more sales to envious neighbors than any similar product in years.

Dayton Rubber Company not long ago developed a new type of foam with infinite use possibilities. The big question: What to make of it? Psychological studies were run to discover the product with likeliest consumer appeals. "Offer comfort," Dayton officials were told, "and you'll get more people to pay more for your product than for one with only utilitarian use." Dayton decided on pillows, called them Koolfoam to stress comfort and get over the hurdle of the popular conception of rubber as hot; developed a slogan: "Gives you the rest of your lifetime." In three years Dayton has become a leader in its field.

Simmons Company, long an industry leader, puzzled by dragging sales, learned through studies that at least one-third of the bedding market currently buys a mattress worth only $60. Today's approach to selling higher-price Beautyrest mattresses is "new comfort hitherto unavailable," rather than stress on spring coils and permanency.

W.A. Sheaffer Pen Company, spent a vast sum to develop its Snorkel when motivation probers came across the fact that a prime objection was the uncomfortable business of dunking and wiping after refill.

The Florsheim Shoe Company, Incorporated, headed in new directions when it put its finger on proof that more and more men wearing loafers at home wanted shoes providing the same comfort, yet dressy enough for town wear. Result: a new type of lighter "Lo-Top" slip-on shoe, combining ease and appearance.

Manufacturers of every kind of home furnishings have found informality, based on the desire for comfort, so strong it has created a whole new "casual period." The National Association of Summer Furniture Manufacturers, for example, eager to increase business beyond seasonal sales, mapped an extensive campaign to sell the idea that summer comfort is available for finished basement playrooms and enclosed porches—and is rolling up year-round sales heretofore believed impossible.

Comfort on the Farm

Not long ago the farmer was the counterpart of the Puritan. Examine his publications today, however, and you'll note that more and more alert manufacturers are, as a result of motivation studies, stressing the comfort their products offer. Farmers are buying everything from mechanical milkers to tape-recorded music for the henhouse. It has been proved that chickens actually lay more eggs when they are made comfortable. And cows, treated like luxury animals rather than duty beasts, increase milk output.

Appliance makers have been most vigorous in developing comfort appeals even over efficiency. When, not long ago, Lewyt Corporation decided to enter the vacuum cleaner field, motivational studies of 5,000 housewives showed that, more than anything else, women often enjoyed a sense of accomplishment in cleaning—but hated the aftermath. So Lewyt created its no-dust-bag-to-empty cleaner and subsequently a low-slung dolly on which cleaner and attachments glide easily from room to room. This, more than anything else, has put Lewyt in top rank.

General Electric Company stresses the comfort appeal for everything from ironers ("no need to sprinkle") to washer-dryer combinations ("do your laundry in less than two hours; start at nine and your washday is over before eleven").

A classic purveyor of the comfort appeal is Carrier Corporation, a leading home air conditioner manufacturer. While always stressing the comfort of the cool house in blazing summer months, with the added motivational appeal of heat for winter, Carrier won over many customers reluctant to spend for a device they believed to be useful only certain months of the year.

How to Use the Comfort Appeal Yourself

Study thoroughly your service or product to determine how it can offer new and different ways to meet consumer desires for comfort—and play up these advantages as fully as possible. Can you show ease of maintenance? Launderability at home? No need to carry, lift, walk? Can you make your product more comfortable by reducing bulk or weight, as have some of the hat, suit, overcoat, shoe and related apparel manufacturers? Or by new design, usage?

Philip Morris, a major cigarette maker, recently spent hundreds of thousands of dollars on its new "Snap-Open Pack" permitting neater, faster opening and refolding, after studies showed that comfort and convenience were a prime consideration in smokers' minds.

The multibillion dollar frozen food industry, and notably orange juice, was built not so much on promises of freshness as of comfort—less work for you, the user. There is little doubt that more industries will, in the next decade, build with the same approach.

Can you find new ways to improve comfort by simple self-demonstrations? General Electric and Maison Blanche Company, New Orleans department store, promoted the idea and topped a $100,000 four-day goal in three by allowing all household appliances to be taken home for ten days on a no-risk, money-back guarantee. The high percentage of keep-it sales overcame minimum spoilage.

Have you made it as comfortable as possible for your customers to shop —given them places to sit, provided undistracting areas to close important sales? Checking 150,000 food transactions, The Coca-Cola Company, not a firm to let grass grow under its feet, found proof that customers who stopped for a soft drink while shopping spent an average of $9.39 compared to $5.20 spent by nonstop shoppers. Then the company put the facts to work—showed super marketers that 80 per cent of the customers accepted offers of free Cokes and increased average purchases to $7.64.

Firms That Have Switched to the Luxury Appeal

Recently the Kudner Agency, Incorporated, asked us to study the "typical high-price car buyer"—and specifically the Buick buyer—his habits, earnings, job, thinking patterns, so the agency could sharpen appeals. Researchers quickly recognized one contradiction to previous statistical research: There just weren't any "typicals." Butchers, grocers, farmers, all kinds of people who traditionally "weren't supposed" to be high-price owners, were. In line with findings of our motivational studies, we advised Buick: "Go beyond customer groups you're appealing to now and into more mass-circulation media. Broaden direct mailings to include all income groups. Don't show cars in unattainable estate settings but adventuring on the open road. And tell dealers not to form snap judgment from shoppers' clothes. The guy in the beat-up pants might buy a Roadmaster convertible, too." Already the advice is paying off, for mass markets not only accept but actively want luxury at every price range.

Heads of Chevrolet's Car Clubs, making their own motivation exploration of sales appeals that closed the deal, found luxury and appearance most important; economy way below; reliability third. Another national study revealed that while customers are still choosy when they buy cars, they want luxury: power brakes and steering, white walls, the extras. Almost the only purchasers of "plain vanilla"—without additionals—are fleet buyers. Cadillac is still a waiting-list product primarily because, with keen insight into buying motivation, it has emphasized the luxury appeal consistently, even when unable to fill orders. And Chrysler, checking to discover why it slipped on sales when other firms moved ahead, found that the answer lay mainly in styling. Engineering-wise, Chrysler is the equal of GM and Ford cars. For most drivers, psychologists learned, getting behind the wheel of an important-looking car lifts morale, increases the feeling of self-importance, enhances gratification. And since they have come to think "long slinky" cars are automatically "better," they have bought the luxury look.

Even in the maintenance end of motoring, our study for Socony-Vacuum Oil Company, Incorporated, showed that price wasn't the primary objective —rather it was the desire for the luxury of *special* service and "being cared for." Proof of findings influenced Socony to shift from strident claims as to what gasoline would do (which, it was found, motorists usually ignore anyway) to better and amplified station facilities.

The Frank H. Lee Company, a leading hatter, has altered its approach from needling men into hat-wearing to avoid that "harried look" to offering luxury— "Nothing makes you look and feel so important as a Lee." Lee has even put rich brocade linings in its hats, adapted from increasingly popular male vests. Though seen only by the wearer when he doffs his sombrero, these linings give him the feeling of the ultimate in the individual luxury—"what a woman gets from a coat lined in mink."

How to Use the Luxury Appeal Yourself

Demonstrate in every possible way how your product or service provides luxury at least cost. The package alone might make the difference: Extensive studies have shown that most women can't tell perfumes by odor—packaging makes more sales than contents. And it works just as well for ice cream. A leading maker had us seek out buyers' reaction to a series of proposed new containers. We found that one in Wedgwood blue, simple in design and pictureless, caused eight out of ten customers to consider its contents more expensive, better tasting, with more flavor than previous packages depicting the ice cream itself. Placed in production, the motivationally chosen design proved to be the best seller.

Similar results came from a study for the Jewel Tea chain. Our probers found that customers did not consider expensive steaks wrapped in plain paper as good as those in special wraps. Some with sliced meat spread out to look richer, others beautifully wrapped ready for the freezer, jumped sales so sharply that Jewel used its research studies to sell butcher groups on prepackaging. The firm has since adapted the system for most of its supermarkets, gaining far higher volume and markup in less space. One California supermarket went even further—found that by creating the idea of luxury through putting a pat of butter atop each of its better steaks, sales increased 15 per cent.

A study for Schenley Distillers, Incorporated, showed the luxury appeal so strong that it lead to introduction of new decanters. Results: The whiskey looks costlier and better in buyers' eyes; new decanters are a powerful merchandising attraction.

Whenever your product is made to look less utilitarian, we have found, the more luxury it usually connotes to the customer.

L. Bamberger & Company, Newark department store, learned that wrapping all possible items in cellophane not only enhanced luxury appeal, but saved on returns, inventory, and soiling particularly with multiplied units. One line of slow-moving linen ensembles, for example, sold out the day after being cellophane-packaged in groups.

Grouping items in kits, or selling associated products together, is another way of appealing to the luxury yen and increasing sales tickets. McGregor Sportswear, for instance, began boxing slacks with shirts, stockings with walking shorts, under the name International Sets. When President Harry Doniger noted that a $5.95 shopper frequently signed a $12 to $15 check, McGregor redesigned its $50 million yearly output. Today almost every item "goes with" other things in color, design, wearability. Sales of wardrobes, instead of individual items, have paid off handsomely.

Variety packs of good cheeses, fine crackers, special occasion components, all express the luxury notion to many customers. Numbers of complete kitchens and bathrooms are sold this way. Often an inquiry for a single item can be built into a complete sale if adequately followed through. Psychologically, buying grouped products provides satisfaction, a sense of completeness and accomplishment, makes most customers feel a little closer to the ultimate perfection we all seek. It also arouses a feeling of "getting a better buy." The carnival pitchman, you'll recall, showed you a kitchen paring utensil, then told you he'd toss in a pear slicer, a carrot grater, a celery shredder, all wrapped up in one package. It was a hard lure to resist; it is as effective today when coupled with a luxury appeal.

Firms That switched to Prestige and Quality Appeal

The desire for prestige, quality, improved social status, as much as for comfort, is the real reason behind purchase of many better homes, apparel, automotive and other products. It's an appeal to the American sense of pride, a desire for recognition; not social climbing in the old sense, but a desire for self-status. Prestige is more social than actual in present-day psychological terms—what people think about a product or service is paramount to what it really is. And your appeals must reflect this to succeed.

For example, seeking clues for Lord Calvert (Calvert Distillers Corporation) we learned that today Americans are less concerned with looking up to outstanding personalities in unquestioning admiration than they were a decade ago. Rather, since most people believe that they can reach the top, they are primarily interested in how Mr. Big did it. Adding "how-to" details in the advertising copy gave the Man of Distinction appeal an extra push.

General Mills, Incorporated, had us check its advertisements for Wheaties to see if they could be made more effective. As a result of psychometric tests for degree of consumer involvement in the appeal, for positive emotional reaction developed, and for degree of mental rehearsal of purchase and use of the product, we advised: "Have a youngster appear in the advertisement with the champion. The kids will identify themselves more readily with your message." Knox Reeves Advertising, Incorporated, Minneapolis, interpreted these findings ingeniously. It has worked out exactly as forecast.

Adding prestige luster to a product or store can be done in many ways. Ohrbach's New York department store, to get away from its one-note price consciousness, not only ran an extensive institutional advertising campaign to stress high fashion, but put on the town's biggest show of Paris originals to drive it home.

Foley's, Federated Department Stores' big Houston store, with a primarily middle-class clientele, advertises $15,000 minks. Doesn't expect to sell many, but tests have proved that such conversation-makers give prestige to labels on lesser items. The same store group spent thousands of additional dollars adding impressive decor to its Fedway Stores to create what President Fred Lazarus, Jr., calls a "$5 blouse atmosphere," though many blouses go at $2.95, because "you can sell a $5 customer a lesser item in better settings, but it's hard to up-trade the other way round."

Prestige in Dime Stores

More and more variety and F.W. Woolworth Company stores have up-graded presentation, store design and appearance, aware that they're not only selling more expensive items than in the past, but that customers choose the store that gives them the satisfaction of prestige.

Radio Corporation of America is stressing the appeal with Limited Edition collections. Assembling sets of Beethoven, Toscanini, and even Glenn Miller, RCA bound them handsomely, had a good explanatory book written and, though most of the recordings had been in the catalog for years and could be bought individually for far less, the prestige albums sold out. Henry Holt & Co., Incorporated, publishers, did the same with several of Robert Frost's poems. A $12.50 fine-binding, numbered collection edition of eightieth-birthday favorites, twice as expensive as his complete works, was gone a week after publication.

C.F. Hathaway Company's eye-patch man gave the shirtmaker national fame in short order because of prestige stress. Snob-appeal advertisements, franchising only top name stores, added an extra prestige value that gradually trickled down. A similar appeal is now being used to sell beverages for "The Man from Schweppes"—red beard and all.

Prestige often stems from what others think of your product. From this premise Caterpillar Tractor Company, Peoria, has developed a unique device: Yearly it invites 200 barbers for a look-see. Since barbers reputedly love to talk, Caterpillar, in giving them something to enthuse about, gets its prestige message across in the most effective manner via word-of-mouth.

The quality appeal is part of this same picture. Williamson–Dickie Manufacturing Company, that sells $18 million of work clothes yearly, found that since factory workers have up-graded their living scale and women come into many plants, the boys are far fussier about the cut of their jib—and willing to pay, if you can show them how to achieve the quality look on the job.

Cluett, Peabody & Company, Incorporated recently checked suburbanites in ten cities; found 94 per cent Mr. Fixits, 80 per cent of whom were dis-satisfied with clothes they wore for do-it-yourself tasks. Result: a newly styled working line, with the quality appeals of the fashion show. McGregor discovered that many men weren't using sportswear for leisure at all, but for work; somehow they felt that sport clothes gave them a quality feeling impossible to get in over-alls. As a result, McGregor has up-graded appear-ance, smartness and color of its sportswear, extended sales to many stores that formerly carried no such items.

The same quality appeal is fully as effective in the mechanical field. R.M. Oakley, sales manager for John Deere Plow Company, Des Moines, formerly showed two evenly matched used products when offering equipment to younger or less prosperous farmers. What we call the "misery of choice" often made the customer hesitate to such an extent that he bought neither. When Oakley concentrated better tires and best paint job on one tractor, the visible quality difference was immediately apparent. In practically every case, the quality product sold first—even though priced higher.

How to Use the Prestige and Quality Appeal Yourself

Anything you can do to dramatize and enhance appearance and focus attention on highlights of your line or service can add prestige. Do it with packages, lights, display, special effects. A Detroit car dealer employed a psychological approach in his showroom by guarding his prestige car with a red plush rope. His trick: telling favorite customers it was O.K. for *them* to duck under and inspect the car closely.

Koch of California thought it had a good approach in stressing how its Fiberglas luggage could take a beating—even if dropped from a plane. Consumer reaction was negative—and our motivation study showed why: It conjured up thoughts of crashing. Another previous appeal, "so strong you can clean it with steel wool," didn't win customers either. Instead of ease, it made them think of the work they might have to do. When studies showed that most people want the admiration of other travelers and of the redcaps handling their bags, a new prestige appeal was put forth and translated by J.J. Weiner Company, San Francisco, advertising agency. It has made sales where other appeals failed to attract. Admiration from others, another way of expressing prestige, has also become the Pacific Mills theme. All its men's clothing advertisements are now additionally directed at women, emphasizing, "Does your husband carry the world on his shoulders? Tell him about the suit with the weightless feel." Enhancing *his* status in *her* eyes has helped to sell both.

Tools of Prestige

If you seek to build prestige by testimonials, endorsements, awards, make sure they are believable and real. Effective publicity in prestige media is another good way of achieving prestige for services or products. Tie-in promotions of nationally advertised brand name merchandise can bring prestige. The manufacturer who omits window and store displays, point-of-purchase and cooperative advertising, and the retailer or service firm that doesn't employ such aids in full, are missing some of selling's best prestige-making tools.

As to use of the quality appeal, remember that, except where real savings are offered on standard price-fixed items, price is the one factor most customers dislike about shopping. Yet so many salespeople repeatedly open with "how much," rather than "here's what this item or service will do for you." To sell quality, you must be able to demonstrate it in terms the customer seeks, expressed or unexpressed. Often, however, explanations are so technical that the customer can't sense the advantage. In fact, our studies proved that in case after case customers, seeing a specific technological claim made for one brand, attributed it to another within 15 minutes. Looking for the little things which denote quality isn't easy. One investigation for the Kwick-Set Lock Company of California showed that home buyers are apt to judge quality less by important basic construction than by hardware and locks. Publicizing its motivational findings, Kwick-Set increased sales to builders. A study for General Motors proved that, realistic or not, it was the "feel" prospects got from slamming doors that made them believe one car to be a quality product, another "tinny" or cheap.

Astute garment manufacturers have learned that women often judge quality by buttonholes or hem depth. And in the men's field, hand-picked stitching on the collar, pearl buttons, non-stick zippers often create the belief that the rest of the item must be of similar quality.

Sometimes quality can be demonstrated by telling how your product is produced. Univis Lens Company, Dayton, for example, skipped nuts-and-bolts details, of interest only to technicians, concentrated on convincing ultimate wearers how each production step meant additional quality for their own benefit. And Luchow's, famed New York restaurant, discovered how one little difference can put across a quality idea: When it began serving a few diners beer in old-world pewter steins instead of glasses, people at other tables immediately asked for the same. Luchow's was happy to oblige—and beer sales have foamed up 40 per cent.

22. OPPORTUNITIES FOR PERSUASION *

by Edward C. Bursk †

It is helpful to know the limits of persuasion: to realize that gains in motivation research techniques are accompanied by gains in individuals' discernment and ability to resist; and to learn that it is difficult, if not impossible, to exert mass control of people through subconscious manipulation. Raymond A. Bauer's article makes this clear.[1] But there is another

* Reprinted from the *Harvard Business Review,* © September–October 1958, pp. 111–19.

† Graduate School of Business Administration, Harvard University.

[1] Raymond A. Bauer, "Limits of Persuasion," *Harvard Business Review,* September–October 1958, pp. 105–10.

way of looking at persuasion—at its opportunities rather than its limitations, particularly when it is practiced openly and rationally.

In fact, I think it can be argued that psychological limitations come into operation only to the extent that persuasion is misapplied. Resistance may be a reaction to attempts at persuasion; however, persuasion does not always produce resistance. I have seen plenty of instances where persuasion is effective largely because it reduces resistance. Sometimes buyers even take positive delight in being sold. And then other times they react unfavorably to too much persuasion or too little persuasion or the wrong kind of persuasion.

What is the right amount and kind of persuasion? That is a difficult question, since different ideas (or different products and brand features) have different reaction factors in people's minds. The potentialities for securing acceptance, as well as the difficulties of overcoming resistance, vary over a wide range. So it is useful to have the clearest possible understanding of why consumers buy or do not buy.

Consumer Motivations

The mistake is to think that knowing consumer motivations means being able to shape them to specific ends, such as getting people to go out and buy a particular product or reach for this brand in preference to that brand. I claim that persuasion is more a matter of strategy than of manipulation; that it is a process of arraying logical forces so that people themselves decide to do what you want them to, rather than of actually changing people's minds; and that any effort to get action by tampering with people's emotions not only runs up against the psychological limitations of resistance but also can be prohibitively time-consuming and expensive.

The way a seller deploys his forces depends of course on the buyer's forces, which include his motives. So the seller needs to take the buyer's motives into account in order to outmaneuver him and get him to move in the desired direction. Here is where the opportunities are; and ironically, they will not be realized until the new motivation research knowledge which makes them such opportunities is reduced to its proper, limited role. I feel it is important to make this crystal-clear before going on to tackle the problem of constructing strategies.

Decision vs. Diagnosis

It is always a temptation for managers to abdicate the functions of analysis and decision-making when some "magical" technique promises to do the work for them. The new techniques we are learning from the mathematical and behaviorial sciences do provide a stronger basis of information for understanding situations on which action is to be taken, and more accurate devices for measuring the results of action once it has been taken; but they cannot prescribe action. Moreover, even for those purposes, management itself must think through its problems, formulate its specific needs, and make explicit its purposes; otherwise the techniques are likely to be pointless, and only fruitful by accident. So it is good to be reminded that motivation research, with all its ballyhoo, is far from providing the "answers" to everything.

The very existence of limitations adds a positive opportunity. Managers should be glad that they must work with imperfect tools—for then other managers, in competing companies, will face the same impossibility of securing perfect results, and the premium will be to those who use the tools more skillfully. Indeed, it is the essence of aggressive management to take up imperfect tools and *make* them work! And the fact that the availability of new techniques may reduce the range of decision-making simply means that, in the narrowing area where judgment and initiative *are* still needed, the effect of relative degree of skill is magnified: the more costly are the mistakes, and the greater is the edge over competitors gained by correct decisions.

So, as we now turn our attention to the *opportunities* for persuasion, the clue is that, however valuable the new research techniques may be for purposes of diagnosis, they are inept for decision-making. It is management that must do the creative part of the selling job. This applies both to products and to ideas; but I shall carry the discussion forward in terms of products, since this area not only is important in its own right but serves to illustrate more concretely the principles that are involved.

Lessons of Experience

I do not think you can discount the lessons of experience. There are certain things that any man who has done much selling knows; he may not understand the reasons, but he can tell you what works. The points that I intend to make are drawn from observation of many salesmen's activities, including my own for a number of years. I have found that the advertising men who have been most successful in *selling* products (in the sense of building consumer demand or brand preference) also subscribe to the same general philosophy.

The fact that consumer motivation experts often disagree violently among themselves (particularly when it comes to recommending action based on their findings) does not make them wrong, but it certainly does not make me wrong in advocating a more direct and realistic view of selling, either. Indeed, it is because I recognize motives as being both so important and so difficult to deal with that I believe we need to approach selling from the practical viewpoint of strategy.

In short, I am convinced that the best way to sell is along the following lines:

It is normal and healthy for people to like to buy, just as it is abnormal and unhealthy for them to dislike to buy; and in selling we should deal with people as if we expected them to be normal and healthy rather than in need of mental hygiene—or at least predominantly on that side of the balance, so they have it *in their own power* to resolve any emotional conflict over buying.

Whether the urge to buy is realized and/or any resistance is overcome depends on management's selling efforts (both on the broad economic scale and for individual companies); and more effort—just plain effort—may be almost as important as new skill.

The way for management to secure the desired results is to employ a strategy that makes use of our best understanding of the psychology of the selling-buying relationship—both as to specific motivations in different situations and, even more important, as to the general phenomenon of people wanting to buy, yet being wary of pressure or trickery, which applies in all situations.

The essence of such a strategy would be to minimize resistance and maximize the urge to buy through selling conducted on the *rational* level—namely, planning and presenting rational goals for people which will lead them to the particular product or brand, in such a way that they satisfy their motivations and even act as their own psychiatrists in the event of any conflict.

Selling of this kind is more effective than deliberate attempts at psychological influencing because it is more in line with the needs and capacities of salesmen, advertising copy writers, and top management; it is more likely to be psychologically sound for the mass of people on the buying end of the relationship; and so secures greater results at less expense.

Apart from the efficiency of the strategy, intensification of selling efforts along lines like these furthers the long-run objectives of both business and society; for it both serves to keep the economy dynamic and contributes to the standard of living of normal, healthy people.

If these concepts hold—and I think those people who have had much firsthand experience in selling would heartily agree—then it is possible to construct a simple (but intensive) strategy for a particular product in a particular market which will handle the complexity and subtlety of the particular motivations involved. In trying to "sell" my ideas in this article I shall make use of some of the same kind of direct, enthusiastic drive.

Urge and Resistance

It hardly needs to be demonstrated that people like to buy. There is a sheer enjoyment in acquiring things, which goes far back to primitive roots. The act of buying is an expression of power, of mastery. Also, people generally like to be nice to people; and if the other person is a salesman, then the inclination is to be nice to him—and the way to be nice to a salesman is to buy from him.

Now, as I understand it, the person who is normal and healthy minded tends to do what society approves of. The purchase of goods and services —not just food and clothing but education, and not just *a* car but a car *of modern fashion*—is part and parcel of our way of life. And it is not only socially right to buy certain kinds of individual products and services; it also is right to buy lots of things in general. Indeed, this is how people's success is usually measured—as individuals or as families, in their own self-opinion or in the eyes of society. Or, at least, this is how *most* people feel, which is what counts.

So there is a positive urge to buy—to buy in general and to buy specific products. But there is also a negative counterforce that can cause resistance —resistance in general and resistance to specific purchases. Right now we are concerned with the general dimensions—with the underlying strategy (which of course then has to be adapted to more specific motivations).

Underlying Strategy

Just as it is socially acceptable to buy, so it is *not* socially acceptable to *overbuy,* that is, to the point where a person appears reckless, improvident, a poor manager of his finances; or to buy *unwisely,* that is, without due regard for price and quality. Admittedly, these are vague terms; in fact they shift with time, and at any one time mean different things to different people. But the idea that there is a point beyond which it is not right to buy is nonetheless very real in every individual's mind, and people are uneasy lest they go beyond it without realizing they are doing so. As far as sellers are concerned, it is the existence of the resistance that is important, not the particular shading of individual buyers' ideas. It will always be operative, and strategy must be pointed to overcome it regardless of how strong it is.

Thus, no matter what that shading, there is the one, single, and over-all fact that for every selling situation the buyer must have some self-approved reason for saying *yes*—whether the affirmation is in terms of handing over the money or signing on the dotted line, or just feeling agreement with an advertising message. For example, a man may want to buy a new car because it is new and sleek and shiny, but he also needs some rationalization like "I'll get a better trade-in if I buy now." Or a woman may want a particular brand of soap because she thinks it will make her seductive to all mankind, but she also must be able to think something like: "If I look prettier, my husband will be pleased"; or more simply, "It will protect my skin"; or still more simply, "It cleans."

This is why it sometimes is difficult for a salesman to close a sale, even though the prospect may seem favorably disposed: the right kind of rationalization has not been offered, even though the actual motivation for buying may have been amply satisfied. The same thing is true in direct-mail selling; a man may want to subscribe to a magazine because it makes him feel important, but the promotional piece must also assure him that by filling out and mailing the subscription order form he will receive some practical help in improving his professional skills or solving his business problems.

I am convinced this is also true in advertising; that of two ads, both of which apply to a product mainly bought for *irrational* reasons, the one that provides in addition some cogent *rational* reason should produce a stronger reaction than the one that does not. I suspect that one explanation of why the combination of an advertising appeal to the image of masculinity *and* a new crush-proof box worked so well for Marlboro cigarettes is that the box offered a generally acceptable rationalization.

Rational *vs.* Irrational

I should like to rescue the terms *rational* and *irrational* from the confusion they seem to have fallen into. If applied carefully, they pose a distinction that can be very useful for selling and advertising:

Rational applies to reasons for buying (or not buying) which are *self-approved*—that is, which the buyer feels to be right and reasonable because they are in line with his own expectations of himself as a thinking man and/or his understanding of what other people (society) would consider to be right and reasonable on the part of a thinking man.

By the same token, *irrational* applies to reasons for buying (or for not buying) which are *not* self-approved and socially acceptable, as just defined.

Not that a buyer thinks this all out, or ever formulates it explicitly, but as a result of all his experiences and the current mores of society he just feels some reasons are "all right" for him, and others are not. Completely independent of this distinction is the distinction between conscious and unconscious, or between economic and noneconomic. The trouble is that the terms do sometimes coincide—e.g., *irrational* with *unconscious, economic* with *rational,* and so on—and that is why a careless tendency to equate them has developed.

True, rational reasons are more *likely* to be conscious than reasons which are not self-approved, because there is no cause for shame or anxiety about them and hence no tendency to push them into the unconscious. This is fortunate, because it means that rational motives are that much easier to identify for selling strategy. However, the fact remains that rational motives *can* be unconscious, particularly when conflicting motives toward a purchase are involved, as in this example:

A man may want to buy a new labor-saving device for his wife, but be very concerned about the money outlay. Prudence in spending money is a rational motive, but the man also likes to think of himself as being good to his wife. So what does he do? He finds fault with the machinery of the proposed new washing machine (or whatever it is)—and does not admit to his wife *or to himself* that a technical defect is *not* the real reason, and he is simply holding back because he doesn't feel right about spending the money.

Even more important, a rational motive may apply also to noneconomic or intangible values, *if* it is self-approved. Most men would consider it reasonable that a man should buy helpful things for his wife, as in the example just cited; the fact that he and society think that it is one of his responsibilities makes it reasonable—even though it may be a self-pleasure, too. Similarly, in this sense, it is rational to want to live in a good neighborhood, to have a modern-style car, to own a television set.

In fact, one of the great buying phenomena of modern times is the way it became almost obligatory to buy a television set so the children of a family could hold their own in their relationships with other children—an intangible but very rational reason. My interpretation is that people already strongly desired TV sets for unapproved, selfish reasons, and it was the overwhelming availability of a good rational reason for justifying the purchase which triggered the buying wave. (Note that the same combination of circumstances does not apply to *color* TV, which has of course not swept in anywhere near so readily.)

It is because of the overlapping of terms that it is absolutely essential to have a separate concept, like rationality, which makes a clear-cut distinction between what is approved and what is not approved, and thus pinpoints the crucial factor in selling strategy. To illustrate:

Suppose a man honestly wants to buy a small car for the sake of economy, but he is afraid he will look like an odd-ball. So he pretends, to the rest of the world *and to himself,* that he is thinking of how easy it will be for his wife to park. Being kind to the weaker sex is his only course; he cannot follow the economic motive because it is not self-approved. At this time and in this neighborhood there is something wrong with a man who doesn't have a big car like everybody else's.

But what is socially acceptable is always changing, and we will do well to keep this in mind as market researchers report "changing" consumer preferences. In fact, I wonder if some of the "changes" recently reported may not simply be due to differences in the freedom with which consumers feel they can *talk* about specific products and advertisements. Thus, in certain regions of the country it now is beginning to be popular to *boast* about the economies offered by small cars.

This does not mean that economy is becoming a more important motive than it used to be. It only means that here and there economy is becoming an accepted or self-approved reason for buying a small car. And the key to understanding the difference between the new and the old situation is not in whether motives have become more or less conscious or more or less economic, but in that change of rationality.

Cause and Effect

We must recognize, too, that a rationalization often is nothing more than a convenient reason for action that actually reflects other motives. To illustrate:

I would agree that it is rational for a woman to patronize a supermarket or a discount house for the sake of economy, but I would argue that this is not altogether her real reason. Certainly she is also influenced by her desire to *appear* (to herself and to the world) as a careful buyer or a shrewd bargainer— perhaps even more so than by her desire for actual money savings. And if she does *not* patronize such outlets, she can always find equally rational reasons— "The meats are so much better where I shop"; or, "They stand back of their products at my store."

There is no doubt that, no matter how rational people pretend to be, very often they buy (or do not buy) things for irrational reasons. But it does not follow that the best way to sell them is by appeals to those irrational motives. The very fact that people insist on devising some rationalization for themselves suggests that it may be effective to supply them with a strong rational reason, so they can follow their irrational bent to the seller's product more surely and speedily. On the other hand, it may actually be ineffective to use irrational appeals because they have more difficulty in securing positive attention rather than just momentary, vague reaction; or, if they do get across, only serve to point out motives the buyer cannot be proud of as the thinking man he wants to be.

There is much discussion these days about brand images and consumers' self-images. I am sure this is a useful way of *describing* relationships between product and buyer, but not necessarily of *creating* such relationships. Is a brand image the cause of buying, or just the effect of selling? Is a self-image a coherent unit, or just a bundle of unsorted, unweighed, and unweighable motivations? Whether behavioral scientists can answer these questions or not, a large part of the job of making the brand image fit the consumer's self-image can be done, and may have to be done, at the rational level. After all, one of the biggest components of a person's self-image is the picture of himself as a reasonable, thinking man.

I know I am doing injustice to the scope and subtlety of psychological analysis, but such oversimplification is basic to the construction of efficient selling strategy. I am convinced that, *no matter what else is done or what other motivations are involved,* to close a sale or make a telling advertising impression the buyer *must* be given a self-approved reason for purchasing the product or preferring the brand. And, as we shall see subsequently, there is still plenty of opportunity, and indeed need, for understanding just what the specific motivations are in specific situations, and whether they are in fact rational or irrational.

Out in the Open

It is on the score of the general dimensions of urge and resistance that I advocate more open selling. People are hard to fool—increasingly so. But there is not just the danger that sly selling will be detected and boomerang —thus ruining that particular attempt *and* impairing all other, more honest attempts. Rather, the trouble is that such selling may be inefficient because it does not make use of the *positive* effect of openly helping people to buy.

Certainly, any apprehension on the part of buyers that someone is trying to sell them something without letting them know it and giving them a fair chance to make their own buying decisions will create almost insurmountable resistance. By the same token, selling that does not try to hide itself or pretend to be something different is reassuring—so long, of course, as it does not go over to the opposite extreme of pushing people to buy through blatant high-pressure techniques, which again will make them feel they do not have a chance to make their own decisions *on the rational basis that is so necessary to them.* There is as much difference between high-pressure selling and good low-pressure selling [2]—open, purposeful, low-pressure selling—as there is between such open selling and hidden selling.

Positive Selling

People expect that a seller who has something to sell will want to sell it; that is rooted in our culture. Further, they respect sellers who have enthusiasm for their products; that too is natural. Indeed it is cause for alarm, and thus for resistance, if a seller apparently is *not* convinced he has a good product. And since the essence of the low-pressure technique is to present the product as the solution to some problem or need of the buyer, the more purposeful the approach, the more the buyer feels he counts.

It is criminal waste of the buyer's own self-interest not to use it to lead him to the product or the brand. Actually, he is likely to be happier if he is so led. I have observed many selling situations where a hopeless seller lost sales while a hopeful buyer in fact wanted to be persuaded to buy. For example:

A middle-aged couple came into an appliance store, asked about a color TV set, and in general showed by the models they looked at and the remarks they made that, without realizing it, they had already made up their minds to spend

[2] See Edward C. Bursk, "Low-Pressure Selling," *Harvard Business Review,* Winter 1947, p. 227; "Thinking Ahead: Drift to No-Pressure Selling," *Harvard Business Review,* September–October 1956, p. 25.

a large amount of money. But every time they raised a question about price, the salesman quickly exhibited a cheaper model, not realizing that what they were asking for was not a better bargain but some assurance there was a rational reason for them to pay the amount in question.

At least three times they were on the verge of saying, "We'll take it." At least three times the salesman lost them by not trying to sell them. They left the store without buying. Although they said—and by this time perhaps thought —that they could not afford the money for one of the small sets, it was obvious that they were completely unhappy because they had not been sold the big set they really wanted.[3]

In Advertising Too

Again, I think this idea also applies to advertising. To illustrate from the extreme: off-beat copy themes which deprecate the product, or act coy or cute, have proved singularly ineffective. Sometimes they achieve some temporary success just because they attract attention by their oddity, but usually people resent the lack of dignity; sellers who take justifiable pride in their products could not possibly talk or think like that.

If anything, the need for open selling is even greater in advertising, which has to depend on fleeting impressions amid the competition of a multitude of sights and sounds. People have developed a defense mechanism against even noticing ads which do not bear on some problem or want they already have in some degree. Today a picture of a refrigerator and a headline of a new feature will attract the attention of those who are refrigerator-minded, while the John-loves-Mary theme where the refrigerator only comes in subsequently is literally passed by.[4] It makes sense that people will see or hear the message that speaks to them in the terms of their own specific everyday interests—and one of the most important of these is the buying of specific products or services. So why not at least try to make a definite selling impact?

The utmost in waste of good dollars and glossy paper would seem to be the nonselling that is characteristic of much advertising of industrial products or services. It may be true that here the burden is on the salesman in the field; but even in the secondary role of seeking inquiries or paving the way for the salesman, the message will come through stronger if it has at least enough "sell" to be pointed specifically and purposefully to the prospective buyer's problems. Why waste the opportunity to do some selling, when that must have more meaning to the buyer than any dull "institutional" generalizations?

[3] Reported in "Northeastern Distributors, Inc., Recording—Part II," a case prepared and copyrighted, 1954, by Harbridge House, Inc., Cambridge, Massachusetts.
[4] See Richard D. Crisp, "Thinking Ahead: Advertising Research," *Harvard Business Review*, March–April 1953, p. 30.

Increased Effort

Even if sellers and advertisers do not sharpen their skills, just doing more selling can be effective because it is actually in line with the general psychology of the buying-selling situation. Indeed, many sellers may be so far short of utilizing the full potential of their present selling approaches that *initially* they can gain more by straightforward increase in effort than by putting the same amount of money and time into new skills. There is a *continuing* gain, too. Increased effort usually brings about a clearer focus on buyers' motivations; it helps the seller to seek the right course instinctively, and so to improve the skill of his selling.

In sum, when a seller approaches a buyer more purposefully, there are two results: (1) The effort itself has a general effect on the buyer's attitude that is favorable. (2) This in turn makes the buyer more receptive to sales strategy designed for the specific situation—and here is where increased skill has its greatest opportunity.

Singular Strategy

People's minds are complex, and every individual's self-image is different from every other individual's self-image. But selling must be a concentrated, focused action. One of the advantages of the open selling just discussed is that it provides a general setting in which the individual—any and every healthy individual—will tend to move himself toward the purchase—any and every approved purchase. Now, it is also possible to take another big step to lead the customer toward the purchase of specific goods and services. It is possible to devise a singular strategy which will be effective in a plural market—plural in the sense of many individuals, and also in the sense that each individual has multiple, varying, and even conflicting motives.

Not that all products or services will have the same strategy. Far from it; each will be different, and this is why it is so important to know what particular motives are involved. So it is wise to make the best possible use of consumer motivation experts. The only question is: "What is the best possible use?" and I do not intend to go into that.[5]

But let me note, just so it does not get left out of the picture, that a good common-sense analysis of consumer motives is much better than nothing, can be better sometimes than a *poor* expert approach, and always is a helpful check against the findings of the social scientists. Let me also note that beyond the *fairly elementary point* of identifying the major motives involved, further research is likely to be marginal for the purpose under

[5] See Joseph W. Newman, "Working With Behavioral Scientists," *Harvard Business Review*, July–August 1958, p. 67.

discussion here; the essence of the singular strategy is a single, central motive (or core of closely related motives), and it therefore avails little to know all the subsidiary, marginal motives in detail.

However—and this is important—that "fairly elementary point" calls for *much more* analysis and investigation than the usual seller employs. It is all too easy to assume that consumers are logical rather than psychological —and especially that they are logical with the seller's identical logic. They just may happen to have their own way of thinking and feeling. So there is always danger that without the stimulus of an objective, inquiring point of view the seller can overlook some *important* motive that could make or break the whole strategy. In selling there must be nothing taken "for granted"—or somebody else will do the taking "for real," such as a competitor out after the same consumers' dollars.

Design for Buying

Once the motivations are known, the design of the strategy is simple: the seller concentrates on the strongest (or most effectively communicable) *rational* buying motive for the particular consumers he plans to sell to. This is calculated to work in all possible combinations of urge and resistance, on the theory that in every instance where there are reasons both for buying and for not buying the most effective procedure is to maximize the urge and/or minimize the resistance. Thus:

Suppose there is a rational buying motive in your favor and no real resistance beyond the routine desire to be sure to make a good buy—as, for example, when a man honestly wants a car that will provide the most economical transportation to work. You just plow ahead and sell—you just demonstrate to him that your car will give him that transportation, reinforcing his existing rational motive.

But suppose the prospect's buying urge is irrational—as, for example, in the case of the "sexy" convertible mentioned by Bauer.[6] You do not aim at the irrational motive. It is in your favor, so why tamper with it? Why run the danger of making the prospect aware of his irrationality (or wickedness, if a sexual drive is in fact operative here), stirring up a conflict in his mind, and actually causing resistance? You just give him a strong rational reason to latch onto—service, trade-in, or sunshine and health—and free his already existing urge to lead him to it.

If, however, there is a strong negative reason present, the problem becomes more subtle. Go back a few years in imagination to the days when the automatic washing machine was first introduced; and take the case of a woman who wants to buy one for the straightforward reason that it will make life easier for her, but for whom this is not a self-approved reason. Moreover, such motivation is sharply in conflict with her unconscious picture of herself as a

---

[6] *Op. cit.,* p. 108.

martyr to drudgery. She hesitates to ask for the product—that is, to ask her husband for it and/or even to ask *herself* for it; hence, resistance.

There are two possible courses of action here: (1) You can present a rational reason that will give strength to her irrational desire for a joyful Monday—such as "washes clothes cleaner" or "less harmful to fabrics"— which will overcome the irrational resistance, and off she will go (with her husband) to buy it. This is just about what happened, and it happened quickly. (2) You also can try to change the non-self-approved to self-approved—in other words, to make it rational. This is a longer, slower process, yet by now I suspect that hundreds of advertisers promoting hundreds of appliances have actually made labor saving for the housewife quite respectable.

The difficulty is compounded when there is no strong motivation already existent and working for you. Negative reasons become correspondingly more significant. If the resistance is on the rational side, it can usually be met rationally. Most rational objections, if anticipated and met head-on, can be turned to advantage by a good salesman operating on the rational level.

This is particularly true in business selling. In the case of a storekeeper hesitating to buy because he has a heavy inventory, the strategy is to show him that the turnover rate of the new product will decrease his investment per dollar of sales. Or, in the case of industrial equipment purchases, the quality or service features that add to price can almost always be translated into long-run dollar savings.

The toughest situation of all is where the cause of resistance is irrational. Usually, it will be expressed rationally, and no amount of meeting the prospect on this ground will change the picture. Even if you win the argument, he simply will shift from one meaningless position to another.

The surest course is, again, the long-run one of changing the irrationality of the resistance to rationality—making it socially acceptable, and thus self-approved. Take this situation: people may hesitate to make more long-distance telephone calls because of a feeling of uneasiness engendered by association with sickness, death, emergency, delayed arrival, and other unpleasant news conveyed by such calls—although they usually explain their reluctance on the ground of expensiveness. This may be one of those situations where irrational resistance is unconscious just because it is irrational and hence at odds with a person's picture of himself.

But the telephone companies by their advertising over a period of time have begun to make the telephoning of friends and members of the family appear a friendly, natural, constructive process—just witness the ease with which today's young people pick up the phone and place a call (usually collect). For the new generation it *is* rational.

My hunch is that this telephone advertising would have been still more effective if all mention of cost had been omitted. Even the claim that "it costs less than you think" calls attention to the fact that there is such a convenient rationalization for having an irrational feeling about long-distance calls. If so, this is a situation where only a long-range rational approach will make a good strategy; and an immediate rational appeal may actually reduce effectiveness. The moral is obvious: even though the selling strategy does not incorporate an irrational appeal, it is necessary to know that a strong irrational motivation is at work against you in order to select the proper rational approach. In other words, here is one more demonstration that motivation research does provide a valuable service when used for diagnostic purposes.

Of course, the strategy will vary for different markets; and where the market is made up of quite varied segments, each segment may have to have its own singular strategy. But, in general, there will be only one rational motive big enough to dominate the other forces involved. The appeals which are built around it may be manifold, but they represent the creative job of translating the motive into selling language, which is another question entirely.

Design for Selling

Note that in all the above examples a rational motive turns out to be the best vehicle for carrying the prospect to the purchase. It is assumed that the prospect will provide some exertion himself, but of course something has to be done to get him started. Now I want to show why basing appeals on a rational motive also provides the best mechanism for the salesman's *action,* so necessary to get the prospect off dead center and actually moving toward the purchase.

For one thing, the salesman can use the rational approach more easily. It is more simple for him to understand, more natural for him to plan, more direct for him to follow. Further, by concentrating on one goal for the prospect and moving toward it purposely, he is likely to end up with an attractive presentation. Since he is thinking in terms of a need or want, rather than a product feature or advantage, he is necessarily concentrating on the prospect as a human being with thoughts and feelings, and will therefore instinctively tend to act so as to *please* the prospect. (That may well be a safer way to get the help of irrational appeals than by deliberately trying to use them; if appropriate, they will come through in gestures, in choice of words, in art work, without undermining the rationality of the approach.)

The fact that the goal is a rational need or want is even more helpful. Since it is acceptable, it gives the salesman the self-respect and confidence he must have if he is to keep on selling. Since it makes sense, he does not become embarrassed or confused. Not being a trained psychologist, he can be very wrong if he tries to figure out all the nuances of irrational motivations; and, even if by chance he is right, he will act self-consciously, and spoil the sincerity that is so essential for good low-pressure selling.

Some of the same demands prevail in mass selling programs and advertising. Sales managers and advertising executives are likely to function more effectively—more spontaneously and more aggressively—if they set out to sell on the basis of the best rational motive and do not get all tangled up with hidden persuaders. The straightforward effort to sell will stimulate their thinking processes, and will add punch to their messages. For example:

The advertising firm of Doyle Dane Bernbach has been attracting much attention lately. It has built its billings to 20 million dollars in less than ten years, eschewing research and emphasizing copy. According to the agency president, William Bernbach, "We get people to look and listen by being good artists and writers. We don't expect of research what it is unable to do. It won't give you a great idea."

The agency stresses a simple but striking idea, a specific selling point. For bread: pictures of nibbled slices, and the message that "New York is eating it up." For an airline: a map of the Atlantic Ocean one-fifth torn away, and the message that "Starting December 23, the Atlantic Ocean will be twenty per cent smaller." And apparently clients have had big increases in sales.[7]

But there is an even more fundamental reason for depending on rational appeals if one is aiming for a plural market—as most sellers are, whether it be a specialized group or the mass market. Everybody's self-images or bundles of motives are a little different, and the trick is to pick an appeal that will best cover the particular market being sought—that will have great positive strength for most of the individuals, moderate to little weight for the balance (it is too much to expect 100 per cent aim), and no deterring effect on any. For these purposes a rational motivation usually serves best. Irrational wants and feelings are diverse and subtle, but rational desires are necessarily shared by a large part of the market since they reflect the norms and customs of society. By the same token, they are unlikely to restrict the market by any deterrent of embarrassment or confusion.

Conclusion

Most people have healthy minds; they like to buy. There is no need to dig into their subconscious to free them from blocks and tensions before they buy. (Indeed, such an effort may be dangerous—may stir up conflict without enough time or skill to remove it—something even psychiatrists worry about.) Irrational resistances, even if in the subconscious, can be handled by the healthy prospect himself—and *will* be, if he is provided with a sufficient *rational* motive as incentive.

But selling is not just satisfying present wants or playing up to old desires. Selling is a process of increasing wants, or even better, creating new wants. This is what keeps our economy dynamic. Further, the more business gets

[7] See *Time,* March 31, 1958, p. 78.

consumers to consider the pursuit of noneconomic values as approved and rational, the more it is building people's potential for a higher, less materialistic way of life. And it is up to education to see to it that consumers say *no* to the more meretricious forms of satisfaction.

The danger of consumer motivation research is that business may rely on "scientific" techniques and forget to go out and sell. As far as getting buying action is concerned, the actual psychological subtleties may just be too tenuous for the hit-and-run of daily life. But we can use our understanding of how people buy to build a lot of little strategies for persuading people to want specific products and services, and one grand strategy of giving people continually bigger and better goals for themselves.

In either case, there is one big, uncomplex psychology at work—the interaction of enthusiastic seller and eager buyer, out in the open where they belong. And whatever irrational forces there are will be released if they are in your favor, contained if they are against you. Such selling is not manipulating people behind their backs; it is giving them rational motives for doing what is in their own best interests as individuals and as society-at-large.

New Insights into Consumer Behavior

23. HOW MUCH THINKING BEFORE BUYING? *

by James K. Blake †

"Automatic repeat buying of the same brand is infrequent regardless of previous experience."

"There is hardly any difference between durable goods purchasers who bought at list price and those who felt they obtained a particularly favorable trade-in allowance. These two groups exhibited approximately the same degree of deliberation (before deciding to buy)."

Only one person in five remembered seeing advertisements about the product they bought and "two-thirds of all durable goods buyers could not recall seeing any advertisements or reading anything about the item they purchased."

A highly deliberate durable goods buyer is likely to have this background: He has been to college; he earns close to $5,000; he is a clerk or in sales; he is between twenty-one and thirty-four years old and he likes to shop around.

These findings and many others in a study made by the Survey Research Center at the University of Michigan will jar the nerves of a good many product designers, marketing executives, and advertising agencies. In "traditional" marketing theory, the consumer is supposed to indulge in impulse buying only for low-cost, fast-moving nondurables. When he spends a hundred dollars or more for a television set, a washing machine, a re-

* Reprinted from *Dun's Review and Modern Industry,* © August 1955, pp. 39–41.
† *Dun's Review and Modern Industry.*

frigerator, or a stove, he is expected to deliberate carefully, weigh alternatives, compare brands and product features, look in several price categories —in other words he is supposed to make a rational decision based on his requirements in relation to the products available.

But does he? According to George Katona, who is the Center's Program Director, "About one-fourth of the purchases of large household goods were found to lack practically all features of careful deliberation and many more exhibited only a limited number of such features."

To get these facts, interviewers were sent to a random sample of about 1,000 families living in all parts of the United States. At least one of the four durables had been purchased by 360 families during the preceding year. The sample was representative of durable goods buyers. The questions were a combination of fixed, direct questions so that replies could be compared and quantified and "open-ended" questions to uncover attitudes and opinions. Data were also collected on income, age, education, and the like. To compensate for the possibility of substantial sampling errors, the researchers analyzed only those findings where the chances were at least two to one that similar findings would reappear in a larger survey.

First of all, what are the components of "deliberation"? The study distinguishes five dimensions, elements in deliberate buying:

1. Extent of circumspectness. A long planning period, extensive family discussion, and consideration of alternatives to the purchase are part of this aspect of deliberation.

Only 51 per cent of durable goods purchasers spent more than two months thinking or talking about making the purchase. Moreover, 36 per cent of the consumers interviewed spent less than a month planning a major purchase! Researchers found that people who plan more than a few months (51 per cent) are divided into two equal groups: people who can't make up their minds or who are anxious to make a good buy, and those who waited for financial reasons and were not necessarily spending this period getting ready to make a shrewd purchase.

Surprising results came from answers to questions probing the extent of family discussion preceding an expensive, major durable good purchase. Roughly one family out of four engaged in extensive discussion—a similar number held no discussion at all.

Nearly 70 per cent of the buyers said they made the decision to buy without hesitating. The choice, in other words, among buying that particular product, buying something else, or simply saving their money was not difficult. Eva Mueller, who directed the study, points out that this particular aspect of circumspectness may be understated, because it is difficult for a person to recall some time after a purchase the nature and content of his doubts then.

2. Extent of information-seeking activity. Buyers were asked about ad-

vertisements, reading material such as newspaper articles, folders, mail order catalogs, reports of testing agencies, discussions with relatives and neighbors, visits to stores, and advice from salesmen.

As might be expected, the researchers found a wide variety of behavior, but several striking findings became apparent. "One-third of the durable goods buyers consulted only one source of information, and that not intensively, or they obtained no information whatsoever." The survey uncovered the fact that more than 50 per cent of durable goods buyers got advice from relatives and neighbors (the largest single information source) and a third of the buyers bought a brand or model they had seen at someone else's house.

The next important source of information was the store itself, or rather several stores. More than 40 per cent of the buyers surveyed went into more than one store to compare models and brands. Of greater significance for marketing executives, however, is the fact that 47 per cent visited only one store and bought before leaving!

In many respects the most astonishing aspect of consumers' information-seeking activities is their lack of conscious response to printed material. Only 20 per cent of durable goods buyers remembered reading advertisements about the product they bought. The researchers comment: "Unless one has an active interest in the purchase of one of these durables (refrigerator, stove, TV, or washing machine), the advertisements may do nothing more than maintain a vague awareness of brand names. The question was whether, several months after the purchase, people remembered having paid attention to advertisements or other reading materials. The chances are that a positive answer was given to this question only where the information received was salient to the purchase decision." If this analysis is substantially correct, about 20 per cent of durable goods buyers receive salient information from advertisements.

For the buyers as a group, one key clue sticks out. The personality type who goes to friends and relatives seeking information about his projected purchase will usually consult other sources of information in addition before making a decision. And persons who do not consult that basic source are less likely to consult others.

The researchers have a strong suspicion, therefore, that information seeking is a cumulative process. For instance, people who reported that they knew what they wanted from the beginning might be expected to look around less than those people who did not know what they wanted, mainly because the first group presumably already had enough data to satisfy itself. The survey revealed, nonetheless, that the two groups were very similar, with the group that knew what it wanted from the outset being somewhat more active than the group which had not made up its mind! Apparently learning a little creates a desire to know more.

3. Choosing with respect to price. The underlying assumption here was that one aspect of careful deliberation involved seeking price information. A deliberate buyer compares a product in several price ranges before purchasing. Discount buying, or sale buying, showed deliberation only if the interviewer found that comparisons had been made. Over half of all buyers did not choose between models in more than one price range. And only 14 per cent considered models both higher and lower priced than the one they purchased.

4. This index distinguished between people who knew what brand they wanted from the beginning and people who considered a large number of brands. A previous question had determined that more than 90 per cent of the buyers interviewed knew the brand name of their new refrigerator, TV set, or washing machine, and 82 per cent knew the brand name of their stove. With brand consciousness well established, direct questioning brought out the fact that only one-third of durable goods buyers limit their attention to a single brand and an equal proportion said their choice at the outset had been wide open. Nearly 20 per cent choose among only two or three brands.

5. The final index was premised on the fact that a deliberate buyer considers many more product features than a casual buyer. Not many consumers measure up to this aspect of deliberation; in fact, only about 35 per cent of durable goods buyers consider more than one feature of the product other than price and brand. With the increasing emphasis upon color and styling and "human engineering" in the design of consumer durables, it is surprising to note that only 13 per cent of all buyers surveyed mentioned appearance as a major consideration. Brand, mechanical properties, and size were the features most commonly mentioned, although 39 per cent (the largest single grouping) of consumers claimed they had no particular features in mind. There is room for considerable speculation in the small percentage (only 2) of consumers who mentioned durability, servicing, guarantees, and reliability as being features they were looking for in durable goods. Only 10 per cent of the buyers even remembered receiving information about these features from printed material or from sales personnel.

What picture emerges when these five indexes are related to each other? First of all, there is a strong relationship between the extent of a consumer's circumspectness (defined under "1") and the degree of information seeking he exercises. Only 9 per cent of those people who were very circumspect, for instance, engaged in no information gathering at all. Moreover, people who were very circumspect were likely to choose among two or more price levels and on the basis of more product features than people who were not circumspect.

The correlation among the three indexes of choosing (brand, price, number of features) was surprisingly weak. Roughly a quarter of the buyers scored at the top on one index, but at the bottom on one or both of the others. The research team defined this situation as "feature substitution" and decided that these buyers either substituted thorough consideration of one attribute of the product for concern with other features, or else were in a situation where their interest in one feature precluded interest in other aspects of a balanced buying decision. If he wants only one price range, for instance, he doesn't bother to look at other models, other features in other price classes.

Combining all of these indexes into a master deliberation index leads to the conclusion that "Any notion that careful planning and choosing, thorough consideration of alternatives, and information seeking accompanied every major purchase was contradicted by the data for each of the four durables. Rather, it appeared that there were great differences among buyers and that many purchases were made in a state of ignorance, or at least indifference."

Another impliction of this type of research on purchasing decisions is that the time is coming when more expensive and larger scale studies will be able to furnish quantified accurate, pinpointed consumer information custom tailored to a product's market. This relatively small study, for instance, suggests that the segment of the population in greatest need of product information are the least likely to look for it. Information seeking increases with education and income up to about the $7,500 bracket. Among durable goods buyers with a grammar-school education and incomes under $3,000, those who neglected to look for product information outnumber active information seekers by about seven to one. And 13 per cent of those who went only to grade school obtained salient information from advertisements as compared with 23 per cent of the college educated consumers.

An old stereotype in marketing clung to by some executives is that the farm and rural market must be handled differently from the suburban and city market. The Survey Research Center's findings lend further emphasis to the argument that the automobile and mass media are making the national market more homogeneous. They discovered that information-seeking was only slightly more active in metropolitan areas than in rural counties and that there was no noticeable difference between medium-sized cities and rural communities.

The study, in fact, challenged a number of seemingly logical marketing concepts. For instance, one might expect that people who buy on credit would be more deliberate than those who pay cash. The survey showed that, although cash buyers were "somewhat" more active information seekers than installment buyers, there was no difference in their degree of circumspectness. Another apparently sound marketing observation might be that the older the consumer, the more deliberate and careful the purchase. Actually, this applies only to around age thirty-four. After this, the "motivation to use financial resources to best advantage becomes weaker. . . ."

Nine Tables Chart Buying Characteristics

Price not an important feature
Question: "Before you started to look for a _____, did you have any clear idea about what you were looking for, or didn't you? What kinds of ideas did you have?"

Types of Features	% of Buyers
Price	6
Brand	21
Mechanical properties	21
Performance	9
Size or capacity	19
Appearance	13
Durability, servicing, guarantees, reliability	2
Operating costs	1
Other	3
No specific features	39
Not ascertained	3
All Cases	*

* More than 100 per cent because some customers mentioned more than one feature.

A little or no family discussion
Question: "Did you discuss what kind of _____ you should buy in your family—at length, only a little, or not at all?"

	% of Buyers
Extensive family discussion	27
A little family discussion	44
No family discussion at all	27
Not ascertained	2
All Cases	100

Information from friends and relatives

Question: "Before buying, did you talk with friends, relatives, or neighbors about different kinds of _____, a lot, a little, or not at all?"

	% of Buyers
Extensive discussion	17
A little discussion	37
No discussion	43
Not ascertained	3
All Cases	100

How much brand switching?

Question: "What brand or make was it? What brand was your old _____?"

	% All Previous Owners
Purchased same brand	22
Different brand	67
Don't know *	8
Not ascertained	3
All Cases	100

* Study comments, "Chances are that most of these people were not brand conscious and bought a different brand."

How long do people think before buying?

Question: "Could you tell me how long you were thinking or talking about buying a _____ before you actually bought it?"

Planning Period	% of Buyers
Several years	8
One or two years	13
Several months	30
One or two months	9
A few weeks	19
A few days	13
One day or less	4
Not ascertained	4
All Cases	100

Little choice exercised on price
Question: "Before deciding on the _____ you bought, did you also consider
_____'s which cost much more or much less than the one you bought?"

	% of Buyers
Considered also more expensive models than the one purchased	16
Considered also less expensive models than the one purchased	9
Considered both	14
Considered only models in one price area	57
Not ascertained	4
All Cases	100

Not much help from reading material
Question: "Did you follow any advertisements or did you read anything else
about _____'s before you bought?"

	% of Buyers
Said they obtained information from reading material	33
Advertisements, circulars	21 *
Magazines, newspaper articles	12
Reports of testing agencies	3
Mail order catalogs	2
Other	6
Said they did not obtain information from reading material	62
Not ascertained	5
All Cases	100

* This column adds to more than 33 per cent because 11 per cent of the respondents got information from two or more types.

Percentage Distribution of Buyers Along Over-All Deliberation Scale

	Four Large Household Goods	TV	Refrigerator	Washing Machine	Stove
Highly deliberate (21–19 points)	*	—	1	—	—
(18–16 points)	6	8	6	3	2
(15–13 points)	14	14	9	16	9
(12–10 points)	21	25	19	21	18
(9– 7 points)	22	22	13	21	38
Nondeliberate (6– 4 points)	15	12	25	13	9
(3– 0 points)	7	6	10	12	4
Not ascertained	15	13	17	14	20
All cases	100%	100%	100%	100%	100%
Number of cases	360	164	87	72	55

* Less than one-half of 1 per cent.

When the purchase decisions of durable good consumers are evaluated according to an intricate set of criteria on a scale ranging from zero to 21, only 20 per cent of all buyers can be called careful purchasers. These people plan, consider alternatives, seek product information, check into a number of different product features, and then reconsider alternatives. For them, a purchase is a problem to be solved.

Nearly half of all durable goods buyers purchase more casually or less intensively than the group above. This group also includes people who deliberate intensively on a few aspects of the purchase, but in so doing ignore other important facets of well-balanced consideration.

This group doesn't seem to care. They buy quickly, don't hesitate on price, brand, or model. In some cases, they seemed to interviewers to be downright indifferent and apathetic. They do little or no information seeking, have no strong motivation to make the right decision.

Few stores before buying new durables
Question: "Did you go to several stores, or to two or three stores, or just to the one where you bought, or none?"

	% of Buyers
Several stores	26
Two or three	15
Only one where bought	47
No stores at all	11
Not ascertained	1
All Cases	100

Brand consciousness limits choice
Question: "Did you know from the beginning what make you wanted, or did you think about two or three brands, or was it a wide-open choice?"

	% of Buyers
Knew from beginning	33
Considered two or three	18
Wide-open choice	31
Paid no attention	6
Not ascertained, inapplicable	12
All Cases	100

24. SOCIAL CLASSES AND SPENDING BEHAVIOR *

by Pierre Martineau †

All societies place emphasis on some one structure which gives form to the total society and integrates all the other structures such as the family, the clique, voluntary association, caste, age, and sex groupings into a social unity.

Social stratification means any system of ranked statuses by which all

* Reprinted from *The Journal of Marketing,* © October 1958, pp. 121–30.
† Chicago Tribune.

the members of a society are placed in some kind of a superordinate and subordinate hierarchy. While money and occupation are important in the ranking process, there are many more factors, and these two alone do not establish social position. The concept of social class was designed to include this process of ranking people in superior and inferior social position by any and all factors.

Class System

It has been argued that there cannot be a class system existent in America when most individuals do not have the slightest idea of its formal structure. Yet in actuality every individual senses that he is more at home with and more acceptable to certain groups than to others. In a study of department stores and shopping behavior, it was found that the lower-status woman is completely aware that, if she goes into high-status department stores, the clerks and the other customers in the store will punish her in various subtle ways.

"The clerks treat you like a crumb," one woman expressed it. After trying vainly to be waited on, another woman bitterly complained that she was loftily told, "We thought you were a clerk."

The woman who is socially mobile gives considerable thought to the external symbols of status, and she frequently tests her status by shopping in department stores which she thinks are commensurate with her changing position. She knows that, if she does not dress correctly, if she does not behave in a certain manner to the clerks, if she is awkward about the proper cues, then the other customers and the clerks will make it very clear that she does not belong.

In another study, very different attitudes in the purchase of furniture and appliances involving this matter of status were found. Middle-class people had no hesitancy in buying refrigerators and other appliances in discount houses and bargain stores because they felt that they could not "go wrong" with the nationally advertised names. But taste in furniture is much more elusive and subtle because the brand names are not known; and, therefore, one's taste is on trial. Rather than commit a glaring error in taste which would exhibit an ignorance of the correct status symbols, the same individual who buys appliances in a discount house generally retreats to a status store for buying furniture. She needs the support of the store's taste.

In a very real sense, every one of us in his consumption patterns and style of life shows an awareness that there is some kind of superiority-inferiority system operating, and that we must observe the symbolic patterns of our own class.

Lloyd Warner and Paul Lunt have described a six-class system: the upper-upper, or old families; lower-upper, or the newly arrived; upper-middle, mostly the professionals and successful businessmen; lower-middle, or the white-collar salaried class; upper-lower, or the wage earner, skilled worker group; and lower-lower, or the unskilled labor group.[1] For practical purposes, in order to determine the individual's class position, Warner and his associates worked out a rating index, not based on amount of income but rather on type of income, type of occupation, house type, and place of residence.

Although the Warner thesis has been widely used in sociology, it has not generally been employed in marketing. As a matter of fact, some critics in the social sciences have held that, since Warner's thesis rested essentially on studies of smaller cities in the 10,000–25,000 class, this same system might not exist in the more complex metropolitan centers, or might not be unraveled by the same techniques. Furthermore, many marketers did not see the application of this dimension to the individual's economic behavior, since the studies of Warner and his associates had mostly been concerned with the differences in the broad patterns of living, the moral codes, etc.

Social Class in Chicago

Under Warner's guidance, the *Chicago Tribune* has undertaken several extensive studies exploring social class in a metropolitan city, and its manifestations specifically in family buying patterns. The problem was to determine if such a social-class system did exist in metropolitan Chicago, if the dimensions and the relationships were at all similar to the smaller cities which were studied before the far-reaching social changes of the past fifteen years. The studies were undertaken to see if there were any class significances in the individual family's spending-saving patterns, retail store loyalties, and his expressions of taste in typical areas such as automobiles, apparel, furniture, and house types.

It seems that many an economist overlooks the possibility of any psychological differences between individuals resulting from different class membership. It is assumed that a rich man is simply a poor man with more money and that, given the same income, the poor man would behave exactly like the rich man. The *Chicago Tribune* studies crystallize a wealth of evidence from other sources that this is just not so, and that the lower-status person is profoundly different in his mode of thinking and his way of handling the world from the middle-class individual. Where he buys and what he buys will differ not only by economics but in symbolic value.

[1] W. Lloyd Warner and Paul Lunt, *The Social Life of a Modern Community* (New Haven: Yale University Press, 1950). Also, W. Lloyd Warner, Marchia Meeker, and Kenneth Eells, *Social Class in America* (Chicago: Science Research Associates, 1949).

It should be understood, of course, that there are no hard and fast lines between the classes. Implicit in the notion of social class in America is the possibility of movement from one class to another. The "office boy-to-president" saga is a cherished part of the American dream. Bobo Rockefeller illustrates the female counterpart: from coal miner's daughter to socialite. As a corollary of the explorations in class, the study also tried to be definitive about the phenomenon of social mobility—the movement from one class to another.

There are numerous studies of vertical mobility from the level of sociological analysis, mostly by comparing the individual's occupational status with that of his father. This study attempted to combine the two levels, to observe the individual's progress and also to understand something of the dynamics of the mobile person as compared to the stable individual. The attempt was to look both backward and forward: tracing such factors as occupation, place of residence, and religion back to parents and grandparents, and then where the family expected to be in the next five or ten years, what were the educational plans for each son, each daughter, a discussion of future goals.

Because this article is confined primarily to social class, this section may be concluded by saying that the studies show a very clear relationship between spend-saving aspirations and the factors of mobility-stability.

Framework of Study

Following are Warner's hypotheses and assumptions for the study:
1. *Assumptions about symbols and values and about saving of money and accumulation of objects.*

Our society is acquisitive and pecuniary. On the one hand, the values and beliefs of Americans are pulled toward the pole of the accumulation of money by increasing the amount of money income and reducing its outgo. On the other hand, American values emphasize the accumulation of objects and products of technology for display and consumption. The self-regard and self-esteem of a person and his family, as well as the public esteem and respect of a valued social world around the accumulator, are increased or not by such symbols of accumulation and consumption.

The two sets of values, the accumulation of product symbols and the accumulation (saving) of money, may be, and usually are, in opposition.

General working hypotheses stemming from these assumptions were: (a) People are distributed along a range according to the two-value components, running from proportionately high savings, through mixed categories, to proportionately high accumulation of objects. (b) These value variations conform to social and personality factors present in all Americans.

2. *Assumptions about product symbols, savers, and accumulations.*

American society is also characterized by social change, particularly technological change that moves in the direction of greater and greater production of more kinds and more numerous objects for consumption and accumulation.

Hypothesis: New varieties of objects will be most readily accepted by the accumulators, and most often opposed by the savers.

3. *Assumptions about the social values of accumulators and savers.*

American society is characterized by basic cultural differences, one of them being social status. Social class levels are occupied by people, some of whom are upward mobile by intent and fact. Others are nonmobile, by intent and fact. The values which dictate judgments about actions, such as the kinds of objects which are consumed and accumulated, will vary by class level and the presence or absence of vertical mobility.

4. *Assumptions about the personal values of accumulators and savers.*

The personality components are distributed through the class levels and through the mobility types. By relating the social and personality components, it is possible to state a series of hypotheses about accumulators and savers as they are related to the object world around them, particularly to objects which are new and old to the culture, those which are imposing or not and those which are predominantly for display or for consumption.

At the direct, practical level, all of these theoretical questions can be summarized by one basic question: *What kinds of things are people likely to buy and not buy if they are in given class positions and if they are or are not socially mobile?* In other words, what is the effect on purchasing behavior of being in a particular social class, and being mobile or nonmobile?

If this is the crucial question, theoretically grounded, then a whole series of hypotheses can be laid out concerning values about money and values about buying various kinds of objects for consumption and for display. Some of these are:

1. There will be a relationship between values held by a particular subject and the extent to which particular products exemplify those values.

2. There is a differential hierarchy of things for which it is worth spending money.

3. Veblen's theory that conspicuous expenditure is largely applied to the upper class is erroneous. It runs all the way through our social system.

From these statements certain other hypotheses follow:

4. At different class levels, symbols of mobility will differ.

There is a differential hierarchy of things on which it is worth spending money. Class and mobility will be two of the dimensions that will differentiate—also personality and cultural background.

5. The place in the home where these symbols will be displayed will shift at different class levels.

The underlying assumption here is that there is a hierarchy of importance in the rooms of the house. This hierarchy varies with social class, mobility, age, ethnicity. The studies also revealed clear-cut patterns of taste for lamps, furnishings, house types, etc.

6. The nonmobile people tend to rationalize purchases in terms of cost or economy.

In other words, nonmobile people tend to be oriented more toward the pole of the accumulation of money. Purchases, then, are rationalized in terms of the savings involved.

The basic thesis of all the hypotheses on mobility is this: Whereas the stable individual would emphasize saving and security, the behavior of the mobile individual is characterized by spending for various symbols of upward movement. All of the evidence turned up indicates that this difference in values does exist, and furthermore that notable differences in personality dynamics are involved. For instance, the analysis of how families would make investments shows that stable people overwhelmingly prefer insurance, the symbol of security. By contrast, the mobile people at all levels prefer stocks, which are risk-taking. In Warner's words, the mobile individual acts as if he were free, white, and twenty-one, completely able to handle the world, and perfectly willing to gamble on himself as a sure bet to succeed.

Class Placement

Returning to the factor of social class, in this study class placement was based on a multistate probability area sample of metropolitan Chicago, involving 3,880 households. It was found that the matter of placement could not be done by the relatively simple scoring sufficient for the smaller cities. To secure house typings, it was necessary to provide the field investigators with photographs covering a wide range of dwelling types, all the way from exclusive apartments to rooms over stores. Because of the very complexity of metropolitan life, occupations provided the biggest problem. To solve this operational problem, it was necessary to construct an exhaustive list of occupational types involving degree of responsibility and training required by each. The data finally used to calculate the Index of Status Characteristics (ISC) were:

(weighted by 5)
    Occupation (from 1 to 7 broad categories)

(weighted by 4)
   Sources of Income (from 1 to 7 types)
(weighted by 3)
   Housing Type (from 1 to 7 types)

The sum of the individual's weighted scores was used to predict his social class level as follows: [2]

ISC Scores	Predicted Social-Class Placement
12–21	Upper Class
22–37	Upper-Middle Class
38–51	Lower-Middle Class
52–66	Upper-Lower Class
67–84	Lower-Lower Class

The study very clearly shows that there is a social-class system operative in a metropolitan area which can be delineated. Furthermore, class membership is an important determinant of the individual's economic behavior, even more so than in the smaller city. The one department store in the smaller city may satisfy almost everyone, whereas in the metropolitan city the stores become sharply differentiated.

This is the social-class structure of metropolitan Chicago, typifying the transformation of the formerly agrarian Midwestern cities from Pittsburgh to Kansas City into a series of big mill-towns:

Upper and Upper-Middle	8.1%
Lower-Middle	28.4%
Upper-Lower	44.0%
Lower-Lower	19.5%

While the Old Families and the Newly Arrived are still recognizable as types, they constitute less than 1 per cent of the population. A similar study in Kansas City turned up so few that they could not be counted at all. On the other hand, we see the emergence of a seventh class, the upper-lower "Stars" or light-blue-collar workers. They are the spokesmen of the upper-lower class groups—high income individuals, who have the income for more ostentatious living than the average factory worker but who lack the personal skills or desire for high status by social mobility.

There is certainly a rough correlation between income and social class. But social class is a much richer dimension of meaning. There are so many facets of behavior which are explicable only on a basis of social-class dynamics. For instance, this analysis of the purchase of household appli-

---

[2] Dr. Bevode McCall helped to solve the ISC scoring problem for metropolitan Chicago.

ances in Chicago over a four-year period shows a very different picture by income and by class:

Nine Appliance Types—Four-Year Period

By Income

Over $7,000	36.2%
4,000–6,999	46.0%
Under 4,000	17.8%

By Social Class

Upper and Upper-Middle	16.6%
Lower-Middle	29.2%
Upper-Lower	45.7%
Lower-Lower	8.5%

Income analysis shows that the lowest income group represents an understandably smaller market, but nevertheless a market. Social-class analysis highlights a fundamental difference in attitudes toward the home between the two lower classes. The upper-lower-class man sees his home as his castle, his anchor to the world, and he loads it down with hardware—solid, heavy appliances—as his symbols of security. The lower-lower-class individual is far less interested in his castle, and is more likely to spend his income for flashy clothes or an automobile. He is less property-minded, and he has less feeling about buying and maintaining a home.

Several *Tribune* studies have explored the way of life and the buying behavior in many new suburbs and communities. All of them quickly become stratified along social-class and mobility dimensions, and, therefore, differ tremendously among themselves. *Fortune* has reported on Park Forest, Illinois, a middle-class suburb of 30,000 and only ten years old. It is characterized by high degrees of both upward and geographical mobility. The people are overwhelmingly those who had moved from other parts of the United States, who had few local roots, and who consequently wanted to integrate themselves in friendship groups. But this was not typical of the new lower-status suburbs where the women did relatively little fraternizing. It was not typical of the new upper-middle-class mobile suburbs where the people were preoccupied with status symbols, not in submerging themselves in the group.

One new community had crystallized as being for higher-status Negroes. This was a resettlement project with relatively high rents for Negroes. Eighty-five per cent of them had come from the South where social class was compressed. But, as soon as they came to Chicago, the class system opened up and they were anxious to establish a social distance between themselves and other Negroes. Almost all of them said they enjoyed the "peace and quiet" of their neighborhood, which was their way of insisting that they were not like the "noisy" lower-class Negroes. They deliberately avoided the stores patronized by other Negroes.

Choice of Store

All of these studies reveal the close relation between choice of store, patterns of spending, and class membership. In the probability sample delineating social class, such questions were asked in the total metropolitan area as:

"If you were shopping for a good dress, at which store would you be most likely to find what you wanted?"

"For an everyday dress?"

"For living room furniture?"

"At which store do you buy most of your groceries?"

To assume that all persons would wish to shop at the glamorous high-status stores is utterly wrong. People are very realistic in the way they match their values and expectations with the status of the store. The woman shopper has a considerable range of ideas about department stores; but these generally become organized on a scale ranking from very high-social status to the lowest-status and prestige. The social status of the department store becomes the primary basis for its definition by the shopper. This is also true of men's and women's apparel stores, and furniture stores, on the basis of customer profiles. The shopper is not going to take a chance feeling out of place by going to a store where she might not fit.

No matter what economics are involved, she asks herself who are the other customers in the store, what sort of treatment can she expect at the hands of the clerks, will the merchandise be the best of everything, or lower priced and hence lower quality? Stores are described as being for the rich, for the average ordinary people, or for those who have to stretch their pennies.

The most important function of retail advertising today, when prices and quality have become so standard, is to permit the shopper to make social-class identification. This she can do from the tone and physical character of the advertising. Of course, there is also the factor of psychological identification. Two people in the same social class may want different stores. One may prefer a conservative store, one may want the most advanced styling. But neither will go to stores where they do not "fit," in a social-class sense.

In contrast to the independent food retailer, who obviously adapts to the status of the neighborhood, the chain grocers generally invade many income areas with their stores. Nevertheless, customer profiles show that each chain acquires a status definition. The two largest grocery chains in the Chicago area are A. & P. and Jewel; yet they draw very different customer bodies. A. & P. is strong with the mass market, whereas Jewel has its strength among the middle class.

While the national brand can and often does cut across classes, one can think of many product types and services which do have social class labels. The upper-middle-class person rarely travels by motor coach because none of his associates do so, even though there is certainly nothing wrong with this mode of transportation. On the other hand, even with low air-coach fares, one does not see many factory workers or day laborers on vacation around airports. Such sales successes as vodka and tonic water, and men's deodorants and foreign sports cars, were accomplished without benefit of much buying from this part of the market.

Communication Skills

There is also a relation between class and communication abilities which has significance for marketing. The kind of supersophisticated and clever advertising which appears in the *New Yorker* and *Esquire* is almost meaningless to lower-status people. They cannot comprehend the stubtle humor; they are baffled by the bizarre art. They have a different symbol system, a very different approach to humor. In no sense does this imply that they lack intelligence or wit. Rather their communication skills have just been pressed into a different mold.

Here again, style of advertising helps the individual to make class identification. Most of the really big local television success stories in Chicago have been achieved by personalities who radiate to the mass that this is where they belong. These self-made businessmen who do the announcing for their own shows communicate wonderfully well with the mass audience. While many listeners switch off their lengthy and personal commercials, these same mannerisms tell the lower-status individual that here is someone just like himself, who understands him.

Social Research, Incorporated has frequently discussed the class problem in marketing by dividing the population into upper-middle or quality market; the middle majority which combines both the lower-middle and upper-lower; and then the lower-lower. The distinction should be drawn between the middle classes and the lower-status groups. In several dozen of these store profiles, there is scarcely an instance where a store has appeal to the lower-middle and the upper-lower classes with anything like the same strength.

It would be better to make the break between the middle class, representing one-third of the population and the lower-status or working-class or wage-earner group, representing two-thirds of metropolitan Chicago. This permits some psychological distinctions to be drawn between the middle-class individual and the individual who is not a part of the middle-class system of values. Even though this is the dominant American value system, even though middle-class Americans have been taught by their parents that it is the only value system, this lower-status individual does not necessarily subscribe to it.

Who Saves, Who Spends?

Another important set of behavioral distinctions related to social class position was revealed in the "save-spend aspiration" study. The question was asked: "Suppose your income was doubled for the next ten years, what would you do with the increased income?" This is a fantasy question taken out of the realm of any pressing economic situation to reflect aspirations about money. The coding broke down the answers to this question into five general categories: (1) the mode of saving, (2) the purpose of saving, (3) spending which would consolidate past gains, meet present defensive needs, prepare for future self-advancement, (4) spending which is "self-indulgent-centered," (5) spending which is "house-centered."

Here are some of our findings: [3] The higher the individual's class position, the more likely is he to express some saving aspirations. Conversely, the lower his class position, the more likely is he to mention spending only. Moreover the higher the status, the more likely is the individual to specify *how* he will save his money, which is indicative of the more elaborate financial learning required of higher status.

Proceeding from the more general categories (such as saving versus spending only) to more specific categories (such as noninvestment versus investment saving and the even more specific stock versus real estate investment, etc.), an increasingly sharper class differentiation is found. It is primarily *noninvestment* saving which appeals to the lower-status person. Investment saving, on the other hand, appeals above all to the upper-status person.

Investors almost always specify how they will invest. And here in mode of investment are examples of the most sharply class-differentiated preferences. Intangible forms of investment like stock and insurance are very clearly distinguished as upper-status investments. Nearly four times as many upper-middles select insurance as would be expected by chance, whereas only one-fifth of the lower-lowers select it as would be expected by chance. By contrast, lower-status people have far greater preference for tangible investments, specifically ownership of real estate, a farm, or a business.

To sum up, middle-class people usually have a place in their aspirations

[3] The saving-spending aspiration analysis was carried out by Roger Coup, graduate student at the University of Chicago.

for some form of saving. This saving is most often in the form of investment, where there is a risk, long-term involvement, and the possibility of higher return. Saving, investment saving, and intangible investment saving—successively each of these become for them increasingly symbols of their higher status.

The aspirations of the lower-status person are just as often for spending as they are for saving. This saving is usually a noninvestment saving where there is almost no risk, funds can be quickly converted to spendable cash, and returns are small. When the lower-status person does invest his savings, he will be specific about the mode of investment, and is very likely to prefer something tangible and concrete—something he can point at and readily display.

Turning from mode of saving to purpose of saving, very significant class relationships are likewise evident. Consider the verbalization of saving purpose. Lower-status people typically explain why one should save— why the very act of saving is important. On the other hand, middle-class people do not, as if saving is an end-in-itself, the merits of which are obvious and need not be justified.

Spending is the other side of the coin. Analysis of what people say they will spend for shows similar class-related desires. All classes mention concrete, material artifacts such as a new car, some new appliance. But the lower-status people stop here. Their accumulations are artifact-centered, whereas middle-class spending-mentions are experience-centered. This is spending where one is left typically with only a memory. It would include hobbies, recreation, self-education, and travel. The wish to travel, and particularly foreign travel, is almost totally a middle-cass aspiration.

Even in their fantasies, people are governed by class membership. In his day-dreaming and wishful thinking, the lower-status individual will aspire in different patterns from the middle-class individual.

Psychological Differences

This spending-saving analysis has very obvious psychological implications to differentiate between the classes. Saving itself generally suggests foresightedness, the ability to perceive long-term needs and goals. Noninvestment saving has the characteristics of little risk-taking and of ready conversion, at no loss, into immediate expenditures—the money can be drawn out of the account whenever the bank is open. Investment spending, on the other hand, has the characteristics of risk-taking (a gamble for greater returns) and of delayed conversion, with possible loss, to expenditures on immediate needs.

Here are some psychological contrasts between two different social groups:

Middle Class

1. Pointed to the future
2. His viewpoint embraces a long expanse of time
3. More urban identification
4. Stresses rationality
5. Has a well-structured sense of the universe
6. Horizons vastly extended or not limited
7. Greater sense of choice-making
8. Self-confident, willing to take risks
9. Immaterial and abstract in his thinking
10. Sees himself tied to national happenings

Lower Status

1. Pointed to the present and past
2. Lives and thinks in a short expanse of time
3. More rural in identification
4. Nonrational essentially
5. Vague and unclear structuring of the world
6. Horizons sharply defined and limited
7. Limited sense of choice-making
8. Very much concerned with security and insecurity
9. Concrete and perceptive in his thinking
10. World revolves around his family and body

25. SYMBOLS FOR SALE *

by Sidney J. Levy †

The thoughtful businessman is undoubtedly aware of the growing use and influence of social science concepts in the business world. Management gives increasing attention to relations between people whether among the management group, down the line, between the manufacturer and the retailer, or between the producer and the consumer. There is less preoccupation with the performance of impersonal economic entities.

The modern assumption is that people are faced with alternatives; that they may be motivated in various directions. From this assumption grows

* Reprinted from *Harvard Business Review*, © July–August 1959, pp. 117–24.
† Social Research, Inc.

the significance of communications and understandings, and the concomitant concern with what the people of the world think—with political public opinion, consumer reactions, and so on. Because of this development the science and practice of marketing have been infused with new life.

Changing Scene

We need not belabor the obvious changes in the American scene. They can be readily enumerated. There are more people. These people have more of all kinds of things—more leisure, more money, more possessions, more pleasure, and more, if not the same, old worries.[1] Sociological and psychological interpretations of the contemporary scene are fashionable now and are, in themselves, a part of the scene—part of the wave of human preoccupation and of self-examination that is growing as we move further and further from grubbing for subsistence.

The less concern there is with the concrete satisfactions of a survival level of existence, the more abstract human responses become. As behavior in the market place is increasingly elaborated, it also becomes increasingly symbolic. This idea needs some examination, because it means that sellers of goods are engaged, whether willfully or not, in selling *symbols,* as well as practical merchandise. It means that marketing managers must attend to more than the relatively superficial facts with which they usually concern themselves when they do not think of their goods as having symbolic significance.

Uneconomic Man

Formerly, when goods tended to mean some essentials of food, clothing, and shelter, practical matters were very important. The consumer was apt to be an "economic man," who was more or less careful of how he distributed his pennies. To do this meant giving closer attention to the concrete value of what he bought, to the durability of the fabric, the quantity of the food, the sturdiness of the building materials.

The philosophy of business was also oriented around these issues, with a few outstanding enterprises intent on creating an individuality of quality and a competitive price. The market place was largely occupied with the things sold and bought. These were often neither packaged nor advertised. Consumers were customers, not audiences.

The modern market place, which is exemplified so dramatically in the vast supermarket (food, drug, or furniture store), reminds us daily of the marketing revolution that has come about. There is an astonishing variety

[1] See Reuel Denney, "The Leisure Society," *Harvard Business Review,* May–June 1959, p. 46; and August Heckscher and Sebastian de Grazia, "Problems in Review: Executive Leisure," *Harvard Business Review,* July–August 1959, p. 6.

of merchandise, all of it displayed in equally astonishing ways. There are frozen foods, precooked foods, plastic containers, and packages with ingenious (often insidious) opening devices.

In this new setting, what kind of man is the consumer? He is hardly an economic man—especially since there is considerable evidence that he does not buy economically. Indeed, he is often vague about the actual price he pays for something; he has few standards for judging the quality of what he buys, and at times winds up not using it anyway!

This is not just a joke. American homes contain many things of unknown price—objects that are bought on time, appliances that would gather dust if not covered, unused basement workshops. Of course, these are extreme examples—they may even be gifts from hostile relatives, who always have furnished homes with undesirable objects. The point is that today, when people shop, they tend to buy lavishly. Consumers still talk about price, quality, and durability, since these are regarded as sensible traditional values. But at the same time, they know that other factors affect them and believe these to be legitimate influences.

New Whys for Buys

This point is worth some emphasis since many people disapprove of the fact that purchases may be made on what they consider to be insubstantial grounds. The fact that people do not buy furniture to last twenty years may be deplored as a sign of the lightheadedness of our times. On the other hand, such massive, stoutly made furniture may be dismissed from the home at the behest of other values such as comfortable living or changing tastes.

Grandmother cherished her furniture for its sensible, practical value, but today people know that it is hardly the practical considerations which determine their choices between Post's and Kellogg's, Camels and Luckies, Oldsmobiles and Buicks, or Arpège and Chanel No. 5. They know that package color, television commercials, and newspaper and magazine advertisements incline them toward one preference or another. And, what is more, when they cannot really tell the difference among competitive brands of the same product, they do not believe that a manufacturer should necessarily go out of business because he is unable to produce a distinguishable product. They do not even mind if Procter & Gamble Company puts out both Tide and Cheer.

Diversity of Spending

At the heart of all this is the fact that the consumer is not as functionally oriented as he used to be—if he ever really was. Esthetic preferences have changed somewhat. For example, we no longer go in for stained glass lamps and antimacassars, although the latter were perhaps more attractive than transparent couch covers. Moreover, the diversity of ways in which people can spend their money has had an impact on motivation:

People Buy Things not only for What They Can Do,
But also for What They Mean

At one level, society has to concern itself with bread for sustenance, and appropriate agencies must see to it that our breads are sufficiently nourishing, enriched, and not poisonously refined. But the consumer is no longer much interested in bread as the staff of life. In the first place, he (or she) is probably on a diet and not eating bread; in the second place, he is apt to be more concerned with whether to buy an exotic twist, to do something "interesting" with a pancake flour, or to pop in a brown-and-serve roll that will come hot to the table to the moderate surprise of the guests.

When People Talk about the Things They Buy
and Why They Buy Them, They Show a Variety of Logics

They refer to convenience, inadvertence, family pressure, other social pressures, complex economic reasonings, advertising, and pretty colors. They try to satisfy many aims, feelings, wishes, and circumstances. The pleasure they gain from buying objects is ever more playful. The question is less: "Do I need this?" More important are the ideas: "Do I want it?" "Do I like it?"

Language of Symbols

Answering the questions asked by today's consumer takes the definition of goods into new realms—at least new in the sense that they are now recognized as questions worthy of serious examination. The things people buy are seen to have personal and social meanings in addition to their functions. To ignore or decry the symbolism of consumer goods does not affect the importance of the fact. The only question is whether the goods are to be symbolized thoughtfully or thoughtlessly.

Specialists in the study of communications, language formation, and semantics make various distinctions between levels of meaning. It is customary to speak of signs, signals, symbols, gestures, and other more technical terms. Many of the distinctions are arbitrary, expressing the specialists' preference for one or another mode of thinking, and need not concern us here. It will suffice to say that in casual usage *symbol* is a general term for all instances where experience is mediated rather than direct; where an object, action, word, picture, or complex behavior is understood to mean not only itself but also some *other* ideas or feelings.

Psychological Things

From this viewpoint, modern goods are recognized as essentially psychological things which are symbolic of personal attributes and goals and of social patterns and strivings.

When going shopping the consumer spends not only money but energy. His attention is stimulated or lies dormant as he moves through the mart. Objects he sees on the shelves are assessed according to standards which he has established for what is important or potentially important to him. For instance.

A saw may be very useful—and there may be things around the house that need to be sawed—but if he feels that a saw is beneath the way he wants to expend his energy, or allot his attention, he passes it idly by. Perhaps he buys a record instead, or he may choose a Hi-Fi component; these are objects in an area where he prefers to invest his psychological energies.

In this sense, all commercial objects have a symbolic character, and making a purchase involves an assessment—implicit or explicit—of this symbolism, to decide whether or not it fits. Energy (and money) will be given when the symbols are appropriate ones, and denied or given parsimoniously when they are not. What determines their appropriateness?

Image Reinforced

A symbol is appropriate (and the product will be used and enjoyed) when it joins with, meshes with, adds to, or reinforces the way the consumer thinks about himself. We are dealing here with a very plain fact of human nature. In the broadest sense, each person aims to enhance his sense of self, and behaves in ways that are consistent with his image of the person he is or wants to be. Prescott Lecky has written an interesting essay on how people behave in consistency with their self-concepts,[2] and many businessmen could doubtless supplement his observations with a number of their own.

Because of their symbolic nature, consumer goods can be chosen with less conflict or indecision than would otherwise be the case. Legend has it that Buridan's ass starved to death equidistant between two piles of equally attractive hay; he would not have had the problem if one pile had been a bit more asinine—let us say—than the other. Modern marketing might have helped him.

Choices are made more easily—either more routinely or more impulsively, seemingly—because one object is symbolically more harmonious with our goals, feelings, and self-definitions than another. The difference

[2] *Self-consistency* (New York: Island Press, 1945).

may not be a large one, nor a very important one in the manufacture of the products; but it may be big enough to dictate a constant direction of preference in the indulgence of one's viewpoint. People feel better when bathroom tissue is pastel blue, the car is a large one (or, at least, until recently), the newspaper is a tabloid size, the trousers have pleats, and so on. It is increasingly fashionable to be a connoisseur or gourmet of *some* kind—that is, to consume with one or another standard of discrimination.

Shrewd Judges

Several years of research into the symbolic nature of products, brands, institutions, and media of communication make it amply clear that consumers are able to gauge grossly and subtly the symbolic language of different objects, and then to translate them into meanings for themselves.

Consumers understand that darker colors are symbolic of more "respectable" products; that browns and yellows are manly; that reds are exciting and provocative. The fact that something is "scientific" means technical merit, an interest in quality, and (probably) less enjoyment. Theatrical references imply glamour and suspension of staid criteria.

The value of a testimonial may depend largely on whether there is an association (logical or illogical) between the man and the product. For instance, people think it is appropriate for Winston Churchill to endorse cigars, whiskey, and books. But if they are *very* average consumers, then they are apt to miss (or ignore) the humor of a testimonial for a Springmaid sheet advertisement altogether.

Dimensions of Distinction

People use symbols to distinguish. As Susanne Langer says in discussing the process of symbolization in *Philosophy in a New Key:*

The power of understanding symbols, i.e. of regarding everything about a sense-datum as irrelevant except a certain *form* that it embodies, is the most characteristic mental trait of mankind. It issues in an unconscious, spontaneous process of *abstraction,* which goes on all the time in the human mind . . .[3]

More or Less Gender

One of the most basic dimensions of symbolism is gender. Almost all societies make some differential disposition of the sexes—deciding who will do what and which objects will be reserved to men and which to women.

Usually it is hard to evade thinking of inanimate things as male or female. Through such personalization, vessels tend to become feminine

[3] Cambridge, Harvard University Press, 1957, p. 72.

and motherly if they are big enough. Men fall in love with their ships and cars, giving them women's names.

In America there has been complaint that some of this differentiation is fading; that women are getting more like men, and men are shifting to meet them, in a movement toward homogeneous togetherness. No doubt there is some basis for this concern if we compare ourselves with past civilizations or with hunting and agricultural societies that make sharper distinctions between what is masculine and what is feminine. But the differences still loom large in the market place—so large that there are even gradations of characterization. For example:

Probably all cigarette brands could be placed on a *continuum* of degrees of gender, as one aspect of their complex symbolic patternings. The same is true for musical compositions and the recorded interpretations of them; of cheeses and the brand versions of each kind.

Sex at Work

Sexual definitions may seem absurd at times, and often have only modest influence in one or another choice. But they're at work and form a natural part of, for instance, the housewife's logic and acquired reactions as she makes her selections in the food store and serves her family. She considers what her husband's preferences are; what a growing boy should have; what is just right for a girl's delicate tastes. To take two simple illustrations:

Since smoothness is generally understood to be more feminine, as foods go, it seems fitting that girls should prefer smooth peanut butter, and boys the chunky. While the overlap is great, a cultivated society teaches such a discrimination, and children, being attentive to their proper sex roles, learn it early. Indeed, the modern family seems to be greatly concerned with the indoctrination of symbolic appropriateness.

In an interview one six-year-old boy protested that he had never liked peanut butter, but his mother and sister had always insisted that he did, and now he loved it. Apparently a violent bias in favor of peanut butter is suitable to little boys, and may be taken as representing something of the rowdy boyishness of childhood, in contrast to more restrained and orderly foods.

Such findings are not idle, since they help explain why "Skippy" is an appropriate name for peanut butter, and why "Peter Pan" was not until he was taken away from Maude Adams and given to Mary Martin and Walt Disney.

Similarly, in a recent study of two cheese advertisements for a certain cheese, one wedge of cheese was shown in a setting of a brown cutting board, dark bread, and a glimpse of a chess game. The cheese wedge was pictured standing erect on its smallest base. Although no people were shown, consumers interpreted the ad as part of a masculine scene, with men playing a game, being served a snack.

The same cheese was also shown in another setting with lighter colors, a suggestion of a floral bowl, and the wedge lying flat on one of its longer sides. This was interpreted by consumers as a feminine scene, probably with ladies lunching in the vicinity. Each ad worked to convey a symbolic impression of the cheese, modifying or enhancing established ideas about the product.

Act Your Symbolical Age

Just as most people usually recognize whether something is addressed to them as a man or as a woman, so are they sensitive to symbols of age.

Teenagers are sensitive to communications which imply childishness. If presented with a soft drink layout showing a family on a picnic, their reaction is apt to be "kid stuff." They are trying to break away from the family bosom. While they might actually enjoy such a picnic, the scene symbolizes restraint and inability to leave in order to be with people of their own age.

Clothing is carefully graded in people's eyes; we normally judge, within a few years' span, whether some garment is fitted to the age of the wearer. Women are particularly astute (and cruel) in such judgments, but men also observe that a pin-striped suit is too mature for one wearer, or that a "collegiate" outfit is too young for a man who should be acting his age.

Class and Caste

Symbols of social participation are among the most dramatic factors in marketing. Like it or not, there are social class groupings formed by the ways people live, the attitudes they have, and the acceptance and exclusiveness of their associations. Most goods say something about the social world of the people who consume them. The things they buy are chosen partly to attest to their social positions.

The possession of mink is hardly a matter of winter warmth alone, as all women know who wear mink with slacks while strolling at a beach resort. The social stature of mink—and its down-grading—leads us to marvel that it is now sold at Sears, Roebuck & Company. On the other hand, Sears has up-graded itself and become more middle class.

Shopping at Sears is symbolic of a certain chic among many middle-class people who used to regard it as much more working-class. People now boast that Sears is especially suitable for certain kinds of merchandise, and their candor in saying they shop at Sears is not so much frankness as it is facetiousness—as if to point out an amusing quirk in one's social behavior.

Membership in a social class tends to affect one's general outlook, modes of communication, concreteness of thinking and understanding.[4]

[4] See Leonard Schatzman and Anselm Strauss, "Social Class and Modes of Communication," *The American Journal of Sociology*, January 1955, p. 329.

Advertising often says different things to people of different social levels. For example, a perfume ad showing an anthropological mask and swirling colors is likely to be incomprehensible to many working-class women, whereas *New Yorker* readers will at least pretend they grasp the symbolism. On the other hand, working-class women will accept a crowded, screaming sale advertisement as meaning urgency and potential interest, while women of higher status will ignore it as signaling inferiority.

Sense and Nonsense

Sometimes advertising symbolism can become confined to a social class *sub*group. For example, some upper-middle-class people are not sure what is being said in liquor ads featuring groups of sinister men wearing red shoes or handsome males riding sidesaddle. While suspecting the symbolic language may be gibberish, they have some undercurrent of anxiety about not being part of the in-group who use "nonsense syllables" to tell each other about vodka.

Discriminating Publics

The choice of the appropriate symbols for advertising a product deserves careful consideration. The symbolic messages conveyed in the ad generally correspond to the advertiser's intention—although consumers may discover meanings additional to or even *contrary* to the intended meaning. A poorly chosen symbol for an advertisement is likely to backfire. For example:

The headline of an advertisement claimed that the product was actually worth one cent more than its price in comparison with competing products. Many housewives interpreted this claim as a sign of cheapness; they needed to see only the one cent in the headline to conclude that it was "one of those penny deals." Even to readers who understood literally what was said the effect of talking about merely one cent somehow suggested the idea of cheapening.

In other words, while the literal aim had been to refer to the greater worth of the product, the symbolic means acted to cheapen it.

Fine Arts and Fine Distinctions

Dramas, particularly the theater shows sponsored by General Electric, Kraft Foods, Procter & Gamble, and United States Steel, are interpreted as serious appeals to responsible intellects, the dramatic theater being a symbol of this as opposed to musical and variety shows. Within the dramatic theater finer distinctions are made. For instance, offerings by Ronald Reagan, a sincere, charming man, are considered in keeping with the institutional nature of the General Electric sponsorship (whereas offerings by Red Skelton probably would conflict).

To Each His Own Conformity

Some comparatively well-defined modes of living and taste patterns tend to combine individual symbols into large clusters of symbols. The separate symbols add to the definition of the whole, and thereby organize purchases along given directions. For example:

The Ivy League cluster of symbols affects the kinds of suits, ties, and, to a lesser degree, the cars and liquors certain people buy.

Being a suburbanite is a broad identification, but it starts one's purchasing ideas moving in certain lines. Name your own suburb, and the ideas leap into sharper focus. Neighbors judge the symbolic significance of how money is spent; they are quick to interpret the appropriateness of your spending pattern for the community. They decide what kind of people you are by making reasonable or unreasonable deductions from what you consume—books, liquor, power mowers, cars, and the gifts you and your children give at birthday parties.

Some objects we buy symbolize such personal qualities as self-control; others expose our self-indulgence. We reason in these directions about people who drink and smoke, or who do not—and such reasoning will play a role in their choices of doing one or the other. A hard mattress is readily justified on pragmatic grounds of health, sound sleep, and the like, but people recognize the austere self-denial at work that will also strengthen the character. Conversely, soft drinks may quench thirst, but people feel that they are also buying an indulgent moment, a bit of ease, a lowering of adult restraints.

Tattletale Patterns

It is easy to overlook the variety of meanings conveyed by objects since they range in their conventionality and self-expressiveness. We ordinarily give little thought to interpreting milk at the table, significant as milk may be (unless, perhaps, at a businessmen's lunch). We are observant of dishes, cups, and silverware, however. True, we have to have them—people expect them. But the patterns tell people things about us—and not always the things that we would expect.

Take books: by and large, books are regarded as highly personal purchases. Guests will respect one personally for *Dr. Zhivago* on the coffee table, and perhaps raise an eyebrow at *Lolita*. Similarly with magazines: there is a world of symbolic difference between such periodicals as, say, *Look, Popular Science,* and *Harvard Business Review.*

Toward Informality

A whole treatise could be written on another symbolic dimension, that of formality and informality. Many of our decisions to buy take into account the degree of formal or informal character of the object. House-wives constantly gauge the hot dogs that they serve, the gifts that they are giving, and the tablecloth that they plan to use with an eye to how informal the occasion is or should be.

The movement toward informality has been a fundamental one in re-cent years, governing the emphasis on casual clothes, backyard and buffet meals, staying at motels, and bright colors (even for telephones).

Currently there seem to be signs of a reaction to this trend—of a seek-ing for more graciousness in living. Again, there is interest in the elegance of a black car; a wish for homes with dining rooms; and a desire for greater individual privacy. But the existence of a countertrend does not cancel out the symbolic meaning of casual clothes, buffet meals, and so on; in fact, it may even sharpen awareness of the implications of these products and customs.

Symbolic Obsolescence

As I have indicated, among all the symbols around us, bidding for our buying attention and energy, there are underlying trends that affect and are affected by the spirit of the times. Every so often there comes along a new symbol, one that makes a leap from the past into the present and that has power because it captures the spirit of the present and makes other on-going symbols old-fashioned. The recent Pepsi-Cola girl was a symbol of this sort. She had precursors, of course, but she distinctly and promi-nently signified a modern phantasy; she established an advertising style somewhat removed from the Clabber girl.

THE SALES MIX

part IV

A successful career in selling requires much more than skill in salesmanship. Advancement also requires understanding the relationship of marketing to production and finance as well as the interaction of personal selling with the other elements of an inclusive promotional program. Acquisition by the salesman of this broader perspective and an ability to think and act in terms of total marketing effort, while covering his territory, will indicate to management his capacity for broader responsibilities. The selections in Part IV were chosen to show these interrelationships.

The section on "Integrated Marketing Effort" reviews alternative channels of distribution and reveals how their selection and administration have a marked effect on selling effectiveness and costs. Also, the broadened responsibilities of marketing managers in corporate enterprise today is explained. No longer is able direction of a sales force adequate for promotion to the higher echelons of management. In the 1960's there will be increasing demand for executives with ability to envisage, direct, and evaluate a total marketing program which is integrated with over-all corporate objectives.

In "Product Communications Strategy," the readings indicate the influence of various promotional tools in the successful consummation of sales negotiations. Personal selling, advertising, sales promotion, publicity, appearance design, and packaging are the key elements of the mix which must be blended properly and coordinated to achieve success in the marketplace.

Channel and Media Choice

26. THE IMPORTANCE OF DISTRIBUTION *

by Thomas J. Kehane †

Choice of Channels

To the manufacturer, the choice of effective channels of distribution can mean the difference between success and failure.

Ours is an economy of mass-production, mass-distribution, and mass-consumption. More people have more purchasing power than ever before and more disposable income to buy more goods. The manufacturer is therefore faced with intensified competition from other producers, and consumer buying is increasingly selective. The steps the producer takes to move his goods into the hands of the ultimate consumer deserve to be studied as carefully as his methods of manufacture or any of the other considerations important to the operation of the total business.

The choice of a channel of distribution for any manufacturer, large or small, will depend largely on two considerations—potential volume of sales and the cost of obtaining this volume. The most effective channel is not necessarily the one which gives the manufacturer the greatest possible volume (which might result in an unprofitably high cost-per-sale), or the lowest possible cost-per-sale (which might be made at the expense of a reasonable volume of sales), but the one which most successfully combines volume and cost, allowing the manufacturer the maximum amount of profit.

* Reprinted from 1957 Turck Lecture Series, Yale University, pp. 38–48.
† Worthington Corporation.

217

The choice of a specific channel of distribution can only be made after analyzing basic factors, such as:

—Nature of the company's business—is it manufacturing, contracting, or service?
—What is the type of product—is it a bulk commodity, consumer goods, or capital or industrial durable goods?
—Value of product.
—Type of market to be reached.
—Mark-up above cost.

Consideration of these and other factors will determine which of the channels discussed today would be best for distribution of the product.

I have been asked to discuss eight of the most commonly used channels of distribution. These are:

1. Selling door-to-door
2. Selling through retailers
3. Selling through company-owned retail stores
4. Selling through wholesalers, jobbers, middlemen, manufacturer's agents, and distributors
5. Selling to industries direct
6. Selling through exporters
7. Selling to importers direct
8. Selling to the government.

Door-to-Door Selling

According to an article in the *Harvard Business Review* (May–June 1954), a surprisingly wide variety of goods are sold door-to-door. Products sold by members of the National Association of Direct Selling Companies include chemicals, clothing, portraits and frames, roofing and siding, foundation garments and shoes, as well as foods, magazines, encyclopedias, brushes, cosmetics, greeting cards, vacuum cleaners, and Girl Scout cookies. Trade associations estimate total door-to-door sales as high as four billion dollars a year. Obviously, then, this is a marketing channel worth investigating for manufacturers with the right kinds of products.

1. What is the right kind of product for door-to-door selling? Size of the product is one limiting factor. Since delivery is expensive, the product should be small enough to be displayed and delivered easily by the salesman. If it is to be sold from samples, it should be deliverable without excessive cost from the manufacturer's warehouses.

The product must have a large margin of gross profit. Costs of door-to-door selling are extremely high. Therefore, products such as cosmetics, with relatively low manufacturing costs and high retail prices, are particularly well-suited for this type of selling. Other suitable products are those for which the customer may not be expected to be aware of the "usual" retail price—e.g., brushes, reference books, specialty foods.

It must be a product of good quality. Since success in this market depends upon repeat sales and upon word-of-mouth endorsement among neighbors, one faulty product can spoil an entire market area.

It should appeal to a large percentage of householders so that the salesman, usually working on straight commission basis, may expect a profitable number of sales each day. If it is a product of limited appeal, the prospective customers should be easy to locate.

The product should be easy to demonstrate by a salesman who may not have had extensive training.

Among the advantages of door-to-door selling are these:

It permits personal, concentrated selling. A salesman selling only one product or product line, on a direct commission basis, can take more interest in each sale than a department store clerk can. Further, because of the inherent courtesy to a guest on the part of most homeowners, once he has gained admittance to a home, the salesman can generally complete his sales pitch without competing distractions and competing product lines.

New distribution for a product is another advantage. In a retail market already crowded with competing products, retailers are unwilling to stock new merchandise for which there is no ready-built consumer demand. Door-to-door selling creates such a demand, without relying on expensive advertising campaigns. (One company selling its products through retailers, according to the *Harvard Business Review* article, actually found that retail sales increased when door-to-door selling was added.)

Costs are more directly related to sales, and therefore, more flexible. Since salesmen are paid commissions only, without salary or traveling expenses, cost of building a new sales force and waiting for it to produce, or of maintaining the sales force during periods of small volume, is relatively low.

Volume of sales remains relatively stable. In depressed times, when sales are off, number of sales-per-salesman may decrease dramatically; but the increase in number-of-salesmen per territory tends to make up the difference for the manufacturer.

Door-to-door selling is suited to the times. For one thing, it takes advantage of the trend to the suburbs. According to *Business Week* (December 8, 1956) "unlike retail stores, it can move to new fields without the heavy expenditures that branch stores or new shopping centers require." Moreover, "in the cities themselves, traffic congestion has worked in favor of the direct sellers who provide services."

Disadvantages of door-to-door selling:

High among the problems of the manufacturer who chooses door-to-door selling is that of obtaining and maintaining an adequate sales force. Earnings tend to be low for salespeople in this field, even considering the fact that many of them work only part time. Obviously, then, except in times of depression or general unemployment, the ablest salesmen are not likely to clamor for door-to-door selling jobs. Still, manufacturers must maintain large sales forces—2,000 to 5,000 is not uncommon. Some companies employ as many as 80,000 at one time. Recruiting sales personnel on such a scale is extremely difficult and often far from selective. Recruiting is done through newspaper and magazine ads, by direct mail, and by other door-to-door salesmen. Once enlisted, the salespeople are often turned out into the field with little or no training. And, since many are selling door-to-door only while waiting for better jobs, for Christmas money, or for other temporary reasons, they may become disenchanted in a short time. Quitting is often a matter of simply not showing up on the route any more, and quit they do—in droves. Turnover of up to 300 per cent a year is not uncommon.

Another difficulty, beyond finding and keeping the sales force, is controlling it. Most manufacturers who distribute door-to-door, because of the size of their sales forces and the high cost of distribution, avoid the costs of Social Security taxes, unemployment taxes, federal withholding taxes and other similar payroll additions by having salesmen function as independent agents. Thus, their lack of proper training coupled with the technical ease of quitting or changing companies makes for a bad sales force and loses customer goodwill.

Another major problem is the high cost—sometimes as high as 60 per cent of selling price—of distributing door-to-door. Commissions often exceed retail-store markup. Classified advertising and record-keeping for a vast sales force with high turnover are expensive. So too are the selling aids for thousands of salesmen. Costs of shipping to tens of thousands of individual customers add their weight. One manufacturer ships about 25,000 orders a week to door-to-door customers, compared with a few hundred a week to his retail accounts. Credit must be extended and records kept. Cost of premiums and other buying incentives go up as competition becomes intense.

The *Harvard Business Review* gives this breakdown for distribution costs of one company selling door-to-door:

Distribution Costs	Per cent of Retail Selling Price
Salesmen's commission	40
Field supervision (managers' commissions, branch expenses)	7
Administrative and other overhead (sales management, clerical, shipping, promotion, selling equipment, credit, etc.)	13
	60 per cent

There is still another troublesome disadvantage. Local ordinances against door-to-door selling, often sponsored by local retailers who resent outside competition, have plagued door-to-door salesmen for years.

Yet despite these serious stumbling blocks this distribution channel persists. New companies and new ideas are constantly added to its roster.

One manufacturer of household products recently added a new wrinkle to door-to-door selling techniques. It began selling to its salesmen for about one dollar a dozen, a new catalog or magazine which displays most of the company's 340 products (brushes and related products). This catalog is designed to add to the salesman's *real* selling time. In the past, the salesman spent about 30 minutes on each home call with two out of three calls paying off in orders. The new catalog makes it possible to spend only five minutes on an average call. The salesman leaves the catalog with the housewife and returns a few days later to take the order. Presumably, he may now shoot for 50 calls a day and thus can get in about five hours of hard selling.

You will note that this technique combines the old-fashioned door-to-door method and the old-fashioned Sears catalog method into a new selling technique. At any rate, the company's sales for 1956 were more than double the 1948 figure.

The firm which accounts for the largest volume of door-to-door cosmetic sales has dropped all other forms of distribution in favor of house-to-house selling except for a small volume in private brands. Sales in 1956 were running 25 per cent ahead of 1955 and, at that rate, will probably top 85 million dollars when the final figures are in. It is interesting that one of their strongest competitors chose completely different channels of distribution—selling cosmetics through normal retail channels supported by heavy TV promotion. We can infer from that, I suspect, that there is no one ideal method of selling any given product and that it is up to the company's management to make the most adroit use of the chosen distribution channel.

Before leaving this discussion of door-to-door selling, I should like to cite two examples which indicate that it can be quite profitable for both the salesmen and the manufacturing firm. I understand that some of the men who sell Compton's Encyclopedia make as much as $20,000 a year. And some Electrolux vacuum cleaner salesmen do as well.

Like other fields of retailing, apparently, the door-to-door business can be a Tiffany operation or submarginal—depending on your products and the people who sell them.

Distributing Through Company-Owned Retail Stores

Food, shoes, paint, furniture, household appliances, tires, and clothing are among the products commonly sold in this way. As with door-to-door selling, certain products are better suited than others. Size is a minor factor though "you wouldn't open your own store to sell safety pins," says one manufacturer. The director of sales promotion for a producer of consumer durables which sells through its own outlets feels that to be successful company-owned retail stores "need a top quality product in broad demand with mass appeal and a reasonably high ticket." He adds that the product should be one in which service is an important factor.

These are some advantages of this kind of distribution:

1. Setting up retail stores can offer a manufacturer entering a market already filled with competing products an opportunity to display his goods when desirable outlets are already committed to other brands. At least one tire manufacturer opened company stores for this reason. When the company began production in 1928, it found that usual outlets for tires were stocked with competing brands, as were the wholesalers who supplied them. Therefore, the company opened its own retail stores in locations of its choice. It now has over 600 successful stores, some of which also carry products purchased from other manufacturers as well as those produced in its own factories.

2. The manufacturer selling through his own stores, with his own trained staff, is assured that sales efforts will be devoted exclusively to his product.

3. Properly trained store personnel take care of special selling and service. As one clothing manufacturer puts it: "We have taken the trouble to make these suits in our own way, and we want to be sure they are fitted and sold properly. Also, department stores would not carry our complete line of haberdashery and might turn out 'hybrid' customers."

4. Adequate stocks of merchandise can be kept. One company distribution man says: "When you want to launch a special promotion tied in with national advertising, you can be sure of having the merchandise in stock in all units at the right time. You can't always rely on independent dealers in this fashion. They may choose not to stock up on the item you are promoting."

5. In some cases, selling through company stores offers the manufacturer a chance to merchandise his line as a whole rather than in separate sections of department stores, thus underlining the importance of his brand name.

6. Sales training and building the manufacturer's organization are facilitated. According to one sales promotion director: "You never have any difficulty with a new training program. We get our message across with training films and meeting outlines at district, agency and shop meetings in about 30 or 40 days. Furthermore, every new man or woman added to our sales force has a ladder to climb and we like to promote from within our organization."

7. Although it is generally expensive, selling through company-owned

stores sometimes provides the right combination of greatest possible volume and lowest possible cost in locations where there is concentrated demand for the product. A manufacturer of fine men's clothing, for example, who prefers to sell through traveling company representatives, has been forced to maintain retail stores in three Eastern locations. "The demand for our clothing in these areas is so great that we would have to keep representatives constantly on the spot, and that doesn't pay."

8. There is still a further reason for selling some products through company-owned outlets. Sometimes customers prefer to buy direct from the manufacturer—either because they like buying from "exclusive" agencies, or because they think it is cheaper.

Disadvantages are also inherent in this channel of distribution. Topping the list of problems for the manufacturer who chooses to sell through his own stores is the cost of such an operation. Among the uncommon distribution costs he will incur are: Building (or renting), equipping and maintaining stores; building and maintaining a large retail sales staff; providing capable supervision of the sales organization; financing and assuming credit risks on goods sold to numerous customers; warehousing goods, and delivering to large numbers of customers at the right time and place. These, plus other unforeseen costs, are constant whether or not business is good, and make for an inflexible method of distribution. Only a manufacturer who is able and willing to supply a large amount of working capital and to assume the problems of manufacturer, wholesaler, and retailer alike may expect to profit from the close contact with his market which this particular channel of distribution affords.

Distributing Direct to Retailer

The 1948 Census of Business estimated some 17 per cent of manufacturers' sales were made direct to retail outlets. No later figure is available but, according to the National Retail Drygoods Association, up to 90 per cent of such items as clothing, greeting cards, neckwear, handbags, furs, and cosmetics distributed through retailers are sold directly by the manufacturer to the retail establishment.

This is a marketing channel used for practically all consumer goods. As the U.S. Department of Commerce notes in its bulletin, "Primary Channels of Distribution for Manufacturers," "It is used because the manufacturer believes he can sell his line better than can a wholesaler with many other lines."

Fortune magazine has pointed out that retailing in the U.S. is undergoing a major shake-up. Supermarkets and discount houses have forced goods onto the open shelves where, to a large extent, they must sell themselves. As a result, manufacturers are assuming more and more of the selling functions traditionally performed by retailers and wholesalers. In order to create demand for their brands, they rely more heavily on national advertising and promotion. They service their own products—a job once done by jobbers and retailers—and they are taking advantage of the "packaging revolution." As *Fortune* says, "Breaking bulk was once the almost exclusive function of wholesalers and retailers, but manufacturers have been taking over more and more of the packaging function. By demonstrating the power of impulse buying, the supermarket has enormously stimulated packaging by manufacturers and the use of package design as a prime selling tool for anything from haberdashery to nails and screws." Even coke briquettes, once notoriously mean to handle and therefore shipped only in bulk lots, are now packaged in paper bags the size of a barbecue grill, so that may be put in the grill and lighted, bag and all.

Kinds of Products

Although there seem to be few products that cannot be sold direct to retailers, certain factors make some products more adaptable to this type of distribution.

1. The product should be one with a wide demand, or for which wide demand can be created through advertising. Retailers, with limited space, are understandably reluctant to order large stocks of slow moving goods which clog their shelves and warehouses.

2. Items like shoes, which must be stocked in many sizes and styles, are well suited to direct-retail shipment, since they must always be ordered in quantity. Some 85 per cent of all shoes sold by retailers are purchased directly from the manufacturer, according to the National Retail Drygoods Association.

3. The product, at least according to tradition, should be one which does not require special selling or servicing. Washing machines, for example, are classified as "conventional" or "automatic." The conventional machines, requiring almost no operating instructions or service, are often sold direct to retailers. Automatic washers, on the other hand, demand special installation and frequent servicing as well as instruction for the operator. Therefore they are usually sold through distributors.

4. Perishable products often must be sold directly to retail outlets in order to save time. This applies to items whose short life expectancy is a matter of style, such as women's fashions, as well as such perishable products as milk and frozen foods.

5. The margin on the product should be high enough to support the cost of specialized selling. Products whose unit purchase price is high— jewelry, rugs, antiques—are customarily sold directly to the retailer.

6. The same is true of products which constitute a large and essential

part of the retailer's stock—such as greeting cards in a stationery store or major food lines in a grocery store.

7. In some industries—men's clothing, for example—the direct-to-retailer channel is so well established that the retailer prefers to buy directly, fearing that the manufacturer who sells through jobbers is not reliable or that he is undercapitalized.

Advantages a manufacturer gains by selling direct to retailers, according to *Marketing Channels,* include these:

1. He maintains closer relationship to the market and is in a better position to learn consumer reactions to products and policies.

2. His salesmen can do a better selling job by concentrating on a single product or line instead of the wide variety a wholesale salesman represents.

3. He obtains closer cooperation from retailers through the use of demonstrators, displays, cooperative advertising, and other merchandising aids.

4. He keeps track of availability and condition of his goods in stores and assures himself of the fresh appearance of his displays—highly essential in "self-service" markets.

5. If he is not seeking "saturation distribution," he can retain close control over the kinds of outlets which sell his product. The sales manager of a large greeting card company says his company prefers to sell only to "legitimate" dealers—stationery stores, bookstores, greeting-card stores, department stores, etc. This company could not expect wholesalers to do the job of selective distribution which, once established, must be maintained. As the sales manager says, "You can't cross channels of distribution in the greeting card business without making somebody mad."

Disadvantages of direct-to-retailer selling, again, have largely to do with costs. (These, of course, vary according to the type of retailers. Chain stores and other "quantity" buyers may be sold at headquarters without salesmen, at little credit risk.) A manufacturer who chooses to deal directly with his retail marketers needs a considerably larger sales force than the wholesale marketer. As in the case of door-to-door and direct-to-consumer selling, the resulting costs are large. Extending credit and assuming financial risks for many customers also result in high cost. A third high cost factor is the necessity of maintaining inventories at a number of strategic locations.

Another problem is that of distributing salesmen's time properly among many kinds of customers—large and small, chains and independents, etc. One food company finds that some 20 per cent of retail stores do about 80 per cent of the business. To be successful, therefore, in distributing direct to many widespread retailers, a company must employ some sort of distribution cost accounting. The previously mentioned Department of Commerce study cites a company which makes small and large industrial products and sells both direct to users and through dealers. Suspecting it was not making the most of the distribution dollar, the company investigated and found that 90 per cent of the direct accounts in one area were responsible for 74 per cent of salesmen's calls and 57 per cent of invoices but for only 35 per cent of dollar sales volume. Deeper prodding turned up the fact that each salesman's call cost the company an average of $5.00 regardless of whether a sale was made; each invoice processed by the clerical staff cost $1.50—whether the invoice was for $5.00 or $500; and delivery costs averaged about $1.50 each, regardless of the size of the order. The company discovered that serving customers in the area of smallest volume meant an expenditure of $1.86 for every dollar taken in. This was remedied by setting up a dealer in the area and eliminating salesmen's calls to the few large customers who accounted for 65 per cent of volume in that area. Although dealer discounts amounted to $16,000 a year, the company saved some $25,000 a year in marketing expenses—a net gain of $9,000.

From this discussion it is apparent that direct-to-retailer selling has its advantages and its drawbacks, like the other seven distribution methods we are considering here. The important thing is that the manufacturer who uses it be aware of its strengths and weaknesses and that he have the wisdom and courage to adopt it or discard it, according to its profitability for him.

Selling Through Wholesalers, Jobbers, Middlemen, Distributors

The term "distributor," as I use it here, includes all the types of selling organizations generally placed under this heading.

In considering this kind of distribution we might ask:

1. Why have a distributor?
2. What function does he serve?
3. Where does he fit into our economy?

Distributors can provide a local service which manufacturers usually lack facilities to provide. Basically then, distributors represent local service.

To visualize the function the distributor serves, let us examine a typical distributor operation. This is a local company with local identity. They serve their local market from stocks in their own warehouse. They provide sales, service and credit. They buy from the manufacturers they represent and sell to the ultimate user.

The distributor has a definite place in our economy for, representing several manufacturers of related items, his sales cost per item is lower than if the manufacturer endeavored to market it directly. The distributor is able to bring the product to the user at a lower selling cost and thus a lower final purchase price. The distributor not only smooths the flow of business but makes more business possible through lower distribution costs.

Types of Distribution

There are three generally accepted types of distribution. These are: (1) saturation; (2) exclusive; (3) selective.

Saturation distribution is usually used in distributing consumer items that are purchased by the user day after day and week after week. Food and household supplies such as soap and paper towels are in this category. The manufacturer allows any number of wholesalers or distributors to handle the same product in order to blanket the market.

Exclusive distribution is used by manufacturers of products having broad acceptance but not purchased repeatedly by the user. Major appliances such as electric ranges and refrigerators are in this category. Depending on the potential market, the manufacturer may appoint one or more exclusive distributors in an area, each with an assigned territory. Manufacturers of specialized equipment with limited application usually market through exclusive distributors. The manufacturer cannot afford the costs of a direct selling organization whereas the distributor selling related lines of equipment can market the specialized product economically.

Selective distribution is used by manufacturers with a broad line of equipment including some large engineered products and other smaller standardized products. The market for engineered products may be large enough to warrant a local sales office staffed by specially trained sales engineers. Marketing the smaller standardized products through these same sales engineers may not be economically sound so it becomes desirable to select a local distributor who, with his related items, can economically market the smaller products.

When selecting a distributor there are five major points, all equally important, that should be considered. These are: (1) stability; (2) standing; (3) sales; (4) stock; (5) service.

Stability includes not only financial and credit responsibility but the character of the people making up the organization. Are they sound people and how well established are they?

What is their standing in the community? Are they well regarded by their neighbors? What do our own customers think of them and do our customers in the area do business with them?

Is the sales organization large enough, alert and aggressive, and with enough "know-how" to provide the distribution the manufacturer wants? This "know-how" may not exist at the outset, for you rarely find a ready-made distributor. However, if the education and background *and inclination* is there, the "know-how" can be developed.

Does the prospective distributor have the facilities and willingness to carry inventory? Customers are attracted when an acceptable product fairly priced is available from local stocks.

Local service is becoming increasingly important. Customers want to buy from companies that not only maintain local stock but can service equipment when service is needed.

Manufacturers seek the best possible distributor in each trading area. However, the manufacturer must recognize that he must have a sound proposition in order to attract good distributors. The good distributor will want to know about:

1. The product
2. The company
3. Inventory requirements
4. Sales cooperation and product education
5. Advertising and sales promotion
6. Distributor policy
7. Distributor Advisory Council.

Inventory requirements must be flexible in both quantity and type in keeping with the territory potential. The distributor must not be loaded with slow-moving stock. Return of slow-moving stock to the manufacturer must be accepted on a fair basis.

Selling Industries Direct

Products sold through this channel are usually capital goods, large in size and dollar value, complex in design and application. They are system items, such as electronic devices or industrial controls. Or they are raw materials such as metals and chemicals.

Selling this market requires technical knowledge and skill. The usual basic requirement for salesmen is a degree in engineering, chemistry, or whatever field the product serves. In addition, most manufacturers have product training programs of three months' to two years' duration.

Selling must be selective. The cost of a sales engineer is high. Twenty-five to thirty-five dollars an hour of selling time is common, depending on size and density of potential in territory.

The channels used in selling the industrial market vary with the size of the manufacturer and with diversity of products, sales potential, breadth of application, and similar factors. Large manufacturers or suppliers of diverse products with wide application usually have their own sales organizations with district sales offices at strategic locations. However, size alone is not the criterion. Often large manufacturers with a limited line applicable to only a segment of specific industries—such as steel producers, foundries, or paper and textile companies—cannot afford the high cost of maintaining their own sales organizations. They customarily use channels of distribution already discussed such as distributors, factory representatives, or other resale outlets. In all cases, however, the selling organization must have adequately trained personnel, well-qualified by education and experience, if they are to be successful.

Small manufacturers with either a limited or broad line of products often choose factory representatives to market their goods. These sales agents usually sell a limited but noncompetitive allied line of product and are paid entirely by commissions. Handling a diversity of products applicable to the industries they serve, they can afford trained organizations, and they operate much the same as the large manufacturers' district offices. However, they sell in a restricted geographical area and not nationally.

Another channel used by both small and medium size companies is a combination of factory representatives and company-operated district offices. District offices are established in certain large cities or areas of greatest demand for the products. Factory representatives are used in all other trading areas.

Industrial customers range from the small company where purchasing decisions rest with the people responsible for the use of the product—for example, the plant engineer—to the very large companies with engineering departments, purchasing departments, and maintenance and plant engineering groups.

You can appreciate, therefore, that the techniques of selling to this market vary widely. With the small customer there are seldom any formal specifications or even formal requests for proposals. The sales engineer may be consulted on the basis of personal acquaintance or past service rendered, or because he represents a manufacturer with a good reputation.

The problem is stated and often a visual examination of the required application is made. Then the sales engineer recommends the size, type, and other specifications of the equipment best suited to fill the need.

Decision to purchase is sometimes made on the spot, but even where several competitive proposals are considered, the decision is often made by the plant engineer and sometimes by the operating engineer.

Selling to larger firms is much more complicated. Large industry buys through several channels:
1. Consulting engineers
2. Industry contractors
3. Original equipment manufacturers
4. Direct from manufacturers.

Consulting engineers prepare detailed specifications, tabulate and evaluate vendors' proposals, make recommendations to the purchaser for desired equipment and, in some cases, actually place the order. Since they are employed as experts, their recommendations are usually accepted.

Industry contractors are often selected by major firms, especially in the chemical and petroleum fields, to build complete plants including all operating equipment. In selecting equipment they act in much the same way as consulting engineers. However, in the case of "turnkey" jobs, they often have the authority to purchase equipment without consulting their principals.

Original equipment manufacturers are sometimes both an important purchaser and a channel of distribution. They purchase equipment necessary to complement their product and make a complete package. An example is the manufacturer of diesel engines or steam turbines who constitutes a major market for the sale of electric generators necessary to make a complete operating unit.

Large industrial customers maintain engineering departments who prepare detailed specifications often containing evaluation formulas as well as guarantee and delivery requirements. These specifications are sent through purchasing departments to a qualified list of bidders, with a time limit for submission of proposals.

Sales engineers representing the bidders are given an opportunity to present an analysis of their proposals to the purchaser's engineers. These conferences, depending on size and type of product, often take many hours of detailed discussions and involve a number of the purchaser's engineering personnel.

The bids are then tabulated and evaluated, and recommendations are made to the purchasing department which may or may not agree, after analysis of the price, to place the order with the recommended supplier. This authority varies from company to company.

This kind of selling requires technical competence, complete knowledge of company product and competitive products, and ability to present logical reasons for the purchase of the proposed equipment. The work is challenging, interesting, and rewarding. It calls for teamwork in most cases and the highest order of salesmanship.

Selling Through Exporters

Development of an export business and selection of channels of distribution in foreign markets require that certain basic factors be analyzed before specific recommendations are made concerning the best method of selling.

A. As in domestic business, basic considerations must be developed first before approaching channels of distribution.

B. To what extent is the company actually participating in foreign business? What is its present export organization and what channels of distribution are being used? Is the company handling its export business in the same manner as the domestic business? That is, does it sell to customers within the country, or has it already developed certain marketing channels overseas, either through exporters or through importers in foreign countries? How important is the export business as now constituted and how far does the company wish to go into it? Is it content to obtain a certain fixed volume in relation to the domestic operations or is it determined to obtain the full share of the market available overseas?

C. From these basic considerations we determine the proper approach to the export business. We must further consider the nature of the services to be performed in the export function before selecting the appropriate channel of distribution. These services are:

1. Research to determine first the importance of the market, second its areas, and third the adaptability of the company's products and services to it

2. Preparation for export shipment, handling of shipments and documentation, reception of products in the foreign market, and the delivery of products to customers

3. Technical applications required of the products to customers' specifications and needs

4. Financing the business and shipments

5. Service and repair parts problems

6. Advertising and sales promotion.

D. Finally in determining relative advantages of the various channels of distribution available to companies in the export market one must analyze the differences in organization and functions of these various channels.

1. Selling through exporters:

a. Export merchants—These are organizations who purchase merchandise outright from the manufacturers and sell it for their own account in foreign markets, undertaking all necessary export functions. They serve in effect as district offices overseas. They offer the advantage of permitting manufacturers to sell in the export market as though they were selling in a domestic market. They have certain disadvantages in that all manufacturer sales are made at the lowest level with no opportunity for greater profits, that they may not be entirely identified in the foreign field with the manufacturer's basic interests and that they build up the business not for the manufacturer but for the exporting organization. Moreover, organizations of this type have decreased considerably in recent years and usually are available now only for commodity exports.

b. Export commission houses—These are organizations which serve as purchasing agents for overseas users and collect commissions from the users for this service. They handle payments to the manufacturers as well as all documentation and details connected with exporting. Again this type of organization offers the manufacturer the advantage of relieving him of most of the responsibilities and problems involved in the export business. They present a distinct disadvantage, however, in that they assume no obligation to market any particular manufacturer's products but buy on behalf of the user at lowest competitive prices. They do not undertake any long-range advertising or sales promotion functions. The manufacturer must handle these directly. Nor do they provide market research and analysis for the manufacturer and its products. Much business is still being done through export commission houses but generally by manufacturers who have no other export channels available.

c. Manufacturers' export agents—These organizations are similar in function to export commission houses. However, instead of operating in favor of the user, they offer their services to small manufacturers not otherwise organized to handle export business. They perform many of the functions of export merchants but to a very limited extent. These export "middle men" contract with manufacturers to promote sales of their products to the exclusion of other competitive lines in foreign markets. They usually enjoy exclusive agency rights for the manufacturer either for the total market or for specified areas. They offer the advantages of promoting manufacturers' names and brands exclusively and of providing a certain amount of market research and analysis. They are, however, limited in their ability to handle adequately an over-all exporting program, and they usually are unable to perform the functions of local service and spare parts. The principal operation is the handling of export shipments, collections, etc.

d. Foreign purchasing agents, commissions and brokers—This type of organization usually deals in either a limited list of products—mainly commodities such as cotton, rubber, grain, coffee, sugar, etc.—or acts as purchasing agents for large foreign enterprises such as railroads, mining companies, and public utilities. They operate on a commission or fee basis and in many ways function as export commission houses—limited, however, to specific products or customer accounts. They offer opportunities to manufacturers to sell their products, but they have no obligation whatever to purchase only from those manufacturers or to promote and develop the sales and service of their products overseas.

Selling to Importers Directly

As an alternative to developing the sale of a company's products in the foreign market through exporters, a company may sell directly to importers overseas. This is a natural development, particularly after a company has gained some know-how in the export business and is desirous of establishing a firm and expanding position in the export market. It must perform the same basic exporting functions as outlined above but does so through its own organization which generally takes one of the following forms:

1. Built-in export department—This is a department which functions usually under the domestic marketing organization but devotes its time exclusively to export sales. It is headed by an export manager and handles especially those functions which are peculiar to export. But it leaves such matters as advertising and sales promotion, credit and collections, traffic and accounting to the corresponding domestic departments.

2. Separate export division—As overseas business is developed, it may be advantageous to establish an export division separate from the domestic marketing organization and place it under the direction of a Vice-President in Charge of Foreign Business, reporting to top management. Such an organization, in addition to direct sales efforts, also undertakes such other functions as export sales promotion and advertising, financing including credit and collections, traffic, and accounting.

It operates on its own profit basis, purchasing products from the manufacturing operations at a fixed cost and selling to the overseas organization at price levels which permit a profit. It differs from the export department of a marketing division in that its profit responsibilities lie with the export division itself and not with the manufacturing divisions.

3. As a further refinement in export business it is sometimes desirable to establish a completely independent international company as a subsidiary of the parent organization. This company has its own integral organization functioning much as the parent organization does except that it does not manufacture in the country of origin. However, it has its own capital structure and administration. It may undertake foreign manufacture in its own name or do so through subsidiary manufacturing companies overseas. Its relation to the parent organization consequently is solely that of returning profit on an investment by the parent organization in its capital structure.

Any of these company export organizations may sell overseas through distributors, dealers, branch officers or subsidiary companies, or direct sales representatives. To varying degrees all of these channels must provide the necessary export functions outlined previously. The degree to which a foreign organization is developed depends on the importance of the market, the nature of the company's products, and the extent of the organization's coverage.

Selling to the Government

The government is the world's largest purchaser of machinery, supplies, and equipment, and the defense program has expanded its requirements tremendously. Government utilizes three basic methods of purchasing:

1. Advertising for competitive bids based on detailed specifications
2. Negotiating bids with selected suppliers, without advertising
3. Negotiating with a single supplier for proprietary equipment or research and development programs.

The first method is normally used. Therefore, in selling to the government it is important for the supplier to contact the bureaus or departments which require his product, providing information on the products he can supply as well as his qualifications for successfully completing any contract he might be awarded. This action qualifies him for the "Bidders List" and will result in invitations to bid on specifications for products he can furnish.

An important source of information for a company which desires to do business with the Federal Government is a publication available at the Government Printing Office titled "Government Purchasing Directory— Who Buys What and Where." This publication contains a list of the thousands of items purchased by the civilian and military branches of the government. It also lists the locations of various procurement agencies, at which point bid invitations are issued and contracts awarded.

Bear in mind that the government has, in the last several years, decentralized its purchasing functions. This means that all government procurement is not concentrated in Washington. However the administrative heads of all government departments are located in Washington, and authorization for purchases are disseminated to the field offices from these administrative heads. The Department of Commerce, through its Office of Field Service in Chicago, issues a daily publication, identified as "Synopsis of the U.S. Government Proposed Procurements, Sales and Contract Awards." This publication is available to anybody interested in doing business with the U.S. Government. It lists proposed procurements, including a synopsis of the material desired, the procurement office, and its location. In addition, it gives a daily summary of contracts awarded, including the material involved, the procurement office, the name of the successful contractor, as well as the contract price. This provides an excellent source of information for those companies who may be interested in subcontract work for prime government contractors. Another source for locating Navy prime contractors is a similar manual published by the Navy Department.

When the procurement office desires a greater number of bids than may be offered by the "Bidders List" in open competitive negotiations, it may advertise extensively in trade papers, the public press, and other forms of advertising media. A time for the bid opening is set when invitations are issued, and all bids are publicly opened and recorded at that time. The contract award is made to the responsible bidder, whose bid is most advantageous to the government, price as well as other factors considered. Upon award, the accepted bid becomes a legally binding contract.

The second method, negotiation, is utilized when there are special conditions such as:

a. The complicated or experimental nature of the material desired

b. Items whose rapid technological advances make it impracticable to prepare detailed and rigid specifications

c. The urgency of the requirement

d. Insufficient competition among suppliers

e. Other situations arising from the best interests of the government.

The third method, negotiation with a single supplier, is basically for research and developmental services where the initial determination of price is impracticable or impossible. Many times these contracts are awarded on the basis of the manufacturer's costs plus a fixed fee. This type of contract protects the manufacturer against the unknowns always present in research or development work and also protects the government against excessive profits.

During emergency periods government procurement agencies have been authorized to increase the practice of negotiated purchase.

Negotiation in placing government contracts is conducted for various factors other than price, such as delivery, quality of material or services, or other elements. This method of procurement helps achieve maximum production and facilitates the handling by the procurement officer. It permits him to give proper consideration to such factors as high quality performance, efficient use of materials and manpower, and encouragement of small business. This negotiation method is used particularly in placing contracts for requirements of the military.

The contract does not necessarily go to the lowest bidder. The only requirement is that purchase be to the best advantage of the government. Price, faster delivery, or ability to meet difficult or unusual specifications may be the deciding factors. After proposals are received from selected manufacturers, they are studied, and firms submitting the best proposals are invited to discuss, review, and revise their quotations. Negotiated contracts usually contain a price redetermination clause, which requires a review of the cost after completion of contract, and establishment of a revised contract price which may be higher or lower than the original bid.

It should be noted that many government requests, primarily for the armed services, require the supplier to have his product qualified by a government laboratory before a bid can be accepted. This means sending the product to the laboratory for exhaustive testing after which, if accepted, the product is placed on the "Qualified Products List." Once the product is on the Q.P.L., it is considered an acceptable product for the future and does not require subsequent requalification.

Such bids usually require a statement from the supplier indicating the specific Q.P.L. for his product. In some cases, the bid will be considered if evidence is presented that the manufacturer is in the process of having his product qualified.

Also, many bid requests—particularly for the Air Force and Navy

Bureau of Aeronautics—require a preproduction sample and complete testing of it prior to production release. This is important since it has a bearing on pricing and shipping commitments.

Further, it is well to remember that a careful analysis should be made of each government specification since such specifications often require special handling or the furnishing of information not usually required by commercial customers. They may call for detailed drawings with a special format, complete instruction books, security provisions, and rather unusual and severe inspection and tests witnessed by a government representative.

The government permits only the manufacturer and his direct representatives, or a dealer or distributor *employed* by the manufacturer on a *permanent basis,* to submit bids. The manufacturer may not have an agreement on a contingent fee basis with agents, dealers, or distributors. You will recognize in these regulations, the determination by the government to eliminate the "five percenters" who operated rather broadly during World War II. A certification in this respect is required on all current government bids.

Normal advertising and sales promotion directed to government agencies is unnecessary and can be eliminated. Commissions to resalers, wholesalers, jobbers, or middlemen are not permissible. Normal entertainment, seller-paid inspection trips to manufacturers' plants or installations also are not permissible.

Costs of selling to government, therefore, with the exception of highly specialized engineered products, are generally lower than to other types of purchasers. However, competition is keener, the award normally is made to the lowest bidder, and profit margins are lower. In the case of the armed services, the percentage of profit is limited by law.

27. THE NEW RESPONSIBILITIES OF
MARKETNG MANAGEMENT *
by John G. McLean †

Changing economic conditions are calling for a new order of things in marketing management. In addition to their traditional responsibility for handling the selling job, marketing managers today must assume responsibility for: (a) planning marketing strategy; (b) hard-headed, realistic

* Reprinted from *The Journal of Marketing,* © July 1958, pp. 1–8.
† Continental Oil Company.

analysis of the business facts about marketing operations; (c) introducing and speeding the adoption of bold innovations in distribution processes; and (d) manning the front lines of defense in our efforts to maintain the private-enterprise system in the United States.

The handling of these multiple-management responsibilities calls for well-balanced application of the skills of an artist and the skills of a scientist. The marketing manager must, therefore, provide for the development of both types of talent in his organization, and must establish organizational and procedural arrangements which will permit each group to play its proper role in the management function.

The job of the top administrator in any field of business management rarely remains constant for any very long period of time. Changing competitive, economic, technological, political, and social conditions continually require revisions in the nature of the responsibilities assumed by the various senior officers of a modern industrial corporation. These revisions do not necessarily take place concurrently in all areas of management; at any given time they may be rapid in one area and moderate or slow in others.

In recent years it has become increasingly apparent that the job of marketing management is now in a period of rapid transition. The top executive in charge of marketing activities is being called upon to handle new and broader responsibilities, and his associates on the management team are tending to measure his performance by a somewhat different set of standards than in earlier years.

It is appropriate, therefore, to take a fresh look at the scope and character of the marketing manager's job as it exists today and to consider some of the organizational and procedural measures which he may employ to handle the new tasks that are being thrust upon him.

The Responsibilities of the Marketing Manager

As a means of examining the new responsibilities of the marketing manager, let us assume that we are sitting behind the president's desk in any large industrial corporation. Let us further assume that we have hired a new marketing vice president and wish to talk with him about the nature and scope of the responsibilities we want him to assume. What shall we tell him?

Responsibility for the Selling Job

First of all, we must, of course, lay heavy stress upon his responsibility for doing the selling job—effectively, economically, and in a highly competitive manner. Given whatever products we may have and wherever we may have them, it is the marketing manager's job to find customers for them and to see that they are sold in such volume and at such prices that we may earn a respectable profit. This is the traditional role of the marketing side of the business—the day-to-day, bread-and-butter job—and it will always be at the core of the marketing manager's responsibilities.

To accomplish this end, our new marketing manager will have to do many things. He will have all the administrative and human responsibilities involved in recruiting, training, building, and supervising a sales organization. He will have the responsibility for such things as selecting sales territories, carrying out sales promotion and advertising campaigns, establishing price policies, developing suitable volume goals and expense budgets, determining adequate methods of compensation for sales personnel, and handling the difficult problems of customer relations which fall outside normal routines, or which are beyond the capacities of his subordinates.

In dealing with these responsibilities, the new marketing manager will be drawing heavily upon the skills of an artist, because his work will be much in the area of human relations and human motivations, where the intangible and illogical are often more important than the tangible and logical and where intuition is frequently a better guide than any amount of rational analysis. In discharging these responsibilities, he will also be managing many people who are largely of an artistic bent—sales-promotion experts, advertising people, and, to a certain extent, the salesmen themselves.

Responsibility for Marketing Strategy

In addition to this traditional responsibility for doing a selling job, the new marketing manager today must also assume certain other responsibilities which are "new" responsibilities in terms of the new importance they are assuming and the new emphasis which is being placed upon them. Foremost among these is the responsibility for *marketing strategy*. In this term is included responsibility for the *tactics* of marketing in relation to a company's over-all program, and responsibility for the logistics of the entire distribution process.

The whole field of marketing strategy has assumed a rapidly growing significance in recent years for many reasons. Among other things, note the following:

—The unusually high rate of business expenditures for new plant facilities in the postwar period, and growing indications that the major economic problem of the near-term future may be that of stimulating consumer demand to the point where it can absorb the output of the new facilities on a continuous basis.

—The steadily increasing scale of the capital investments required for manufacturing and distribution facilities, which because of the high fixed costs associated therewith, place a high premium on the ability of marketing organizations to predict future sales volume with precision and to deliver results in accordance with forecasts.

—The proliferation of new products springing from accelerated technological research, which has resulted in a high rate of product obsolescence and accentuated all the problems associated with product-line planning, inventory management, and the introduction of new products to the market.

—The growing trend toward product diversification as a means of gaining stability in over-all corporate income, which has tended to complicate the problems of marketing management at all levels of the organization from the bottom to the top.

—The generally rising standard of living, which has tended to make consumers more discriminating in their wants and more exacting with respect to quality, price, and the range of products from which they wish to make selections.

—Finally, the steadily rising costs for labor and other factors of production which have attached a new significance to profit planning and profit analysis, and have created an urgent need to see that each dollar of capital invested in the marketing department is earning a satisfactory rate of return.

All of these circumstances are combining to bring about a fundamental change in the character of the marketing-management job. A new and major emphasis is being placed upon the strategic, tactical, planning, and analytical aspects of the marketing manager's work. Today, perhaps more than ever before, he must conduct a relentless search for new logistic arrangements and new distribution techniques which will improve his cost position in the market relative to competitors. He must likewise ruthlessly comb his existing operations for "profit leaks" and for situations which are at the low end of the scale in terms of profitability.

In dealing with these matters, it will be necessary for the marketing manager to set some new standards for himself and his organization. It has long been recognized that volume considerations must give way to profit considerations in appraising marketing department performance. Today some further transitions are necessary. Profits must be related to capital investments in the marketing area—not only in the headquarters offices, but likewise at nearly all operating levels in the marketing organization. Finally, the senior members of the marketing-management team must be prepared to appraise and evaluate returns earned on invested capital in the marketing department in the light of those earned in other parts of the business.

In short, the circumstances of today are calling upon marketing managers to function in increasing degree as *scientists* in conceiving the business strategy of marketing operations, as well as *artists* in carrying out that strategy.

Responsibility for Facing Business Facts

A third responsibility of the new marketing manager is one closely associated with that discussed above, namely, the responsibility for facing business facts in a hard-headed, realistic manner.

This involves several different things. First, it is necessary to establish the organization and procedures to collect the facts—clearly we cannot face them until we have them. Accordingly, the new marketing manager must employ effectively all the techniques of market research, control reporting, and associated information-gathering activities. The information must then be digested and interpreted, and a constructive plan of action must be developed from the findings. Finally, it is up to the marketing manager to see that something is *actually done* about the results.

These things are not easy for the ordinary selling organization to do. This matter of facing business facts realistically does not "come naturally" to the ordinary salesman. In the normal course of his selling experience, he learns to talk around adverse facts which may be raised by unreceptive customers. He also learns to brush aside the unhappy circumstance of a lost sale and to approach each new prospect with spirit and enthusiasm.

A good salesman thus automatically develops a "good forgetter" and learns not to let his mind be cluttered, or his work be influenced, by negative experiences. He learns to look at the world through some special "salesmen's glasses" which shut out the negative and accentuate the positive. Later on, when he reaches higher management levels and when control reports containing negative information begin to come across his desk, he intuitively closes his mind to them and searches for, or has his subordinates prepare, some other kinds of figures that will be more satisfying to him.[1]

There is, therefore, an important psychological transition which a good salesman must make as he moves up the organization ladder and assumes in increasing degree the broader responsibilities of marketing management. In short, he must become a cold, hard realist in the world of business facts.

Responsibility for Innovations

The new marketing manager should next be charged with the responsibility for introducing and speeding the adoption of innovations in distribution methods. This task is essential for competitive reasons, and also because a constant stream of innovations is necessary for the economic progress of the nation. Only by finding new and more efficient ways of doing things can we realize a steadily advancing standard of living for our population as a whole. The responsibility for innovation is, therefore, important from both a business and social standpoint.

[1] The author is indebted to Mr. Harry J. Kennedy, Senior Vice President of the Continental Oil Company, for the interpretations in this section.

For the marketing manager to discharge adequately his responsibilities in this area, at least three things are necessary:

Receptivity to Changes. First of all, the marketing manager must develop within himself and his organization a receptive attitude with respect to new ideas and new developments.

The individuals in any business group usually fall into two general categories. First, there are those who tend to regard any change in the accepted order of things as a threat to their personal security or happiness, and hence their first response to any change in plans or circumstances is usually negative. Second, there are those who regard changes as a fertile field for new opportunities, and hence their characteristic response is to view changes as desirable until proved otherwise.

Clearly the new marketing manager, and his associates, must be primarily of the second type, because if there is anything we can predict with certainty about the future of business affairs, it is simply that there will be plenty of changes in the present order of things.

Creative Imagination. Next, the new marketing manager must insist upon a very high order of creative imagination on the part of at least some of his subordinates—the power to dream up completely new ways of handling distribution processes.

As we review the history of the past quarter of a century, we can find ample evidence of enormous progress in the fields of science and engineering: radio, television, atomic energy, guided missiles that do their own stellar navigation, jet air transports that will permit us to take off in New York as the sun touches the horizon in the West and arrive in San Francisco before it completely disappears, airplanes that take off and land on their tails, and earth satellites heralding the new era of interplanetary travel! These developments seem fantastic and incredible, but nonetheless they are fast becoming commonplace realities.

As we look about us in the field of marketing management (or indeed, in the field of business administration generally), we can see a number of important new developments, but rarely do we find anything of the breath-taking, awe-inspiring significance of many of the recent changes in the field of the natural sciences. And it is long past time we raised the question, why should this be so? We must, therefore, charge our new marketing manager with the responsibility of finding ways and means of stimulating changes in the distribution field, parallel in importance and scope to those going on in technical areas.

Awareness of Obsolescence. Finally, if the new marketing manager is to discharge his responsibility for innovation, he must develop in himself and his organization the capacity to perceive obsolescence in business policies.

Professor Malcolm P. McNair of the Harvard Business School opened a recent address before the National Retail Dry Goods Association with the following statement: [2]

The trail of business progress is littered with the debris of outworn management devices. One of the great truths of human experience is that management plans, systems, and concepts have a rate of obsolescence just as does a piece of machinery. . . . Originally serving fully appropriate purposes, they tend to become encrusted with habit and tradition to a point where they actually become deterrents to fresh thinking.

In keeping with this thought, the new marketing manager should accept a high order of responsibility for perceiving the points at which *business policies* in the marketing area undergo economic obsolescence and, in effect, degenerate into *business prejudices*.

Responsibility for Defense of Our Economic System

Finally, the new marketing manager should be charged with the responsibility for manning the front lines of defense in our efforts to maintain in this country the private enterprise system which has contributed so much to the high standard of living enjoyed by the American public. The threat to our present economic order which lies in the steadily growing role the federal government is playing in American business life is all too apparent. The experiences of almost every European nation demonstrate that the threat is not an idle one and that it is a very easy thing to drift down the road toward some form or another of socialism.

The political attacks upon business organizations and the growing tendency toward the exercise of various kinds of government intervention and control have their roots, of course, in deep-seated and long-standing misgivings on the part of the public with respect to the motives of business managers and the human and social values of business enterprises, and particularly large-scale enterprises.

In meeting this problem, we must first of all make certain that business practices and methods meet very high standards from a social, moral, and ethical standpoint. We must then resist with vigor and skill the attacks which spring from misguided, ill-informed, or politically inspired sources.

The marketing manager is necessarily in the forefront of this battle, because the marketing department is the one which normally has the closest association with the public. Moreover, the marketing manager is the one who has the responsibility for the matters which have most frequently been the focal points of political attack, namely, price and product policies and business relationships with dealers, jobbers, and the many other small business units involved in the distribution process.

[2] Before the Controller's Congress and Merchandising Division Joint Session, National Retail Dry Goods Association, forty-sixth Annual Convention, New York, New York, January 9, 1957.

If he is to be successful in discharging his responsibilities in this area, the new marketing manager must recognize that it is not sufficient merely to extol the economic and materialistic contributions of our present business system. Good products, in large volumes, at low prices—this is an old story, and the public has long since come to regard these things as minimum standards of performance. The attack today is being made on social, moral, and ethical grounds—and these are the grounds on which it must be met.

The marketing manager must also recognize the importance of taking a consistent position before the public. We cannot, on the one hand, sing the praises of free, unfettered business competition, and on the other hand, seek the pseudoprotection of the so-called fair-trade laws, excessive restraints on foreign imports, and government support of agricultural prices at unrealistic levels. Nor can we clamor for reductions in taxes and federal spending and at the same time plead for government building programs to stimulate trade in areas where we do business. These are inconsistencies which the public will not accept as a steady diet.

Finally, the marketing manager must realize that much of the pressure for government intervention and control comes, unwittingly, from within our own ranks! All too often when competitive pressures become a little more painful than usual, businessmen are inclined to run to Washington for some kind of federal protection or control. Each group, of course, wants only a little bit of federal help—at the points where it is experiencing competitive pressure or having other difficulties—and vigorously *resists* government intervention in other areas. But in the aggregate, this adds up to a tremendous clamor for federal intervention and control—here, there, and everywhere in our economic life! We must recognize that true business competition sometimes achieves its ends by painful means, and we must learn to accept the bitter along with the sweet.

Means of Handling the Marketing Jobs

The new marketing manager might well say: "This is all well and good. I understand and appreciate the significance of the points you have been discussing. Do you now have any suggestions as to how I should go about handling these 'global' responsibilities you have assigned to me?"

Two suggestions might be made in response to this question.

A Problem of Eugenics

The first problem to be faced is one of eugenics. We must do some crossbreeding in our marketing organizations. The handling of these responsibilities clearly calls for a diversity of human talents. We need men who have the personality traits and human characteristics which will enable them to do an effective job in dealing with customers and the public; we need artistic and imaginative people to create effective advertising and sales programs and to develop new ideas with regard to distribution methods; and we need men with strong analytical abilities to cope with the strategic and logistic aspects of marketing operations.

All of these capacities, of course, are not easily found in any one individual. We must, therefore, establish recruiting programs which will continually feed into marketing organizations at least two different types of individuals: a group of "artists" whose primary *forte* will be the problems of personal selling, advertising, and sales promotion, and a group of "scientists" whose primary *forte* will be analysis, interpretation, and logistic planning. In time, these two streams will influence and educate each other, and out of the intermingling will come the new generation of marketing managers.

The task of bringing a sufficient number of analytically minded people into our sales organizations will not be accomplished easily, because any management group is always prone to do recruiting in its own "image."

Organization Arrangements

Beyond well-balanced recruiting, the next step in handling these new responsibilities of marketing management is organizing to do the job. Suitable staff units must, of course, be set up to handle such things as market research, sales analysis, product planning, price analysis, supply and distribution arrangements, and similar matters. It matters little whether all these analytical, planning, and service groups are actually part of the marketing department or attached to other groups, providing they are competently manned and available to the market department when needed. In addition, the senior officers of the marketing department must, of course, be placed on appropriate general committees where they will have an opportunity to participate in the formulation of plans and programs for the company as a whole.

After a suitable plan of organization has been worked out, procedures must be set up, formal or informal, which will enable each part of the organization to play its proper role in the management function. This is a point which is frequently overlooked. All too often we establish a market research unit, or some similar staff group, and then assume that the job is done and that the function will be handled automatically. Actually, continual effort is necessary to make sure that such units participate effectively in the day-to-day stream of management affairs and that appropriate analytical and research experience will be brought to bear upon management problems at the appropriate time.

Conclusion

In one sense, there is nothing "new" at all about the responsibilities of marketing management discussed in the preceding pages. To some degree, it has long been recognized that they were a part of the marketing job. But these responsibilities are *new* today in terms of the new emphasis that is being placed upon them, the new organizations and procedures that are being set up in company after company to assure that they will be handled effectively, the new courses of instruction that are being established in colleges and universities to provide training in these matters, and the new importance they are assuming in the strategy of business competition.

The task of reorienting selling organizations in these new directions will not be easy. Philosophers, historians, and theologians tell us that our greatest strengths often prove to be the source of our most serious weaknesses. This holds true for entire civilizations, small social groups, and individual personalities. Consider, for example, the company executive who has outstanding ability and great capacity for personal leadership—so talented, in fact, that he has no need to develop strong subordinates around him, or, if developing them, fails to use them effectively. Here indeed great strength carries the seeds of serious weakness.

So, too, it will be in the case of many selling organizations. The greater their capacity to do an aggressive, hard-hitting, personal selling job, the less likely they will be to appreciate the importance of, and to assume the responsibilities for, the strategic aspects of marketing and the other new responsibilities discussed above. The task of overcoming this natural tendency and of developing strength with respect to both the old and the new responsibilities is the essence of the job that lies ahead.

28. SELLING WILL BECOME MARKETING *

by Peter F. Drucker †

Our mass market as much as our mass production underlies the American economic miracle, with its high standards of living, its rapid expansion and its full employment. To get the customer to buy is central to the success of any business and to the prosperity of our economy.

* Reprinted from *Nation's Business,* © November 1955, pp. 79–84.
† New York University.

But more and more thoughtful businessmen are beginning to wonder whether our concern with selling and with the salesman is not in large measure a result of our neglect of marketing; whether indeed we do not expect from the sales force and its selling effort results which only marketing can deliver. More and more businesses are, as a result, developing systematic marketing efforts and organized marketing organizations.

One example is the General Electric Company where the former sales vice president is now called a marketing vice president, the former sales managers have become marketing managers and where selling, though still important, is only one function among many others that a new marketing organization is expected to discharge.

The salesman is, so to speak, the combat soldier of business. But combat troops are not much good if they attack the wrong enemy or if they are 2,000 miles from the front where they are needed. And giving the combat soldier the right equipment and the right supplies for his job, when and where they are needed, will multiply his effectiveness many times over. Sending him out poorly equipped and undersupplied may destroy his effectiveness.

Marketing, as we are coming to understand the term, is the organized effort of a business to make sure that its sales efforts go after the right customer and are directed at the right market; to make sure that it applies the right sales strategy and uses its sales efforts where the sales are. Finally, marketing is the organized effort to get the sales force the best equipment at the place and at the time at which it is needed.

Most businesses already do a good deal of marketing—whether they use the term or not. But few of them do an organized job. Even fewer get the most out of the marketing work they are doing.

Here are the main things which companies that are doing a successful marketing job consider essential:

Research, Market Research, Customer Research, and Sales Forecasting. This is the area of marketing that has grown the fastest in American business during the past 25 years.

Product Planning and Testing. These are the newest areas of marketing and the ones where we so far mostly know what should be done rather than how it could be done. A great many marketing people, in all kinds of businesses, feel strongly that these may be, in the long run, the most important areas of marketing.

Product planning does not try to design a new product. This is the job of the engineer, the chemist, or the designer—or in an insurance company, for instance, of the actuary. But product planning tries to bring to the designers the knowledge of marketing needs and marketing opportunities. What products does the customer want? What products does the customer need? What does the product have to do for the customer? How much

can he afford to pay? Is there any good marketing reason why two different kinds of customers should be offered two different models of the same
product, or can the design be unified for both markets, thus making possible real cuts in cost? Product planning, in other words, is the intelligence
service of marketing and of designing, the organization that brings together
all the knowledge about the customer's needs and the market demand,
sifts them, appraises them, evaluates them and then reports the conclusions to the men who are responsible for designing and turning out the
product.

Product testing is the reconnaissance force of the business. It is charged
with testing out a new product or changes in a product, with finding out
where the market for this new product is likely to be and what it demands
of the product. It also tries to find out how the product should be introduced, how it should be advertised, how it should be sold and serviced.
Even the best product testing efforts will not eliminate entirely the risk
that introducing a new product or changing a well-established old product
always entails. But the risk can be greatly cut down. There is real need for
this. Figures indicate that only two out of every ten new products introduced—even by the most powerful and most experienced large corporations—really succeed or are thoroughly thought through and worked out
to the point where they satisfy market needs.

Pricing. "Nothing," the president of a large company said recently, "so
directly influences our sales volume and our profit as the pricing of our
product. Yet we'd be better off using a crystal ball for our pricing decisions
than to use the yardsticks we now have. We really know nothing about
what prices we ought to charge, what prices we ought to design our product
for and, above all, what the price differentials between our different product lines should be. We either just follow the competition in the hope that
somebody else knows better than we do what our price should be, or we
take our production costs hoping that the market will accept them as a
good foundation. Or we go just by tradition or hunch."

Perhaps this is an exaggeration—but only a slight one. Pricing is really
the darkest Africa of management. Here we operate by hunch, by looking
over our shoulders at the competitor or by just adding a fixed margin on
what we think are our costs of production in the hope that the market will
accept our figures. Of course, if the product is overpriced, we soon find
out though rarely soon enough to prevent damage. But many competent
people, businessmen as well as economists, believe that a great many products today are underpriced simply for lack of knowledge as to what the
price should be. And there is even less doubt that few businesses have even
studied the relationship between their prices, their sales volume, their costs
and their profit—let alone have aligned these four pillars of their business
success with each other.

Sales Strategy and Selection of Distribution Channels. Should a business sell to jobbers or directly to retailers? Or should it do both? Should it try to sell by mail or through salesmen? Should it aim at the luxury market and at building an exclusive name for itself? Or should it aim at the mass market and perhaps not even brand its goods but sell them to wholesalers who distribute under their own brand names? Should it have franchised dealers and give the franchise only to a few people in each area? Or should it sell to all who are willing and able to pay the price?

All these are familiar questions. The right answers are different for each industry and each company. Yet the American distributive system has always changed rapidly and it has perhaps never changed quite as fast as today. To determine what a company's sales strategy and distributive channels should be, to develop them, and to determine when a new sales strategy or different channel is needed, is therefore a major problem facing business today.

Advertising and Sales Promotion. This is another familiar category. But advertising, especially advertising beyond a small local neighborhood, is becoming so expensive that a business must know both whether it spends the right amount on its advertising and sales promotion—and too much can be as damaging as too little—and whether it gets the most for its money.

There is one crucial question which few businesses know even how to ask, let alone how to answer. That is: When should one advertise to get results at the time at which they are needed? Most advertising budgets are determined simply by setting aside a fixed percentage of current sales. It may, however, be much more intelligent for, let us say a manufacturer of pumps, to increase his advertising when sales are fairly low and to decrease it—or at least not to increase it further—when sales are high. Another difficult and important question which few businesses would feel capable of answering with confidence is: To whom should the advertising be directed and where should sales promotion take place?

A large department store which tried to answer this question by hunch shows how wrong such a method can be. This store tried to promote the lagging sales of men's wear by displaying men's wear in its women's fashion department. The thought was that the women buy most of the apparel their husbands wear. Hence displaying the men's suits, shirts and ties amidst the women's dresses, blouses and skirts would induce them to go to the men's wear department and pick out a tie or a shirt for their husbands. The result, however, was that the women not only did not buy more men's wear but bought much less women's wear as well. They apparently felt that mixing men's wear with women's fashion goods cheapened and coarsened the entire atmosphere of the store. Yet another store in a neighboring city used the same sales-promotion approach successfully. But it catered to a much lower income group which of necessity calculated men's wear purchases in the household budget—with the wife usually deciding both when and what to buy.

Customer Service. This is important not only where a product requires actual servicing in the customer's home, office, or plant but also where the product apparently requires no service. The customer never buys a product—unless he is a dealer aiming to sell it again. He buys what the product will do for him. Therefore the customer always buys service. It is important to make sure that the product actually gives this service, though there are many ways in which it can do that.

Selling, finally, while obviously of vital importance, is only one phase of the marketing effort.

The first reaction of many businessmen—when they hear talk about the need for marketing—is to say: "Maybe General Electric needs this and maybe General Electric can afford this, but we neither need it, nor can we afford it. Our selling problems are simple and anyway, how can we possibly add to selling costs which are already way too high?"

But there are a few things which any business, even the smallest, can do; a few things which in any business are likely to pay substantial dividends. Five fairly simple things are possible in practically every business and profitable in most of them.

1. The first one—and one which almost any business can do without running into additional costs or effort—is to make a price-cost-volume-profit analysis of its sales effort. What this might be, and what it might do, is shown by an example which, though somewhat simplified, is taken from the experience of a medium-sized manufacturing company.

The company had four major products. Product A sold at $1.00 each. It cost 87 cents to produce it and 6 cents to sell it to distributors. The company sold annually about 2,000,000 pieces making total sales of Product A of $2,000,000 and total profit (before any overhead allocation) of $140,000.

Product B, an improved version of Product A, was priced at $1.50. Manufacturing cost was $1.02. Selling costs were eight cents. Volume was 500,000 pieces a year, making total sales of $750,000 and gross profits of $200,000.

Product C was a different product which, though based on the same engineering principles, served different uses. It was priced at $1.75, cost $1.40 to produce and 14 cents to distribute; 500,000 pieces were sold each year with total sales of $875,000. Total gross profit before overhead was $105,000.

Product D, an improved version of Product C, sold for $2.00, cost $1.58 to produce and 19 cents to distribute; 300,000 pieces were sold, making total sales per year of $600,000 and a gross profit of $69,000. Altogether the company sold about $4,225,000 worth of goods a year and made a gross profit before overhead of just a little more than $500,000. After overhead of $240,000 only $260,000—less than 7 per cent of sales—remained after taxes.

The first thing this analysis revealed was that the sales efforts were not directed where the company would stand to profit the most. The sales manager, in his desire to build volume, pushed his men to sell more of Product A, the one easiest to sell and the one in which the company had a position of leadership. He was only slightly less concerned with pushing Product D where the gross profit margin, before sales costs and overhead allocation, looked so much better than it did on Product C, and where any improvements in sales would seem to promise such great improvement in total sales volume.

Actually the product that needed pushing the most, the product on which the company stood to gain the most from any increase in sales, was Product B. The salesmen would have to sell two pieces of Product A to get the increase in profit which an additional sale of one piece of Product B would have produced. In fact it is doubtful whether the company would have benefited at all from any increase in the sales of Product A. For with a margin between selling price and manufacturing cost of only 13 per cent and with selling costs of 6 per cent, this product actually at best broke even, if overhead costs are taken into account. Product B, on the other hand, had almost double the margin.

This analysis also brought out the question whether there was any point in trying to push both C and D. Was the company actually competing with itself trying to sell both? Was there any point in trying to sell an improved version if the profit on it was actually no larger, in view of the higher sales and distribution expenses? At least it would seem logical to price Product D a good deal higher—perhaps at $2.25—to make up for the high distribution cost and the high overhead which low volume entailed. Or, if this should prove impractical, Product D might be dropped and real sales effort be put behind Product C, especially if, as the small difference in price indicated, there was not enough difference in performance to justify a higher price.

Another conclusion was that, while no major effort should be made to push Product A, improvements were needed in manufacturing to cut costs and make this company staple profitable again.

Finally, this simple analysis raised two important questions. First, where should the company's advertising and sales promotion effort go? Should it go toward pushing Product A, or for pushing those products that promised the greatest profit if successful, that is, B and C? Another question—a product-planning question rather than a sales strategy question—arose in respect to product design.

Should the company concentrate its small and limited engineering effort on changing the design of Product A to make lower manufacturing costs possible? Should it concentrate on cutting manufacturing costs for Product D—which also obviously were high in relation to price? Or should it, which in the end seemed the most intelligent answer, concentrate on merging C and D into a product which, for the manufacturing costs of C, would give the performance of D, and thereby justify a higher price than C was getting at the time?

Obviously much more information than such a summary tabulation can give is needed to answer these questions. And the answers usually will be hotly disputed. Final decision will be on the basis of judgment rather than on the basis of figures. Yet such an analysis, despite its simplicity, is a diagnostic tool of great impact and immediate usefulness. Even in the simplest business, experience has shown, it will bring up possibilities for improvement which, though they seem obvious after they have been noticed, would otherwise not have been noticed at all.

2. Not so simple but equally productive is an analysis of the sales strategy of the business. What distribution channels do we use? What distribution channels do our competitors use? What distribution channels do we not use—and are we right in not using them? On what basis do we organize our sales efforts? Are we aiming, for instance, at getting the cream with the minimum cost? Or are we aiming at mass penetration of the market and at getting the maximum percentage of the potential business regardless of selling cost?

For different businesses different answers will be right. Usually the people who run the business, and especially the people who run the sales end of the business, have a pretty good idea what the answers should be. But without asking themselves the questions they are likely to go on doing things which, if they would only think about them, they would want to change or improve.

A simple illustration is the case of a company that publishes a salesman training program for business. In its own publication the company stressed the need to think through one's sales strategy. But it had never applied its own medicine to its own business. Yet while sales were good profit began to do poorly. Then the company looked at its own sales strategy to find that it had concentrated 80 per cent of its sales effort on small businesses—in other words aimed at mass penetration of the market.

However, only one out of every 25 small businesses visited ever bought. Most of the sales were made only after eight or ten calls. Worse still, almost no repeat orders came from small business even though the small business customer asked for a great deal of help in using the material and in presenting it to his own salesmen.

By contrast companies with 2,000 or more employees either bought on the first or second call or made it clear immediately that they were not interested. Actually one out of every ten such companies called upon bought; and it took only 25 calls on large companies to make a sale whereas it took up to 150 calls on small companies to make one. The cost of a call is the same whether the customer is large or small. More important, one out of every three large customers gave a repeat order without an additional sales call.

A change in the sales strategy which eliminated calls on any potential customer with fewer than 1,500 or 2,000 employees enabled the company to cut its sales costs by almost 70 per cent. But volume or sales did not fall at all—because the large company also gives a bigger order. Repeat sales—on which a business like this actually makes its profit—increased fourfold within twelve months and now require only the minimum sales effort.

This may be considered an extreme example—though I have heard of quite a few like it. But, every sales manager knows that one can either try to reach a specific audience, or one can try to reach everybody. One cannot, however, try successfully to do both—and yet, unless sales strategy is carefully analyzed, this is exactly what a business is likely to try to do.

3. Another simple and productive approach to marketing which even the smallest business can successfully apply, is to ask: What are the customers' unsatisfied wants, wants which neither our product nor that of any competitor really satisfies? The greatest chance to obtain profitable sales in volume lies in the satisfaction of such wants.

A small manufacturer of fuse boxes, safety switches, circuit breakers, mainly for homes, recently scored a nationwide coup when he introduced a better wiring kit for the use of his customers. There is really nothing in this kit that has not been in his line before.

This kit was the result of asking: What is it our customer, the electrical contractor, needs and wants that he does not get? The answer was simple. The greatest potential business in this field lies in strengthening electrical wiring and controls to make homes—most of them at least twenty years old—capable of handling all the new appliances that have come into use since they were built. Yet the contractor had nothing available for this job. In every case he had to figure out what was needed and then had to get together, often from a variety of manufacturers, the pieces he needed for the job. Putting these pieces together into one kit supplied one of the customers' unsatisfied wants—practically without expense other than that of some hard and honest thinking.

4. A related question is: What does our customer consider value to be and how do we give him the greatest value for his money?

In many cases the answer will be "low price." But even price is not as simple as it sounds, as the following examples show clearly.

This is the story of a manufacturer of plumbing equipment which is bought by plumbing contractors who then install it in buildings. The plumbing contractor is, like every contractor, extremely price-conscious. He will buy the product that will enable him to quote the lowest price for a job. But this does not necessarily mean the lowest-priced equipment. Two factors enter into the contractor's price to his customer, the price of equipment and the price of the labor used to install it. And the contractor, customarily, makes his profit primarily on the price of equipment which he passes on to the customer with a mark-up. The cost of the labor he employs is usually passed on with little, if any, mark-up.

Therefore lowest price to the contractor really means that equipment that gives him the lowest price to the ultimate customer, the builder or home owner, with the lowest labor cost ingredient. Products that enable him to cut installation time—and installation skill—can therefore be a good deal more expensive in this day of high wages and scarcity of skilled help. By focusing on the design of equipment that requires little time for installation and even less skill, the manufacturer has been able to increase his market greatly, even though his prices intentionally are somewhat above those of his competitors. In addition to the contractor this manufacturer has been able to tap the new, rich "do it yourself" market.

5. The final simple but effective marketing task which even the small business can carry out, is to think through the service expectations of its customers and the service promise of its product. This service may be built into the product; and this may be the only way to get it. The service may be given in helping the customer use the product or adapt it to his needs. Finally there is the service rendered after the sale, the service with which the housewife is most familiar and the absence of which she resents so much.

Every business can therefore ask: What kind of service do our customers expect? How good does it have to be to live up to their expectations? Do we actually give it or not?

Here are two examples of successful answers. One manufacturer of dictating machines is able to sell his machines at a high price, both absolutely and by comparison with the prices of competitive products. He bases his sales appeal on the promise that he will keep the machine going no matter what happens and at no extra cost to the buyer. He figures that nothing is as annoying to a businessman as to sit down to dictate, only to find that the machine is out of order. Since the sales appeal of any dictating machine is precisely that the owner can dictate in a hotel room, at home after dinner, or while his secretary does other chores, the manufacturer decided that low price was not as important as the guarantee that the machine would always be in working order or would be repaired within half an hour or an hour after a call for help.

Conversely, a leading manufacturer of x-ray machines for medical practitioners owes his position largely to a realization, 30 years ago or so, that
his major service task was to guarantee that no one would be harmed by
his machines. It is of course annoying if an x-ray machine goes out of order.
But it is rarely a major problem. Except in small communities there are
a good many x-ray machines in every town. If the machine in one doctor's
office goes out of order the doctor can have his patient x-rayed at the
hospital. Or he can, without too much trouble, use the x-ray equipment
of a colleague. But an x-ray machine, with its radiation, is potentially a
dangerous thing. Doctor, nurse, technician and patient must be absolutely
certain that the safe level of radiation will not be exceeded. The manufacturer does keep spare machines all over the country which can be lent
to a doctor in an emergency. Otherwise he has made no special effort to
have ailing machines serviced; it may be a week or more before one of the
service men gets around to the repair job. But every machine is built in
such a manner that it will cease to function the moment the safety level
of radiation is exceeded by the smallest amount. In other words service
in a medical x-ray machine consists in building in breakdowns.

These five things, which even the small business can do fairly easily
and effectively, are of course not what a large company today means when
it talks of a systematic marketing effort. Yet they do come to grips with
practically every major effort of marketing; with the job of finding out
systematic and reliable facts about market, customer and sales volume;
with product planning; with pricing; with sales strategy; with advertising
and sales promotion; and with customer service.

Together, in other words, they constitute a package—which will at least
show a business whether it does a reasonably good marketing job and will
enable it to do a good deal to supply its sales force with the direction, the
equipment, and the marketing strategies needed to make sales efforts pay
off.

But there is one more thing to be done. Even if every single part of
the marketing job is done and done well, the question still remains: Do
these efforts hang together and is the sales force really using them to yield
more profitable and cheaper selling?

First the head of a business might ask his sales manager to set down
the objectives of the sales organization. Next he should ask for the assumptions on which the sales efforts are based. Is the sales effort, for instance, based on the assumption that to get more volume is always good
in itself? Is it based on the assumption that more volume will automatically
mean lower sales costs—and does the company's experience bear out this
rather common (and usually dubious) assumption? Is the sales effort
based on the assumption that sales volume is directly proportionate to the
number of calls made by the salesmen? Or is there reason to believe that,

beyond a certain number of calls on any given customer, the salesman is wasting his time and that of the customer?

In other words what are the guidelines which the sales manager himself applies to his marketing effort?

Finally, the most important and usually the most difficult question, the sales manager should outline who is responsible for each piece of the marketing job and what other responsibilities the same man carries, that is, how much of his time and effort he can reasonably be expected to give to marketing.

That is, frankly, a painful thing to do—searching one's own conscience usually is. But wherever it has been used, it has been found—practically without exception—that even in companies that are marketing-conscious, important marketing areas are slighted. Basic marketing information, information that could easily be gotten, simply does not exist; marketing and selling efforts are based on contradictory and conflicting objectives and on inconsistent assumptions; half measures are only too common. Finally, responsibility for the marketing effort is diluted, spread over far too many people, uncoordinated and often left hanging in the air.

A good many people have lately been talking of push-button selling and have made it appear that marketing is a way of getting goods and services distributed without having to use selling and salesmen. There are several examples of such push-button selling—the supermarket or the vending machine for instance.

But there is little doubt that for a long time to come—probably forever—it will take people to sell goods and services and it will take selling to make the customer buy. Marketing is not an attempt to make the salesman superfluous and to make selling automatic. On the contrary it is primarily an attempt to strengthen the salesman and to make his selling effort more effective.

We need such attempts urgently in every business. In the first place the great technological changes today, such as automation, all depend for their success on our ability to establish both stable and expanding markets. Second, one of the biggest opportunities for economic advance now probably lies in reducing distribution costs. There are cost-cutting possibilities in the physical distribution of goods, their movement from plant to warehouse, and from warehouse to distributor, and from distributor to customer; but the greatest opportunities for cutting distribution costs lie in reducing selling costs—that is, in more effective, more planned, more purposeful selling effort. Finally American business will have to learn to sell a much larger volume of goods and services with the same—or perhaps even with a smaller—number of sales people. We anticipate a doubling of national production within the next twenty years but our labor force will grow only a little.

We will not therefore be able to rely on additional people for the additional selling effort needed. Instead, we will have to learn how to increase —perhaps to double—the effectiveness of the sales effort of the individual salesman. In light of this fact alone the belief that all we need are more salesmen is somehow reminiscent of that old joke about the mountain tribe in the Balkans who made a living by stealing each other's sheep.

An individual business might indeed be able to increase its sales force —though only at great increase in cost. The American economy as a whole cannot hope to do so. Even if the individual business can solve its problems by harder selling, the American economy as a whole will have to solve them through marketing.

For the individual business, too, the cheapest and most successful— probably the only successful—way to solve the selling problem is to give some of the time, attention, and money now spent on selling to the marketing tasks, the tasks of finding, developing, and servicing market and customers, on the accomplishment of which the effectiveness and performance of sales force and salesman ultimately depends.

29. THE REVOLUTION IN THE JOB OF SELLING *

by Joseph Lorin †

Strange things, as a TV comic of a few seasons ago used to say, are happening.

—The Grand Union supermarket chain is installing dressing rooms to spur profitable apparel sales.

—Gas stations, which now account for more retail volume than department stores, are starting to use mobile vending carts for household goods.

—Woolworth's is experimenting with selling TV sets; S.S. Kresge has taken on sewing machines. Newberry's "five-and-dimes" now offer charge accounts, free delivery, upgraded lines, and top brands.

—More than 20 per cent of all ladies' hosiery sold last year was bought in supermarkets.

—Discount houses are rushing into the food business; "Two Guys from Harrison," a large Eastern chain, has opened two food supers, plans to add them to all fifteen of their units.

—More than 80 per cent of all major appliance dealers now stock other categories. Between 5,000 and 8,000 are selling soaps, detergents, and looking around for other lines.

—Apparel supermarkets are booming in New England. Housed in empty

* Reprinted with permission from the April 1958 issue of *The American Salesman*, 355 Lexington Avenue, New York 17, New York.
† Grey Advertising Agency, Inc.

textile mills on the edge of town, they have a low-cost "pipe-rack" operation and are starting to add hard lines. Idea is spreading to South and West.

And while these retail outlets were flourishing during the first nine months of 1957, business failures shot up to 300 a week. Half of them are retail stores.

These are some of the latest symptoms of what has by now become a full-fledged revolution in marketing. Reaching every level of the economic structure, this revolution is sweeping away many of the traditional ways of doing things, profoundly changing others. It has affected, and will further affect, consumers, producers, retailers and, perhaps more than anyone else, salesmen.

For the salesman, the single most dramatic effect of the revolution has been to make him in effect an ally, if not almost an outright partner, of the retailer. Time was when salesmen and their customers were in the position of good-natured opponents; a sale was a contest and the size of the order was the only measure of a salesman's victory. Now, a salesman is in the position of being able best to help himself by helping *his customer* sell.

Diversification

The underlying theme of the revolution is the widest possible diversification of lines, sometimes so wide as to cause doubletakes. Drug chains now sell small appliances. Discount houses, which started out by selling appliances, now sell drugs, along with almost everything else. Apparel houses are stocking sporting goods.

The logical conclusion of this game of musical chairs—and they are beginning to appear all over the country—are the giant shopping centers designed to offer one-stop shopping.

The diversification is not just to sell more, but also to increase markup. Supermarkets add drugs because drugs carry a higher profit margin than most food items.

It costs the retailer just as much, in overhead, salaries and the rest, to bring a shopper into his store whether that shopper buys one item, four items, or no items at all. Retailers who understand this naturally try to put as many things on their shelves as they can. For the salesman, this means that he has new opportunities but also that he faces formidable new competition, not only from other brands of his own product, but from entirely different products competing for space and for the retailer's dollar. Each year some 5,000 items never before available in supermarkets are put on sale there alone. There is obviously not room in each store for all of them so the battle for shelf space is rough.

Salesmen as Merchandising Experts

Going back to the old axiom that a full shelf means no repeat orders, the salesman now finds that shelf space itself is at a premium. It is the most valuable commodity in a modern, well-run store. If he wants to get that repeat order, and in many cases the original order too, the salesman and his company have to help the retailer sell his product. In so doing, he becomes himself a merchant. Tie-ins, promotions, related sales, all the techniques of the alert merchandiser are now becoming the operating equipment of successful salesmen.

Examples? A brand of cookies which may not be too lively by itself, possibly because of better-advertised competitors, may suddenly spurt when placed on sale as part of a "Make that next coffee break a coffee-and-cookie break." A hand lotion, which is a high-profit item for the store, may suddenly start selling better if placed on the same shelf as soaps and liquid detergents. Other combinations suggest themselves almost automatically: measuring spoons, mixing implements and houseware baking items (also high-profit generators) occupy shelves alongside prepared cake mixes; baby foods are next to toys; cleaning supplies are next to work gloves.

Thinking up such sales ideas is part of merchandising and generally considered the work of the retailer. Until recently it was not thought to be the responsibility of the salesman who comes to call on him. There is no law, however, barring the salesman from having good ideas about how to promote his own product.

Outlets, Outlets, Outlets

Just as widespread diversification has given the salesman new problems in the form of increased competition, it has also given him tremendous new opportunities. The fact that more things are sold in more places automatically opens up new prospects for him. Whereas a given territory might have included 30 places where lawn furniture was sold, there may now be 100, including gas stations, supermarkets, discount houses, variety stores and, quite possibly, drug stores. There are also many places where lawn furniture isn't sold. Not yet, that is. They too are prospects, likely ones for a salesman who can explain to a merchant how he could make a profit by selling lawn furniture. And very likely ones for a salesman who has a bright idea that can help a merchant sell lawn furniture. Diversification of lines has opened the door wide; anybody can walk through it.

The marketing revolution is not only turning salesmen into merchandisers; it is also making market analysts out of them. One of the revolution's effects, mentioned earlier, is the failure of about 150 retail stores a week. Since the over-all retail volume has not diminished, the buyers are, obviously, moving their trade elsewhere. It's good business for a salesman to know where. He can do this by keeping a finger on the economic pulse of his own market. He should know when a mortality is about to take place and be able to anticipate its effect. No region or community is sitting still these days. As the population shifts and increases, the pattern of retail trade shifts with it.

Price and Preselling

Next to diversification, the most profound effect of the marketing revolution is probably to increase importance of price in retailing. All the spectacular monuments of the revolution, the huge supermarkets, the burgeoning discount houses, the so-called farmer's markets, are essentially elaborate attempts to cut overhead, trim markups, and proudly tell the shopper, "We'll sell it to you cheaper here." High selling volume and rapid inventory turnover are the essential ingredients of the recipe, and depend in large part on the shopper's already having been "sold" on his prospective purchase before he enters the store. The discount manager's dream customer is one who rushes into the store, calls for his wants by brand name, and rushes out with his purchases.

Only advertising came make this dream come true. No customer will rush in to order something he hasn't heard about frequently. Lesser-known brands will therefore sit on a shelf, or would do so if the manager had put them there in the first place. His shelf space is his stock-in-trade; he measures it by the dollar-foot and guards it jealously against slow-movers. When he adds new items to his stock, he carefully assesses their use of the shelf or floor space against other possible uses. Display space and markup are his two main criteria for accepting or rejecting a new item.

Retail experts have a phrase, "the meat of the market," which they use to describe that particular *assortment of different brands of a single item which will generate the highest volume of sales per unit of shelf space.*

Increasingly, salesmen trying to get orders for products which may not be as widely advertised as their competitors' are running up against this "pre-sold," "meat of the market" barrier. To some degree, the barrier is inevitable. The most eloquent sales talk delivered to a store manager in behalf of an off-brand can't change his inventory turnover figures, because his customers, who *could* change it, don't hear the talk.

A salesman can do several things to sell his product even if it isn't included in the "meat of the market."

—One of them, described earlier in connection with supermarkets, is to sell merchandising ideas along with his product. A prospect who is reluctant to take on an order may suddenly warm up if he sees a possibility of staging a store-wide promotion or a profitable tie-in.

—Another thing the salesman can do is to avoid the mistake of assuming that, just because they all look alike, all high-volume, rapid-turnover outlets are alike. In this connection, the man who walks into the discount house and walks out again because the carefully assorted selection doesn't please him, is the salesman's best friend. Somebody will sell him, too.

In a small New England town, an independent supermarket recently moved in and is beating the long-established local branch of a national chain all hollow. How? By better service to be sure, but especially by

Selling the Presold Product

The Marketing Revolution has forced companies to engage in more and more preselling. In modern marketing, the salesman and his company share the sales job.[1]

What the Company Did	*What the Salesman Does*
1. It provided a skillfully designed, thoroughly tested product.	1. He *knows* his product and is an expert at demonstrating it.
2. It packaged the product to be attractive to the customer, and to fit the retailer's shelf plans.	2. He understands the packaging, can point out its superior design, color, function, shape, etc.
3. It carefully determined outlets for maximum efficient exposure to customers.	3. He covers them all, looks for new outlets, and reports back on which ones do best.
4. It paved the way by planned trade ads and promotion.	4. With no need to introduce his product, the salesman has more time to offer the prospect selling ideas.
5. It provided a carefully wrought presentation that saves time and effort.	5. He takes full advantage of it, using it as a base on which to build personal selling.
6. Its sales manager supplied helpful guidance on new lines, new items, new uses and selling points, examples of successful promotions, and threats from competition.	6. Again, he takes full advantage of the guidance to generate sales, and he reciprocates by reporting on competitors' promotions in his own territory.
7. It placed dramatic advertising, preselling the product to consumers.	7. He shows the ads and makes them work for him and his customers by suggesting merchandising keyed to their themes.
8. It generated sales speed by periodic merchandising and promotional activities like premiums, coupons, tie-ins, contests.	8. He puts these devices to work, developing specific ideas that his customers can use to boost sales.
9. It understood the importance of display, provided point-of-sale material for the retailer.	9. He keeps an eye out for the most effective display opportunities.
10. It set up an efficient delivery and reorder system to insure that customers have good service.	10. As his own sales promotion manager, he flushes out thin stock or out-of-stock conditions, fights for good shelf spots.

[1] Outlined by Arthur C. Fatt, President of the Grey Advertising Agency in *The American Salesman,* June 1957.

stocking items which the chain disdains to offer because they aren't sufficiently "presold." There is something called "store-image." It is, substantially, the idea that people have about the character or type of the store that they shop, or don't shop. Price is, of course, an important part of the image, but there are other factors just as important, like prestige appeal.

It is up to the salesman to recognize what store images his prospects are trying to develop, and to suit his presentation and his ideas to their purpose. The manager of the independent market whose store is beating the chain is an ideal prospect. An eloquent sales talk *will* sell him, if it shows him how he can make a profit by buying what the salesman has to sell. Fortunately for salesmen, there are thousands of independents like him, not only in the supermarket field, but also among variety stores, discount houses, drug, and department stores.

To Whom to Sell

Investigating what his outlets are really like, the salesman will make still other discoveries. He will find, for instance, that some supermarkets are wholesaler-owned, that others are cooperatives. Many of the larger chains are setting up buying committees. Superseding even departmental buyers, these committees are in effect multimillion-dollar purchasing agencies that will buy for national distribution, largely on the basis of statistical studies (tonnage moved per man-hour, volume-store space equations, sales productivity per employee, etc.). The committees are hard to crack, but there are also thousands of small chains and independent stores, some very large, and also rack jobbers.

A rack jobber is a man, usually a wholesaler, who will undertake to arrange, stock, and operate a specific nonfood unit inside a store. His "rent" consists of an agreed-upon percentage of his gross. Since he makes his own stock purchases and sets his own price pattern, he is in effect an independent storekeeper much like the operator of a leased department in a department store. For the alert salesman he's a prospective customer-within-a-customer.

Private Labels

Many chains, and independents too, sell products under their own private labels. This practice offers the salesman a wide area of opportunities, especially since it may afford him a competitive price edge, or may hold out the prospect of a better markup for the merchant. Depending on company policy, private branding need not be limited to the obvious food and toiletry lines. A sporting goods retailer probably has trouble meeting price competition from discount houses on well-advertised roller skates or tennis rackets. He could meet it with his own brand, however. A salesman who made it possible for him to do so could expect to have no great trouble with repeat-orders. No revolution will ever change the principle expressed by this sign posted in a large buyer's office: "If you can help us sell it, we'll be more anxious to buy than you are to sell."

So many of the examples cited here have involved supermarkets because supermarkets are probably the most spectacular products of the revolution. The same rules about merchandising, about coping with diversification, about studying the pattern of retail trade, about recognizing and capitalizing on store images, all hold true for other outlets. Every time a hardware dealer decides to clear out some floor space and stock home ceramics or leather-craft kits—and it was probably a salesman who helped him decide to do it—another chapter is added to the continuing revolution.

Two-Way Funnel

In keeping up with these market changes, the salesman has to act as a conduit to feed products, ideas, and services to customers, and to send information about the market and about prospects and customers back to his company. The success of the preselling which the company does to help the salesmen place its products depends in good part on the company's own information about what is actually happening out where the transactions take place. The salesman is the one on the spot who can report. He is both the active missionary of the company and the intelligence agent. And, at the same time, he is the customer's adviser and merchandising consultant.

The marketing revolution has certainly made his job a more complex and challenging one. Just how far the changes will go is anyone's guess. But right now, the whole distribution system in this country is moving so fast, that accepted sales practices of yesterday may be disastrous tomorrow. The major outlets of a few years ago may not even be in the same business tomorrow. In the meantime the salesman is becoming more than ever a key factor in marketing, both for the supplier and for the retailer.

Product Communication Strategy

30. PRODUCT COMMUNICATION PAVES WAY
FOR GREATER SALES *

"American motors will get a larger share of the automobile business in 1955 than in 1954.[1] We are not asking for help from Congress or the Federal Trade Commission or the antitrust people at the Department of Justice. We believe we can do it on our own . . ."

Would you like to attribute that degree of self-help to the sales destiny of your company? Would you like to assign that degree of certainty to your sales promotion program?

You can. The man who spoke those words of conviction, George Romney, the president of American Motors Corporation, doesn't have a guaranteed crystal ball. He has the obvious in mind, but he has the faculty of vocalizing the obvious at the appropriate moment.

The Secret—Mr. Romney is sure his company can meet the challenge "by doing a more effective merchandising and selling job (and) by *articulating* what we have to sell better than in the past."

"Sales articulation" is Mr. Romney's way of characterizing the inseparable link between direct sales and product promotion. Hudson and Nash always have been good products, he explains, "but we have done a terrible job of letting the public know about it."

* Reprinted from *Steel,* February 14, 1955, pp. 73–80. Copyright 1955 by the Penton Publishing Co., Cleveland 13, Ohio.
[1] Editor's Note: This prediction was correct and American Motors continued to increase its market share.

263

Mr. Romney isn't alone in his estimate of the importance of "letting the public know about it" through the media of product communication —catalogs, direct mail, radio, television, publication advertising, trade shows, public relations, trademarks, etc. The nation's product communication budget and the value placed on all passenger cars shipped by the auto industry last year ran neck and neck. Both figures bulked well over the eight billion dollar mark!

Question—With this kind of money being spent "to tell the public about it," metalworking management is asking: How can we get maximum mileage out of our product communication dollar?

To get an informed answer, *Steel* talked to advertising and sales executives in a number of metalworking companies which are doing an outstanding product communication job. Leading authorities in the field of industrial advertising also were interviewed. This is what we found:

Answer—Progressive management is going to the grass roots of product communication, taking a fresh look at what it is, how it operates, what it can do. The exact role of each instrument of product communication is being defined.

Concepts that were "blue sky" yesterday are being accepted today. Production, sales, and product communication are being viewed as integrated rather than separate functions. Product communication budgets are being based on integrated objectives rather than an arbitrary per cent of sales. More realistic ways of measuring product communication results are taking hold.

Where do you start this self-appraisal? Taking first things first, you can ask . . .

What Is It?

Sales Information—A chief engineer heard of a special machine through a friend at a technical meeting. Going to the vice president in charge of production, he recommended that they take a look at it.

"I've never heard of the company," were the veep's first words. "Their salesmen have never been around. What is their line? What is their reputation?" After checking his favorite business papers, he added: "And they don't advertise either."

The company did purchase the machine, but it wasn't until some time later when the vice president happened to see it in action at a trade show and had the opportunity to sound out the company's sales representatives.

Crow About It—The moral is obvious. Direct selling alone is like keeping a secret. You tell one person at a time. Product communication talks to the mass audience.

Properly aimed, it reaches all your customers and potential customers.

It not only talks to the vast number of men who buy your kind of product but also to the even greater number who influence its purchase.

Message—Call it customer education. Your curriculum must drive home three points: Who you are, what you make, what your reputation is.

It sounds simple, but how many of your customers and potential customers can answer the three questions?

How It Operates

Opens Doors—Unless you sell supplies or standards that do not require engineering application, you can't count on product communication to make too many actual sales. Substantial expenditures call for studied purchases. Product communication does its job by paving the way for your salesmen.

It reaches the men who buy and those who influence purchases. A study by U.S. Steel Corporation shows that 1,850 men in 33 customer plants influence purchases. An additional 105 men are buyers. U.S. Steel salesmen see only the latter. With the exception of two buyers, all read business publications in which U.S. Steel advertises.

There is always the question: Who are the key men to contact? One man puts it this way: ". . . it is particularly difficult to pinpoint all the men who influence the purchase of equipment. Our market research reveals as many as 34 men in one company have direct or indirect influence in buying important equipment. It indeed would be difficult for a salesman to cultivate all 34."

Most salesman agree. Koppers Company, Incorporated asked its sales force: (1) Do you consider your company's advertising an important tool in helping you make sales? (115 of 121 salesmen said YES); (2) Do you feel you could do as good a sales job if your company did not advertise? (113 said NO); (3) On making first calls do you find the prospect is familiar with the company because of its advertising? (81 salesmen said OFTEN; 46 said SOMETIMES; no salesman reported a prospect who had NEVER heard of Koppers.)

Why is it important for people to know who you are, what you make, what your reputation is?

Time Lag—You buy a tube of tooth paste on impulse. Most industrial sales must wait for a need or the creation of one. If your product has a life expectancy of ten or twenty years (barring obsolescence), it's a long time between needs. In the interim, you must condition your prospects through constant product communication.

"If you analyze the motivation behind most industrial purchases," says an industrial advertising authority, "you'll find it is the result of an *ac-*

cumulation of impressions. It is impossible to pin it down to this ad or that sales call."

Of course, many products and supplies are standards. One brand doesn't have a price or quality advantage over the other. Sales generally are traced to good service and personal relations. Here product communication can help to get the customer to think well of your company and accept your brand.

No doubt about it, product communication gets into intangibles, but you can prove . . .

What It Can Do

Many Things—Durez Plastics & Chemicals Incorporated used product communication to invade a new field. The company's advertising manager says the foundryman who didn't know his firm existed eight years ago is probably a customer today.

Jarecki Machine & Tool Company was selling all it could produce in 1953, but it launched a national advertising campaign in business publications to build up a backlog of customers.

The same year the National Electrical Contractors Association saw the end of the defense construction boom and allocated $500,000 for a "business development program" to smooth out the industry's traditional feast and famine cycle.

Cheaper—Product communication reduces the cost of making sales. In a 1953 survey of firms selling to product design, plant engineering and metalworking markets, the Sales Executive Club of New York deduced from 228 returns:

The average cost of a sales call was $17.24. Out of every 100 cold calls an average of 9.2 orders were written. The number of orders jumped to 16 when salesmen were following up publication advertising inquiries. In terms of cost per order, this was the breakdown: Cold calls, $187.39; advertising inquiry followups, $107.75.

Gets Around—The head of a successful company (call it company A) tells about the time it was negotiating a long-term loan, which was to be handled through the issuance of debentures. At the same time, its bank was arranging a similar loan to a much larger company (call it company B) in the same area.

Company B was charged 0.25 per cent more interest than company A, which regularly used advertising for many years to advise industry and the public of its facilities.

When the president of company B complained to his banker, he was told that his company was not so well known as company A; that the market for his company's securities was not so broad as company A's.

Proving Ground—Product communication speeds sales. In the acceleration process you'll also get a good idea of how your product will be accepted by the market over the long pull. One vice president in charge of merchandising puts it this way:

"In the long run no product sells because of advertising that would not have sold without it. If the product is not worthy, advertising simply hastens the day when the whole market has sampled and rejected it. Advertising cannot make a permanent success of any product not fit for success of its own."

This vice president views product communication as a phase of market research. The point: Your product must have a need or desire value; it must have a market or a potential market; it must be competitively priced. Unless these qualifications are filled, you probably haven't got a job for product communication to do.

Economics—Have you ever considered the consequences of dropping your product communication efforts?

A survey of 696 industrial companies showed: 220 said there would be an immediate drop in sales if business paper advertising alone were cut. Predictions ranged from an estimated 5 per cent decrease in sales to "it would put us out of business." A qualified or eventual drop in sales was indicated by 177 respondents. And 166 said they would need a larger sales force or would find difficulty entering new markets.

Over-all Economy—Some people go farther. In late 1953, this editorial appeared in *Printers' Ink*. It said in part:

We are not among those who believe that our economy needs the prop of heavy expenditures for national defense or war to keep it strong.

We are among those who believe that advertising has the power—if management will use it—to offset any decline in defense spending that may be in sight.

Today, some of our major industries are running into their first real sales problems since World War II. We believe that in most cases they will be able to lick those problems by increasing or at least maintaining their advertising.

Indications are that they did. But the question remains: How can you be sure you are getting . . .

Your Money's Worth

Facts of Life—Product communication pays—if you know how to use it.

Say you are the proud manufacturer of machinery which makes the only left-handed widget in captivity. You call in advertising: "I'm giving you $500,000 to push this baby. Get a spot on Garroway's morning TV show. Get a spread in the *Post*."

If advertising is worth its salt, it will dig up some facts of business life before spending a cent: Does industry need the machine? Is there a potential market? How big is it? Where is it? Is the price right? Who are the people we want to talk to? Which media of product communication will reach them most efficiently?

Report—If the machine has only 53 potential customers, you won't get much of a return by telling housewives and preschool children about it on Garroway's morning show. The *Post* is a fine magazine, but how many of its readers *aren't* interested in the widget machine?

In this case, specialized business publication advertising is the logical choice. Remember the findings of the U.S. Steel survey? Your advertising finds and influences all the men who may have a part in buying your machines—even if you don't know them.

The Point—Generally speaking, the nature of your product determines the scope of your audience, which breaks down into customers, potential customers, buyers, those who influence purchases.

The question becomes: Which men do you want to reach? Certainly, you won't catch the eye of top brass with a catalog containing information for purchasing agents. Conversely, your four-color ad proclaiming that the widget machine does it better, faster, cheaper doesn't contain the details the engineer wants when he is shopping for a machine to do a specific job.

Or, if you want to converse with top brass and purchasing agents at the same time use the media that reaches both.

Before you can use them effectively, it is important to know . . .

How They Serve

Catalogs

Silent Salesmen—A good catalog is generally regarded as the equivalent of a run-of-the-mill salesman. It contains all the facts: Specifications, dimensions, weights, applications, prices, etc. Further, when the catalog is opened, the customer is in a buying mood. The need is there. He is comparing brands, prices, delivery dates, etc. It is at this point that the good salesman can step in and convince your customer that your product can do it better, faster, cheaper.

Most catalogs reach the men at the production and engineering levels. Many companies also use special-purpose catalogs—books, bulletins, brochures, etc. Say you are a supplier many steps remote from the ultimate use of your product. It may pay to promote end use through a how-to handbook.

Direct Mail

The Rifle—The "personal message to the exact man you want to talk to" is doing a good job for a lot of people. But there is some question whether it will sell a $98,000 machine. As one man puts it: "That kind of customer needs a lot of lovin'. I rate the value of the medium in direct proportion to the price of the product and the degree to which it is a standard."

Other people say: "Direct mail is no better than your mailing list." Then they add: "The next problem is to get by the man's secretary. She generally has authority to screen his mail; 80 to 85 per cent of it winds up in the wastebasket before it gets to him." To get by the secretary or get to "the man," some people use "substantial-looking" house organs as direct mail pieces.

Time

Radio–TV—These instruments of wholesale telling come at premium prices. Both do yeoman's work for consumer items, but a lot of industrial companies say: "We've thought of using them at one time or another, but we can't afford this luxury until we have licked the day-to-day problems of doing business."

Notable exceptions: Local radio and TV have been used to recruit skilled employees when the labor supply is short. On the rare occasion, a company going into a new city may sponsor a local radio or TV show to "get acquainted" with the community.

Space

The Big Plus—Subtle psychology plays an unseen but powerful hand in publication advertising. The editorial acceptance of the publication is transferred to your product. Editorial content determines the publication's audience. The quality of its circulation—the men it reaches—determines how well the audience is covered.

Most people use the over-all approach, choosing the paper with the "best" reputation that talks to the greatest number of customers and potential customers. People who can afford it often combine their efforts, aiming at the big audience in some publications, sniping at special groups in others. Everybody says: "You must advertise with regularity on a continuous basis to get your money's worth."

Trade Shows

The Big Look—This is the one time the men who buy and those who influence purchases come to you. You are generally previewed by an executive who is on the make for ideas. If what he sees, touches, and hears hits a responsive note, he will send production or engineering men around to get down to cases.

"Choose your show by the quality of its audience," is the usual advice.

Companies also like to have home office people and key executives in the booth: "It's about the only time they can meet the customer."

Movies

Magic Carpet—A good movie is the next thing to getting the customer into your plant. You can show him what you make, how you make it, where you make it. When you have a movie, you become a publisher. You have to find ways to circulate it.

One manufacturer is making a smash hit with "show parties." Salesmen arrange to show the company movie at the customer's plant after hours and at the convenience of key personnel. After dinner (which the seller furnishes) movies are shown; and when the lights are turned on, company exhibits are rolled out. When questions are asked, sales and engineering people are on hand to answer them.

Public Relations

Operation Snowball—Here is the opportunity to make the editorial pages. Your product is removed from the resistance of the market place. It has been passed upon by editors and deemed worthy to share in the publication's editorial reputation.

Because of the desirability of speaking through this "approved" medium, most companies keep their news releases on a quality rather than a quantity basis. Editorial needs are carefully studied. The new product release that gets "printed" is universally regarded as the grand prize.

. . . with the fundamentals of product communication and the roles its media play out of the way, the problem boils down to one of proper . . .

Planning

All Together—Progressive management is taking cognizance of incidents like the following and revamping its thinking and planning accordingly:

Research and production spent several years perfecting and making the first whoosis. Sales is called in and told to "go out and sell it." Advertising is called in and told to "back up sales." Both report back in a hurry: "There is no visible market for the whoosis."

Two Lessons: Before turning a gear, go out into the market place and find out what your customers need. If they want it and you can make and sell it at a profit, have research, production, sales and advertising plan a coordinated program. For the best over-all result, their functions must be integrated.

Integrated planning will prompt you to take a new look at . . .

Budgeting

Not Enough—The traditional method of basing your product communication budget on a flat per cent of sales probably won't give you enough money to attain your integrated objectives.

Suppose your sales volume is one million dollars a year. You generally spend 1.25 per cent of sales on product communication. This year you decide to double your sales over the next five years. Next year your sales should be about $1.2 million.

Your objectives call for $35,000 a year to do your product communication job. A flat 1.25 per cent of sales ($1.2 million) will give you only $15,000.

Of course, when you are spending $35,000, you like to see what you are getting for it. You look for ways to . . .

Measure Results

Proof Positive—Ideally, you would like to trace the number of orders that $35,000 brought in. But, remember, salesmen close most of the sales.

The role of product communication is to pave the way for your salesmen. It is a never-ending educational process. Its prime objectives are to inform the men who buy and the men who influence purchases among your customers and potential customers:

1. Who you are.
2. What you make.
3. What your reputation is.

If you want to test the effectiveness of your product communication campaign, have an outside agency ask your customers and potential customers those questions. You'll have to wait two years for a good indication of how well you are known.

Say you find 25 per cent know you this year. If the rating is 35 per cent next year, you know product communication is doing an effective job.

Is this enough?

The Payoff

L.M. Cole, sales manager, Warner & Swasey Company, says:

Through our sales managers and officers it is our business to be in touch with as many customers and prospective customers as we can. We all have the same experience—wherever we go and talk to key executives, we are told that our product is being favorably considered or that the sale actually has been consummated because of the reputation our advertising has built for our company.

Mr. Cole concludes:

Through this advertising Warner & Swasey has sat in thousands of directors' meetings, executive committee meetings, production executive meetings, where no Warner & Swasey man could ever sit—but Warner & Swasey, I repeat, has sat there and has spoken forcefully because our philosophy has spoken for us—our philosophy as expressed in our advertising.

George Romney had something like this in mind when he said: "We believe we can do it on our own."

31. ADVERTISING AND THE MARKETING CONCEPT *

by Robert E. Kenyon, Jr.†

Stripped to bare essentials, business consists of making or selling. In the very early days you made what you could and found a buyer for it with not too much difficulty. As production methods improved and more goods were made, salesmen were employed to locate the buyers. In this period of modern manufacturing demand for goods generally exceeded the supply.

As our productive capacity increased still further, the supply of goods tended to exceed the demand, even though that demand had also increased through higher wages, greater leisure, more wants and desires.

That's when the need became apparent for a greater sales effort backed by more advertising and sales promotion. The attention of business management necessarily shifted from making goods to selling them. Management soon found, however, that selling was no longer a simple operation. Selling had become marketing.

A company's objective today must be to produce goods in kind and quantity that will meet the demands of the market. Managements are coming to realize that a marketing-minded, rather than a production-minded, attitude is the right one to have toward their customers. With this point-of-view management can hope to achieve a profitable balance between production capacity and market demand.

It might be said that a marketing executive thinks of the customer first, whereas a sales executive thinks of the company first.

Another distinction is that the marketing executive is primarily engaged in planning, whereas a sales executive is primarily concerned with doing.

Selling has usually meant getting the order and doing those things which are directly concerned with salesmen and sales management in the development of the greatest possible sales volume. Marketing means the use of all company resources in creating profits through an adequate sales volume.

The best marketing men are those who have an understanding of the key importance of marketing in the making of profits. They may be called

* Reprinted from *Boston Conference on Distribution,* © 1956, pp. 37–40.
† *Printers' Ink.*

"sales directors" or "marketing directors." Titles mean less than an understanding of the strategic importance of marketing in their company operation.

Marketing is a basic business function. Therefore it occurs in a one-man shop as well as in a billion-dollar corporation. The differences are in degree—though admittedly a great degree. The progress of an industrial giant of today from a backyard factory of yesterday illustrates the growth in size and complexity of both the manufacturing and the marketing operation. Manufacturing and marketing are basic to that company, whatever its size.

In a small company, the owner-operator is the maker and the seller. When the company gets bigger, more workers and more salesmen are needed. Then a sales manager. Then advertising and an advertising manager.

In a big company, the man who is responsible for the total marketing operation may be called the "marketing vice president."

Growth in business has created another concept which is essential to the proper functioning of modern business, and that is "integration."

The concept of integration means that all parts of today's complex business enterprises must be correlated, coordinated, integrated so that each part contributes its share to the success of the whole.

Integration occurs all up and down the corporate ladder. The various manufacturing operations must be integrated. The different marketing activities must be integrated. Advertising, sales promotion, personal selling, research, product design, packaging, public relations—all must be interrelated. These specific activities must be integrated so that the whole marketing operation effectively makes its contribution to a company's profits.

The way in which the various activities are used to achieve a given marketing objective has been called the "marketing mix." One marketing mix might include a large amount of advertising; another might depend more on personal selling; still another might have research as its principal component for the current year.

In companies where marketing is a particularly vital operation and where the marketing mix may change from year to year, the head man could, I suppose, be called the "marketing-mix master."

Another characteristic of marketing is that it must be a team operation. The specific activities of advertising, sales promotion, research, product design, etc., demand executives with experience and knowledge in these areas. This group must work together as a team under the leadership of a marketing man in order to achieve the goals the company has set. The title of this man is not as important as his function. He could be president, sales vice president—or marketing vice president. He must be the one to determine what shall be done in the marketing operation. His knowledge of advertising, selling, marketing techniques must be exceeded only by his skill in human relations because he must see that the marketing job is done by the people on his team.

A particularly good result of this team operation is greater mutual understanding among those who must work together. Advertising and sales people, for instance, come to have a better grasp of each other's jobs.

The marketing concept, therefore, is the result of growth in the size and complexity of business, especially in the selling of products. It is a basic business function, and so must be an ingrained part of management thinking.

While marketing includes many specific activities designed to create customers, advertising is a key factor.

Indeed, in this present day economy of tremendous production potential, high earnings, and varied desires or wants, advertising must dominate marketing.

This reason is, I think, simple.

Our productive capacity is so great that prosperity could be hamstrung if people do not continue to buy and consume, buy and consume.

Personal selling, as I have noted before, is not adequate to this task. Customers must be created in as great a quantity as products are mass-produced. Advertising is the mechanized process by which prospects are created for countless products, converted into customers and kept as steady consumers. Advertising is to marketing what the machine is to manufacturing.

The advertising task is complicated today by the new products coming out of new discoveries and processes; by more brands in every product category; by self-service and the consequent need to presell a product before the purchaser even gets to the point of purchase; by the indifferent personal selling in many conventional stores.

Advertising even complicates its own task because there are more advertisements, more media and so greater difficulty in getting through to the readers' and listeners' minds.

The growth of advertising is truly remarkable.

In 1945, the total volume was $3 billion.

In 1955, the volume was $9 billion.

In 1959 it was just short of $12 billion.

By 1965, I'd say it could easily reach *25 billion dollars*.

This fantastically greater volume means that advertising must take on a strategic task in the marketing operations of our companies. Advertising must mass-produce customers as factories mass-produce products in a growing economy.

I'd like to suggest five basic points to guide advertising into its decade of greatest impact and value to our welfare.

1. Advertising campaigns and every ad in a campaign should have a specific objective so that the time, talent, and money invested in it will be a positive contribution to the over-all marketing objective.

2. Advertising must create customers. Every ad must therefore contain a sales idea that will move people, and so move merchandise. The creative people in advertising must be trained and encouraged to develop fresh, new ideas that will make their words ring—and make the cash register ring, too!

3. Advertising must be truthful. Copy must tell a good story and tell it straight. Sharp copy blunts an advertiser's reputation.

Advertisers must not relax their efforts to keep their houses in order. Recent activity on the part of legislation to enact statutes leveled against bait advertisers reflects the public attitude toward questionable advertising practices.

Rather than resort to new legislative methods, it would seem better that advertising itself be a more effective policeman with advertisers, agencies, and media who lean toward the fast buck instead of truth in advertising. The code of ethics established by the many associations in advertising and marketing, the *Printers' Ink* Model Statute in most of the 48 states and the activities of the Better Business Bureaus certainly give us the necessary instruments with which to discipline offensive members.

4. Advertising must be integrated with the marketing program. Advertising, selling, sales promotion, research, packaging, pricing—these and all other marketing activities must be tied together, correlated and integrated so they will all be working smoothly toward their common goal. They should not be pulling in different directions through lack of a master plan or because each executive works out his own destiny.

Packaging, for instance, is no longer just a matter of putting a product in a container. If a product is sold in retail stores, the package should be designed to reach out for the buyer from the store shelf. It must also register a distinct sales impression from the magazine page and the TV screen. The design of the package, the kind of illustration, the color used are decisions that must be shared by the entire marketing team.

5. Advertising should recruit talent for its development. Good people can be found in other areas of a company's operation and in other kinds of work. They should be sought out and sold on making advertising their career.

Education in advertising is getting more attention from all quarters. Universities, colleges, and business schools are improving their curricula and enrolling more students. Those who have received such education in advertising should be brought into the field so they can contribute to its further growth.

Advertisers, agencies, and media are developing on-the-job training courses. People who have received this help should certainly be kept in the field.

May I conclude by quoting three leaders in three widely separated fields.

Paul Mazur, senior partner in the Wall Street firm, Lehman Brothers said in his book, *The Standards We Raise:* "The power of advertising is one of the great persuasive forces not only in educating men and women to a higher standard of living but also in providing industry with its necessary sales volume and workers with their high wages and purchasing power."

Professor David Potter of Yale, in his book *People of Plenty,* says that modern advertising was brought into being by and is peculiarly identified with American abundance. ". . . advertising now compares with such long standing institutions as the school and the church in the magnitude of its social influence."

In his very stimulating discussion of Advertising as the Institution of Abundance, [Potter] points out that "Advertising is not badly needed in an economy of scarcity, because total demand is usually equal to or in excess of total supply, and every producer can normally sell as much as he produces. It is when potential supply outstrips demand—that is, when abundance prevails—that advertising begins to fulfill a really essential economic function."

Hal Stebbins, one of America's great copy writers, sums up in a fine piece of copy the place I think that advertising occupies in the marketing concept:

> It's up to us to show what a dynamic force can do in an atomic age:
> Let's move products by moving people.
> Let's make the truth exciting.
> Let's bear in mind that people buy what they want, not what they need; and that our American economy can't keep in high gear unless the nation's products are not only produced but consumed.
> Let's create advertising that not only sells but builds integrity and prestige for the company that sponsors it—and, in the process, builds believability in all advertising.
> Let's quit apologizing for being in advertising—and for spending money for advertising.
> Let's not be content with rubber-stamp ideas and frigid-formula phrases; with headlines that are dead lines; with body copy that has no body.
> Let's spark our creative power so we get more out of the space and time we use; so we influence more people with less money—and thus reduce our selling costs.
> Let's remember that advertising isn't just a clothes-horse but a work-horse; and that every advertising dollar must yield its pennymost return.
> And let's not forget that nothing is more important in advertising than advertising itself.
> Advertising is a great force. It is we who are not great enough to use it.

32. SALES PROMOTION COMES INTO ITS OWN *

Face-to-face selling is the oldest form of marketing, and advertising, which came into its own with the advent of newspapers and periodicals, got its start long before in the form of shop signs. Sales promotion, by contrast, is a newcomer—and many companies, knowing its importance, still have trouble deciding exactly what it is and where it belongs in the marketing set-up.

To clarify the status of sales promotion in the modern marketing organization, Professor Albert W. Frey of the Amos Tuck School of Business Administration, Dartmouth College, recently conducted a study among producers of consumer and industrial goods. Ninety-three sales promotion managers and 139 sales promotion managers who were also their company's advertising managers cooperated in the survey.

Most Make the Distinction

Judging from their replies, most companies now consider sales promotion an activity in its own right, distinct from advertising. In 77 per cent of the 232 companies, the distinction is formal, and in many others it is informally recognized. One hundred of the companies have separate sales promotion budgets.

Some comments from those who see sales promotion as a separate function in the total marketing effort:

—Neither advertising agencies nor sales departments have a full understanding of what is involved.

—A sales promotion manager's responsibilities are to do the thinking, to negotiate the marketing program which the sales manager is too busy to do and the advertising manager doesn't know how to do.

—Sales promotion is the other half of the job begun by national advertising which, by itself, cannot complete the sale—at least in our business.

—Sales promotion should always be treated as a separate function—no matter how interrelated and connected to advertising it becomes—because it's so important to support sales on a broad front, and the whole idea of sales promotion is conducive to the broader thinking and action that modern merchandising requires.

* Reprinted from *Dun's Review and Modern Industry,* © November 1957, pp. 126–9.

The minority who thought the function should be part of advertising or sales argued that sales promotion was so closely related to the other marketing functions that separation was artificial.

I feel that it's a question of interpretation that can have no effect on the job to be done. . . . It's strictly academic.

My university professor taught me that advertising and sales promotion were separate functions, and it was desirable to have them separated in the sales organization. . . . Years of experience have shown me that quite the contrary is desirable. The problems of each are so similar and they work so closely together that I now hold that a single person should head both functions, reporting directly to the top sales executive. This is so in my case, and I would not be a part of any program otherwise set up.

In my opinion separation is appropriate principally as a budget convenience only. . . . Some of the so-called sales promotion activities are hardly distinguishable from advertising activities.

As to a definition of the function, and the way in which it differs from advertising—which is, of course, also designed to promote sales—the great majority of the sales promotion executives participating in Professor Frey's survey felt that the term "advertising" should cover only (1) selection of the media through which a company will transmit its message to consumers and the trade; (2) buying space or time for the message; and (3) composing and presenting the message. Sales promotion, on the other hand, was defined as the effort to "educate and arouse the interest of salesmen, middlemen, consumers, and perhaps others through a variety of materials, tools, and devices controlled by the company itself."

Place in the Organization

Where does the sales promotion department fit into the company organization? Of the 162 sales promotion managers who answered this question, 74 reported to sales executives, 49 to general management executives, 10 to advertising executives, and 5 to executives responsible for sales and advertising or sales and merchandising.

To whom the sales promotion executive reports seems to depend largely on what groups his efforts are mainly designed to influence. Where sales promotion is part of sales, the reason is generally that the promotion is designed primarily to inform and interest the company's own salesmen.

Usually, however, companies direct only about one-fifth of the sales promotion effort at their own salesman, as the table (based on survey findings) shows.

Where the Sales Promotion Effort Is Directed

Kind of Product Manufactured	Number of Companies	Sales Promotion Targets (% of total effort)			
		Salesmen	Middlemen	Consumers	Others
Consumer Goods	70	22.4	44.8	32.4	0.4
Industrial Goods	32	21.7	26.0	44.3	8.0
Both	59	18.0	40.4	32.8	8.8
Unspecified	5	23.0	26.0	31.0	20.0
Weighted Averages		20.7	39.1	34.8	5.4

The middleman is usually the prime target of the consumer goods companies, while industrial goods promotions are aimed mostly at the consumers—probably because most producers of industrial goods sell directly to the user.

Where *should* the sales promotion department report? In Professor Frey's view, the most logical and rewarding arrangement is to put sales promotion, advertising, selling, and merchandising under a single top marketing executive, perhaps a vice president for marketing.

Wanted: Idea Men

What qualifications should the sales promotion man possess? Above all, said the men who answered this question, he must be creative, capable of producing new ideas—and he needs to develop more of them, perhaps, than anyone else in the organization. Ability to work under constant pressure and enjoy it also ranked high in the responses. It was also agreed that he must know his product and his market.

It may not, of course, be strictly necessary to have a special department to produce sales aids, bulletins, product information sheets, and other promotional tools. A company can get along without a separate sales promotion activity, says Professor Frey, and a good many do. But "sales promotion buttresses and strengthens a marketing operation, magnifying a company's profits and position."

33. BALANCED SALES STRATEGY:

HOW CAN IT BE ACHIEVED? *

"Effective strategy is marketing management's key responsibility," said John R. Sargent, a partner in Cresap, McCormick & Paget, a management consulting firm in New York.

He was outlining for *Printers' Ink* last week the reasons it is so vital in today's competitive markets to have a well-balanced, long-term master plan for marketing.

"The trouble all too often," Sargent continued, "is that a company has a single strong point and it rests easy on it"—for instance, a patent-protected product, or a hot-shot sales manager. Things are going along fine, so the firm's management doesn't worry about market research, product development, advertising, sales promotion, and the other ingredients needed for the long pull. Then, suddenly, a competitor comes out with a new and better product, or the sales manager is hired away by somebody else. And they're in trouble. Example: The carpet industry awoke one day to discover that a bedspread manufacturer had found he could make tufted carpeting on his looms faster and cheaper than the traditional methods of carpet-making could. Today 54 per cent of all sales are tufted carpets. Another example: Where once 20 companies dominated the old reel-type lawn-mower field, there are now more than 250 firms turning out powered, rotary-bladed lawn-mowers.

Why Strategy Is Important

These, of course, are only a few of the ways a company that bases its future on a single strength can someday find itself in difficulty. There are many others. For that reason, Sargent says, it is impossible to emphasize strongly enough the importance and necessity of good, long-term marketing strategy.

What are its ingredients? The prime step is sound forecasting on which to base the long-term sales plan. Then, Sargent feels, there are eight steps that make for well-coordinated and imaginative marketing activity. They are:

Selling: The salesman is well trained; he has a strong story and a plan in contacting customers; he is backed up by executive calls, district mana-

* Reprinted from *Printers' Ink,* © July 17, 1959, pp. 50–1.

ger calls, and specialist attention, all according to the master balanced marketing plan.

Promotion: The advertising and sales departments work closely together in achieving an agreed-upon goal and, recognizing their interdependence, each works with the other. All other activities important to effective marketing are well tied in with the promotion program.

Research: Marketing research is in the process of preparing current data on the size of the market and the competitive situation for both existing and new lines.

Products: New-product development activities are geared to known customer needs and preferences, and are scheduled on a long-term basis.

Competition: Pricing and inventory policies are carefully calculated to implement the marketing plan, including matters of packaging, units of sale, and credit terms required to meet competition.

Service: The company is set up to provide rapid and courteous dealer or customer service on inquiries, orders, and correspondence, as well as technical service whenever it is required by a customer.

Public relations: The company's public relations program is well coordinated with the activities of its marketing program.

Sargent makes the point that there is a substantial difference between "total marketing," about which much is being said and written these days, and marketing strategy.

"We think," he says, "that management's attention should be focused on the end to be reached, not necessarily on just one of the variety of means that can play a part in reaching that end."

Don't Neglect the Intangibles

"Organizational integration of marketing functions may be an important first step in meeting the challenge for some companies, but it is usually only a part of the means." Put another way: there are also many intangibles involved. They include:

Leadership exercised in developing and executing marketing plans and programs.

Imagination in developing and communicating new ideas, particularly an open-mindedness and lack of rigidity in marketing thinking.

Teamwork and coordination by company personnel on all pertinent marketing activities.

Enthusiasm and high morale for all personnel concerned with the marketing operation.

"In other words," Sargent says, "good marketing strategy is represented in a company where all the important tangible marketing activities are set up to function efficiently, and where they are melded harmoniously through the exercise of the intangible elements of leadership, good communications, strong coordination, and the development of a high level of enthusiasm and morale."

Sargent prefers the word "strategy" to "planning" for a definite reason. Planning, he feels, all too often is thought of as a staff job, and a differentiation is made between planners and doers. Strategy doesn't have that stigma attached to it.

"Strategy is laid out by a man who is both a planner and a doer," he says. "Strategy suggests aggressive thinking. In a good, well-balanced marketing program you are on the offensive," Sargent concludes.

34. A THEORY OF PACKAGING IN THE SELLING MIX °

by William R. Mason †

It is axiomatic that the job of packaging is to sell. But after that banality has been voiced, what guides to management judgment—what theories, if you will—influence the choice of a package?

This article is not a check list of features that should be built into a package, but a rough guide to basic judgments management must bring to bear in its choice of packaging before the particulars of type face, combination of colors, package count, or printing method are up for decision.

The critical judgments that must be made on the packaging choice concern the "mix" of packaging attributes best able to perform, in different degrees, the particular functions of the package that are believed to be important to sales. The basic judgment in choice of packaging is "What jobs should the package do, and how completely should it do each?" The answers to the lesser decisions can fall into place once the "mix" of desirable packaging attributes has been determined, once the assignment of basic functions desired of the package has been made. Frequently, too much effort and time are devoted to making lesser decisions, usually on questions of graphic art, rather than this basic judgment.

The packager may accept as a guide, when making basic decisions on product "mix," that:

The major purpose of any package is to influence or control the location of product storage within the marketing channel.

"Storage," as I am using the term, means the holding of goods for future use at any level along the marketing channel, *including the level of the*

* Reprinted from *Business Horizons*, © Summer 1958, pp. 62–6.
† Nashua Corporation.

ultimate consumer. Even at the ultimate consumer level, the product may be stored in several places—sugar, for example, may be stored on a shelf or on the table. The packager is interested in getting the bulk of his product's storage as near as possible to the point of ultimate use.

The functions of the product's package are:

Protecting the product

Adapting to production line speeds

Promoting the product

Increasing product density [1]

Facilitating the use of the product

Having re-use value for the consumer

The performance of a package in the first two of these basic functions is relatively easy to measure through physical testing procedures. And, because it is comparatively easy to evaluate the degrees to which these functions are fulfilled by any package under consideration, such measurement is very common. Today, it must be a rare package that reaches its market without being rated objectively on its degrees of protection and production line adaptability. However, these ratings seem to be applied too often without consideration of the package's ability to fulfill its other possible functions.

There are four other major jobs that the package can do at least partially; these should be assigned priority by company management, but often they seem to be neglected.

All packages have the opportunity to perform, at least partially, each of these functions. But it is an unusual package that performs each to the same degree. That the package gives a superior performance of one function does not necessarily mean that it will give a superior performance of another. Because he needs to choose a package, the packager, whether he recognizes it or not, must assign priorities to the value of each of these functions to further his product's sale and use.

To illustrate, it is usually easy to create a package that has uniquely promotable features quite aside from graphic arts; that is, a package that could eminently perform the promotional function. But something else has to give. Using such a package may require sacrificing a good job in one of the other areas, for example in adaptability to production line speeds or in failure to increase package density. In like fashion, it is frequently possible to build a feature facilitating product use into a package—but not always without sacrificing some measure of product protection.

After all, when a package is criticized as a poor sales- or use-builder, it can be criticized fairly only when its performance of *each* of the basic functions is evaluated. A product may seem "overpackaged" simply because the packager's assignment of priorities differs from the critic's.

[1] That is, increasing the ratio of product volume to package volume.

Interrelationships

Let's examine in a little more detail the way each function impinges on the others.

Protecting the Product

Beyond the requirements imposed by various governmental, carrier, and trade practice rulings, there usually are a substantial number of alternatives open to management with regard to product protection—even during the period when the product is in its distribution channel. To illustrate, even though a carrier ruling may require the product's 24-count carton to have a minimum corrugated fiberboard strength of, say, a 100-pound test, a company's management may choose board that meets more severe tests in order to permit higher stacking or use of mechanized materials-handling equipment by certain important handlers at various levels in the product's distribution channel. Accordingly, in such a situation, an opportunity to tailor the product's package to its product-protection job alone is relinquished because of a desire to better the package's performance of its density-increasing and promotional jobs.

But perhaps a more important range of product-protection considerations occurs at the time of product use—especially when the product is partially used. How much protection should the bread wrapper give a partially used loaf of bread? Will incorporating the use-facilitating features of a pouring spout or a tear tape opening require yielding too much product protection?

Adapting to Production Line Speeds

Sometimes the operating speeds of packaging equipment do not match the speeds of other equipment in the production line. Until recently, for instance, the normal operating speeds of wrapping machinery that would handle polyethylene film did not match the normal production line speeds for many products. Two or more wrapping machines were often required in a production line, and the results were poor space utilization, greater capital investment, and sometimes greater labor costs. As an alternative to these wastes, the packager "made do" with other types of film that could be handled by high-speed wrapping equipment but lacked some of polyethylene's protective attributes. New types of wrapping machines have largely corrected this situation. But the point is that the freedom of the packagers to better their packages' protective attributes was limited.

The question of a package's adaptability to production line speeds, however, usually crops up before the package is actually used. The packager's advertising agency or his sales department suggests a new package with striking promise of being able to fulfill the promotional or use-facilitating function better than current packaging; but, upon analysis, the suggested new package is found to require either slowdowns in production line speeds or investment in new packaging equipment. The company's management is then obliged to judge whether or not the suggested package's better performance of the promotional or use-facilitating functions justifies the slower line speed or the different packaging equipment.

Promoting the Product

Features may be built into a package which are promotable to consumers, to customers, and to intermediaries in its product's distribution channel. But sometimes a feature desirable for promotion to one of the three is not desirable for one of the others. Features that minimize a retailer's loss or pilferage are, presumably, important to him; but they are not necessarily of any interest to consumers. Features that minimize a consumer's embarrassment at purchase can increase a retailer's stacking or display difficulties and make inventory control more trying.

Even granting a package feature that is promotable regardless of level in its product's distribution or use, incorporation of the feature into the package frequently requires sacrificing some good package performance of one of the other basic package functions. For example, a gift-wrapped set-up box complete with nosegay of artificial flowers is a highly promotable candy package, as is a rigid plastic, re-usable package for razors that is large enough to hold a fishing lure. But both packages sacrifice density for better promotion.

Increasing Product Density

This seems to be the area where the packager's sales department on the one hand, and his purchasing and production departments on the other, are most often in disagreement about the choice of packaging. Except on those occasions when the sales department recommends yielding a package's higher density in order to improve its promotional value, the sales department is usually advocating increased package density. It improves relations with carriers; it permits better utilization of space throughout the distribution channel, thus encouraging fuller inventory stocks in the pipeline; and it permits more units to be displayed per assigned running foot of self-service display space. But it frequently slows production line speeds and increases per-unit packaging cost.

Usually this issue turns on package shape. The cylinder, for instance, is an efficient package shape for liquids; a given measure of liquid can be packaged cylindrically with less material than is necessary for any rectangular container holding the same amount of liquid. But the normal 12-count (3 × 4 put-up) layer of a 24-count carton will occupy significantly less shelf space if it holds rectangular packages rather than the same number of cylindrical packages with the same amount of liquid.

But bettering a package's performance of its density-increasing function can inhibit good performance in other areas too. The density of many candy packages, for instance, could be improved significantly, but not without loss of their value as items specifically tailored for re-use as sewing baskets or cookie tins. Increasing density could also lessen the package's value as a promotional vehicle or as a promotable item in itself. Package designers seem better able to build points of brand differentiation into a 12-ounce beer bottle than into the higher-density 12-ounce beer can.

Facilitating the Use of the Product

Excluding changes in the graphic art of packages, most package changes in recent years have been in facilitating the product's use. All the changes to tear tapes, pouring spouts, squeeze bottles, aerosol cans, and so forth would have to be included here. And, as is obvious to anyone exposed to the mass advertising media, bettering the package's fulfillment of this function has proved to be a means of bettering the package's performance in promotion.

In many cases, however, where the use-facilitating function of a package has been improved, a case can be built that some degree of product protection has been sacrificed. And, bettering the package's use-facilitating job sometimes means relinquishing some package value as a re-use container for the consumer. The flow of a viscous liquid perhaps can be directed a little more accurately or easily from the mouth of a narrow-necked glass jar than from a tin can, but packaging the liquid in the glass jar means sacrificing the protection against impact provided by the tin can. The tear tape makes a corrugated carton easier to open but, for many purposes, lessens its value as a re-usable container. Some shaker openings make cleanser or spice packages easy to use but, once used, leave the product exposed.

Having Re-Use Value for the Consumer

Perhaps the competition of the various functions of the package for recognition by company managements is most apparent in this area. In recent years, according much recognition to this function of the package seems not to have been in vogue. Typically, designing a package to do its other jobs well has meant slighting its re-use value—the previous illustrations of candy and razors notwithstanding. A package's re-use value generally has suffered with successive changes unless its re-usability has been very promotable.

The Principle, the Corollary, and Recent Trends

Assuming that two "mixes" are in conflict or partial conflict, management may find the answer by deciding which will be more likely to push product storage as far from the packager as possible. This is, of course, another way of saying that the basic purpose of a product's package should be as much as possible to maximize product inventory near the point of use or possible use. If neither "mix" holds promise of increasing product inventory at the point of use, does either hold promise of increasing product storage at the next level back from the point of use? If neither "mix" aids in getting the product stored on the dining-room table, does either help in getting more of the product inventoried on the kitchen shelves? If neither helps there, which encourages the greater amount of well-placed open display at retail? If it is a tie between the two package "mixes" at this level, which of the two has promise of encouraging the greater retailer inventory—regardless whether in open display or not?

It follows, then, that the most successful package changes are those whose impact is greatest at a level in the product's marketing one step forward from the level currently storing the channel's largest share of the product.

Most recent packaging changes can be understood a little better if viewed against the backdrop of these generalizations. Interestingly, they explain current trends in package design that, on the surface, seem to be running in opposite directions. For instance, recently some company managements have been increasing package size or package count. Other managements have unit-packaged, lessened package size, or reduced package count. But both apparently contradictory approaches have the same purpose—*to maximize product inventory as close to a point of use as possible.* Let's examine a few recent package changes in light of these generalizations (I am referring to those changes that typically affect more than just the package's graphic art).

Changes Involving Package Size or Count

Proprietary medicine, soap powder or detergent, beverages, and toilet tissue are among those widely distributed consumer products whose recent package changes have included addition of "king" or "giant economy" size packages to their lines. Table salt, facial tissue, crackers, and cereal on the other hand are among the items, distributed in large part through the same marketing channel, which have added smaller-size packages or "unitized" packages to their lines. In each case, promotion turning on "convenience" to the user frequently has accompanied the introduction of the new package size. Where the move has been to increase the package size, packagers are trying to encourage the consumer to maintain inventories of their particular brands far in excess of the consumer's normal needs for the product during any reasonable time span between shopping trips. In effect, the packagers are trying to move a greater share of their channel's total storage function closer to the point of use—from retailer to consumer in this particular illustration. Where the move has been to lessen package size, it is apparent that the packagers are trying to move storage location further forward: to get facial tissues into purses as well as on the vanity; to get brand-identified salt on the dining-room breakfast, TV, or barbecue table as well as on the pantry shelf; to get half a dozen varieties of cereal in the home rather than in the store in anticipation of a family's vacillating demands. Again, the packagers are trying to move a greater share of the channel's total storage closer to the point of use.

Changes Involving Package Shape

Ice cream and milk, in both powdered and liquid forms, are examples of items that have been undergoing changes from cylindrical to space-saving rectangular packages. In part, at least, the change has been precipitated by increased recognition of the marketing channel's limited capacity to store items under refrigeration and of its eagerness to husband its shelf space. In effect, the change permits a greater share of the inventory to be moved forward.

Changes Involving Packaging Materials

This is the area where packagers' desires to push storage forward probably have been most apparent. And, incidentally, it is in this area that the lie is put to the belief that a package's prime job is protection of the product. If product protection were the prevailing consideration, few if any of certain kinds of change in packaging materials would ever have taken place. For example:

1. *Changes from opaque to transparent materials* usually have been represented as irrefutable evidence of the packager's good faith in allowing his customers to see his product. Understandably, the suppliers of transparent packaging materials have done what they could to further this impression. But conversion from opaque to transparent packaging typically has meant something else as well: *It has been a means of obtaining favorable open display shelf space at retail,* where the product could be seen by the consumers. In effect, it has meant moving part of the storage function forward in the channel from concealed storage or low-traffic locations to prominent, high-traffic locations. Small wonder that such a premium has come to be placed on transparency—even for products not especially attractive to the eye.

2. *Changes from rigid to flexible materials* have almost always meant re-

linquishing some measure of product protection—and the recent changes from rigid to semirigid or flexible packaging are legion. The changes, while requiring some loss of product-protection value, typically have given the product an especially promotable package, one with conspicuous promise of moving product storage closer to a point of use.

Changes Involving Addition of "Ease-of-Opening" or "Ease-of-Use" Attributes

I believe that, where they have been successful, package changes incorporating this kind of feature have tended to move product storage increasingly closer—however slightly—to the point of use. Typically, the movement of storage effected by such "ease-of-opening" package changes has not been at the consumer level in the product's marketing channel; it has been at the retail level. Perhaps it could be argued that the extremely successful rigid flip-top cigarette package has helped move the smoker's storage of his cigarettes a little closer to the point of their use, but the main value of the package with regard to its movement of product storage has been at the retail level. The package, again, was a means of obtaining a good, high-traffic position in open display for the particular brands of cigarette that pioneered this packaging change. It was something distinctively new that could be promoted to the marketing channel itself—quite aside from its being amenable to use in effective promotion to smokers— for brands not having so extensive or complete retail inventories as those enjoyed by more popular brands.

In summary, the choice of a product's package, no less than the choice of the total selling effort brought to bear on the product, has to represent a reconciliation of a variety of functions, each of which has potential merit in furthering the sale of the product, but all of which are, in part at least, mutually exclusive.

The most successful reconciliation will be the one that, to return to our original axiom, produces the most sales. It will emphasize that function which pushes the bulk of product storage one step farther along the marketing channel and one step closer to the ultimate consumer.

THE SALES PROCESS

part V

Much has been written about how to sell. Techniques and methods for use in prospecting, making the approach, planning presentations, dealing with objections, and closing sales are covered well in standard texts. The articles in Part V under "Improving Sales Effectiveness" shed new light on the subtler aspects of salesmanship. Making the customer want to buy through the creation of confidence and receptivity is stressed. The views of purchasing agents about the effectiveness of salesmen are explained. Also noted, is the growing use of new approaches such as sales seminars where customers are invited into the plant to learn more about problems, and to discuss their problems with sales engineers.

Fundamentals of the sale and improved self management in selling are the key topics covered in the selections under "Planning, Organizing, and Controlling Sales Effort." Experienced salesmen as well as tyros need to review basic selling principles frequently in order to enhance or freshen their knowledge. Part V provides the basis for a self audit of sales insight by those interested or engaged in the field. And because salesmen are often under less direct control by management than those engaged in other phases of a firm's operations, they have greater responsibility to direct intelligently their own activities. The articles in this section help one to sales manage himself to achieve maximum productivity from his time and effort.

Improving Selling Effectiveness

35. SUCCESSFUL SALES TECHNIQUES *

by J.M. Hickerson †

It may be true, as Robert A. Whitney, recently said, that salesmanship is an "American specialty." Certainly salesmanship typifies the competitive spirit of our economy; and if any one person symbolizes the difference between the capitalist and communist systems, it is probably the salesman. Yet few subjects in this country are more widely misunderstood. Misconceptions range the whole way from the popular notion that successful salesmen are rare individuals who somehow have been born with natural qualities of glibness and smooth talk to the equally errant idea that salesmanship is a science, a kind of push-button psychology which anyone can practice if he is let in on the secrets.

Sophisticated sales executives know differently. They are becoming increasingly selective in their employment and promotion policies, demanding salesmen with greater aptitude and ability. They are also becoming increasingly aware of the values and potentialities of training. Management's part in a salesman's development can be planned, positive. There are sound criteria for educating, leading, prodding, and inspiring an average young man with courage, initiative, and interest to become a better salesman.

Why should the selection and training of these men be left to luck or

* Reprinted from *Harvard Business Review,* © September–October 1952, pp. 33–46.
† J.M. Hickerson, Incorporated.

spur-of-the-moment inspiration any more than that of, say, accountants or industrial relations men? They represent the company personally to the public. Moreover, probably no function of the average company has traditionally—and deservedly—contributed so many men to top management as has sales. The bread-and-butter end of the business, it is also a first-class training ground for human relations, knowledge of consumer viewpoints, and understanding of the competitive picture.

Today business is good. To be sure, there are "soft spots" in the economy, but by and large the companies with reasonably good products to offer are able to sell them with comparatively little difficulty. In such circumstances, the need for aggressive, heads-up marketing policy is not so well recognized as it should be. *Most* firms are getting their share of the market. It may not be long, however, before production catches up again as it almost did in 1949 and early 1950. When this happens, the men will be separated from the boys, the professionals from the amateurs, so far as selling is concerned.

What is the difference between the approach of a good salesman and that of a mediocre or poor one? What are the secrets of salesmanship? Certainly these are questions of great significance to the sales manager who seeks to increase the effectiveness of his force—and to the top-management team of which he is a part. Any attempt to answer such questions precisely would, of course, be doomed from the start. There *are* intangibles, there *are* mysteries of human interaction, and there *are,* furthermore, infinitely varied possibilities both of sales problems and of sales approaches. At the same time, the experience of successful salesmen does point up a number of definite object lessons which are of general application—if only to the extent that they indicate the fundamentals involved in meeting sales situations, rather than any ready-made techniques.

Accordingly, in this article I have attempted to take the experience of a number of successful salesmen and to present it in such a way that it will be useful to others. The cases discussed are drawn from a collection of 60 sales stories, contributed by men who are all leaders in their fields.

Analyzing the Sales Problem

Although the art of persuasion may play the dramatic role in making a sale, the primary and really important thing for a salesman to do is on a more mundane, common-sense level. That job is to learn the prospect's viewpoint and adapt to it. In the words of L. Morton Morley, Vice-President in Charge of Sales, Brown Industrial Division, Minneapolis-Honeywell Regulator Company:

I believe that all the other qualities of a true salesman are of lesser importance. He can have enthusiasm, stamina, intelligence, personality, sincerity, and all the other attributes of a salesman, and still be a failure if he does not have the knack of finding the *points of common interest.*

And the important points, Mr. Morley adds, are those which are of chief interest to the prospect—not to the salesman. What Mr. Morley is saying is that each sales problem must be analyzed before one can go to work on it successfully, just as in dealing with any other type of problem.

Learning the Customer's Viewpoint

At the risk of deflating the romance of selling right at the start, therefore, let us take Mr. Morley's experience as an illustration:

Morley's company and another firm were locked in a last-ditch struggle to sell a control system for bleaching processes to one of the largest cotton mills in the South. When Morley was called in to help the district salesman, the prospect mill's purchasing agent—an engineer—was on the verge of signing up with the other firm.

Together with the local salesman and district sales manager, Morley went to the small town where the mill was located. They put up in a local hotel and thrashed the problem over thoroughly. Unless he knew precisely what the problem was, Morley reasoned, he would have very little opportunity of solving it when the psychological moment in the sales interview came. Thus, at the outset, he began getting the facts necessary to orient himself to the customer's point of view.

At the bleaching mill the next day, Morley and his associates entered a large unfurnished room in which about a dozen people were hard at work. They saw the purchasing agent, their "target," sitting at a corner desk bent over his work. He was a huge man, partly bald, with his shirt collar open and sleeves rolled up, and he was perspiring profusely. He beckoned Morley over and indicated chairs. He tiredly asked to be excused for a minute so that he could finish an important bit of work. Obviously he thought he was in for another session of high-pressure salesmanship such as he had been going through with the rival salesmen.

Finally the purchasing agent finished his paper work and opened the conversation by saying: "I've just about made up my mind, but I'm willing to listen to what you have to say."

Now, instead of launching into a glowing and probably disastrous talk about the virtues of his firm's equipment, Morley opened by explaining that he wasn't an engineer but would appreciate it if the purchasing agent would describe the new bleaching operation that was being installed.

The purchasing agent—an engineer, remember—started talking about the process, obviously his pride and joy. Within a few minutes he had become quite enthusiastic and began calling to his secretary for charts and blueprints to illustrate how the new operation would work. The tone of the meeting began mellowing considerably. More important than that, additional facts about the mill's needs in a control system began to appear.

As a result, when the purchasing agent raised the question of servicing and the fact that Morley's electronic control equipment was too delicate for an ordinary workman to fix, Morley, who had been listening carefully, was able to answer him. He could point out several places in which the electronic equipment would actually be easier to repair than a conventional control system.

Although the purchasing agent seemed impressed, Morley kept remembering that he would have to justify his opinion to his superiors. So Morley gave him, not a long song and dance about the technical virtues of the electronic system as such, but the facts that would enable him to support a recommendation to buy it—how it had been tested, tried, and rebought by some of the largest instrument users in the country, how it could save much more than its 30 per cent greater cost over the control systems of Morley's competitors.

Significantly, Morley finally clinched this sale by again keeping the prospect's viewpoint in mind. Knowing that the purchasing agent was not trying to select a batch of instruments but looking for a means of running the plant efficiently, Morley emphasized the reliable, quick service which would be available on a continuing basis. "You've made a deal," the purchasing agent said, and after settlement of the details the contract was signed.

A good salesman will do everything he can to learn the prospect's viewpoint. But remember that he will not, any more than a physician, be able to diagnose the case without seeing the patient too. Opportunities to learn about the sales problem both in advance of the meeting with the prospect and in the actual sales conversation are important. The ability to create and take advantage of such opportunities may mean, as Morley's story illustrates, the difference between a sales attempt that ends "It's a deal" and the one ending "I'm sorry, Mr. Salesman, but . . ."

Preparing for the Sales Conference

Granting the importance of preparation for the sales conference, there is the question of *how* the salesman should go about it. Here is an area in which management can do a great deal to train and improve salesmen and, incidentally, make significant evaluations of a salesman's creative imagination, initiative, and other important qualities.

As might be expected, again there is no easy answer. The extent of preparation needed varies not only with the relative importance of the hoped-for sale and with the situation of the prospect himself but also with the kind of product and industry. A salesman of heavy industrial equipment needs to make a radically different type of preparation, obviously, from that of a salesman of wearing apparel. Nevertheless, concrete illustrations of the ways in which successful salesmen have prepared for representative types of problems ought to be helpful in suggesting the approach needed in betwixt-and-between situations.

In this connection let us consider one of the most interesting of all the 60 cases. The story is told by the thirty-two-year-old head of what is probably the best-known company in the men's wear field—Hickok Manufacturing Company, Incorporated. President since 1945, Ray Hickok was trained by his father to be a salesman, and he still makes salesmanship his chief interest.

When Ray Hickok learned there was a chance that the president of a chain of stores who was dividing the stores' belt business among Hickok and two other concerns might be lined up as a Hickok exclusive, he found the temptation too strong. He decided to try to make the deal himself. Characteristically, he first talked with his "guides," as he calls them, about the president's situation. He came to the conclusion that this man's big interest was inventory, and sales volume was secondary. Then he went out to make the sale.

"I wasn't content with just listening to what my guides told me," Hickok relates. "The first step I took when I reached the headquarters city of Mr. Jones, we shall call him, was to take a trip through his stores. I wanted to study his method of display, the amount of space allotted, the method of presentation, what he was doing about training his clerks, and last, but most important, the inventory. In other words, because I knew his chief concern was inventory, I wanted to see with my own eyes just how much duplication there was, how many styles he was carrying that were unnecessary. Then I wanted to check up to see if he had all our best selling numbers in stock."

The next day Hickok kept the appointment he had made in advance with Mr. Jones, and after the "traditional warm up" he got down to business.

"Mr. Jones," he began, "I had a most interesting day yesterday. I spent about ten hours visiting some of your stores here. Looks like you have a lot of money tied up in inventory."

That remark hit home. Hickok's advance conclusion was right; Mr. Jones was the inventory type. But he was a good merchant, too, or he wouldn't have been occupying the office marked "President."

The conversation went on to some of the merchandising problems of the chain. Then Hickok began relating these problems to the specific matter of men's belts. Where only one brown belt was needed at $2.50, he asked, why have two or three? Why not have one good brown belt that the stores could be sure of having in stock at all times?

From his on-the-ground survey Hickok could be specific on a number of styles the stores were carrying that were unnecessary. The president himself began to comment, as Hickok wanted him to, that it was all adding up to excess inventory. "I could almost see him," says Hickok, "multiplying in his head the specific instances I mentioned by the number of stores in his chain."

The conversation continued, covering numerous other points, but all the time Hickok kept the point about the heavy inventory in the president's mind. This approach, hit upon as the result of careful advance thinking, was largely responsible for the president's being won over when the conference ended. (It might be added, as a rueful postscript, that the deal never materialized. Shortly after, Mr. Jones resigned and was succeeded by a new president who had very different ideas.)

Knowing the Market

Preparing for the sales conference may mean walking through the prospect's store, as in the foregoing case, or a tortuous research job. The latter is most likely to be the case in the technological industries, where a good deal of technical proficiency may be needed before the salesman can get even to first base. The management implications of this difference, however, are not that only technicians should be hired as salesmen. This would be fallacious reasoning, for the "art" elements of salesmanship are no less important in the technological industries—particularly as the point of closing the sale approaches—than in others. Personality, manner, enthusiasm, and appearance count whether one is selling tractors or toothbrushes. Rather, the implications are that men should be picked for sales who have native technical curiosity, who are willing to "sweat blood," if necessary, for needed information about the products and their applications. Technical training may be an asset, but its importance is as a means to an end and not as an end in itself—a fact which should not be disregarded.

An illuminating story of sales preparation in a technological industry is provided by Richard H. DeMott, President of SKF Industries, Incorporated. Incidentally, the sales history of this company, of which this case is one small part, is a good example of the significance of salesmanship to American economic progress. Some 30 years ago, when the incidents described by DeMott took place, the antifriction bearing industry in this country was in its infancy; hardly a machine—or, for that matter, hardly a piece of equipment with a shaft that turned—rolled on ball or roller bearings. Today, modern industry is dependent on these marvels of engineering science and precision. The fact that their use is so widespread is due in no small part to the sales ability and pioneering efforts of people like DeMott in such fields as paper-making, textiles, electric motors, and railroads.

DeMott was district manager in SKF's New York office, and the management of a Brooklyn paper mill wanted his scalp. The SKF people had just installed ball and roller bearings in the mill's Fourdrinier papermaking machine, and in their overconfidence (typical in those days) in the ability of antifriction bearings to cure everything, they had failed to account for wire pull, weight of the roll, thrust load, and other factors. The machine soon broke down irreparably, and neither DeMott nor anyone else could solve the problem. This set him to thinking.

"We don't know enough about the paper industry, so how can we suggest workable applications and make sales?" he asked his staff. "Our information about papermaking machinery is pitifully inadequate. We do not know, for example, the operating characteristics of the equipment, nor do we have data on loads, speeds, temperatures, or moisture conditions under which many of the rolls on these machines operate. In fact," he summed up, "we know next to nothing about the industry that we hope to make a major market for antifriction bearings."

To get this information was not easy, DeMott recalls. "It was not just sitting in a public library and boning up. Armed with a 'little black book' (no personal phone numbers) I spent the better part of a year away from home. I met people I had never known existed, doing work I had never known was done, and I recorded information on paper industry equipment such as jack ladders, barkers, chippers, pulp grinders, refiners, stock pumps, and various rolls on Fourdrinier and cylinder-type machines such as breast rolls, table rolls, press rolls, felt rolls, drier cylinder, calender stacks, and many other shaft-turning locations on which ball and roller bearings might be used."

About one year, dozens of hotel rooms, and approximately 50,000 miles of automobile, horse-and-buggy, and plain horseback travel later, DeMott had the answers. It was a lot of work, but it turned out to be worth it many, many times. It was the big first step in subsequently selling to a machinery manufacturer—a company that didn't even want to let DeMott in at first. That company's installation, in turn, was an entering wedge in cracking an entire lucrative industry as a market.

Everybody who has been a salesman or listened to one appreciates the importance in salesmanship of being able to sound convincing. The practical problem, of course, is how to get that way. DeMott's case points up a relevant moral: part of the problem of sounding convincing is familiarity with one's market. Especially in the technological field, the salesman has to know what his product will do in the customer's plant and why. Let the salesman demonstrate to clients that he knows their point of view, and he will not have to worry about being heard up to the point of his clinching arguments.

But suppose, as often happens, that the prospect's point of view is at odds with the salesman's? For instance, when prices are going down, merchants often defer buying the usual merchandise quantities on the understandable basis that it is foolish to buy today if the purchase can be put off until tomorrow when prices will be lower. The manufacturer, on the other hand, is obviously interested in steady orders. In such a case, the salesman's job is not only to be familiar with the facts of the prospect's business but to be able to interpret those facts—at least the ones that concern the sale—in better management terms than the prospect himself.

Road to Executive Success

The road to success for the sales executive—the salesman nobody meets—is just as long as for the salesman with the sample case, if not longer. There is no royal road—at least none that top sales managers can agree on yet. As an adage, that may sound innocuous. But when we begin to break the sales executive's job down (as best we can) into its main components, and see that one of its components is the ability and interest to plan contacts and associations carefully, tediously, and often over long periods of time, we see that the "pattern of greatness" in selling is not what it is often popularly believed to be as a result of movies, books, and plays.

We may even find that our conception of the ideal sales executive—our mental image of what he should look like, act like, and say—is due for a change. One of the best illustrations of this point is the story told by Harry A. McDonald, a prominent figure in the investment business who in 1949 became the first Republican Chairman of the Securities and Exchange Commission and who, more recently, was appointed Administrator of the Reconstruction Finance Corporation.

My best inspirations and insights come from people. Not long after I left the Navy I began to hear about Grant of Chevrolet. He had done the miraculous, pushed Chevrolet sales to the point where they had outstripped Ford. His name was magic; his reputation glowed; he was the greatest salesman of them all. To see him and to hear him became one of my ambitions. Grant was to speak at a local dinner, and I looked forward to hearing him then as I have later looked forward to meeting the President.

My first sight of that man was one of my deepest lessons in salesmanship. Instead of the majestic figure I had expected, I saw a man who would have been lost in a small crowd. What, I wondered, did he have that had enabled him to bring his product into the forefront of the giants? I soon found out. It was not dynamic radiance, although Grant had an intense charm. His speech was not in parables or that of the orator but one of simple declaration. His achievement was not in the play of personalities but in the power of planning and of ideas.

The sales manager whose planned, intense, creative effort bears fruit in the accomplishments of others, not in making the sale himself, has a new sort of thrill. Using research and psychology, and drawing upon the services of experts who may never have sold a dime's worth of merchandise, he may be like the general who masterminds the successful campaign without seeing a single enemy soldier.

Creating Confidence and Receptivity

Preparing to make a sale is part of the salesman's job and usually a very important part. But adequate preparation alone never made a sale. Far from it. When a salesman comes face to face with his prospect, the make-or-break part of his job begins in earnest. First, he must win the confidence of the prospect, develop a receptive attitude, pave the way for his clinching arguments. How does he do this?

The stories of a securities salesman, a former car salesman, a movie producer, a former wax salesman, and a former newspaper boy may throw some light on that question.

Making the Customer Want to Buy

Most salesmen do not have the luxury of clients coming to them; they have to seek out the clients, and often they are lucky if they can get in the door. A great many salesmen, furthermore, do not sell products or services which can be easily distinguished from those of competitors. Still, the experience of one of the country's top securities salesmen, who was *not* confronted with these disadvantages or (perhaps better) challenges, is an outstanding example of one of the leading principles of salesmanship:

The career of Gerald M. Loeb, partner in E.F. Hutton & Company, New York, is not a dramatic one. It is a repetitious tale of building brick by brick. It is a story of personal devotion to an austere, back-breaking schedule in Wall Street. Loeb rises so early that by the time he reaches Schrafft's at 31 Broadway, where for twenty years he has breakfasted at precisely 7:30 A.M., he has already read all the morning newspapers from beginning to end. By the time the Stock Exchange opens at 10:00 A.M., Loeb has spent two hours at his desk digesting the bulletins on late developments flashed him by branch offices and correspondents all over the globe. He maintains a very heavy correspondence with corporation officials, makes many personal calls on business leaders, and keeps almost as well-posted on developments in a number of industries as do many insiders.

"I remember one top California executive who told me a great deal about his company," Loeb recalls. "I liked it, and altogether my friends and I came to buy and own about 10 per cent of his outstanding shares, which turned out to be a fine purchase. But suddenly this man shut off his information. At first I could not find out what was wrong, but later he told me that I had scared him. 'You knew so much about my affairs I wondered what your real aim was,' he said. Somehow he feared a sinister motive, such as questioning the quality of his management. Of course, his fears were unfounded, and this was the only time that I have ever encountered such a reaction. Usually after I see the executives of a company, I try to see their competitors, their suppliers, and those whom they sell to in order to get a well-rounded and unbiased view of their situation. This procedure may not sound like salesmanship, but of course it is. People buy more from 'the man who knows' than from any high-pressure sales talk that is given them."

From management's point of view, there are important implications in the moral of this story. Management's challenge is to educate its salesmen to such a belief in the product or service that they can confidently orient their approach and thinking to developing the *customer's* interest in the product—not breaking his resistance with "high-pressure" selling. Put in another way, it is making the prospect want to buy, not "selling" him. As Loeb expressed his own attitude, "I don't sell. People buy from me."

A salesman can be encouraged to grow into this kind of thinking. Do the management "higher-ups" set a good example for him of belief in the company? Is he given opportunities to be "in the know" about product development and problems, sales thinking, management policies, and so on; and is he encouraged to come up with new ideas and criticisms? But questions such as these are only the beginning. There are sterner tests. For instance, how much discretion does the salesman have as to what he sells and how much? And how does management react if, after intelligently studying a prospect's interest in the product or service, he encourages him to buy less than first intended? On the answers to questions such as these depend in no small part the salesman's initiative in attempting to gain the customer's confidence.

Use of Discrimination

Of course, there are all sorts of ways to inspire confidence. Indeed, there is probably no form of selling that does not have a place in some situation or other. The prospect may *want* to be mesmerized, may *want* to see an exhibition of cleverness, may *want* to have the heat turned on. Where one individual (say a businessman) can only be sold a truck by a car salesman talking straight performance facts, another individual (perhaps, but not necessarily, a woman) may have to be sold a car on emotional appeal—design, color, comfort, and reminders about what the Joneses have.

In other words, discrimination must be used—discrimination not only as to *how* but as to *when* and even *whether* to try for the sale. On these points, William A. Blees, Vice-President and General Sales Manager of the Crosley Division, Avco Manufacturing Corporation, has some relevant words of advice based on his years as an automobile salesman:

Selling cars is one of the most competitive occupations. Every town in America has automobile dealers cheek-to-cheek, practically, along Main Street. Every one of these entrepreneurs has a tremendous investment in his dealership. To get it, he must be a man of substance. He probably belongs to the Rotary, Kiwanis, Lions, Elks, or some other fraternal organization; possibly to the American Legion and a local country club. He probably has connections in town politics, is active in community affairs and the church. Consequently, each dealer has as many good friends or contacts as another. The sooner auto salesmen realize that the better. There's no point at all, if you want to remain a successful salesman, in persisting in badgering a brother Elk to buy your Chevrolet if his brother-in-law is the local Ford dealer. You have to watch for different types of opportunities. If you're a Cadillac representative, for example, you must know when the veteran Buick owner is ready to step up out of his range.

Encouraging salesmen to use discrimination in deciding when, how, and whether to approach prospective customers does *not* mean, it needs to be emphasized, that management should take the pressure off salesmen to sell, to produce results. Rather, the meaning is in the kind and method of pressure management uses. Blees has some helpful advice on this point, too:

One of my earliest associates taught me another good lesson: "Never grab a lion by the tail." He was a Chevrolet dealer. He said that there was no point in trying to buck the local Ford dealer, his biggest competitor, in a harmful way. Instead, he concentrated on getting *some* of the sales away from Ford, some from Chrysler, some from Nash, etc. There's plenty of business for everyone, he reasoned.

Right now, while I'm selling refrigerators, among many other things, I am applying my friend's philosophy. I don't worry about whether Crosley displaces Norge or Westinghouse. They all have good products and I'm proud to be in their company. We want to beat the leader. I try to teach our dealers how to snag *one* or *two* sales from *each* of our competitors. That way, none of them is hurt, and we increase our sales.

By teaching salesmen to "snag" a sale here and another there (in contrast to putting the pressure on them to sell *every* prospect), management helps to instill the kind of attitude in the salesman which makes it easier for the prospect to gain confidence in him. It is the management way of teaching salesmen to "stop, look, and listen" before jumping into their talks. It makes it easier for the salesman to think he can afford to gamble on a "low-pressure" approach when his instinct suggests it.

A pefect example of the pay-off to the salesman and his company of the selective approach is given by Mr. John Orr Young, retired co-founder of Young & Rubicam, Advertising, and now of John Orr Young and Associates, Incorporated, New York:

A number of years ago, Young & Rubicam decided to broaden its clientele beyond the food field, where it was then specialized, and Young put Parke Davis at the top of his carefully selected list of prospective clients. The subsequent story involved many stages and transactions, but the long and short of it was that Parke Davis became a customer.

Explaining how "this conservative manufacturer" was sold, Young says: "I should characterize it as strictly a low-pressure selling job. I was careful in my approach. I did not strain my adjectives, and I did not make the Parke Davis executives feel that I was trying too hard to 'sell' them."

In his book, *Adventures in Advertising,* Young remembers that "Dr. Lescohier, soft-spoken and poker-faced, then vice president and now chief executive of that great company . . . listened courteously but gave no encouraging words or smiles. I thought, however, that occasionally I detected the faintest sort of gleam in his eyes as I talked. I told him that *if* he should ever have occasion to make a change, *if* he were not happy over every advertisement now being produced for his company, *then* I should like him to give Young & Rubicam a trial.

"Had I employed the stage version of hammer-and-tongs agency selling, this prospect probably would have backed away from me," Young thinks. "Had I tried to do a complete and obvious sales job during those first interviews as I was tempted to do, I probably would not have been asked to call again.

"At this point in my selling experience, because I had once failed to sell a good many of my prospects, I had learned the hard way to cut my selling cloth to the pattern of the buyer's personality instead of tearing into every solicitation with a standardized, cut-and-dried, high-powered selling technique. I had started to learn when to turn on the heat and when to use restraint."

Just as this story illustrates something that *can* be taught about salesmanship, it points up one of the critical values that *cannot.* A salesman may be well aware of the nature and importance of both high-pressure and low-pressure approaches. But unless he is astute about human nature, unless he is able to sense when and upon whom to use one type of approach instead of the other, anything else that he knows is next to useless.

Making a Friendly Impression

One very important secret of creating customer confidence and interest might be summed up simply in a single word—friendship. Perhaps, however, this is not so much a different problem as it is a different way of saying some of the same things that have already been said. For example, in 1939, when Richard de Rochemont was producer of *The March of Time,* he "sold" the Vatican, which up till then had been sacrosanct so far as movie cameras were concerned, on the idea of letting him make a documentary film of

Vatican City; and he did it by winning friendship at the top level—not through professional arrangers and middlemen, all of whom he by-passed, but "on the basis of legitimate common interest" (astutely presented in his conversations, of course).

There are many ways in which friendship can be demonstrated, and none of them need to seem contrived or artificial. Contrary to what some poor or mediocre salesmen seem to believe, most executives—purchasing agents included!—are pretty nice people. They appreciate the same human gestures as anyone else. The salesman who has a feeling for this fact will not find it difficult to show his friendliness.

Probably one of the strongest illustrations of the value of acts of friendship is the story told by Harold Schafer, President of the Gold Seal Company. This company, now a prosperous sales organization with headquarters in North Dakota, was principally a three-man outfit—and a struggling one at that—back in 1945 when Schafer was trying to sell self-polishing wax to the merchants of Aberdeen, South Dakota.

Stores just weren't buying. Schafer felt on the brink of failure as a salesman when, thinking back over the last few days' work, he decided to take a new approach.

"When I called on a store, if the man who owned the store was washing windows, I started helping him wash windows," Schafer says. "If the storekeeper was unloading a truck load of flour in the back of the store, I helped him unload flour. In one lumber yard I helped unload a couple hundred sacks of cement. In one store I helped wash shelving with soap and water and put on display competitive merchandise. I helped several men sweep their floors on my early morning and late evening calls. A lot of people will say that this is not the right approach, but believe me it works. In every case I stepped right into this work without bothering with the formality of an introduction."

This approach brought tremendous results—sales to 41 of the 44 independent retail stores in Aberdeen. Gold Seal has found that it continues to work. Accordingly, in sales training the company makes it a point not to give its men canned sales talks, not to make them practice before mirrors on their approach, but, rather, concentrates on getting each salesman to develop his own "personal touch."

Finally, the problem of getting the prospect to "stop, look, and listen" can be stated in still another way. Mortimer Berkowitz, formerly Vice-President of the Hearst Publishing Company, found it out years ago when he was selling newspapers after school in New York's Union Square. He learned that the boy who simply yells, "Mister, buy a newspaper," does not sell many. But the boy who calls, "Full account of the big fire on Fourteenth Street," or "Society woman jumps out of hotel window," or "President signs new tax bill," does make sales. Why? Because he arouses people's curiosity. He gets them intrigued with what he has to sell. What happens from there on may be a different story, and the problems involved are discussed in the next section.

Making the Sale

Lest the preceding pages with their emphasis on sales-problem analysis, careful planning, and close attention to prospects' viewpoints create any impression that the dramatic and suspenseful elements of salesmanship are not recognized as important by top salesmen, we can promptly point out that this is not the case. Indeed, just the opposite is true. There *is* a romance in selling, and the salesmen who figure in the stories related in the following pages prove it.

Capturing Attention

Originality in salesmanship can take as many forms as there are sales situations. Samuel F. Rolph, General Manager of the Berrien Springs Division of the Yale & Towne Manufacturing Company, once sold a large order of door knobs to the Robert E. Lee Hotel by having his company make up a sample of a knob with General Lee's face modeled on it. Up to that point the competition for the order had been on a price basis; Yale & Towne seemed out of the running, but Rolph's ingenuity made his product stand out, and he got his order.

In some businesses, of course, there is very little opportunity for product differentiation. The originality of an insurance salesman may have to be in his manner or approach; in the prospect's mind, this often distinguishes the company much more than any clause in the contract. Again, washing machines may be sold—or not—on the basis of the service that the customer is assured of; so may many types of industrial equipment.

Dramatic devices are no substitute for sound selling, but sometimes they help. R.L. Hockley, Vice-President of the Davison Chemical Corporation, recalls an associate who began tossing $20.00 bills, one by one, in the general direction of the door. When the prospect, an automobile dealer to whom they had not been able to sell undercoating, asked what the idea was, Hockley's friend answered: "That's what you're losing every time a car goes out of here without an undercoating job." The sale was made. Here again an appeal to the senses was partly responsible.

Perceptual senses are not the only ones that count. In a situation where a demonstration with $20.00 bills is inappropriate, the salesman can appeal to his prospect's sense of humor, or his patriotism, or his sportsmanship. David F. Austin, Vice-President—Sales, United States Steel Corporation, once won his company a good account by helping the prospect straighten out a mix-up with an important customer. When the prospect lets the salesman do a good turn for him, it is difficult not to reciprocate. Buying on this basis may not be "logical," but it is human nature.

It should not be necessary to emphasize that appeals (sometimes "techniques" is a better word) of this sort, even when they work, are only a part —and often a very small part—of the process leading to a sale. Their importance is nonetheless great because they usually have to do with the decisive period when the prospect makes up his mind. Basic to everything, it must always be remembered, is whether the product *as the salesman presents it* is in the buyer's self-interest.

A Basic Principle of Making a Sale

If possible, let the prospect convince himself. There are many ways of doing this. Some of the best ways would be classified as indirect. They involve suggestion, restatements of customer viewpoints, anecdotes, and so on.

One of the best of them is asking questions. Frank Bettger, regarded by Dale Carnegie as the best teacher of sales training in America today, learned this years ago from a top salesman of an earlier generation, J. Elliott Hall. Bettger was electrified by Hall's demonstration of meeting objections by asking questions. According to Hall, if the prospect said he couldn't make up his mind, the salesman should ask questions to help him pinpoint the trouble spots. If the prospect said he wanted to go home and "think it over," the salesman should ask questions to help him find out just what it *was* he wanted to think over. The idea, in other words, was to help the prospect recognize what he wanted and then to help him decide how to get it—not to persuade or influence him in the usual sense.

But no approach works all the time. Sometimes the only solution is the exact opposite of indirection and restraint. Graham Patterson, the publishing head of the *Farm Journal* and *Pathfinder,* once managed to get General Wood of Sears, Roebuck interested in farm-journal advertising, after the ordinary means had failed, by openly challenging him to do better than Montgomery Ward if he *didn't* advertise in farm journals. (Patterson did not go away with the order he wanted that time, but his tactics brought him a lot closer to doing so.)

Conclusion

Salesmanship seems to be a great defier of logic. The outcome of any given sales conference is affected by intangibles and luck. Prospects may add up to averages or percentages, but each one is an unpredictable human being when you are dealing with him individually. Furthermore, whether the man who failed to make a sale did the best anyone could, or whether the man who succeeded could have done better, are questions which can seldom definitely be answered by either the salesman or his sales manager.

It is clearly important for a salesman to make the most of as much experience—his own *and* others—as he can. He never does the *best* that could be done, but by constantly searching, examining, and evaluating sales experience he can sometimes come close to it. Horace B. Van Dorn, Vice-President of the Joseph Dixon Crucible Company, Pencil Sales Division, expressed the top salesman's attitude this way:

"Selling is one of the subtle arts, which throws mind against mind, tongue against tongue, firmness against firmness. Salesmen are in conference all day long, and as Bacon has said, 'Conference maketh a ready man.' The ebb and flow of conference is a joy to me. It always is to a salesman. He has much to accomplish with spoken words. As I reflected upon a life of selling contracts, the experiences that leap out are those made memorable by something said, something said to me or something I replied. Such experiences are educative, disciplinary, and wholesome."

To the many points which can be perceived from the experiences quoted in these pages—the value of little things, the role played by fate or circumstance, the fact that people are not "sold" but that they "buy," the value of perseverance and creative imagination, and all the rest—we must add, therefore, one more: the priceless value to the salesman of actual selling experience.

36. STARTING THE NEW SALESMAN OUT RIGHT *

by D. Maynard Phelps †

For some new salesmen, probably many of them, the first few weeks or months on the job are a period of discouragement and frustration. If a new salesman becomes too discouraged, he quits; if he is too ineffective, he may be fired. This is a regrettable outcome, both for the salesman and for the company which employs him. The salesman has lost some of his self-assurance; the company has lost its investment in the man, including the cost of recruitment, selection, and preliminary training.

In many cases, a large part of the blame can be laid to faulty selection. The man just was not the right type to sell merchandise successfully. In other cases, however, the man was well adapted to selling work, but he didn't get a good start. If new salesmen can be started right, if they can become really

* Reprinted by permission from the May 1956 issue of the *Michigan Business Review,* published by the School of Business Administration, University of Michigan.
† University of Michigan.

productive in their job before many months have passed, if they can largely avoid frustration and discouragement, they will soon become well-adjusted members of our economic society. Human abilities will be well used and human values will be preserved.

Adjusting Men to Jobs

The above problem is one of adjusting individuals to jobs. In recruitment and selection, the problem is one of predicting human behavior. Estimating what a man is likely to do on the job, if hired, is essentially a predictive task, followed by employment of some men, rejection of others. After a man is hired, the problem is one of controlling human behavior insofar as possible to induce greater productivity.

How can the company be helpful in getting its new salesmen started right? What are its responsibilities to the new salesman? What is the salesman's responsibility to the company which hires him? What are their several contributions to the process of adjustment of the salesman to his job? Starting the new salesman out right is a *joint* responsibility. Both the company and the salesman contribute to the process, and success can only come if both the salesman and the company fully recognize this important fact.

The Company's Responsibilities

It seems to me that the salesman can reasonably expect that the company will assume the following responsibilities:

1. Give the new salesman a feeling of confidence in the company and respect for its executives, its policies and its products.

2. Convince the new salesman that selling is a dignified human activity, that representing the company before potential buyers is a task worthy of a person of high caliber and good training.

3. Convince the new salesman that he can sell merchandise effectively, that it is a job which can be accomplished, that it is not an impossible task for him.

4. Assure the new salesman that he will get help when needed, particularly during the orientation period when he is first contacting potential customers.

5. Provide satisfactory means of training and supervision which help to increase the salesman's productivity on the job.

It will be noted that these items largely deal with *attitudes;* and, therefore, the question arises whether positive attitudes can, in some manner, be instilled in salesmen, either while in educational institutions or during the induction and orientation period. It is my feeling that this can be done; likewise that proper attitudes can be destroyed by poor personnel practices.

People have patterns of reaction to stimuli, and these patterns are in the nature of habits. Psychologists speak of acquired ways of feeling and of acquired attitudes as habits. Some people have essentially negative attitudes. They always think of reasons why certain things *cannot* be done. Other people, in contrast, are not fazed by any problem. They are always thinking of ways in which things *can* be done. Salesmen need habitually affirmative attitudes. They need positive, not negative responses to stimuli of all sorts.

Now let us take up each of these five areas of responsibility previously mentioned, with a few comments on each.

A Feeling of Confidence and Respect

The first of these responsibilities is to give the new salesman a feeling of confidence in the company and respect for its executives, policies, and products. It is doubtful whether any reputable person can sell merchandise effectively for any considerable period unless, deep down within his consciousness, he feels "right" toward his company and its products. How can a salesman sell effectively if he feels doubtful about the quality of his company's line of merchandise?

In order to instill this attitude of respect and confidence, the salesman must be given information on company history, the company's accomplishments over the years, its research and new-product development, and finally, its prospects for the future. What is needed, according to the psychologists, is a feeling of "belonging," one of identification with the company, its past, present, and, particularly, its future. When I ask salesmen about their jobs, some of them first tell me that they are representing an excellent company, and are selling top-level products. If a salesman feels this way about his company, this particular responsibility has probably been met well.

Attitude Toward Selling

The second responsibility is to convince the new salesman that selling is a dignified activity, one which is worthy of a person of high caliber and good training. It should not be assumed that he feels this way about selling activities simply because he has accepted a job, or that his conviction is firm that selling is a worthy profession.

We hear much these days about a negative attitude toward selling in the universities and colleges. There is such a negative attitude, but it is not so pronounced as commonly thought. Nevertheless, it is the joint responsibility of the universities and colleges, particularly of the business schools, and of business concerns, to overcome this attitude. Considerable progress is being made in doing so, but it has not been fully overcome as yet.

If the salesman is not firmly convinced on this point, he will never be fully satisfied with his job. Moreover, he may adopt a cringing attitude before prospects, i.e., a self-defeating attitude. It is well to assure the new salesman that he is representing his company as well as attempting to sell its products; also that selling is a dignified calling, and just as much so as accounting, finance, industrial relations, or other fields of business activity.

Confidence in His Ability to Sell

The third responsibility is to convince the salesman that he can sell merchandise effectively, that it is not an impossible task for him. Most young salesmen seriously doubt their ability to sell merchandise. Therefore, they must discover this ability and develop greater self-assurance. Some initial success in selling is very important to get over this initial hurdle.

In my opinion, there is nothing better than time spent in the field with a senior salesman. The new salesman watches the selling process at work. He sees it done. In this connection it should be noted that the senior men should be "orthodox" salesmen—careful, painstaking individuals who plan well, are well disciplined, and at least reasonably successful.

Availability of Abundant Help

The fourth responsibility of management is to assure the new salesman that he will get help when needed, and to give that help in reasonable abundance. In this connection I am thinking of immediate supervision and guidance, particularly of a personal type.

Every young salesman needs some particular person in the organization to whom he can go for sympathetic understanding and guidance. Some companies, particularly those in the office equipment field, have sales training directors at their branch sales offices. In one such instance, the new salesman spends at least one hour each day with the sales training director, usually after some actual selling experience in the morning hours. Therefore, the help is given when it is needed most, and when adverse experience is uppermost in mind.

Signs and Characteristics of Frustration

During the first weeks and months, supervisors and directors of training should look for signs of frustration, and the characteristics which frustration may develop in salesmen. These characteristics have been classified as regression, fixation, resignation, and overaggression. They are all concerned with a change in the pattern of attitudes toward the prospect occasioned by frustration.

The psychologists tell us that variability is often replaced by stereotyped behavior, and that constructive behavior is replaced by nonconstructive regression or destructive aggression on the part of the salesman.

With the recognition that frustrated behavior may have these characteristics supervisors may become more tolerant of new salesmen, and may learn how to deal with frustration. Perhaps the salesman himself can recognize his own symptoms of frustration and learn to control them if they are unfortunate from the point of view of effectiveness in the selling process.

Illustrations of overaggression brought on by frustration are numerous and of great interest to sales managers. It is often illustrated during the last few minutes of athletic contests. A team which is very likely to be beaten may well become overly aggressive, commit many fouls, and be penalized frequently during the last few moments of play.

Frustration is particularly apparent in these individuals who are naturally strong competitors, and their reaction is very likely to be overly aggressive. Another illustration of this phenomenon comes to mind. A sales manager received a telephone call from a purchasing agent one day during which the agent strongly protested the actions of a young salesman who had just called upon him. He said that the salesman virtually demanded an order, and his conduct was described as insufferable. Therefore by means of this telephone call he protested to the salesman's immediate superior, the sales manager. Apparently the new salesman had made a somewhat favorable impression, nevertheless, for the purchasing agent instructed the sales manager to give the new salesman a "dressing down" and then have him return a few weeks later for an order.

Undoubtedly this new salesman was overly aggressive. He did not have a regressive or resigned attitude which would have been even less desirable. He did not give up easily, in fact he tried harder, but surely not in the right way.

Of course, what I'm really saying is that sales managers and supervisors should attempt to understand human beings, and the way they react under particular circumstances. In this connection, I remember a particular sales training director who, over a long and fruitful lifetime, was a keen observer of human behavior. He understood people well and, in fact, was a practicing psychologist, for psychology is the science of human behavior.

Overcoming Frustration

The question arises as to how frustration can be overcome. First, let me say that it helps a great deal to understand it, and to recognize that it is present through changes in patterns of human behavior. If a person can be told why he is behaving in a certain manner, he may be well on the way toward correcting unfortunate behavior.

The psychologists also tell us that one way to relieve frustration is to talk about it. A sales manager or supervisor may serve as a good "sounding board" for people in difficulties. Even slight success in selling is also helpful to overcome frustration. Perhaps, at times, the sales manager or supervisor can aid the salesman in making a few sales, and thus overcome frustration and unfortunate action patterns which result from it.

Training and Supervision

The fifth responsibility of management is to provide the means of training and supervision which help the salesman to increase his productivity on the job. Sales training is really a three-way problem: (1) to impart knowledge in such a manner that it can be comprehended and acquired by the trainee; (2) to aid the salesman to develop proper work habits; (3) to attempt to instill in salesmen proper attitudes.

The development of good habits is very important because bad habits are very difficult to overcome. Older people, in particular, have great difficulty in overcoming bad habits acquired many years previously. It is generally recognized that it is much better to start right, and to acquire good habits of work early in life.

The Company's Attitude

Finally, in reference to this question of what salesmen can reasonably expect from their companies early in their careers, let me quote Mr. Clarence Francis, President of General Foods Corporation. He said, "But you cannot buy enthusiasm; you cannot buy initiative; you cannot buy loyalty; you cannot buy the devotion of hearts, minds and souls—you have to earn these things."

It seems to me that business concerns "earn these things" to a large extent during the induction and orientation period, for attitudes toward the company, toward the job of selling, and toward others in the company's employ are developed largely at that time.

Companies differ markedly in regard to questions of loyalty and devotion. This is well illustrated by the situation of two large, competing companies. These two companies have much the same products, the same sources of raw materials, and the same markets, but over the years one has been much more successful than the other. While there are probably many reasons for this fact, I would ascribe it largely to a difference in the attitudes of executives. One company is a really democratic concern, and democratic procedures are followed. The other is much less democratic. Executives are more autocratic, and there is less spirit of cooperation present. Perhaps the executives of the first company have earned enthusiasm, loyalty, initiative and devotion throughout the years. Perhaps it has contributed markedly to the success of the company.

Attitudes of the New Salesmen

Now we turn to our other principal influence—the contribution of the salesman to the adjustment process.

We hear much these days to the effect that the attitude of young men from the universities and colleges, especially in regard to selling careers, is not right. It is said that they expect too much too quickly, and are not content to proceed at a reasonable pace toward higher incomes and positions of authority and responsibility.

People who have come up the "hard way" are often a bit resentful of young people who wish to get ahead too quickly in any organization, especially of those who wish to become top executives in something less than par figures. They often resent younger people from universities and colleges who are given unusual opportunities for advancement through special training programs.

Perhaps the younger men *are* somewhat maligned just because they *are* ambitious and want to get ahead rapidly. The fact that they are well trained, confident, and ambitious is held against them rather than in their favor. In view of these conditions new men need a certain sensitiveness to the attitudes of older people in the company and restraint when necessary to avoid irritations. In this connection the mental question, "How does he (the older employee) feel about it?" is a most pertinent one.

Humility and Hard Work

As a second requisite, a company can reasonably expect that a new salesman will have humility in relation to his job. He should recognize that, through his educational training alone, he is still very imperfectly prepared for his job, that he has only a start toward real understanding of business and particularly of the marketing field. Every new salesman, at least one who is selling for the first time, has much to learn, and humility is much in order.

As a third requisite, a company can reasonably expect that the new salesman will be willing to work and work hard. There is no good substitute for the attribute of industriousness. A "clock watcher" has no business in the selling field. Opportunities for success are great, but success will not be attained easily. In this connection it is a significant fact that success, if attained, is very apparent—much more so than in many other fields of activity.

Willingness to Learn

The fourth requisite which can be reasonably expected is the willingness to learn, to take advantage of every training opportunity offered by the company, and thus to become more proficient on the job. The company should be able to take it for granted that new salesmen from the universities and colleges have developed at least reasonably good study habits, and that they will not abandon them when on the job.

It can be expected that new salesmen will study their jobs and make improvements in performance by means of self-training. Many people have said that salesmen cannot be depended upon to develop effective methods of work. This may be true of many salesmen but not, in my opinion, of those who have had good training, particularly in business schools. Such people have analytical abilities and will probably use them.

Most of these people will, I think, be constantly on the lookout for deficiencies in their work, and will strive for more effective work habits. Of course, this does not mean that they will not need instruction in regard to the performance of particular tasks, only that they should seek improvement in work habits by whatever means is available.

Good Faith

Finally the company can reasonably expect an individual to show good faith in accepting a job initially. In this connection I have little patience with students who say that they want to accept a job with a large concern in order to get effective training, but that they expect to go into private business shortly thereafter. Good faith demands that a person who accepts a job consider it as a business career opportunity. The likelihood should be that the individual will stay with the company for an extended period.

We all know that costs are great in the recruitment, selection, orientation and training of salesmen. The investment of a company in a man may be thousands of dollars before the man becomes really productive in his job. Therefore, a man is acting under false pretenses if he accepts all the benefits proffered during the first few months and does not expect, at the time he is hired, to stay with the company indefinitely.

Of course, this does not mean that there will be no terminations of employment for good reasons. Nevertheless, a company can expect good faith on the part of salesmen when initially employed with all that term implies.

Progress Report

It is my confirmed belief that most college men can become effective in selling work if they have a proper attitude toward their jobs, and if they accept their responsibilities well during the induction and orientation period. In recent years, management has more fully recognized the nature of the problems present during this period and has attempted to solve these problems. Progress is being made, both in relation to attitudes and the acceptance of responsibilities, which argues well for the future.

37. BASIC SELLING *

by Cason Rucker †

A recent movie tells the story of a famous stage star, who received a Hollywood contract. Some months later, after working with screen techniques, he returned to Broadway and went into stage rehearsals for a new play. The producer then accused him of having lost his basic acting ability, and forced him to thoroughly review and practice all over again the basic fundamentals of stage acting before a live audience. He even went so far as to draw chalk lines on the stage to show the matinee idol how to walk.

A good many salesmen have "been to Hollywood" in the recent heyday of easy selling, and are finding it hard to get back into the groove. Many salesmen are first class actors, though it may be hard to picture them as John Barrymores. However, all should realize the need of going back to the basic principles and procedures of selling at periodic intervals.

Many manuals and sales-training movies have been prepared to show the buying motives and how to shape a sale around them. They are very clear and inspiring at the time, particularly when one is new at the game. Yet, for how long do we consciously follow them?

All of us slant our sales presentation in accordance with our own personality and experience. Yet, by placing undue emphasis on a minor facet, one's whole approach can be distorted to a marked degree. Sometimes I wonder if a salesman isn't obtaining orders in spite of himself. Occasionally he gets into a slump of "no orders" without knowing exactly what is wrong. In such a case it is best to go straight back to the basic selling methods and see whether he isn't falling into one or more of the common traps.

* Reprinted from *Purchasing*, © October 1954, pp. 120–2.
† General American Transportation Corporation.

Rules and Exceptions

One principle that I have heard repeated time after time is: never call on a purchasing agent until he has had an opportunity to read his mail and become organized for the day. Yet, one successful salesman has always made it a practice to start his day by being in the lobby before starting time, awaiting the arrival of the purchasing agent. He is almost invariably kidded, invited in, interviewed, and ushered out before the daily headaches start to pile up. If appointments with other members of the organization are required, the purchasing agent can make them before they too, become tied up.

These calls are never long, and they are straight to the point. The salesman is thereby enabled to save important hours of his own time, and still leave the purchasing agent with the pleasant feeling of having successfully completed and eliminated one of the day's problems at the very start. This early calling was not always appreciated, but it was successful to the extent of trying until discouraged and discontinued at certain places.

Calls and Calling Hours

Another shibboleth, in buying as well as in selling, is that the salesman and purchasing agent must see one another at every call, regardless of the time involved. A warm feeling was aroused by a very busy purchasing agent one day when a salesman was making a routine call. The receptionist announced the salesman in the regular way over the telephone. Without hesitating, the buyer asked to speak to the salesman. "I'm busy as the dickens today," he said, "and will have to keep you waiting a long time. Would you mind excusing me until your next trip?"

The very cordiality and regret in his voice spoke volumes. In a sense, the salesman failed in his objective—he didn't get his interview. But it was really the start of a beautiful, understanding friendship that lasted for years, to the mutual benefit of both sides. It did not happen very often, but the very honesty and spontaneity was penetrating.

A purchasing department's office hours for salesmen are planned for the best interest of both sides. They are generally respected. Yet a salesman should not hesitate to infringe upon those hours if he is sure that it is to the best interest of the buyer for him to do so, and if it cannot be avoided. Whenever possible, it is best to call ahead.

But don't make it a habit. The salesman should be careful not to place himself in the position of the boy who cried "Wolf" when there was no real cause.

On the other hand, when immediate information is required, the purchasing agent should have no compunction about demanding instantaneous service. It works both ways. And there's the same danger that abuse of the practice will lead to indifference and failure when the service is most needed.

How to Handle Inquiries

An extremely time-consuming trap is the feeling that every inquiry should be answered in great detail. The salesman wants to give service, of course. But it is often good policy to call the inquirer to obtain more background on the particular case. Frequently, an approximate "order of magnitude" figure, or a routine catalog description is sufficient and serves the purpose quite adequately. The purchasing agent, since he himself is so burdened with detail, is usually eager to help the salesman simplify his work. This is particularly true where the salesman has similarly demonstrated his desire to cooperate, in the past.

An inquiry for a special machine came in last fall. It would have been a nice order, completely justifying the large amount of detail work involved in getting out an estimate and a quotation. However, a telephone call to the buyer revealed that a short delivery was required, which could be met by a competitor, but not by the manufacturer in question. Upon learning the facts, the salesman asked to be excused from quoting, and explained why. The buyer appreciated the prompt answer which enabled him to proceed immediately with the competitor and get the order under way without loss of time. This straightforward handling was appreciated by and helpful to both.

Another such call to a purchasing agent indicated that the salesman didn't have a chance in a million to obtain the order, and that the inquiry was simply a matter of courtesy. Again, time-consuming effort was eliminated. To do his best work, a salesman must not only feel that he has an even chance to obtain the order, but must have time to do a conscientious job. By sorting out the inquiries, and actually obtaining the over-all buying picture, the salesman avoids spreading himself too thin. He is then able to perform satisfactorily and promptly, as he should.

Orders That Don't Materialize

For four consecutive years, a buyer requested a detailed new proposal for practically the same set of conditions. Every time, when the project came up for an actual appropriation, the Board of Directors rejected the request for money expenditures. Some day it will pass and the equipment will be ordered. In the meantime, the buyer's file is so crammed and mixed up with detailed proposals in triplicate that it is a mess. Much of the data are already obsolete. What he needed at this stage was only a letter listing the equipment and an approximate figure of cost. Then, when the project was OK'd, the detailed specifications and specific quotations could have been requested. To be sure, the salesmen's eagerness may have been partly responsible for this situation. He had a "hot lead" which he didn't want to lose by default; but he didn't know the extent to which competition was in the picture and how hard he had to fight it.

After having worked hard on an order and lost it, a salesman is entitled to know the reasons for his failure—price, delivery, quality, special features, somebody's antagonism, or whatever else may have swayed the decision. In this way he can try to correct his deficiencies and improve his proposals for the buyer's benefit as well as for his own. Thus true competition is maintained. A salesman's endeavor should never be belittled. It represents considerable work which should be recognized and appreciated by all the parties involved, no matter who gets the order.

When selling equipment that is not ordered every day, it is possible for a salesman to get into the habit of friendly, pointless calls. They need not be pointless. A refrigerator salesman in a retail store, during the depression of the thirties, had a stock approach whenever a prospective customer came in. "Can I wrap one up for you?" His question was always accompanied by a broad grin, and invariably aroused attention. He was attentive, too, and was quick to follow up any response; very frequently the other sales steps of interest, desire, and action followed.

It is nice to pay friendly calls on old customer friends, but they can never be allowed to forget that your visit has one basic purpose—to obtain an order, either now or in the future. The salesman doesn't have to be as blunt as our refrigerator salesman, but he has to put the point across. It's directly in line with the principle, "Ask for the order." This procedure certainly brings the case down to bedrock. Not only does it help in getting orders; it also filters out calls that are uneconomical and potentially unfruitful.

How Much Technical Information?

The advice of one experienced sales manager was to require his salesmen to periodically reread the technical and sales bulletins provided by the company, that the salesmen routinely sent out by the dozens. His experience had been that a salesman is prone to concentrate on one or two sales points to the exclusion of the others.

He did not mean that the salesman should recite every feature at every opportunity. His thought was rather that his men should be so familiar with the broad scope of the product that the proper point or argument should naturally pop up as needed. This avoided the tendency to inadequately tailor all objections to a stock answer, which was frequently beside the point and consequently unconvincing.

Such primary sales bulletin reading is tough medicine for an old timer to take. Nevertheless, it is essential. Why, even the expert who writes the bulletins has to refresh himself by periodically rereading his own words.

Great stress has always been placed on conscientiousness, but it can be carried to a detrimental climax. Other departments exist in his company, and a salesman should take advantage of them. Unless a definite sales need is involved, it is wasteful for the salesman to try to attend and supervise laboratory or service work. Those departments are set up to assist him, and they are manned by capable men. His responsibility is to so plan and coordinate the work that it can be carried out purposefully, objectively, thoroughly, and expeditiously.

It is a common failing to expect a laboratory to develop a hundred proved answers "day before yesterday." The salesman must determine what answer is wanted, and point the laboratory specifically toward that goal. It is then the laboratory's task to use their specialized training and facilities to determine the necessary data and findings. These data should be quickly tabulated and explained in a simple report, so that they can be used in solving the sales problem involved. Correspondingly, any mechanical troubles requiring service should be immediately reported to and corrected by the service department, with a prompt report going to the salesman. Laboratory personnel, service men, and salesmen should feel free to criticize each other—freely, but above all constructively. A close degree of cooperation works wonders, to the ultimate benefit of the customer.

Before or After?

After leaving the doctor's office, I always think of more symptoms or additional questions that I should have asked, but it is then too late. My time is up. This problem was eventually overcome by writing out the pertinent facts on a slip of paper for reference, or to be handed to the doctor on arrival. Now the visits are complete, to the point, and more beneficial.

The same feeling of futility sometimes comes over a salesman after leaving a customer's office. There was something more that he should have said, or done, or performed differently. An explanatory or confirming letter is sent to complete the call that should have been completed at the time. This is time-consuming for both sides. Often, in the stress of work, it is not properly read or understood, or related to what has gone on before.

The solution may well be the same as in the case of the call on the doctor. Before each call, a short outline of the points to be brought out is noted. This is followed during the interview, and the points are checked off as covered. Additional points are marked as required during the conversation. This procedure is handled openly, but as unobtrusively as possible. It helps considerably in completing points while they are hot, and in eliminating a later review and rehash of cold turkey. When calculations are required, they are usually made at the time, with a carbon copy for the seller's office record. The whole object is to leave the customer's office with a feeling of completeness on both sides, with no loose ends to be gathered up later. There is often an inner pressure to hurry up the call by glossing over a lot of this. Still, in sticking to this procedure, the end of the day usually finds the important calls made and much of the need for calling back eliminated. In most cases, ordinary delays in lining up and carrying through a greater number of routine or half-calls will offset the extra time required for complete interviews.

To do this satisfactorily, one must have a good set of up-to-date records, an excellent memory, and an inquiring mind. To develop these is a stimulating challenge. They are particularly useful in building up the best tool of all—experience. Experience gives one the ability to discard the impractical, and allows one to concentrate clearly, in a straight line, on the best method toward attaining the objective. When a man has that, plus a sympathetic understanding and feeling for the customer's needs, he need never worry about a welcome.

Good Working Relationships

Experience will also tell the salesman when he is fighting a lost cause, when his best move is to beat a fast retreat to other pastures. The old simile of the overstaying guest certainly applies to sales calls. When he is outsitting his welcome and usefulness, he is no longer a good salesman.

One of the nicest ways to develop a good working relationship is to compliment a man to his boss, when the remark is in order. By that I mean in a sincere, natural way, as the recognition and appreciation of competence, courtesy, and fair dealing.

The points mentioned above have been helpful in a number of cases toward maintaining a consistently fruitful and professional approach to selling. They may stimulate other thoughts, pro or con, toward that objective.

The salesman must always be in a flexible position. He must be able to take advantage of changing conditions as they occur. His work does not nail him down to a static, unstimulating, unsatisfactory routine. To a great extent, it's his own show to handle. But if he strays too far from the basic principles, he's likely to lose his audience—and his orders.

38. INDUSTRY TRIES SELLING BY SEMINAR *

Nobody needs to be told that the heavy machinery that is putting so large a part of the verve into the U.S. economy is getting more and more complex. But as this is happening, the selling job that heavy industry has to do is getting more and more complicated, too. So much hard cash, so much advance planning, so much heavy betting is involved in purchases of heavy machinery nowadays that the men who make big and expensive equipment are having to work up new marketing methods if they're to sell their products.

Right now, they think they've found one answer to their selling problems: Don't send your salesmen to your customers, bring your customers to your own plant.

In one form or another, this is a time-honored device. It may turn up as a "casual" (yet carefully timed) invitation to "drop in and see us when you are in our neighborhood." It may be an open-house to show off a new plant, or a tour designed for supervisory personnel. A research plant— Purina Ralston's Research Farm is a case in point (*BW*—March 13, 1954, p. 48)—may make special bids to customers to bring their problems with them and find their solutions in the host's products.

Refined Approach

More and more companies find that when they refine these occasional invitations they gain an important selling pitch. The refinement is the regularly staged seminar, lasting one, two, three, or more days, put on for the customers' technical men, the design and product engineers. Some of these seminars, like Westinghouse Electric Corporation's Machine Tool Electrification Forum, give experts from a number of companies a chance to pool their knowledge. Other companies—especially in the aviation field —use such seminars as their prime sales tools.

One of the newcomers at the seminar game is Electro-Alloys Division of American Brake Shoe Company. Over the past two years this outfit has held nearly a dozen seminars on the manufacture, metallurgy, and engineering of alloy at its Elyria (Ohio) plant. Guests come from such blue-chip operations as Chrysler Corporation, International Harvester, Bethlehem Steel, Oliver Iron & Steel, U.S. Steel Research, Pickands Mather, Link Belt. They spend two days touring the facilities of Electro-Alloys and

* Reprinted from *Business Week,* © July 14, 1956, pp. 45–9.

getting down to brass-tacks discussions of design principles for trays, rails, retorts, hearth rolls, chain belt testing, and the like.

No Sample Cases

There are plenty of reasons why this kind of selling is growing. The sheer bulk of much of heavy industry's product makes it an unlikely package for a salesman to tote from door to door. And a customer who is sinking tens or hundreds of thousands of dollars in new equipment wants to be sure what he is getting, and wants to know a lot about his supplier before he lays down his money. The quickest way for him to get the answers is to visit his supplier's plant.

Twin Coach Company, in Buffalo, tells how it operates before it bids for a subcontract supplying components to large aircraft manufacturers. Before it gets an invitation to bid, Twin Coach has a team of six to twelve experts come in to visit its plant. The team investigates nook and cranny: finances, cost accounting, engineering and technical personnel, traffic management, packaging, even water supply, and cost and supply of power.

Customers, of course, have always wanted to know these things. But today—in an era of huge industrial expansion, calling for new equipment that daily becomes more complex and more expensive—there is extra pressure to have all the answers before signing the purchasing contract.

Equipment Race

It would be dangerous for a customer to buy much of today's heavy industrial equipment from a catalog or a salesman's description. Innovations and improvements of old techniques and a constant flow of new processes and machinery keep customers hopping to stay abreast of the times. Seminars at which the beauties of these new industrial babies are expounded are a good way to introduce the new machines and new processes.

It's no accident that the aviation industry has gone in heavily for seminars, that International Business Machines has set up a Computer College for potential customers at Elmira, N.Y., or that Taylor Instrument Company holds special demonstrations of its gasoline refinery automation equipment at its Rochester (N.Y.) headquarters.

Customers are responding enthusiastically to these seminars. They're sending representatives from all over the U.S. and Canada, and some even from overseas.

The host company usually picks up the tab for incidental entertaining, but the guests usually pay for their own transportation.

There are some exceptions, especially when the host company has its

own airplane. And the NesTier Division of Charles William Doepke Manufacturing Company, near Cincinnati, finds that hiring a helicopter to fly
potential customers from the airport to its plant pays off in good customer
relations.

Costs

It is hard to say whether this form of selling costs more than the old
doorbell-ringing technique. Some concerns believe it is much cheaper than
keeping up a field sales force. In some cases, they can cut out the field
force altogether. This is what happened when a group of three companies
set up Alden Research Laboratory, in Westboro, Mass. The laboratory
is a promotional demonstration center for Alfax Paper & Engineering Company, Alden Electronics & Impulse Recording Equipment Company, and
Alden Systems, Incorporated, and these companies keep no field sales
forces. All their selling is done when prospective customers visit their laboratory demonstrations.

The new technique hasn't been pushed quite so far by most other companies. Westinghouse's electronic and x-ray divisions in Baltimore, for
example, give their prospects a complete sales pitch, but they do have
a field sales force as well.

Soft-Selling

For the most part, though, selling at seminars is held to a very muted
key. Most companies emphasize that the salesmen who follow up the seminars are the men who write the orders. Of course, the salesmen are able
to write their orders far more readily if the customer has seen the product
and has had a detailed explanation of its accomplishments.

One reason for the difference in the intensity of the sales pitch is that
in many cases seminars serve more than one purpose. General Electric
Company, an old pro at the seminar game, makes a distinction here. "Developing a market is quite different from developing sales, although the
two complement each other," says J.J. Heuther, manager of GE's Market
Planning and Development Section of User Industries Sales Department.
For companies seeking market development rather than immediate sales
the sales pitch at seminars is soft.

Results

Few companies care to make any estimates of the practical dollar returns in sales of such programs. Electro-Alloys believes there has been
enough increase in orders from its older customers to warrant continuing

its new program. But company after company points to the fact that it has no difficulty in filling its roster for a seminar.

There are certain pitfalls, some companies admit. One problem, says Bendix Aviation, is to get together at the right time the correct composite group from all over the country. Occasionally, companies have stubbed their toes by forgetting to include some concern with a stake in their products—and have made enemies instead of making friends. Worse yet, one extrusion supplier ruefully notes, customers sometimes will come in, watch an extrusion process, and after soaking up all available information, will buy presses of their own so they can turn out extrusions for themselves.

Gains

But the overwhelming vote among manufacturers who put on such shows is favorable. Whether the effort aims at developing new markets—which may entail product development—as in the case of Monsanto Chemical Company (*BW*—June 16, 1956, p. 185)—or immediate sales, they cite these advantages:

1. There's nothing like a captive market, and a customer under your own roof is a complete captive.

2. Customer-supplier understanding improves significantly, says Electro-Alloys' sales manager, William D. Raddatz. Customers, with their new understanding of the processes involved in turning out the products they buy, are less likely to ask the unnecessary—or the impossible—from the equipment they buy.

3. The feedback of information works both ways. Companies that hold seminars often get tips from their customers. One seminar guest at Electro-Alloys asked the host company's engineers, "Why do you use such a high nickel content in the alloy on that unit?" The engineers discovered they had no good answer—and that there was no good reason for using so much expensive nickel. Joy Manufacturing Company, Pittsburgh machinery producer, is another one that reports customers often come up with ideas. From Joy's viewpoint, this has the pleasant result that the customers are apt to buy equipment when they feel it embodies their own ideas.

4. Seminars open doors for salesmen who have had trouble getting to see potential customers. They establish the personal contacts that count for so much in this kind of custom selling. Electro-Alloys thinks this is significant: In its two-year experiment with seminars, it has watched the caliber of its visitors move from engineers and metallurgists to chief engineers and top technicians.

Sales managers in many heavy equipment companies feel that the whole selling approach in their industry is changing. The older "seat-of-my-pants" salesmen who are low on technical knowhow and strong on selling are disappearing fast. Replacing them are the younger engineering graduates, perhaps less qualified from the sales point of view, but with more factual knowledge and a better understanding of the customer's problems.

39. SALES AND PURCHASING: HERE'S HOW
THEY LOOK TO EACH OTHER *

by James K. Blake †

One of the key facts turned up in a new attitude study of 400 salesmen and purchasing agents is that neither now regards the other as an antagonist. If current attitudes can be summed up in one phrase, their feeling is that they are more like sparring partners, teammates with different functions.

As the questions and answers below show, not all points of friction have been eliminated. The likelihood is that not all ever will be or even should be. The very fact that purchasing agents, as shown by their write-in comments, are aware that they could buy more efficiently if they were able to provide salesmen with a more explicit summary of current and future needs, and the fact that salesmen recognize personally (more important than management's awareness of this) that more emphasis should be placed on knowing the customer's organization intimately is a long step toward frictionless sales transactions.

The material for this article was drawn from two survey-based studies conducted by a New York management consulting firm, Management Development Associates. Purpose is to help management create greater job understanding on the part of sales and purchasing personnel as a basis for more effective buying and marketing practices. Comments below explore areas where these crucial relationships frequently run on the shoals.

The Salesmen

In your opinion, what percentage of the purchasing agents and buyers that you call on understand their jobs?
Fewer than one out of two purchasing agents understand their functions, according to 41 per cent of the salesmen. But 22 per cent of the salesmen thought that at least three out of four purchasing agents understand their

* Reprinted from *Dun's Review and Modern Industry*, © June 1955, pp. 45–7.
† *Dun's Review and Modern Industry*.

jobs in relation to the story the salesmen were trying to get across. One salesman commented, "To be an order taker and service complaints and requests is easy enough. However, to sell a merchandising idea, and through it, your product, is extremely difficult."

What percentage of purchasing agents that you call on have unqualified recognition and authority from their top management?
Only 43 per cent of the salesmen think that more than 50 per cent of purchasing agents operated under these conditions. And 23 per cent of the salesmen believe that fewer than one out of four purchasing agents have "unqualified recognition and authority."

How often do you deliberately avoid the purchasing agent in making your calls?
A whopping 53 per cent said they by-pass the P.A. more than 20 per cent of the time and more than a quarter of the salesmen avoid the purchasing agent in half their calls. Typical response: "Problem is really created by management who set up ill-trained P.A. without knowledge of anything beyond basic material requirements to handle all procurement. This mans acts as a buffer. The effect is to prevent method changes from reaching management. Our policy: direct mail to Engineering, Accounting, Production executives. Initial approach to P.A., by-pass if no results."

Why do you avoid the purchasing agent?
"He is a dead end who won't refer you to the management, engineering, or operating people who have authority to requisition" is a paraphrase of the opinion of 55 per cent of the salesmen. About a quarter of the salesmen believe the purchasing agent is not qualified to evaluate their product because it is an intangible or else a technical product needing engineering department specifications.

Have you run into serious prejudice from companies because you avoided the purchasing agent?
Only 11 per cent had had trouble often enough to make it detrimental. About 43 per cent of the salesmen experienced trouble now and then, and 36 per cent hardly ever had any difficulty.

In what percentage of the purchasing departments which you contact do you consider inadequate anticipation of needs resulting in excessive demands for "service," rush orders, too many small orders, no coordination in ordering similar items to be serious problems?
These were active problems in more than 50 per cent of purchasing departments according to 28 per cent of the salesmen. But 35 per cent of the responding salesmen said these problems existed in fewer than 25 per cent of contacted purchasing agents.

In what percentage of purchasing departments do you consider poor handling of relationships with salesmen, waiting for interviews, unnecessary call backs, broken appointments, and so on, to be serious problems?
Nearly 20 per cent of the salesmen thought this was serious in more than 75 per cent of the departments they contacted; but 49 per cent thought it was a problem in fewer than 25 per cent of their calls.

Where you think your visit merits it, are you promptly referred to the proper engineering or operating personnel by purchasing?
Nearly 40 per cent of the salesmen estimated that the P.A. puts them on the trail of the right man promptly less than 50 per cent of the time. Only 28 per cent of the salesmen were lucky enough to meet the contact they needed in more than 75 per cent of the companies they called on.

How often have you made presentations or repeated calls on purchasing without success only to find that as soon as you managed to by-pass the purchasing agent and talk to the key men in engineering or operations, you got your order?
"A number of times" responded about 45 per cent of the salesmen, and 21 per cent thought it happened "frequently." But 30 per cent replied this happened very rarely or never.

What percentage of the plants that you call on have clear-cut regulations in writing with regard to back-door selling?
A minor 14 per cent of the salesmen thought that more than 50 per cent of their customers had definite policies in writing, and 56 per cent thought that fewer than 25 per cent of their customers had written regulations.

Are regulations in writing regarding back door selling made known to all who call on the company?
Only 5 per cent of the salesmen replied, "always," and 41 per cent thought regulations were usually relayed to the salesman.

Are these regulations equitably enforced?
Here the number becomes smaller—only 3 per cent responded "always."

Have you ever received requisitions that by-passed the purchasing agent deliberately?
"Yes," said 51 per cent of the salesmen; "No," echoed 40 per cent. But 46 per cent said they have received this type of order more than once or twice.

To what was this due?
The answers of about 35 per cent of the salesmen showed that deliberate by-passing was due to the nature of the material or product or special conditions surrounding the sale. But nearly 40 per cent wrote in comments

like these, "friction and politics . . . no regard for P.A. . . . inability of operating executives to get action out of P.A. . . . engineer trying to carry the ball . . . jealous individual trying to develop buying authority . . . avoid red tape and simplify."

What do you do about this situation (receiving orders that deliberately by-pass the purchasing agent)?
About one third of the salesmen let the P.A. know about it in order to maintain good understanding, but about the same proportion continue to by-pass, hoping the whole thing will work out somehow.

Do you feel restrictions of salesmen's interviews to definite hours or days is a serious impediment to your effectiveness?
Nearly a quarter of the salesmen checked off "in every case," about 35 per cent thought it depended on the company and the particular situation, and 40 per cent thought it depended on the degree of regulation. About two-thirds of the salesmen thought these regulations were increasing, and over 40 per cent believed that salesmen themselves were to blame because they made too much routine and unnecessary calls. Their write-in comments showed that most salesmen appreciate that buying is only one of the purchasing agent's tasks, but a broadly held view was that it is his most important task.

What has been done by your sales department in recognition of the need for better buyer-seller understanding?
Only 12 per cent of the salesmen stated that their managements have made formal studies of relationship problems. Devices, techniques, and procedures specifically designed to anticipate the buyer's needs, questions, and difficulties were employed by 27 per cent of the companies; sales training programs emphasizing the buyer's problems were used by 29 per cent; and 25 per cent of the salesmen replied that their firm makes honest efforts to determine scientifically the buyer's problems and unique ways of doing business.

Any other general comments on the subject of the relationship of sales to purchasing?
These comments are representative. They give a fairly explicit picture of the purchasing agent as seen through the salesmen's eyes. "In general P.A.'s are not paid enough to attract high caliber material, and being 'small' men with a lot of power, they get a superiority complex which the salesman feels instinctively and so holds back information that might help the buyer."

"Every P.A. should serve three to six months as a salesman and each salesman should know the P.A.'s problems. His own company has salesmen, and he should treat the people calling on him as he would want his own people treated."

"In most cases lack of authority in purchasing departments is due to the fact that they do not have top management backing."

"Too many P.A.'s buy price only—a clerk can pick the low figure."

"Compared with 25 years ago, to-day's P.A.'s are saints."

Purchasing Agents

In your opinion, what percentage of the salesmen calling on you know their product thoroughly?
Nearly 30 per cent of the purchasing agents think that fewer than 50 per cent of the salesmen were product specialists. Only 22 per cent think that more than three out of four salesmen know their product thoroughly, and 48 per cent think that 50 to 75 per cent of the salesmen have expert product know-how. One P.A. qualified his answer by noting that 100 per cent of the salesmen "from whom we buy" have thorough product knowledge.

In your opinion what percentage of salesmen calling on you have authority to make reasonable agreements that their company will back up?
Only 14 per cent of the P.A.'s thought that three out of four salesmen have this authority, and 50 per cent believed that only one salesman out of two calling on them had it.

Does top management in your company permit salesmen to by-pass purchasing?
"Never," said 22 per cent; "some times," replied 37 per cent; and 32 per cent of the P.A.'s claimed it happened only in extreme emergencies.

What happens to the salesman who by-passes purchasing?
"Investigation, explanation and warning," checked off 58 per cent of the replies, but 28 per cent said "nothing." Only 3 per cent take specific punitive action.

Do people in your own company by-pass the purchasing department and place orders or requisitions directly with vendors on the outside?
This happens once in a while replied 36 per cent of the P.A.'s, only in emergencies said 52 per cent. Asked for explanations of this by-passing, 25 per cent of the purchasing agents thought there was lack of understanding of company policy forbidding it, 39 per cent attributed the by-passing to behaviour habits of operating personnel, and only 2 per cent thought it reflected lack of confidence in the efficiency of purchasing department procedures.

What are your biggest problems in dealing with salesmen?
A flat "Waste too much of your time" was the response of one third of the purchasing agents, and 30 per cent replied similarly, "nothing con-

structive to offer." The biggest problem of about 15 per cent is that salesmen, they think, do not understand their problems. Undependability on
agreements, deliveries, and emergency service is the biggest headache of
14 per cent of the P.A.'s.

*What percentage of the salesmen you do business with would you rate
"good" on immediately rectifying errors?*
A fat 60 per cent of the purchasing agents thought that more than 75 per
cent of the salesmen rate high on this one, and 25 per cent thought that
between 50 and 75 per cent of salesmen rate "good."

*What percentage of the salesmen would you rate "good" on furnishing
technical assistance in the use of the product where necessary?*
Over 75 per cent of the salesmen, thought 56 per cent of the P.A.'s. Between 50 and 75 per cent, thought 28 per cent of the buyers. Typical comment: "Takes too much time to get technical data . . . get us *more* technical data at or after the first interview and cut out all nonsense of price
dilly-dally by offering at once the best price based on known or anticipated
volume." Another frequent comment: "The majority of salesmen know
little more about their product than the buyer. This is not good."

*What percentage of the salesmen would you rate "good on furnishing
replacement parts from stock—or who do everything in their power to
expedite delivery when you are in a jam"?*
More than 50 per cent of the salesmen, think 86 per cent of the purchasing agents, and 53 per cent of them think that more than 75 per cent of
the salesmen rate "good" in furnishing names of individuals to telephone
for expediting.

*If you cannot directly help a salesman or understand the technical aspects
of his story, do you immediately refer him to the appropriate management, engineering, or operating personnel?*
"Always," said 46 per cent of the purchasing agents surveyed, and 47 per
cent checked off "usually."

*What percentage of the salesmen would you rate "good" whose primary
sales asset is technical training or product knowledge?*
More than 50 per cent, thought a similar percentage of the P.A.'s. Typical
comment: "A large percentage of the men who call on us are top men
who move up in their company. They are better trained than 25 years ago
—however, not as forceful." Another comment: "Sales gives up too easily.
The first call is to introduce himself. If he sees nothing for him, the next
time will be six months hence."

*What percentage of the salesmen would you rate "good" on showing
good understanding of sales techniques, behavior, grooming, and so on?*
Fewer than 75 per cent, thought more than two-thirds of the purchasing

agents. One comment was: "Most larger companies or companies that sell engineered material have salesmen who are adequate either personally or technically. However, it is criminal, the percentage of salesmen from other businesses that lack know-how, technical data, veracity, and in some cases common decency."

Do you restrict salesmen's interviews to definite hours of the day or days of the week?
No restrictions, said 70 per cent of the purchasing agents, and to the question, "Why was this restriction necessary?" 66 per cent responded, "too many idle calls." Many purchasing agents commented, however, that their policy was to interview any salesman from out-of-town immediately. It may be significant that only 16 per cent felt that limiting salesmen's calls to definite hours and days of the week completely solved the problem.

How many salesmen, on the average, do you see each week?
More than 70 per cent of the purchasing agents see more than twenty salesmen a week—11 per cent see more than 50 salesmen each week! Average interview time runs from ten to twenty minutes. Only about 8 per cent of the P.A.'s average more than 30 minutes.

What percentage of the salesmen calling on you are unquestionably reliable so that you hardly ever hesitate to accept their word on price, delivery, etc.?
More than three out of four, thought 30 per cent of the purchasing agents. But a significant 27 per cent thought that fewer than 50 per cent of the salesmen were sufficiently reliable. One respondent noted that 100 per cent of salesmen calling on him were reliable on price but only 75 per cent on delivery.

What percentage of the salesmen calling on you make a sincere effort to be helpful and do not just try to make a sale?
More than 75 per cent, thought 28 per cent of the P.A.'s, although the largest grouping (46 per cent) thought that 50 to 75 per cent tried to be helpful. One purchasing agent noted that salesmen generally spend most time with higher volume accounts, giving them the better service.

Specifically what attempts have been made in your company's purchasing department to foster better relationships with suppliers?
"Organization of current needs for orderly consideration by suppliers' salesmen" is a technique used by 36 per cent of the companies. About one-third of the firms have organized information on future requirements and about 14 per cent have established written policies designed to improve relations with salesmen. Only 13 per cent of the companies have prepared a buyers' guide for salesmen, listing the categories that individual buyers handle.

What other general comments have you on the subject of the relationship of sales to purchasing?

These candid remarks are typical of comments made: "A small shop can have so many requirements and no more, and usually it has its regular line of vendors. Too many sales people do not recognize this fact. I try to put myself in the salesman's place when he calls and realize that for a new salesman in a new territory or a new company, he's up against a stone wall. There is nothing for them to offer outside of service."

"Many salesmen would help themselves if they had more information about the companies on which they plan to call."

"A weakness of 50 per cent of the companies is lack of a good 'inside man' to answer questions over the phone when salesman is out."

"Reciprocity is brought up too often."

Planning, Organizing, and Controlling Selling Effort

40. SELLING AND THE SALESMAN *

by Samuel N. Stevens †

In one of the most penetrating studies of America as a civilization,[1] Max Lerner defines the distinguishing characteristic of our American tradition as "the emphasis placed on dynamism." "This dynamism," he observes, "cannot be chastely selective, with its elements chosen or rejected on the basis of class outlook and political belief. . . . The fact is that the American experience has operated in every area. There has been the dynamism of the pioneer and the mechanic, the independent farmer and the trade-union worker; of the toolmaker, the inventory, the financier. There has been the dynamism of the 'company men'—the managers, the factory organizers, the salesmen who have made the irrepressible practical imagination of Americans world-famous."

The psychologist, the sociologist, and the economist have all recognized that the saga of American success is vested in the willingness of men of vision to dare to dream, and of hard-headed entrepreneurs to take the calculated risk. At the center of our business enterprise has been the man who sold the products of our mines, rivers, forests, and factories. Since the early days of the twentieth century, when the American people began to develop needs beyond the most primitive, it has been the peddler, wander-

* Reprinted from *Aspects of Modern Marketing,* AMA Management Report No. 15 (New York: American Management Association, 1958), pp. 85–94.
† Stevens, Thurow and Associates, Inc.
[1] Max Lerner, *America as a Civilization* (New York: Simon & Schuster, 1957).
334

ing over the countryside with his cart of wares; the drummer, traveling by horse and buggy to visit the general stores along the highways and by-ways of our country; and the fast-talking, lone-wolf specialty salesman who, even as they sold their goods, created expanding needs and opened up ever larger markets. It is no exaggeration to say that, from an economic point of view, selling has been the most dramatic symbol of American dynamism. And the salesman has been called the last but most enduring social symbol of a restless, hungry, growing American culture.

A Historical Perspective

In the early years of the twentieth century, the psychologist and the economist were the social scientists most interested in selling as a social phenomenon and the salesman as an economic factor in modern society. From 1900 to 1925, the psychologist's interest in these areas was focused primarily upon three problems:

1. The selection of men who would succeed as salesmen.
2. The psychological nature of selling as a form of behavior.
3. The training and supervision of the salesman as aspects of learning and motivation.

During these years, advertising, sales promotion, and what there was of market research were thought of primarily as supporting mechanisms for the payoff work of the face-to-face salesman. In 1907 Walter Dill Scott [2] published the first systematic analysis of the problems of advertising and selling from the psychological point of view. From that time until the present, the books and articles written on the subject have been legion. The fact that much of this literature has been superficial, trite, and sterile need not cause us to overlook the important facts which underlie the problems as they were defined by both the psychologist and the economist.

The first important research in the selection of salesmen was carried on by Walter Dill Scott for the American Tobacco Company. Scott's search for important differences in the psychological characteristics of good and poor salesmen and of salesmen and nonsalesmen was a pioneering effort. The fact that no significant results were achieved should surprise no one with any time perspective, for instruments capable of the precise measurement of individual differences in areas of sales significance did not then exist. Since that time, of course, the persistent quest for psychological understanding in this area has met with more success. Gradually we have developed a valid analytic concept of the sales environment and reliable instruments for the measurement of most of the important differences which distinguish the persuasive, hyperkinetic individual who can sell

---

[2] Walter Dill Scott, *The Psychology of Advertising* (Boston: Small, Maynard & Co., 1907).

from the more analytical, less aggressive person who will find more stable occupational patterns more congenial.

The interest of psychologists in the problems of training and motivation began to be expressed in research form after World War I. The impressive psychological instruments and the greater understanding of the psychology of learning developed through research on military problems during the war led both professional and businessmen to be overly optimistic about the successful application of these tools and insights to the sales training situation. Yet continued research in the field of communication has since produced a body of technical and scientific knowledge which has taken most of the guesswork out of the organization of materials for sales training purposes. And the growth of clinical psychology, with its intensive studies of the personalities and social motivations of individuals, has made the supervision of salesmen a much more creative management function than it had been possible to achieve through the purely statistical and analytical approach taken prior to World War I.

Sociopsychological Characteristics of Salesmen

At this point, let us consider, in rather general terms, the major conclusions which social scientists have reached in regard to the social and psychological characteristics of salesmen; later, we shall deal in the same manner with conclusions reached in regard to the sales environment.

1. *There is no significant relationship between intelligence test scores and sales success.* The requirements for ability to learn, to solve problems, and to adjust quickly to the sales situation obviously differ widely in practice, depending upon the nature of the product, the type of selling involved, the competitive nature of the market, and many other such factors. Specialty selling and engineering selling, for example, make such different demands of the salesman that they can hardly be classified as being of the same order of experience.

2. *No significant relationship has been found between independent measures of personality traits and sales success.* Many of our "classical" notions of what makes a salesman do not appear to have any validity when put to psychological test. As selling has become more professional, the successful salesman has become less of a stereotype.

3. *No correlation exists between age and sales success.* Many research studies have revealed that, in companies which have established fairly rigid age ranges for the selection of salesmen, these standards have been almost as frequently ignored by the field sales managers as they have been recognized. The simple fact is that age, although theoretically related to maturity, is not absolutely correlated with it. In short, many young men are more mature than older men.

4. *There is no correlation between measurable character traits and sales success.* Many "typical" character traits ascribed to salesmen since the early days of the hard sell have been found to have little basis in reality. We find that the traits which make for success in selling are the same as those which win the approval of employers in other occupations.

5. *There is no significant correlation between level of education and sales success.* Respect for education as an important tool in selling has grown by leaps and bounds. There has, in fact, been a tendency to set artificial levels of educational achievement for many sales positions. Yet careful statistical analysis of the educational backgrounds of individuals who are succeeding as salesmen reveals no such firm relationship between the amount of formal learning and the strict educational requirements for success in a given sales job. This does not mean that education is of no importance; it simply re-emphasizes the fact that there are many factors other than education which ultimately determine the success or failure of the salesman.

6. *No significant correlation exists between level of sales activity and sales success among individual salesmen.* This finding may be very difficult for many sales managers to accept. By tradition as well as by inclination there has been an understandable tendency for managers to believe that increased day-to-day activity will more or less inevitably produce increased sales volume. Theoretically, this is, of course, correct: A given man with a given selling method will produce more through sustained activity. Yet the fact is that attempts to increase the level of sales activity generally contribute less to increased sales volume than an equal amount of attention directed toward improving the selling method. Research clearly indicates that better selling techniques applied to carefully selected prospects are more likely to produce results.

7. *Each of the above factors has significance when studied in relation to all of the others in individual salesmen.* While no one of the factors cited above—age, education, personality, level of activity, and the rest—seems to have predictive significance, research indicates that when such social and psychological variables are studied in relation to one another the resulting profiles are valid guides for the selection of men who are likely to become successful salesmen. It was not until a very large number of important psychological instruments had been developed and more sophisticated statistical methods for the treatment of data had come into being that we were able to secure significantly useful results from our research in the evaluation of sales potential. Today it is possible to combine the social and psychological factors in such a way as to determine with considerable accuracy, in advance of employment, the likelihood of success in selling.

8. *Such study as that indicated in point 7 above can provide a useful*

tool for selection and development. When, on the basis of research which compares the successful with the unsuccessful salesmen, a profile is built which reflects the unique characteristics of the successful men, it becomes possible to upgrade the sales force progressively through the use of the profile as a critical standard for the selection of new men.

9. *Salesmen are more likely to succeed when chosen with regard to the kinds of customers they will deal with than in terms of the types of products sold.* We must recognize that the salesman does not operate in a vacuum. He works in a sales environment in which he and the potential customer are important factors. When the salesman is compatible with his customer, he has a much greater chance of success than when he is not. Therefore, an important part of the analysis upon which a sales profile is based should be a study of the kinds of customers the potential or prospective salesman will deal with.

10. *Salesmen differ from nonsalesmen in four important ways:*
   a. Salesmen are persuasive rather than critical.
   b. Salesmen are intuitive rather than analytical.
   c. Salesmen have higher average energy levels (expressed in activity).
   d. Salesmen are more strongly motivated by the desire for prestige, power, and material gain than by a service ideal or the need for security.

11. *Salesmen's interests cluster around a dominantly persuasive common core.* Almost all of the important research into the interests of salesmen and marketing people substantiates this finding. The role of secondary interests varies with the nature of the product sold and the peculiarities of the sales environment itself. For instance, people engaged in technical and scientific selling almost always have a secondary interest that is either engineering or scientific, or both, while a man who is successful as a feed salesman will have a range of interests of relatively minor strength compared with his persuasive interest. In both cases the product and the sales environment give validity to the interest pattern.

These points represent the major findings of research on the sociopsychological characteristics of salesmen. The extent to which a manager of salesmen can creatively and imaginatively apply this knowledge in finding and developing men who can sell is the measure of his managerial success.

Nature of the Sales Environment

Turning our attention now to the environment in which the salesman works, let us consider those environmental characteristics which psychological research indicates contribute most strongly to successful selling.

1. *An atmosphere of mutual compatibility must be achieved.* As we have already indicated, it is wise to select the salesman with primary consideration for the kind of customer he will deal with. When this is done, one of the most important aspects of natural environmental compatibility is realized. When the salesman knowingly plans his call to meet the convenience of the customer and makes his presentation in terms of known customer needs, a further development of a compatible environment takes place. Finally, the achievement of a mutually agreed-upon sales decision involves the realization by both the customer and the salesman of an increased sense of personal worth. Compatibility therefore begins with a sense of community between salesman and customer based on congenial personality factors; it develops as a skilled salesman molds the sales environment; and it achieves its climax through the experience of a heightened sense of personal worth as a sales decision is mutually arrived at.

2. *The customer's attention must be focused on the salesman and his message.* The psychological factors involved in the making of a sale have long been recognized. The structuring of the sales environment so that the salesman and his message become the focal points for the attention of the prospective customer is one of the most widely acknowledged fundamentals of sales training.

3. *An atmosphere of permissiveness must be established by evoking a felt need on the part of the customer.* Successful selling results when the sales environment is permissive rather than hostile or indifferent. Usually, such a positive, permissive environment is achieved as a direct result of felt need on the part of the customer.

4. *The natural aggressiveness of the salesman must be channeled to enhance the customer's ego; it should not be allowed to express itself in self-assertion, dominance, or hostility.* We must recognize that in any sales situation there is an element of psychological competition and a striving for ego-dominance on the part of both the salesman and the customer. That salesman is most likely to be successful who is able to achieve control by enhancing the ego of the customer rather than by asserting his own dominance.

5. *An atmosphere conducive to decision and action toward the resolution of the customer's felt need must be established through the development of feelings of satisfaction and profit.* The closing of a sale has long been considered the central problem in sales training. A great deal of research has been devoted to determining the most effective techniques by which the customer can be led to sign on the dotted line. Whatever the techniques recommended by the professional experts in the field, one essential psychological condition must be achieved. This may be described as the resolution of felt need through the development of feelings of satis-

faction and profit. The psychological as well as the economic benefits of affirmative action in line with the desires and recommendations of the salesman become compelling conditioning factors to direct action.

The good salesman is aware, implicitly, of these things. He has an intuitive feel for them. A subtle aspect of sales training is the development of an *explicit* understanding of these factors, so that the salesman can manipulate the sales environment with more sureness and awareness.

Basic Selling Tools

There are a number of basic tools with which the salesman must be equipped in order to implement the social science findings described above in the way that will be most productive for his particular company and its particular products. In general, these basic tools are of three major types, as described below.

1. *Technical product knowledge.* Tangible and concrete information concerning his company's products, processes, and services constitutes the salesman's basic tool. This type of knowledge can be effectively communicated to salesmen in groups by means of demonstrations and discussion, or individually by means of well-prepared brochures, booklets, and the like. Adequacy and correctness of product knowledge must be constantly checked and evaluated by the sales supervisor. Research has revealed that many times the failure of the salesman is the result of inadequate or incorrect product knowledge. It cannot be assumed that because a salesman is told once he will remember forever.

2. *Administrative techniques* (organization of territory, development of call pattern, record keeping, etc.). Good sales management today attempts to develop wisdom and know-how in this area through extremely concentrated training and close face-to-face supervision. It is not natural for a salesman to consistently reorganize his detailed knowledge of territory changes; neither will he readily accept the discipline of highly structured call patterns; and he simply is not temperamentally suited to the correct maintenance of a large number of records. The better the man is as a salesman, in fact, the less congenial he is likely to find the necessity for close and constant record keeping. Management, therefore, must develop a number of highly effective motivational methods to secure the kind of cooperation from the salesman that good sales control requires.

3. *Group training* (face-to-face sales strategy and motivation, demonstration, directed practice, side-by-side field practice). Many studies have been carried on to determine the relative effectiveness of field demonstration and role playing in teaching selling strategy. The consensus at the present time is that both of these methods are highly effective. In view of the central psychological principles we have discussed, it is clear that

the salesman must *do* in order to learn. Listening and observing are, of course, forms of doing, yet they do not have the same efficiency-producing effect as actual field performance under observation. It does not seem likely that there will ever be an effective substitute for side-by-side field practice carried on sympathetically by the sales manager and his salesman.

Changing Times, Changing Needs

Today, only a small segment of the total sales environment presents a congenial condition for direct selling. The needs and wants of the consuming public are being predetermined through the use of advertising and sales promotion in magazines and on radio and television. In the consumer area, for example, the sales merchandiser no longer deals directly with a customer; instead, he deals with a buyer or a buying panel. His problem is not to influence the ultimate consumer to buy, but rather to convince the professional buyer that the other functions of marketing have already created a demand for the product, and that he can profitably make precious shelf space available. This situation presents the consumer salesman with an entirely different challenge, to meet which he requires an entirely different selling approach. He must be able to talk technically in terms of frontages, shelf space, product movement, supporting promotions, the economic effects of couponing, the secondary services which the manufacturer will render the distributor, and the influence of displays on the impulse buyer.

In the industrial field the same kind of problem exists, although it has a slightly different psychological context. The industrial salesman must sell to a professional purchasing agent who has received his product specifications from some other company official. As a result, the industrial salesman must establish friendly relations with management users in order that they will specify his product when requisitioning through the purchasing office. With regard to the psychology of selling, this means that the industrial salesman must be a good public relations man and a good service engineer far in advance of the occasion of actual felt need on the part of the business.

It becomes obvious that today's salesmen are not entrepreneurs but professional communicators, working within the framework of a fairly rigid management system. Thus, they are not wholly dependent on individual performance or productivity for income or economic advantage. The psychological problems, therefore, not only continue to be related to the selection of the kind of man who will accept the challenge of professional persuasiveness in a highly structured situation but also have to do with the development of techniques by which the use of incentives and internal and external motivations can be rationalized and made effective.

The salesman must be able not only to understand his product and his customer but to relate this understanding to the economics of marketing and to such institutional problems as pricing and profit.

The typical problems which interest the psychologist and the sociologist today derive from an appreciation of the dynamic elements which comprise the marketing complex. "Motivation research" is a phrase symbolic of the new focus of interest. Projective techniques, as applied to both the salesman and the customer, are new devices. The nature of the corporate image, the power of the brand name, and the maintenance of a consumer franchise are all attracting the research time and interest of the social scientist. Morale studies, as they reveal the attitudes of salesmen toward the sales process and the company product, are assuming new and increased significance. The professionalization of sales training—with its highly operational definitions, its use of double and sometimes triple stimuli as learning facilitators, and its dynamic implementation of other incentives than money alone—is of increasing sociopsychological importance.

Hovering over these more highly individualistic problems are many which have to do with the sheer economics of distribution. The costs of doing business today threaten to eat up the ever-narrowing margin of profitability. Basic and applied research on products, packaging, and production techniques take an increasing toll from the consumer's dollar. Fringe benefits, pensions, and unemployment compensation involve added administrative costs which throw the traditional corporate concepts of doing business out of balance. These considerations cannot fail to affect the salesman and his selling effort.

Toward a Psychology of Marketing

Clearly, great changes have occurred in our economy during the past fifteen years. The impact of these changes must be appreciated if sales management is to meet the challenge. The economic and social character of the mid-twentieth-century marketplace is the direct result of the fact that American dynamism has continued to work steadily toward the adaptation of our capitalistic, competitive society to the increasing complexities of a world-wide revolution. The more complex our economic society becomes, the more unstable it is. The greater our economic resources to meet our expanding needs are, the more fierce competition becomes and the more critical the role of selling appears to be in the marketing complex.

Free enterprise, symbolized by the freewheeling entrepreneur of an earlier day, has been subject to many social and political controls. Government has assumed the role of the father-protector of the consumer. Sheer economic power is no longer looked upon with approval by many highly placed government officials. Efforts to place limitations on competition through the use of arbitrary economic power have been most vigorous at the very time when competition itself has been most bitter. The very tentative and uncertain balance between demonstrated need and capacity to produce is in constant danger of being lost. We observe, with a growing sense of frustration and concern, a spiraling gross national product and a tightening margin of gross profit.

It is in the light of these dynamic changes that midcentury selling has been forced to become an integral part of a larger and more complex economic process. We call this larger process "marketing." In an earlier day, advertising, sales promotion, credit and deferred-payment plans, and product development were supplementary aids to direct selling. Today these functions of marketing are themselves aspects of a total sales effort, and face-to-face selling is no longer the dominant causative factor in the distribution of goods.

This transformation is not entirely accepted by salesmen and their sales managers. Many of the frustrations now being experienced are the direct result of the failure of sales management realistically to adjust the role of the salesman to the changing patterns of modern marketing. Unless new insights are quickly gained, we may find ourselves in a declining economy. We may see a depression in the midst of plenty—a "profitless prosperity," as some have ominously called it.

Because selling has become marketing and because the entrepreneur salesman has of necessity become a professional, the need for more exact and more discriminating selection of sales personnel has become more pressing than ever. Our research into the characteristics of the "new" mid-twentieth-century sales-marketer has produced results which are most encouraging. The selection profiles which we have developed, in both the consumer and the industrial fields, reflect the changes in the sales job and in the characteristics of the successful salesman.

We are sure that, at most levels of selling, the sales-marketer must be more educable and have a higher intelligence potential than the salesman of the past. He must be less of an individualist and more of a team player. He must be as strongly motivated for personal success as salesmen ever were. He must be a more disciplined person, with greater control over his energy output. He must be more of a student, using his fund of marketing and sales knowledge with greater intuitional skill. He must be capable of more precise analysis of the marketing variables which affect his sales effort, and he must acquire additional skills in organizing, planning, and scheduling his sales work.

It will be obvious to all thoughtful sales managers that this type of salesman will require more guidance and will profit more from well-scheduled training. His economic requirements will be greater. His chances for professional growth will have to be more carefully spelled out. Sales supervision will require a higher degree of real managerial leadership. From every point of view it is reasonable to suggest that, *as selling becomes marketing, it also comes of age.* An expanding economy and an enlarged opportunity for personal financial achievement go hand in hand.

The psychologist and the sociologist may become true servants of management as they assist it, through research and consultation, in achieving increased understanding of the nature of the marketing process and the role of the salesman in it.

41. HOW TO MAKE SALESMEN GOOD PROSPECTORS *

by Willard M. Fox †

Time is a salesman's most precious asset. The hours a salesman can spend with prospects are few. They are eaten into by travel, by waiting, by service activities for customers, and by calls wasted on nonprospects. Even those paragons who do all their reading, planning, report writing, and other nonselling work outside of office hours can and do waste golden selling hours unless they are good prospectors.

Who Is a Prospect?

Teaching salesmen how to be good prospectors is an important and too often neglected part of sales training. The reasons are not hard to find. One is psychological.

Enthusiastic sales executives are sold on the value and importance of their products. They know and believe in their user-benefits. They exaggerate the number of their prospects. I have heard sales executives say sincerely that every smokestack, every screw machine, every office, every advertiser is a prospect. Such statements simply are not true.

The first requirement for salesmen is the ability to recognize prospects.

Nobody is a prospect unless he has the ability to absorb and the capacity to pay for profitable quantities of what is offered him. Without those powers

* Reprinted from *Printers' Ink,* © December 3, 1954, pp. 38–41.
† TradeWays, Inc.

he cannot be a prospect. He can be a suspect. He can be an unprofitable account. He cannot be made a profitable account. Therefore, he cannot be a prospect.

Next, one must know the sales strengths and weakness of each salesman. Every prospect can be sold by somebody. No salesman can sell every prospect. Salesmen must be taught to select those prospects they themselves can sell. This aspect of account assignment deserves much more attention than it usually gets. It is a key element of statute sales management.

To recognize prospects, one must first describe or define profitable customers. Fortunately, this is not a difficult task if it is approached objectively. Having a well-organized and well-managed sales control system simplifies the job. Lacking that tool, one must go to somewhat more trouble; but the reward is worth the effort, and a workable sales control record is a by-product. The definition or description must be in terms of characteristics and preferably in terms of characteristics that can be recognized from directories or lists. What these characteristics are depends upon such things as the products, their applications, and the channels or methods of their distribution.

In a direct selling organization, such as an industrial products manufacturing company, they include such things as:
Location (distance from service facilities)
Nature of operations of customer
Usage of products offered (including competitive, substitute, and alternate products)
Size of operation, measured in appropriate units (employment, plant area, as a check on use data)
Buying practices and policies
Identity of buying factors (individuals, by titles or functions).

In an indirect selling organization, such as a manufacturer selling through industrial distributors or wholesalers. They include:
Area served
Number of outside salesmen
Product classifications handled
Product classifications emphasized
Proportion of business in vendor's product lines
Competitive lines handled
Competitive line featured, if any
Number of customers (industrial establishments or retailers on books)
Kinds of customers served.

In a wholesaling or distributing organization, interest in retailing customers and prospects might center on:

Kind of store
Number of selling employees
Departments operated
Departments emphasized
Number of selling employees in department handling line
Location of department
Class of trade served
Branch stores operated
Price lines featured
Services rendered
Store volume
Department volume.

Those are not exhaustive suggestions. They are merely indicative of classification that may be important in defining profitable customers and setting them off from unprofitable customers. Once done, the sales executives can use this information to weed out the unprofitable accounts and the suspects, and to divert the effort now wasted on cultivating losses to the cultivation of prospects and development of profitable customers.

One manufacturer to whom every smokestack had been a prospect got a definition of prospects and cut his prospects to members of four industries whose establishments employed 500 or more.

He eliminated about 90 per cent of his accounts and went after prospects like the remaining 10 per cent. And he speedily increased his volume and his profits with far less commotion, fewer salesmen, and fewer but larger shipments to profitable customers.

Another who distributed through wholesalers increased sales and earnings by concentrating on a certain type of narrowly specialized jobbers of relatively medium size who could and did do a volume job for him.

Putting Square Pegs into Square Holes

I have never heard a sales executive talk about empathy. Maybe I just don't know the right sales executive. Yet empathy (which is mental-entering-into the feeling or spirit of a person or thing) is no less valuable to a salesman than to a doctor. It cannot be turned off and on at will. It is natural and spontaneous between some people and alien and impossible between others.

That is why no salesman can sell everybody, and there is some salesman who can sell anybody. And it is why recognition of a prospect for a company or a product is not the same as recognition of a prospect for an individual salesman.

It is the reason why sales executives must be able to recognize the strengths and weaknesses of their men. You can't reduce to arithmetic the way people feel about each other. This does not mean that thorough analysis of salesmen's performance cannot assist sales executives to match men and sales assignments. It can.

In the course of defining profitable customers and identifying prospects like them who are being solicited by salesmen, it is not troublesome (and by some methods it is more convenient) to take off subtotals by salesmen and to run off the percentage of profitable customers to prospects by the classifications used. When these profiles are made, they often show as much or more difference than the physical appearances of their possessors. I have seen case after case in which successful men in very similar areas have entirely different success patterns.

Some salesmen work the front door and some the back. Some automatically go on the principle that the boss has the power to say *Yes* and the time to listen to anybody who can show him a way to accomplish what he has in mind with less cost or less effort. Other men who write just as much business work through channels from the purchasing department. They are different. But since both succeed, neither is right and neither is wrong.

What is wrong is to try to make either into the image of the other. What is wrong is to put a man into a territory (or on a class of prospects) made up to a considerable extent of prospects for whom he has no empathy. If he has no understanding and no feeling for the problems of certain classes of trade, he cannot be effective with them, and his ineffectiveness will sooner or later frustrate him.

Separating Territories

At least to a limited extent, metropolitan and rural territories can be separated, and boundaries can be drawn along county or other suitable lines to make them reasonably compact and homogeneous. In the metropolitan areas, the Fifth Avenues and the State Streets can be assigned to men whose performance in the past shows they have a flair for such prospects. The men who tend to shy away from the big fellows—and they are the majority— can have rural and outlying or second-string metropolitan territories. In the case of newly recruited salesmen, until such time as they have the depth of knowledge to make them competent technically, reliance must be placed on observation and testing to determine their natural bent.

Even in those industries in which considerable reliance can be placed on directories and lists for initial prospecting, it is still necessary for salesmen by personal calls to qualify and evaluate prospects. In this work, if it is skillfully organized and supervised, salesmen cannot avoid typing themselves.

Given a list of 100 or 150 names to work on and a basic call-report form to complete, the sequence in which he covers his list, the kinds of people he picks to call upon, the completeness and the emphasis of the information he reports, his evaluation of potentialities and even the date of the callback he establishes tell much about the empathy he has for different types of prospects.

Sales training and supervision can do much to check the formation of bad sales habits and the inculcation of the patterns that his seniors have found profitable and efficient. Nevertheless, almost from his first day on a territory, what he does, how he does it and his specific accomplishments will build up a body of evidence about the kind of territory he can handle to best advantage for himself and for his firm, or they will demonstrate that he is miscast as a territory salesman.

42. HOW THE PROFESSIONAL SALESMAN
MAKES HIS APPROACH *
by J.N. Bauman †

There isn't anything very mysterious about two people getting together to discuss something of mutual interest. And that, basically, is what the approach to a sale amounts to.

But before a salesman can approach a prospect properly for that purpose, he has to do a number of things:

He has to get himself in the right mental state. He has to make up his mind to *like* the man he is dealing with.

It is essential that a salesman build up within himself this liking for his prospect. He cannot talk convincingly in terms of the prospect's self-interest unless his whole attitude conveys the impression that he is interested in him and wants to help him . . . in short, that he likes him and wants to do him a favor as a friend.

Nothing telegraphs itself so quickly to a prospect as a feeling of animosity on the part of a salesman . . . or superiority . . . or just plain disinterest in the prospect *as a person*.

So whether a salesman is trying to make a capital goods sale, amounting to thousands of dollars, or selling insurance, a service, or an Arrow shirt, the first thing he must do is make up his mind to *like* the person doing the buying—and reflect this feeling in his expression, tone of voice, and attitude.

* Reprinted from *Sales Management,* © June 15, 1955, pp. 58–63.
† The White Motor Company.

It helps to keep in mind the admonition of one of America's great salesmen: *"Put your prospect on a pedestal."*

If necessary, a salesman should force himself to look up to the prospect as a worthwhile individual he wants to serve.

People today are pretty highly regimented in their daily lives. When they are buying something, they have practically their only opportunity to play king—or exercise freedom. This, in turn, is the salesman's opportunity—to recognize the reaction to modern pressures and to capitalize on it.

Let the buyer be king. Let him exercise his freedom. This doesn't mean he should walk all over the salesman but the salesman, by actions as much as by words, should let the buyer know he has been *put on a pedestal;* he should know that the salesman recognizes his problems and wants to help him solve them, because he likes him as a person.

Crucial Ten Seconds

Remember that *the first ten seconds before a customer are critical.*

In other words, first impressions are important.

And the approach deals with first impressions.

The customer is slow to change a first impression—and a wrong one can become a permanent prejudice.

First impressions, of course, are based on many things—tangible and intangible. Some are quite unreasonable and beyond the individual's power to change.

I don't intend to say anything about dress. That is, of course, a basic element in the impression a man creates. Salesmen all know the canons of good taste on that score. Clothes should be neat, well-pressed and, as someone has said, "your tie shouldn't be any brighter than your smile."

Sales experts all have quite a bit to say about the importance of voice in making a good first impression.

It helps a salesman to take home a dictating or recording machine and find out just what his selling-voice sounds like.

Of course, it shouldn't be high-pitched and squeaking; neither should it be too deep and funereal. Words should be spoken slowly enough to be clearly understood but, again, not so slowly as to arouse impatience.

Almost anyone can cultivate a voice that reflects pleasant feelings and helps to lift the customer to what psychologists call the "participating, enthusiastic, accepting side of life."

There is a definite rule to follow in this connection: Keep the voice *up* on the last syllable.

An *up*-rising voice holds attention. A dying-out voice loses attention and gives a sound of unwelcome.

Macy's in New York conducted a store-wide experiment on this very point and discovered that when salespeople greeted customers with "Good Morn*ing*"—keeping their voices up on the last syllable—there was a marked warming up of customers and an increase in sales tickets.

Emphasis does not mean shouting.

Yelling is not selling.

A noisy greeting is often obnoxious and resented.

A voice of conversational intimacy draws people together; this is desirable.

A prospect will "open up" and discuss his problems much more freely when the interview is carried on in ordinary conversational tones.

Most of us have had the experience of hearing our voice on a tape recorder for the first time and being surprised by its sound. It's perfectly true that most people are unaware of what their voices sound like to others, and for that reason salesmen should find it advantageous to practice their selling voices on a tape recorder at home.

An entire sales presentation cannot be rehearsed on a voice recorder, because questions and answers in a regular interview are spontaneous, but a great deal can be learned about the pitch of one's own voice, and the speed of diction, which may be much too fast or slow for pleasant listening.

These machines, too, are a great help in guiding salespeople on how to put warmth and emphasis into the way they greet their prospects.

A man's own shaving mirror is also a good sales training tool. The best actors are not ashamed to practice before mirrors. Their purpose is not only to practice pleasant expressions but, particularly, to learn to use their lips and enunciate properly.

Many salesmen make a bad first impression because they are lip-lazy. We are supposed to use our lips in saying *good morning,* for instance. But it is amazing how many people say it with their mouths half open, scarcely moving their lips at all. Try it in front of the shaving mirror. It might surprise us to see what a pleasant, animated expression we get just saying it.

Remember, a salesman has only ten seconds to make a good impression.

His Bald Spot?

What does he look at, in the first instant of contact with his prospect— his necktie . . . his left ear . . . his bald spot . . . the lodge pin in his lapel? Or does he look him straight in the eye, wait for him to extend his hand—if there is to be a handshake—then start to talk?

That's what he should do. A good salesman always looks his prospect in the eye on meeting.

The eye—more than the ear—is the best receptor of the friendly feeling. The friendly-eye expression when old friends meet is the best proof of that. So, the eye is to be used not simply to appraise or estimate a prospect's reaction. The eye, as much as the voice, should be used to promote mutual understanding and friendliness.

Just as a matter of personal curiosity, a salesman might make it a matter of routine to note the color of the eyes of every prospect he approaches in, say, the next ten days.

I think it would be a very interesting experiment.

Incidentally, one of our most successful fleet salesmen in New York has made a habit of this for years.

He can tell you the color of the eyes of every truck operator he calls on. He told me that he acquired this habit years ago, as a young salesman, to force himself to look directly into a new prospect's eyes at the moment of meeting him for the first time.

Obviously, different kinds of selling call for different approaches. Nevertheless, they all have in common the human relationships I have mentioned.

But I do not wish to oversimplify this matter of the approach to a sale.

Important as it is to get on a basis of friendly understanding with a buyer —as a background for presenting the story effectively—there is much more to it than that.

The salesman has to be a good student of human nature.

He has to be able to size up the prospect quickly.

And, after making a good impression, he must go on to win his prospect's *confidence*.

In the case of retail, over-the-counter selling, this must be done quickly.

Two Confidence Builders

Building confidence usually consists of just two elements in retail selling —the salesman shows interest in the customer's wants and quickly demonstrates a knowledge of his stock.

If the salesman has correctly sized up the customer's need and produces a proper product to meet it, confidence is automatically established in the customer's mind and the sale is half made.

In other types of selling, it is not possible to establish this feeling of confidence as quickly. The more a product or service costs, or the more important it is to the business or daily lives of prospects, the more a salesman has to build up buyer confidence in him as an honest, competent adviser, as well as a seller of merchandise.

If the product is insurance, he deals with a prospect's ultimate financial security. Not many things could be more important to the prospect. He, naturally, will buy only from one in whom he has confidence.

If the product is something that requires a rather large capital expenditure, but will return itself in future savings or extra earnings, the same is true. A prospect will buy only if he has confidence, first, in a salesman's ability to analyze his business correctly and, second, in his ability to prescribe for the future.

It is this growing element of confidence that, more than anything else, makes salesmanship a profession.

Horse-and-buggy salesmanship methods of yesterday have given way to the highly developed counseling methods of today.

The modern salesman does not rely on a bag of tricks to make a good first impression only. It is part of his approach—part of his basic selling technique—to win the confidence of his customer, to make his customer regard him as a counselor—in much the same way he regards his lawyer or doctor, or any professional man.

There are four basic rules a salesman should follow to gain a prospect's interest—and win his confidence:

1. Prove that he knows something about the prospect's business and his problems.

2. Give the prospect a chance to talk to him.

3. Never make a quick, glib, unconsidered remark.

4. Be sure the prospect understands his statements.

A salesman can be sure that he will never inspire confidence in his prospect unless he convinces him that he knows something about his business and can help him with at least some phase of his problem.

After he has done this, it is extremely helpful if he can get the prospect to "open up" and talk about his business.

If he wants to talk, let him: A man in the mood to talk isn't in the mood to listen.

There is another reason for letting a prospect talk—or, if necessary, trying to encourage him to talk: Information gained in this way may change the whole direction of the later approach and follow-through.

The Art of Talk

The salesman who discovers the art of getting his prospect to talk is not likely to talk too much himself.

And that is one good reason for learning and practicing the art of listening to the prospect.

Such training also helps the salesman to refrain from making quick, glib, off-the-cuff comments.

An inconsiderate statement by a salesman can go a long way toward weakening a buyer's confidence in him.

Similarly, a statement made by a salesman, which the buyer does not fully understand, can be equally harmful. It may be entirely true, but sound boastful—or even fantastic—if the buyer hasn't been taken through the steps leading up to it, and doesn't understand it.

A distinction should be made between statements made to gain *interest* and those made to gain *confidence*.

A salesman may arouse interest by some such statement as this: "Mr. Prospect, this machine will pay for itself in your service in thirty days."

But if he makes such a statement in his approach, he must go on to build enough confidence to convince the buyer of its truth later in the sale, or more harm than good results.

The winning of a prospect's confidence, as early in the approach as possible, is important to the salesman not only in making the sale, but often in selling what the buyer needs, rather than what he has in mind to buy.

In most cases, the buyer wants to keep his purchase at a *minimum level of cost*.

A salesman must have specific knowledge of the buyer's business and problems to recommend—and sell convincingly—above the minimum concept the buyer has in his mind.

Change Experienced Buyer

Very often, what he should buy is quite different from what he has in mind to buy, but unless a salesman has won his complete confidence, it is virtually impossible for him to change the mind of an experienced buyer.

Yet all the great changes that have come about in our mode of living in recent years are the result of successfully selling *above people's minimum needs*.

This applies to our homes, transformed by our many labor-saving devices, as well as to stores, offices and factories—from cash registers that make change to electronic accounting and automation on the production line.

All are the result of selling, constantly, *above people's minimum needs*.

Today's miracle performer becomes tomorrow's minimum need.

This principle is the mainspring of our economy.

Industry can confidently bring out new and constantly improved materials, products and models—as rapidly as ever-widening horizons of research disclose them—because the salesmen of this country have proved that they can win markets for them quickly.

Without this creative aspect of salesmanship—and if it did not function as powerfully and successfully as it does at all levels of trade—new and better materials, products and models, *above the minimum concept of need in buyers' minds,* could only be developed laboriously.

If a salesman is to achieve his main purpose and sell every prospect what he should buy—and not merely take his order for the minimum concept he has in mind—he should pay attention to the approach.

43. WHY EVERY SALE MUST HAVE TWO PARTS *

There Are Two Parts to Every Sale

Let's put the "sale" on the analyst's couch and do a little probing. For the better we understand the nature and character of modern selling, the better salesmen we're bound to be.

When we examine a "sale" we find that it has a dual personality: two parts which merge into a single organism:

1. The part of the sale which is done *for* the salesman
2. The part of the sale which the salesman does *himself*.

If selling were only using that part of the sale which the company has prepared, even a boy could be a "salesman." (Pardon us, we mean an order-taker.)

If making a sale meant only taking an order for what the customer needs, there would really be no need for *salesmen*. Most selling could almost be done by mail.

But, as every good salesman knows, the true test of good selling is not in getting a *minimum* order. The big orders for important retail efforts are not *bought* by the stores. They're *sold* by salesmen . . . by men who regard a sale as much more than filling the gaps in a customer's stocks.

The salesman who is satisfied with just taking an order does a disservice to himself, his company, yes, even to his customer. For he has failed to make that *extra* sale for his own company, and to help bring to his customer that *extra volume* which he is seeking so desperately in today's razor-edged competition.

The Same Start but a Different End

Let's take two salesmen. Both have the same product, backed by the same advertising, the same promotional and merchandising aids, in territories of equal potential. John Jones gets a 10 per cent increase in sales. Sam Smith reaches 50 per cent.

The difference is not in the company's part of the sale, but in the *creative* ability of the salesman. Yes, we *mean* "creative." For the truly creative salesman can make sales sprout where no sales grew before, and reap a rich harvest where only scrubby plants grew.

The test of the true salesman then is in the "No. 2" part of the sale . . .

* Reprinted from *Sales Management,* © March 15, 1957, pp. 88–90.

the part which calls upon his own resourcefulness, ingenuity, imagination, and enthusiasm.

Let's examine the "dual personality" of the sale more closely:

The Two Parts of Every Sale

The part which is done for you (the salesman).

The part which you (the salesman) do.

1. Your company provides you with a product *skillfully designed* and *thoroughly tested* to stand up against competition.

1. Know *everything there is to know* about your product, its selling features, its points of superiority, its uses. Be *expert* in demonstrating it.

2. Your product has been *packaged* so that it will attract the customer, and also fit in the retailer's shelf or floor plans.

2. Know and understand the why and wherefore of your *product's packaging,* why it's superior in design, coloring, shape, function.

3. Your product has been priced to *compare favorably* with competitive products.

3. Start with a *sincere belief* in your product's value. If a cheaper price is the whole story, would there be a need for good salesmen . . . or any salesmen?

4. Your outlets have been *carefully determined* to make your product available to the largest number of customers.

4. Your job is to *cover every single prospect* in your territory rather than deciding independently which type of outlet to solicit and which to ignore.

5. *Doors to the trade* have been opened for you by planned trade advertising and promotion. You never have to call "cold turkey" with an unknown product by an unknown company.

5. Use time thus saved for you to give your prospect *sound selling ideas.* A good idea may turn a reticent buyer into a rabid booster.

6. You are provided with *efficient selling tools.* Even your presentation has been thought out, blueprinted and put into graphic form to save you time and effort in telling your story.

6. Don't shortchange your company by deciding to tell only part of the story or glossing over it. A good salesman, like a good workman, *uses his tools* efficiently.

7. Your sales or product manager is your *helpful guide and leader.* He keeps you constantly informed on

7. Your part of the sale is to *take advantage* of this guidance and leadership enthusiastically and in-

new items, new lines, new uses for the product, new selling points, examples of successful promotions by dealers, threats by competition, opportunities for new accounts.

8. *Dramatic advertising* creates acceptance or desire for your product on the part of the consumer.

9. Added sales speed is given to your product from time to time by *merchandising* and *promotion* devices such as premiums, couponing, tie-ins, contests, dealers' and salespeople's incentives.

10. Since display is so vital in moving merchandise out of the store, your company provides point-of-purchase material to *help the retailer sell*.

11. Your company has set up efficient reorder and delivery systems to *insure* that your customers have plenty of merchandise on the selling floor and in reserve at all times.

telligently. Reciprocate, too, by keeping your leader informed about successful promotions in your territory and of competitive products.

8. Appreciate that your company's advertising is like a *modern machine*. It produces customers faster and cheaper. Show it. Dramatize it. *Make it work for you.*

9. What *you* do with these merchandising and sales-accelerating devices makes the difference. *You* hold the throttle. Their speed and their power to produce depend on *your* success in getting your customers to use them. Help your customers plan promotions.

10. Keep a sharp eye on *display opportunities*. Suggest ideas for using the material your company has created. Accept as a personal challenge any display preference given to competitive brands.

11. As the *sales promotion manager* of your company in your territory, be a "hounddog" in flushing out thin stock and out-of-stock conditions; in fighting for shelf position; and in striving for those *extra sales* which will mean extra volume for your customers.

The Crucial Part of the Sale is YOURS

Two illustrations which demonstrate our point:

Here's a sign seen outside the major appliance buyer's office at Macy's, San Francisco:

"SO HELP US. If you want to sell us something, be sure your product is accompanied by a plan which will so help us that we will be more anxious to buy than you are to sell."

And here's what a food buyer says a salesman should present to him:

1. Have your proposition in writing.
2. Be prepared to give the buyer statistical facts on the position of your product in the market.
3. Talk about your own product and its potential as opposed to sales effort that aims only to "replace" a competing product.
4. Important: Don't "run away after you have a big order." Follow the order all the way through personally.
5. Buyers welcome merchandising suggestions and sales IDEAS.

Did you note how both emphasized that the *salesman is to help them sell?* For on *you* rests the *crucial* part of the sale . . . the part of helping your customer *sell* more so that he will *buy* more.

44. HOW TO SALES-MANAGE YOUR TERRITORY *

by Merrill DeVoe †

J.O. Vance, of McKinsey and Company, the famous firm of management consultants, tells of a salesman who prepared himself for advancement in a way that it will pay you to remember.[1]

The salesman that Mr. Vance tells about was selling a few years ago for a national distributor of food products. The unusual thing about him was that he managed his territory as though it were a sales district.

He allocated his calls on the basis of customer groups and subareas within his territory. He made estimates of his firm's share of the market by product lines, and classified customer potentials on the same basis. He kept careful records for purposes of sales control—including records of competitive activity and of sales expense in relation to volume.

Today, this man is a highly successful sales executive.

Many other men who are now sales managers achieved their present position because, when they were salesmen, they cultivated their territory in the manner of an executive.

Should you aspire to executive responsibilities, you will improve the chances of reaching your goal if you follow the advice of Sidney Weil, president of the American Safety Razor Corporation. "Every salesman," he says, "should look upon himself as the sales manager of his territory,

* Reprinted from *Effective Self-Management in Selling* (New York: Prentice-Hall, Inc., © 1956), pp. 165–72.
† Consultant.
[1] J.O. Vance, "How Adept Are You in Spotting Five Traits in Young Potential Managers?" *Sales Management,* February 1, 1954, p. 72. (See p. 391.)

duplicating at his level all the things that make for successful sales management at the top of the organization." [2]

Managing your territory systematically can easily prove to be the biggest single factor in promoting your selling career. It will multiply your sales and earnings. If you cover your territory methodically, you will be able to make many more calls than are possible when you cover it haphazardly. A larger percentage of your calls will be productive. You will lose less selling time, lower your selling expenses, give customers better service, and strengthen your hand in relation to competitive salesmen.

Your Opportunity for Territory Management

A survey of more than 100 companies showed that the majority of them permit the salesman to cover his territory as he sees fit.

This policy is based on the reasonable premise that sales management knows less than the salesman about market conditions in his territory, the buying habits of customers, distances between accounts, and facilities for travel. Since the salesman is closer to his territory and more familiar with it, he is considered better able to plan thorough coverage.

Even though your firm may leave you comparatively free to make intra-territorial decisions, it wants you to operate systematically. It expects you to classify customers on the basis of sales potential and devise a call pattern that will result in balanced coverage.

Many companies do not assign salesmen specific territories. Each salesman is allowed to go wherever he pleases, and see whomever he chooses. He is not tied to any particular area. He is free to call wherever he thinks business possibilities are the best.

You may find yourself in this situation. It is especially likely if you are representing a small firm, introducing a new product for which the market is undeveloped, or selling highly competitive specialties or intangibles, like automobiles or investments.

The salesman who is an independent agent or dealer is the freest of all. He is able to select his territory, set its boundaries, and sell within it according to his desires and judgment.

Whether you are assigned a specific territory or are at liberty to preempt one, you have a big opportunity for selling like an executive.

Define Your Territory

"My territory is wherever I drive my car," says a direct-to-consumer salesman. "If I'm in Florida in January and February, that's my territory.

[2] " 'Good Old-Fashioned Selling' . . . What Is It?", *Sales Management,* December 15, 1953, pp. 24-5.

If I decide to drive through Michigan in August, my territory is Michigan."

This salesman is using the term "territory" very loosely. What he has in mind is such a vague and tenuous thing that it does not lend itself to being "managed."

It is undoubtedly pleasant and delightful for this salesman to drive casually and leisurely from place to place. He may even do fairly well financially. But he cannot begin to earn the money he would if he concentrated his efforts in a limited, well-defined area. Before you can manage your territory, you must have a specific territory to manage. You must have some concrete unit—something you can visualize.

If someone hasn't defined a selling area for you, define one for yourself. Get a map and mark off the area that you plan to work during the next six months or year. If you have a long-range view, you may want to designate an area for development during the next ten years.

Define your territory in terms of states, counties, trading areas, cities, or some other convenient, logical unit. It may be desirable to think in terms of blocks within a city.

Another approach is to view your territory as being made up of certain classes of firms or people who need your product or use it, and who can pay for it.

But it is better to go farther and define the territory from the standpoint of potential consumers, retailers, wholesalers, factories, institutions, or other kinds of prospects that are located in a definite, circumscribed area.

How Territory Definition Helps You

Defining your territory specifically provides you with a management unit that can be used in planning and controlling your field operations. It facilitates the location of customers and prospects, and aids in classifying and evaluating them. It makes it possible to adjust your calls and interviews to the needs that are imposed by the market and competition.

By providing a basis for systematic call patterns and planned routings, territory definition helps you in covering your sales opportunities thoroughly and economically, and with proper balance and frequency.

When you relate your selling task to a specific geographic area on the map or to a specific number of prospects in a given area, you make the task clear and "visible." You can "see" it. As a result, making calls becomes more interesting and challenging.

Try to do a good job in a sharply delineated area and you will turn in a better selling performance than would be possible if you simply tried to sell as much as you could wherever you might go at random.

Eight Keys to Greater Territorial Rewards

If you wish to reap the benefits of a well-managed territory, you must become adept at sales planning and control. You must work with figures and make analyses to a degree unknown to a run-of-the-mill salesman. You must become less preoccupied with *gross* sales and more concerned with *profitable* sales and with selling expense. You must become cost-conscious and records-conscious.

More specifically, here are eight keys to getting more out of your territory:

Become Intimately Acquainted with Your Territory

Study its topography and its geographic structure. Study it as a market. Learn the location of population groups or of clusters of dealers or of other nuclei of sales potential. Find out what kinds of people or firms comprise your best prospects. Determine the quantity of your product or line that your territory can be expected to absorb. To get good facts on these points, you might want to make some careful market analyses, especially of the "quantitative" variety.

In addition to knowing the market aspects of your territory, you will want to keep in touch with business conditions and competitive activities, and to be ever on the outlook for opportunities to improve your selling position.

Work Out a Territory-Coverage Pattern

This should be based upon a long-term territorial goal. It should focus upon your calling activities for one full year. To give the plan content, you will have to decide upon the classes of customers and prospects to be contacted, the aggregate number of calls or contacts to be made in the area, and the desirable frequency of contact for the different classes of accounts.

In developing the coverage plan, give proper consideration to the comparative merits of high-spotting the territory and of covering it intensively. Try for a balanced coverage, as between present accounts and prospective buyers, and for an allocation of calls and interviews consistent with the relative sales value of various groups of accounts or of various subareas within your territory.

Baby Your Present Customers

Contact them regularly. On the better ones, call more frequently. Give them good service—within limits. Try to keep every account satisfied, as long as it doesn't cost you more time and expense than its worth to you warrants.

Every time you sell a new account, attempt to establish a strong friendship. Take every reasonable action that will bring you that account's repeat business.

In all your customer relations, work to instill good will and to achieve loyal and cooperative support. This is especially important when you sell to wholesalers or dealers. Their willingness to push your product and to find new customers for it may be more essential than their willingness to stock it in the first place.

Keep Striving to Develop New Business

Follow a systematic prospecting procedure—one that will assure you of a continuous supply of good, well-qualified prospects.

Give thought to possible favorable times for expanding your territory, preferably by adding one new subterritory at a time. Be careful not to take on a larger additional area than you can service economically.

Prepare Weekly or Monthly Call Schedules

These are developed within the framework of your over-all calling pattern and are the means for putting it into operation.

Your call schedules should be tied to the calendar by preparing them from week to week or month to month. They should include the total calls to be made each week or month and a breakdown for different customer groups or subterritories.

Adopt A System of Routing Calls

Study the basic methods of call-routing with a view toward setting up a system that permits thorough coverage of the territory with the planned frequency of contact, and at the same time minimizes unproductive travel time, unnecessary distances, criss-crossing, and back-tracking.

Before adopting any particular method, study a map of the whole territory in relation to the coverage plan and the location of customers and accounts. You may find it advisable to divide the territory into subterritories containing approximately the same number of people, retail stores, wholesale establishments, offices, or other kinds of prospects.

Become Cost Conscious

Become aware of the costs incurred in selling throughout your territory. Find out what your major costs are. Know what you spend for transportation, hotel accommodations, meals in restaurants, and for all other activities involved in your selling operation.

Analyze your expenses in relation to sales. Determine which of your field expenses vary with your volume or the number of calls, and which ones are independent.

Adopt a system of expense control. Keep good records of your expenses. Take every possible step to eliminate unnecessary or wasteful expenditures.

Convert Territorial Intentions into Realities

Don't allow your plans for territory development to remain only good intentions. Convert them into realities. To insure carrying out your plans as intended, with the least possible deviation, and to provide a factual basis for measuring your territorial progress, set up a good system of territory-management records that provide:

1. A classification of customers and prospects, based upon present or potential sales value

2. A coverage pattern that can guide you in scheduling calls

3. A tickler arrangement that reminds you of what prospects are to be seen when

4. A follow-up plan for interviews

5. An automatic check of your performance against your plan

6. A means of reviewing and re-evaluating customers and prospects so you can adjust the coverage pattern, call schedules, and routing plans to changing conditions.

Use these keys to unlock treasures that will remain buried as long as you work only the easy-to-get-at surface of your territory.

Know Your Territory as a Market

People with money, places to spend it, and the desire to buy make a market.

This frequently used definition of a market stresses four basic factors that you should appraise in relation to your territory. The factors are: population, purchasing power, number of retail stores, and the need or desire for the kind of product you are selling.

Perhaps I should add that these factors apply to the consumer-goods type of market. If you sell an industrial product, you will want to use other factors, such as the number of manufacturing establishments or factory payrolls, to measure the size of your territory as a market.

When you are assigned a new territory or when you are laying one out, try to get a mental picture of the over-all business potential, and of the potentials of various subareas within the territory.

Look for the main concentrations of population, or of purchasing power, or of retailers, or of other market indicators. To aid you in locating them, study all readily available market facts and market maps.

In selling a new product in a new territory, it's helpful to get answers to questions like these:

1. What is the extent of the available business?

2. Roughly, how many prospective buyers are there in the territory?

3. Where are they concentrated?

4. What is their probable interest in or attitude toward the product?

5. Is there some class of prospects that might buy more readily or offer less sales resistance than others?

6. Are there many competitive salesmen in the territory?

In selling an established product in a territory you are already working, estimate the possibilities for getting additional volume. Where does the greater sales opportunity lie—in getting present accounts to increase their purchases, or in extending your sales efforts to new groups of consumers or middlemen?

KEYS TO

CAREER SUCCESS

part VI

The final group of readings is devoted to consideration of the personal characteristics and attitudes which advance or inhibit career success in selling. The ability to think logically and creatively, combined with skill in oral expression, are invaluable attributes for success in any field. They are essential in selling where human relations and business judgment play a paramount role.

In addition to covering "Creative Thinking and Speaking" Part VI also contains a review of the traits and training that management is looking for in those being considered for increased responsibilities. The salesman does not abruptly shift over to management; he advances up the administrative ladder. In his day-to-day activities as a field salesman at the bottom rung, he must plan, execute, and evaluate, and must constantly make decisions within the framework of company policy. These managerial responsibilities are inherent in his primary mission of creative selling.

The successful salesman may be promoted to supervisor, district manager, regional manager, and on to the home office, or he may move into one of the other aspects of the selling mix: advertising, sales promotion, product or brand management, or export sales, as examples. Other successful men choose to remain in the field. Their advancement takes the form of an increasing market share in their territories, or in transfers to more challenging and lucrative areas. In all cases, however, salesmen are managers.

Creative Thinking and Speaking

45. THE CREATIVE THINKING PROCESS *

by John F. Mee †

The creative thinking process is in wide use today for purposes of stimulating scientific research in both the physical sciences and the social sciences. It is used also to help executives and employees discover better ways to achieve desired results. Individuals can use it to solve personal problems. There is strong evidence that anyone can increase his creativity if he has the desire and patience to master the creative process. The success of numerous creative thinking training programs for executives supplies the evidence.

Operative Definition

Creative thinking is the process of bringing a problem before one's mind clearly as by imagining, visualizing, supposing, musing, contemplating, or the like, and then originating or inventing an idea, concept, realization, or picture along new or unconventional lines. It involves study and reflection rather than action.

Subject Areas for Creative Thinking

Some of the most fruitful areas for applying the process of creative thinking are:

* Reprinted from *Indiana Business Review,* February 1956.
† School of Business, Indiana University.

Good. The creation and introduction of a new good or service which is unfamiliar to consumers.

Method. The invention and introduction of a new method of production, one not yet tested in the branch of manufacture concerned. A new method also may be a new way to market a product commercially or a new method for financing.

Market. The creation and opening of a new market into which the particular branch of manufacture or product has not previously entered.

Supply. The creation and conquest of a new source of supply of raw material or manufactured goods.

Organization. The establishment or formulation of a new way of organizing, such as the trend toward organizational decentralization into many individual profit centers with central policy and decentralized authority for decision-making by individual managers, indicating that creative thinking has been done in this area.

Management or Administration. The creation and development of a new philosophy for more effectively achieving objectives through human effort is a possible area for consideration. For example, attention given to the administrative point of view or the management process may result in creative thinking in this area.[1]

Examples of Creative Thinking

Creation of a New Good

In Hamilton, Ohio, a young man who had inherited a strongbox factory looked at a minnow bucket. He got a new idea. He brought into his mind clearly the visualization of insulation between the two cans, a cover, and ice cubes. He imagined a picnic container that would keep drinks or food cold for a long period of time. He brought into his mind the concept of the now well-known Skotch Kooler. His factory now has a gross volume of over $5 million a year.

Creation of a New Method

A former second baseman of the Washington Senators at the end of his playing career got a job with the Consolidated Vultee aircraft plant in Nashville, Tennessee. He had only a high school education and worked on the assembly line. The plant was not meeting its quota of engines, and the obvious waste of manpower irritated him. In his spare time, he designed a new assembly line procedural method which gave each worker a simple, timed assignment. When the general foreman was on vacation, he obtained consent to try his procedure. The result was the meeting of the plant's quota

---

[1] The areas presented were adapted from Schumpeter's *The Theory of Economic Development* (Cambridge: Harvard University Press, 1934).

with less manpower. This man had no formal engineering education; but he did have the ability to use the creative process of thinking.

Creation of a New Market

A salesman some time ago was forced to spend the night in Harrisburg, Pennsylvania. He looked in vain for a television set to see a special program. There was none. Although Harrisburg was within normal reach of several television stations, the mountains cut off the signals. This salesman brought into his mind the idea of a community antenna on a nearby mountain top which could serve those homes desiring television. He formed a new business which has erected over 290 community antennas and is a million-dollar business. He created a new market for television as well as a new product.[2]

Many examples could be given of products, methods, and markets with which we are now familiar but which first had to be created in someone's imagination. Without composers, musicians would have to make up their own music to play on instruments. Without architects, builders would be very limited. Without engineers, we could not shift so well from physical to mechanical energy. However, creativity is not limited to mechanical or artistic inventiveness. Creativity is being sought and used in marketing, advertising, production, transportation, financing, real estate, and personnel relations. A.C. Monteith, Vice-President of Westinghouse, has stated, "Creative thinking has become the spark plug of American business. If we don't find enough imaginative men to supply that spark plug, the machine will run down."[3]

Main Levels of Thinking

Three main levels of thinking have been advanced by Professor B.H. Jarman of George Washington University. They are the habit level, the problem-solving level, and the creative or insight level.[4]

The habit level of thinking results from either the conditioned response or trial and error methods. It is routine and unimaginative. Those who work at the habit level are following "beaten paths for beaten men." They work from plans of other men's minds by performing standard operating procedures or methods. They depend upon memory of techniques and formulae. The well-known poem by Sam W. Foss, "The Calf-Path," describes the thinking of such individuals.

Thinking on the problem-solving level is logical because it proceeds from facts which are either given or obtained. The scientific method of attack

---

[2] The preceding three examples were adapted from Bill Davidson, "How to Think Your Way to the Top," *Collier's,* CXXXV, No. 3 (February 4, 1955), pp. 26, 27.
[3] *Ibid.,* p. 26.
[4] B.H. Jarman, "Can Executives Be Taught to Think," *Advanced Management* (January 1954), p. 6.

may be used at this level. The well-known "case study" approach to education, in which certain business situations are simulated, is used to provoke
problem-solving thinking. A problem is discovered. Analysis and evaluation
of the facts are made. Then a decision is made to resolve the problem.

Thinking on the creative or insight level may not be logical because it
is done when only some facts are known and others are missing. Creative
thinking occurs when sound conclusions or judgments are reached when
some important facts or data are either unknown or withheld. Creative
thinking results from a partial knowledge of a situation. Combinations and
eliminations of associated facts begin to clarify the imagery or idea that will
lead to a solution. Insight then provides the imagination with the searched-
for concept or idea. The imagination is required to set up a number of
hypotheses that can be checked, compared, and evaluated, so that a superior solution can be developed from the best elements of the competing
hypotheses. Examples of such insight were Trudeau's flash of inspiration
that tuberculosis could be cured if a victim's environment could be controlled; and Finlay's insight that yellow fever was associated with mos-
quitoes.

There is a close relationship between these levels of thinking and the
levels of management practice as described by Barnard.[5]

Levels of Management Practice	Levels of Thinking
1. Job know-how	1. Routine or habit
2. Specific organization practice	2. Problem-solving
3. Principles and fundamentals	3. Creative

Steps in the Creative Thinking Process

The creative thinking process has been described in the literature of the
field by numerous authorities and practitioners. The presentation here represents a selection and combination of the best elements of all these methods
for creative thinking.

> When 'Omer smote 'is bloomin' lyre,
> He'd 'eard men sing by land an' sea;
> An' what 'e thought 'e might require,
> 'E went an' took—the same as me!
> —KIPLING,
> "When 'Omer Smote 'is Bloomin' Lyre"

Attitude and Concentration

There should be established in one's mind a positive attitude toward
complete freedom of ideas even though they may seem impractical or un-

---

[5] Herbert A. Simon, *Administrative Behavior*, Foreward by Chester I. Barnard
(New York: The Macmillan Co., 1948), pp. x–xii.

orthodox at first. Attempts to criticize or evaluate should be held in abeyance. Concentration for periods of about 30 minutes' duration should be practiced each day. To become proficient in the creative thinking process, it is essential that one develop the desire and the will to concentrate on a problem for a period of time without interrupting by getting a drink, turning on the radio or television, making a phone call, or looking out the window. A positive attitude and the ability to concentrate are basic essentials for a climate friendly to creative thinking.

Selecting or Defining a Problem

First, determine your purpose. Ignore ideas until you have determined why you want or need ideas. Find out what needs to be done or what you want to accomplish. You will not get started on the creative process by looking around for ideas that are new. To try to be creative by random search for original ideas will result only in futile frustration. C.F. Kettering, a very creative person, once stated that "All research is simply finding out what is wrong with something, and then fixing it." Therefore, start by selecting a problem in your area, and make sure that you know what the problem is. Define the problem clearly; then write it down as a "fix point" for the start of the creative process. It is suggested that "limiting factors" be listed and a "difficulty inventory" and a "difficulty analysis" be used in getting a "fix point" on the problem at the start of the creative process.

C.F. Kettering set out to develop the electric self-starter for motors, and he did it. In a demonstration, objection was made to his invention because he used more current through the wires than established formulae allowed. Kettering stated that his problem was to start an automobile. He was not interested in formulae. He had defined and picked his problem; then he stayed with it until a solution was reached. Previous failures of others to develop the electric starter did not bother him. He considered other failures an opportunity for him.

In selecting a problem, remember that the positive attitude and concentration climate are important. Regardless of the difficulty or the apparent impracticability of the problem, a solution can be reached through the creative process. Have the courage to depart from traditional formulae or thinking. Remember the plight of the bumblebee: "According to theory of aerodynamics and as may be readily demonstrated through laboratory tests and wind tunnel experiments, the bumblebee is unable to fly. This is because the size, weight, and shape of his body, in relation to the total wing spread, makes flying impossible. But—the bumblebee, being ignorant of these profound truths, goes ahead and flies anyway—and manages to make a little honey every day!" The world of business is filled with opportunity for those who will and can select problems that impede economic or technological progress and solve them through the process of creative thinking.

Exploration and Preparation

New or unconventional ideas are not created by wishing. They must be laboriously and carefully created from raw materials. The raw materials may be called knowledge. In the creative thinking process, ideas are originated by associations of existing ideas and factual information. New combinations and eliminations are brought about. Facts are matched against facts.

The exploration and preparation step in the creative process involves gathering, refining, and organizing all of the obtainable raw materials and knowledge that bear upon the problem selected. The purpose is to enable one to soak up information that will be grist for the mind later. One is not concerned with new ideas in this step—they come later. Raw materials and knowledge may be obtained from journals, books, magazines, research reports, associations with informed people, personal observations, lectures, and experience. In the exploration and preparation step, one should search for knowledge over as broad a field as possible. Every effort should be made to determine what underlies the facts and whether or not fundamentals or principles are apparent. For best results the raw materials or knowledge gathered should be written down for proper organization and refinement.

The exploration and preparation work is probably the most difficult of all of the steps in the creative thinking process because it involves a great amount of painstaking mental and physical effort. There are no short cuts. One must force oneself to gather, refine, and organize raw material and knowledge pertaining to the problem until every source is exhausted. This requires great self-discipline and tenacity of purpose. The lazy or the indolent will fail in this step. One must continue the exploration and preparation step until no new or additional raw materials and knowledge are obtainable. Remember, in creative thinking some facts are known and some are missing. Therefore, all possible facts and information must be obtained. Furthermore, the facts should be classified on some logical basis for later analysis and evaluation. Otherwise, the gaps in the later mental configuration may be too great for insight to bridge.

Hypotheses, Brainstorming, or Wild Thinking

This step involves the application of all existing ideas or knowledge to the solution of the problem in all possible combinations. Pareto's concept of "instinct of combinations" in *Mind and Society* describes the method for this step.[6] It is during this step of the creative thinking process that one gives his mind full freedom to range for a new idea to resolve the problem.

All possible relationships of existing raw materials and knowledge are combined. Some will be very wild and impractical; but the more the better, because of the increased probability that one will hit on the solution. All

[6] Vilfredo Pareto, *Mind and Society* (New York: Harcourt, Brace, 1935).

should be written down and preserved for later reference. Charles S. Whiting of McCann-Erickson, Incorporated, has described some operational techniques for this step: the analytical technique, the forced relationship technique, and the free association technique.[7]

The analytical technique involves the use of a pattern for establishing all possible relationships of knowledge to a problem. Alex F. Osborn's check list illustrates this technique by asking the following questions. Let's take an existing product or service as an example. (1) Can it be put to other uses? (2) Can it be adapted? (3) Can it be modified? (4) Can it be magnified? (5) Can it be minified? (6) Can it be substituted for others? (7) Can it be rearranged? (8) Can it be reversed? (9) Can it be combined with something? [8] This technique is well known for methods work and work simplification.

The forced relationship technique involves making a list of objects or ideas which may have some possible relationship, and then considering each object or idea in relation to every other one on the list. An example of this technique in action would be forcing the combination of all chemical elements in all possible relationships in an attempt to find a cure for cancer or the common cold. Obviously this is a laborious and time-consuming effort, although the use of electronic machines can be helpful.

The free association technique involves wild thinking or brainstorming. This technique is based on values which come from allowing any idea which comes to mind on a problem to be recorded. No attempt is made to evaluate ideas until all possible ideas have been expressed. A positive attitude and a receptive climate are essential for this technique because the purpose is to write down all possible ideas generated on a problem regardless of how silly or impractical they at first seem to be.

If a brainstorming session is to be held, the exploration or preparation step is minimized because the raw materials or knowledge obtainable exist in the experience and minds of the members of the group that participates. The group is presented with a problem, and everyone is encouraged to contribute ideas. For example, in the General Motors A C Spark Plug Division, one brainstorming session produced over 100 ideas on how to finish off a casting. The Ethyl Corporation got 71 ideas in less than an hour on a new booklet for employee benefit plans.

The digestion of the raw materials and knowledge obtained in exploration and preparation should continue by wild thinking on relationships, the establishment of possible hypotheses, brainstorming, and the like until a feeling of frustration appears. When all possible relationships have been combined and mental fatigue occurs, it is time for diversion—the next step.

[7] Whiting, "Operational Techniques of Creative Thinking," *Advanced Management*, XX, No. 10 (October 1955), p. 25.
[8] Adapted from Alex F. Osborn, *Applied Imagination* (New York: Charles Scribner's, 1953), p. 284.

When Sherlock Holmes seemingly ceased work on a case and dragged his friend, Dr. Watson, to a concert or played his violin, he was actually moving up a step in his brilliant creative thinking.

Incubation or Gestation

This step involves unconscious cerebration. One can contribute little to this step directly. One must either arrange to think about other subjects or problems, or even rest from any form of conscious thought by seeking recreation or entertainment. When those responsible for assignments requiring creative thinking indulge in reading wild west or detective stories, or listen to jazz music, don't malign or belittle them. They are probably engaging in this step of the creative process. Likewise, a hobby is a valuable asset to a creative thinker. During this step of incubation or gestation, one's mind will continue to operate on the problem unconsciously. However, it is important to prevent emotional or mental blocks by some form of diversion which will result in one's not thinking about the problem or associated ideas. This is important because the next step should result in illumination or insight which brings to mind the idea sought to solve the problem.

Illumination

This step often occurs when least expected. The idea will appear when one is eating, bathing, relaxing, driving, or engaging in some similar activity. If the previous steps of exploration and preparation, digestion of relationships, and incubation or gestation have been accomplished properly, the new idea will be brought to mind. However, other ideas will follow in quick order. Many fail in the creative thinking process on this step because ideas come to mind faster than one's memory can absorb or retain them. Therefore, it is important that some means of writing down the ideas as they occur be devised. Otherwise, they will be lost and the previous work in the creative process nullified.

Verification and Application

The final step in the creative process of thinking is that of verifying, modifying, or applying the idea toward the solution of the problem selected and defined. However, the same freedom of thinking and imagination should be used in verifying or applying the new idea brought to mind as in the other steps of the creative process. This step is essential if one is to get his ideas accepted and used.

The creative thinking process is based upon three essential elements: knowledge, proficiency, and attitude. Knowledge supplies the grist for the mental process. Proficiency in all steps of the creative thinking process is vital for success in using it. There must be a positive attitude and a receptive climate for using the process.

They copied all they could follow,
but they couldn't copy my mind,
And I left 'em sweating and stealing
a year and a half behind.
—KIPLING,
"The Mary Gloster"

Business Research and the Creative Thinking Process

Willard A. Pleuthner, Vice-President of BBD&O, has stated:

In too many cases, nothing is done creatively about research findings. Sound research has provided the knowledge which is a potential power for the business. But research itself seldom puts that power to work in providing all the answers, or the best answers, to the problems. This is exactly where creative thinking should move into the research picture. In that move, the mental climate should change . . . some of the faces around the table should change. The transmission of thinking should shift from the third gear of judicial judgment into the free wheeling of creative imagination.

Sound business research carried on according to valid methods is essential to the creative thinking process. The all-important step of exploration and preparation in the creative thinking process depends upon research to provide the basic knowledge upon which the subsequent steps depend.

One may be able to follow a career and earn a living by operating on the routine or problem-solving levels of thinking. However, the highest rewards in recognition and income will be offered to those who will contribute to economic, business, and technological progress through creative thinking about the world's problems. Fortunately, the process of creative thinking is not patented or withheld from anyone. It is available and free for all to use.

46. IMPROVING THE COMMUNICATION PROCESS *

by Rupert L. Cortright and George L. Hinds †

Poise

The Italian painter, sculptor, and architect, Michelangelo, has been called the Shakespeare of art. The greater part of four years of his life was de-

* Reprinted from *Creative Discussion* (New York: The Macmillan Company, © 1959), pp. 89–103.
† Both of Wayne State University.

voted to the magnificent mural paintings on the ceiling of the Sistine Chapel
in Rome. His statue of Moses, his painting of the Last Judgment, and his
design of the dome of St. Peter's are among his most famous works. Each
is a masterpiece. Each is a product of painstaking skill. To those who used
generous adjectives to describe the wonder of his art, Michelangelo had a
simple answer: "If people knew how hard I have had to work to gain my
mastery, it would not seem wonderful at all." Many an effective speaker
would express similar feeling. You may observe a person who is skillful in
the art of speaking, and you may say, "How wonderful to be so generously
endowed." But if you knew how hard he had worked to gain his mastery
and to perfect his skill, you would not think of it as a wonder but as *well
earned.* Each person is endowed with certain potential abilities for speech.
How well these potentialities become realized depends upon right practice.

Poise may well be a by-product of such qualities as maturity, confidence,
and preparedness. Yet many can testify from personal experience that it
does not spring spontaneously from these. Poise generally implies composure—knowing both *what* one should do under the circumstances and
how to do it. There is also implied in the word poise a *readiness for right
action.* These implications give us our clues to the ways to improved poise
for ourselves in all speaking situations, whether conversation, interview, discussion, or public speaking. Nervousness is one enemy of composure and
thus of poise. We make progress toward lessening its inhibiting effects in
two ways. *First,* we direct our attention away from those aspects of the
situation which destroy our confidence by positively directing our attention
to those aspects which build our confidence. We remind ourselves of our
thorough preparation, of our knowledge of what we are to talk about, of
the respect which our listeners already have for us, of the high confidence
we would feel in discussing this subject with close friends, and of the likely
fact that our listeners know less about the subject than do we.

Second, if in spite of all this wise direction of our attention we feel all of
the physical manifestations of nervousness mounting steadily and threaten-
ing to go out of control, then we take direct muscular command. This is
where another definition of poise takes on significance. When uncontrolled
nervousness overwhelms us we are like a huge machine that has lost its
balance wheel. Poise also implies balance, control, and purposiveness. A
good place to begin to apply balance and control over mounting nervousness
is in the conscious control we have over breathing. Slow down the breathing rate. Take steady, long, deep breaths. As a result, the heart beat slows
and its pounding lessens. The whole nervous tempo of body functioning
comes under control and balance. Poise takes over. The difference between
the person who acts as though unafraid and the person who acts as though
afraid is not in the *situation* but in the *person.* When we know *from actual
practice* that nervousness begotten by fear can be kept under control by

the simple expedient of controlling the breathing; when we know that the nervous symptom of a dry mouth, making us feel as though we could "spit cotton," may be controlled by the power of our imagination to stimulate the salivary glands into action—in short, by a pleasant thought of a juicy steak, strawberry shortcake, or whatever may be our favorite food; when we know that the scared speaker's pounding knees may be quickly relaxed and brought under control by purposeful movement on the platform; when we *know* these things *by having experienced them* we have the *key to poise*. All that is required to make the key work is determined and persistent effort. It is as simple, yet as difficult, as the master artist Michelangelo said: "If people knew how hard I have had to work to gain my mastery, it would not seem wonderful at all."

Gesture

You need only observe a group in conversation to realize that gesture and facial expression enter importantly into the processes of communicating meaning and feeling. Many theories as to the origin of speech in the history of man explain gestures as having been used before voice. According to these theories, voice came to be used in order that the hands might be freed for other activities, and because a voice can be heard when gestures might not be seen. We might add that the oral code has made possible finer shades of meaning. Yet gestures have continued to facilitate the process of expression, and to supplement the voice with added meanings and, particularly, shades of feeling. Speech, whether in conversation, conference, discussion, or public speaking, employs two codes: both the oral and the visual. The visual code is communicated by gestures, principally of the hands, arms, and head. Gestures serve primarily three functions: (1) description, (2) emphasis, and (3) suggestion.

Gestures help us to describe the length of fish we caught, the size and shape of some object, the mannerisms of another person, how to make a baseball curve, or how to use a can opener. Descriptive gestures are good if they convey the intended meaning clearly, if they are easily seen, and if they do not call attention to themselves rather than to the idea they seek to convey. Practice in demonstrations of a how-to-do-it nature is a helpful way of checking on one's use of gesture. The same can be achieved by the use of visual aids: charts, blackboard, pictures, and objects. A little experience even before small groups will make you aware of the importance of such fundamentals as keeping gestures and visual aids up where they can be seen, tending to exaggerate action a bit to make it more obvious, and getting the right gesture to convey the intended idea. The still popular game of charades can provide excellent practice. For accurate and vivid description, remember that gestures are natural, normal, and needed.

Not only are gestures needed for descriptive purposes, but they also give emphasis to ideas. The clenched fist or the extended index finger are examples. In a sense, thus, gestures may be thought of as underlining or setting in italics certain words. You will have noticed that when emphatic gestures are either under used or over used they tend to lose effectiveness. It is perhaps unnecessary to note that emphatic gestures, like emphatic words, should be appropriate and in good taste. Noisy table-pounding, for example, may more often be a sign of immaturity or lack of poise than of effective emphatic gesturing. Variety, timing, and change are important principles of emphasis. Just as sudden quietness in voice may be far more attention-getting than extreme loudness, so restrained and poised gesture may carry far greater weight than would excessive flailing of the arms. There is no more reason to be concerned about building one's vocabulary of useful words, than there is to consider one's repertoire of gestures to convey positiveness, for instance. Experiment to find the most effective gesture to make positive such a statement as:

> This much I know!
> I mean every word of it.
> There is but one price too high to pay for peace!
> Call it what you will—it is fraud, or worse.

Ask another person to experiment similarly, but without having seen your gestures. Note that each individual must discover the type of gesture which accomplishes emphasis, in each case, for him. While there will be similarities, in keeping with a kind of universal code which we all understand in gesture, there will also be important differences.

We use gestures not only for description and emphasis but also to accomplish suggestion. We may wish to suggest smoke rising on the horizon, or a flag being unfurled to the breeze. This is a form of description to be sure, but only to suggest things to the listener's imagination. The speaker's eye follows the really descriptive gesture because he wishes the listeners to see what he is accurately and exactly describing. But neither speaker nor listener looks at the guesture of suggestion because that would inject realism instead of imagination. The listener would see cracks in the wall or ceiling instead of a flag unfurling. We may use a gesture simply to suggest an image which exists only in the listener's imagination. The listener is aware of the gesture in this instance not as itself but for what it suggests.

Imitation plays a considerable part in all learning. We imitate the way another person handles a tool or holds a golf club. It is only natural, therefore, for us to imitate the way another person speaks, particularly another person whom we very much admire. Yet our words and our gestures are, and ought to be, uniquely our own. They constitute perhaps the most significant traits of our *individual* personalities. This fact certainly suggests that any imitation of the gestures of others should be discriminatingly done so that we do not sacrifice all individuality for the element of uniformity so necessary for understandability.

What we share in common with others, in word, voice, and action, makes us quickly and easily understood. Yet what each individual adds beyond this constitutes his personal style, introduces richer shadings of meaning, and gives unique worth to the ideas expressed. We win and hold the respect of others not alone for what we know and express in common with them, but above and beyond this for what we know and express more deeply and more richly than they. So our gestures will benefit from the elements of imitation of what all gesture language needs to have in common. And just as one looks in a mirror to adjust dress or make-up, so one may profitably use the mirror to improve the personal expressiveness of gestures. You can find real help from others, too, as you request their criticisms and suggestions. You may well be reticent about changing in response to a single critic; but when several make a similar suggestion you may feel more certain that you have a representative reaction.

Finally, we have four specific suggestions for improving your use of gestures.

1. With but rare exceptions, *gestures precede the words or ideas they picture.* You first point to a picture, then describe it. A frown precedes, in fact announces words of disapproval. You smile as you recall some humorous experience, then you tell it. You say, "I caught a fish——" and pause while you show how long, before you finish the sentence. Remember also the point already made that your listeners are not only *first* but *more importantly* lookers. If your actions are inconsistent with your words, they will believe your actions and disregard your words. So heed Hamlet's advice: "Suit the action to the word, the word to the action." Smile when you are joking but not when you are serious. Use more action in the informal situation, less in the formal; more action in the large gathering, less in the small. Timing and appropriateness are two of the more important attributes of effective gesturing.

2. *Each gesture should be a product of your whole being,* of all your muscles, all your thought, and all your feeling. Gestures at best are a product of total bodily reaction. Unless you really feel and believe what you are saying, faulty gestures will reveal your insincerity or lack of conviction. Some people seem to be talking only from the shoulders up, occasionally a hand makes a feeble attempt at movement—the only evidence that the rest of the body is still alive! Overuse of distracting head movement often results as the body struggles in vain for expression. Even thinking is an active process. We think with our muscles. So we must learn to speak with

them—with *all* of them. Don't let your gesture come just from the wrist, or elbow, or shoulder. As in boxing or fencing, so in speaking, the whole body must be alert and involved.

3. *Poor gestures most often result from inhibition, restraint, and lack of confidence.* This is true because gestures are by nature an inherent part of us. They are more basic even, and more universal, than speech itself. They try to assert themselves even with the most nervous, ill-at-ease, and inexperienced speaker. But he inhibits them by clasping his hands tightly in front, or behind his back, or hiding them in his pockets. He doesn't give them a chance. Of course he is self-conscious, afraid he will make the wrong gesture (whatever that may be), or that he will be considered awkward. And the latter is just exactly what he is considered, because he makes it inevitable! When, after more than enough of agony, he makes the discovery that gesturing is many times easier than not gesturing, more than half the battle is won.

4. *Any gestures overused tend to lose effectiveness.* This is a mistake more common among overconfident speakers than among the timid. The very laws of learning, and particularly the powerful effect of practice, make a speaker tend to overuse those few gestures he has used most, or the ones which seem to him to have gained the more satisfying responses. We have the same tendency in conversation or extemporaneous speaking to overuse certain favorite words or phrases. In action this may result in far too many gestures with the right hand, or almost entirely in some set pattern. In reality, what this speaker is asking is that the same gesture convey a great variety of different meanings. The result can be only monotony, confusion, and meaninglessness.

Movement

The term *movement* as distinguished from *gesture* refers to total bodily movement or actual change of position on the platform. For many conference and discussion situations it has little, if any, significance. But in the symposium and open forum situation and in most other speaking situations it merits serious attention. Many aspects of movement have been referred to in the discussion of *poise*. There remain for mention here but a few positive suggestions.

The four suggestions just made with regard to gesture certainly hold also for movement. Movement assists, as do gestures, in giving emphasis and otherwise aiding meaning. A change of position, or movement, often means to the listener what a new paragraph implies for a reader: a new idea, or an additional point. Thus effective movement during a talk serves to set off main transitions in thought in the speech outline. An easy and graceful speaking position tends to have the weight of the body so distributed upon both feet that readiness of movement and quickness of response is not only made easy but also natural. This certainly is not true of a position, so commonly seen in inexperienced speakers, with the feet fairly wide apart and parallel. Effective speaking is *active*. The speaker must *appear, act,* and *be* alert.

The principle of empathic response, listener with speaker, adds to the importance of the speaker's movement. It is a kind of sympathetic muscular reaction which occurs when a speaker has established rapport with his audience. You may have felt it sometime while watching a juggler: he almost drops one of the balls; and you find yourself involuntarily responding muscularly as if to aid him. Studies show that an audience which is really attentive and responsive tends to synchronize its breathing rate with that of the speaker. Like begets like. The movement of the speaker tends to predispose the nature of the reaction he will get from his listener. It is important, therefore, that the speaker's movement be graceful, purposeful, and impelling to the mood and feeling desired.

Movement, as already suggested, helps the inexperienced speaker to dissipate harmful tension. It must be varied so as not to contribute to monotony. It must be suitable to the audience, the occasion, and the speaker's purpose. This suitability is both in kind and amount of action. Movement too, like gesture, must be appropriate to the individual personality of the speaker. But let us note that this means: appropriate to the individual personality *at its best!*

Finally, often it appears that both a speaker's movement and gestures seem merely random and somehow for the exclusive purpose of facilitating his process of thinking out loud. As such they are only distracting for the listener. All gesture and all movement should serve a definitely purposeful function in facilitating the process of communicating meaning.

Voice

Unpleasant to the Ear. Human judgments and values differ. Likes and dislikes from individual to individual are unlike. This is true of our senses of taste, smell, temperature, pain, or touch. It is also true that our eyes and ears have *individual*—and therefore differing—senses of value. This simple and obvious fact about human nature, which all of us have experienced and observed, should make us realize that what sounds to us like a pleasant voice may appear to others either as less pleasant or more pleasant. To a certain extent, then, the description of a given voice as pleasant is a subjective evaluation dependent upon the individual listener. Granting all this, however, there will yet be general agreement in rating some voices as pleasant, and others as unpleasant. Are the ladies even partly justified in their large annual expenditure for cosmetics? Are both male and female well advised in their expenditure of that considerable part of the total clothing budget which goes beyond the needs of comfort and propriety to add the often more costly attributes of style? Then we should not overlook the value of paying at least the cost of that little effort which might make our voice more attractive, more pleasant to the ear.

What makes a voice unpleasant? Ask yourself what qualities you find annoying in the voices you hear. No doubt you will respond with such adjectives as high-pitched, harsh, tense, strident, raucous, coarse, rough, shrill, or piercing. It would be well to reassure one's self that others are not having such reactions to one's voice. There are two ways of finding out. You may ask the opinion of some qualified critic of voice, or you may have a recording made and judge for yourself. Remember that except upon the basis of a recording one cannot evaluate one's own voice, for the simple reason that no one can hear his own voice as others hear it. The biological and physical facts of hearing make this impossible.

Lacking in Variety. Another common voice fault interfering with communication and favorable impressions is the lack of variety. This is commonly described as monotony. Except for individuals extremely low on the intelligence scale, a few types of glandular malfunction, some cases of psychosomatic illness, or specific neurological or muscular abnormalities, the usual cause of a monotonous voice is to be found in the failure to use the wide range of its potentiality. One should think of one's voice as an instrument of almost unlimited possibility, like an expensive pipe organ of which one would be taking most inadequate advantage if one merely constantly overused two or three pipes. The cause of monotony, however, may be complex. It can be a by-product of one's personality. Voice inevitably mirrors one's attitude toward life. A vibrant personality, an earnest and enthusiastic workman will tend to use his voice to more nearly its optimum. Yet all will recognize that incentive and right attitude are not alone enough to make a great baseball pitcher, for example. Some long and careful right practice is also necessary. It is no different with the muscles of the human voice than it is with the muscles of the arm. The combination of enthusiasm, of a sense of vitality, and of right practice will make of any one's voice a finer, a more serviceable, and a more pleasing instrument of expression and communication.

Rhythmical Patterns That Detract from Meaning. Cadence, staccato, and sing-song are distracting rhythmical patterns into which some voices seem to have become habituated. It will be a rare listener who hasn't suffered through a preacher's cadence, an announcer's fatiguing staccato, or a classroom lecturer's sing-song manner. All are bad because they annoy the sensitive ear, distract from one's best efforts to pay attention to the message, and have a repetitive lullaby effect inducing sleep or, at best, day dreams. Perhaps the saddest fact about these cadences is that apparently in some academic settings, in some church congregations, and in some political conventions they are mistaken for effective speaking!

Poorly Adapted to the Listeners. A good practical measure of the speaker's use of voice is afforded by the question: Is he easily heard? Particularly in a conversation or in a discussion, it is difficult for all to hear a voice that is too low, too quiet, and poorly projected. The listeners not only fail to get the speaker's point but they have a subconscious feeling of resentment that the speaker hasn't even enough respect either for them or for his own ideas to *speak up*. The opposite fault of the person who speaks too loudly and indirectly stamps him as no less considerate, particularly to your ear drums. After all, the human voice has an excellent built-in volume control. Would-be listeners wish it were better used.

Careful Practice with Criticism. We have sought to make clear that speech is a product of action—of moving muscles. This is no less true of voice than of any other phase of speech. It follows clearly, then, that the way to improvement of voice is the way of right practice. Reading aloud—even the daily newspaper—before others capable of giving helpful criticism is a practice opportunity available to everyone. If you have access to a recorder of any kind you can record your voice as you read or speak into the microphone—we would recommend speaking rather than reading for this—and then you can play back and evaluate how well you have done. You can set goals for improvement and repeat the process. Whenever you have opportunities to participate in conferences or discussions, be aware, keep reminding yourself of specific improvements in voice which you need to be making. Awareness of need and well-directed effort toward its fulfillment will be certain to bring results. Do not become overly self-conscious about this either. That would only make matters worse. Asking others too often for criticism or suggestions can readily be misinterpreted as egotism seeking praise.

Finally, never lose sight of the fact that you are developing a voice that is to be uniquely and characteristically yours, neither a copy of some other single individual's, nor of some imagined perfect composite. Each voice mechanism, physique, and personality is and ought to be unique. The voice should contribute in the most positive possible way to this uniqueness. It is that distinctive part of YOU which you wish others to find pleasant, and which will contribute in every finest possible way to your effectiveness.

The Road Up — Sales Management and Beyond

47. WHAT DOES A SALES EXECUTIVE HAVE TO DO TO MOVE HIGHER UP IN MANAGEMENT? *

by Charles W. Smith †

There are at least six important answers:

1. He must keep his sights high enough to avoid total preoccupation with sales.
2. He must acquire a substantial understanding of other corporate activities: finance, engineering, personnel relations, for instance.
3. He must balance devotion to volume with an equally intensive concern for profits.
4. He must learn to analyze facts for use as the basis of decisions.
5. He must develop and maintain a broad interest in economics and philosophy.
6. He must keep abreast of developments in scientific management.

Long-range marketing strategy has become so important to corporate growth that men who have demonstrated their ability to plan sound sales programs are moving rapidly into the top echelons of management. The best evidence of this trend is the growing list of corporate chief executives who have come up through sales.

However, many sales executives are failing to capitalize fully on career development opportunities. Furthermore, companies that are spending sizable sums in recruiting candidates for promotion to higher executive po-

* Reprinted from *Sales Management,* © September 20, 1957, pp. 33–5.
† McKinsey & Company.

sitions have not exploited the full growth potential of their sales chiefs. Many able sales executives have been repeatedly passed over for promotion to jobs that provide stepping stones to top echelon positions. Why does this situation exist and what can a sales executive do to increase his chances of being tapped for a top-drawer management job?

Set Your Sights Higher

One of the factors that keeps many able sales executives from being considered for a top-drawer job is simply that they have set their sights too low. They seem to feel they have reached the top of the ladder when they become sales manager. They do not aspire to more responsibility.

This attitude limits their thinking to sales problems. They refuse to expand their interest horizons to the broader problems of top management, but confine their efforts to technical matters related to their immediate assignment.

Develop Your Technical Background

Sales executives who have been graduated to top management positions are well-rounded men who know the basic problems of their companies in manufacturing, accounting, engineering, finance, and personnel relations. In addition, they know the principles of organization and have studied the science of administration. Thus, they understand and can deal effectively with problems that fall outside the area of responsibility normally assigned to the sales department.

Become Profit-Minded and Cost-Conscious

One weakness commonly attributed to sales executives is that they are so volume-minded that they pay too little attention to costs or profits. To some extent this criticism is valid, particularly in companies in which top management withholds profit information from them.

Nevertheless, any alert sales executive who thinks about profits, as well as about getting an order, has many opportunities to show he understands what is involved in increasing profits in his industry. Such an attitude helps him to "talk the language" of top management.

Learn to Use Facts

Another criticism commonly voiced regarding many sales executives is that they do not know how to use facts in reaching decisions, but rely too much on personal experience.

Good judgment is required of any executive, particularly of chief executives. However, the most successful chief executives have nearly all been good fact-and-figure men. Because they realize the impossibility of making decisions in areas of business where their personal experience is limited, they have learned to ask for figures that disclose basic facts about a specific situation requiring a decision. They have also learned how to check figures so as to catch any covering up—either intentional or unintentional. In many instances, this checking is done by getting opinions of informed people with a variety of interests in the problem under consideration. In other cases, it involves personal inspection of key situations, but always against a background of previously developed information.

Many sales executives, however, instinctively dislike to work with figures. Many of them have become so expert in manipulating statistics to prove a point that they distrust all figures. Such men have great difficulty in convincing top management that they possess the skills required for promotion to a top echelon position.

Become Interested in Economics and Philosophy

Ability to sense the underlying causes of change in our economy is an important qualification of a chief executive. Men who aspire to such positions typically have a broad interest in both economics and philosophy.

Some have become interested in these subjects through formal education; others have acquired their knowledge through broad reading. Unless a man has such background, however, he is ill-equipped to interpret the basic trends that can influence a company's health and growth.

Learn More About Scientific Management

As companies have grown, there has been a greater and greater need for professional managers. Thus, a new class of executives skilled in the arts of scientific management has been gradually assuming greater responsibility in our major corporations.

Many sales executives do not understand the language used by the scientific management group. Those who have developed such an understanding, however, have found the knowledge extremely helpful in interpreting current developments in corporate organization structure and operating practice. Such concepts as "span of control," "line and staff," "management by exception," and "long-range planning" stem directly from the scientific management group. All of these concepts have been applied in reorganizations of sales departments in many companies without the sales executives being fully aware of what was being done.

As a result, many sales executives have failed to take advantage of opportunities to contribute to the development of important new management concepts. This is particularly true of companies that have begun to apply the "total marketing" concept, thereby creating many new marketing management positions for which sales experience is a primary qualification.

Who is Responsible for Your Development?

The concept of the self-made man seems to have been losing ground rapidly as company after company has initiated some type of executive development program. A number of leading companies have established their own executive training colleges; many middle management men are now being enrolled in advanced management courses at leading universities.

These moves by top management are in the right direction. But they in no way shift the primary responsibility for an executive's development. In the final analysis, the most that any company can do is create a climate favorable to self-development. For unless an individual wants to grow, no training program that has ever been devised will be effective.

Furthermore, an executive with his feet on the ground does not wait for a formal training program to begin preparing himself for promotion. Unless a man has demonstrated some capacity for development on his own, he is not likely to be chosen for advanced training.

The first step any sales executive should take toward a higher level job, therefore, is to assume responsibility for shaping his own development program.

Elements of a Personal Development Program

The elements that a sales executive's personal development program should include will be determined by what he needs most to learn. This reflects his formal education, the extent of his work experience, and the caliber of the executives with whom he has had personal contact.

Anyone with graduate training in business administration has been exposed to many of the basic concepts involved in becoming a successful executive. It is going to become increasingly difficult for anyone to achieve a top management position without having had some formal business training. Perhaps the best evidence of this trend is that a number of foreign countries have begun to develop their own graduate schools of business administration with the help of American professors.

Yet many top executives have achieved their positions without the benefit of graduate training. Some have developed their know-how by taking correspondence courses. Others have attended evening classes in local universities. And most of them are avid readers of business literature.

Every sales executive should inventory his skills and define his development needs. For instance, the sales executive who recognizes a weakness in his knowledge of accounting should think about taking a course in accounting. There are excellent correspondence courses that can be taken even by a man who must be constantly on the road in his present job.

Such an inventory can also point up the need for different types of work experience. A man who has had only field experience may thus come to recognize the importance of taking a staff job, when it is offered to him. He may even take steps to get himself transferred into such a job at the right stage in his career. Knowledge of what kind of experience is most needed can also be of help should it become necessary to move to another job.

Finally, the caliber of a sales executive's contacts can have a tremendous influence on his rate of development. One advantage of well-born men is the opportunity they have from an early age to rub shoulders with top executives in a wide variety of fields. Such contacts develop valuable insights that come much more slowly to those who have not had the privilege of such associations.

In some cases, a man can do little to develop such contacts. But every sales executive should be alert to opportunities to do so. Participation in trade and professional association activities or in local community projects often provide such opportunities. Writing or speaking on subjects of interest to other executives is another way of attracting the favorable attention of key people.

Thus, each individual can chart his own program of self-development. Pursued effectively and in a relaxed frame of mind over a period of time, such a program is bound to produce results. Why then are more sales executives not pursuing a course of personal career development?

Limitations on Personal Growth of Sales Executives

Limitations on the personal growth of sales executives are generally of two kinds: internal and external. The strength of the limitations depends in most instances on the individual's willingness to pay the price required to overcome them.

Internal limitations include such things as:
1. Self-satisfaction
2. Unwillingness to recognize shortcomings
3. Laziness
4. Lack of imagination
5. Inability to think analytically.

The first step toward personal growth is to be dissatisfied with things as they are. Many sales executives are satisfied simply because they have never thought of themselves as potential top executive material.

On the other hand, many sales executives are ambitious to achieve promotion, but are unwilling to recognize their limitations. As a consequence, they fail to take the steps necessary to prepare themselves for advancement. In many cases, this stems from lack of humility. In other cases, it is simply a form of rationalization to avoid the effort required to correct personal shortcomings.

Laziness is a fault to which few sales executives will admit. But many sales executives are always too busy to take the time to think about their personal career development problems. Intense activity on routine responsibilities is often used as an excuse for failing to take action on the much tougher problems involved in career development. Essentially this is just mental laziness.

On the other hand, some sales executives simply lack the imagination to see themselves as top management executives. They are so limited in vision that they are unable to project themselves into higher level positions, to "try them on for size." Thus, they never can see clearly their own shortcomings for such positions.

Finally, many sales executives cannot think analytically. They grow up in their jobs either taking orders or relying on past experience. When conditions change and create new problems, they are unable to devise sound solutions on their own. Such men can't see the forest for the trees, particularly with regard to their own career development problems.

The able sales executive who has none of these limitations usually finds it possible to move ahead in his company over a period of time to higher level jobs. Some companies, however, are still putting roadblocks in the way of able men. Such roadblocks include:

1. Withholding all responsibility for profits
2. Discouraging any effort to develop broader experience or knowledge of the business as a whole
3. Failing to provide needed educational opportunities.

When a company is organized along strictly functional lines, sales executives may be given little opportunity to think about the over-all problems. For instance, in some companies information about costs and margins is so closely held by a few key men that the average sales executive has no knowledge of the factors that influence the profit structure of the business. This policy tends to create one-sided sales executives who can think only in terms of sales volume.

The trend toward adoption of the "total marketing" concept is helping to remove this roadblock. For as teamwork is encouraged in profit planning, sales executives have an opportunity to learn the economics of their industries as they come up through the ranks.

Other companies limit the development of their sales executives by discouraging any effort to broaden experience or knowledge of the business as a whole. Some companies frown on a sales executive who seeks to become active in any outside organization on the principle that such effort diverts his attention from the business at hand. Other companies place restrictions on writing or speaking which make it difficult for a sales executive to develop a personal reputation beyond his assigned area. Still others keep sales executives too long in one job, and deprive them of the chance to expand their know-how through periodic job rotation.

Some companies are not even aware of the problem, so they are doing nothing. Their executives are becoming older, with no adequate replacements in sight. Under intense competitive pressure, such companies are likely to experience great difficulty in maintaining their share of market in the future.

Finally, many companies still have no formal training or development programs for sales executives. Sales executives are not encouraged to take courses to broaden their experience. They are not given opportunities to participate in advanced management training programs. Fortunately, the number of such companies is rapidly decreasing.

What About the Future?

Looking ahead, astute observers are beginning to ask: "Where are our executives going to come from in the next five to ten years?" "Is the present shortage of capable marketing executives going to become more severe?" "What are companies going to do to increase the pool of promotable men?"

As businesses grow, the need for more and better executive manpower grows. This reflects not only the larger number of transactions, but also the fact that planning and coordination problems seem to multiply in geometric, rather than arithmetic, proportions as a business expands.

Schools of business administration have been rapidly expanding their operations to train more potential executives and to provide advanced programs for promotable men. But schools aren't growing fast enough to keep pace with the demands of industry. They have neither the facilities nor the staff required, and cannot get them quickly. What then will companies do to insure their future supply of executive manpower?

Some managements recruit executive manpower from other companies. This creates great morale problems as older employees are denied opportunities for advancement, even though they are obviously not qualified to fill the openings. Such a policy tends to increase costs by forcing up the levels of executive compensation. It also dries up the initiative of able younger men who see little chance for promotion.

Other companies have planned programs for developing executive manpower. General Electric has long had a policy of recruiting men from colleges and training them. Recently, the company organized its own advanced management school. Additional steps have been taken to encourage individual employees at every level to develop their own executive abilities. A number of other leading companies have been working along similar lines. As a result, men are being advanced quickly to positions where they can demonstrate their potential executive ability at an earlier age. Men who show such ability are helped to broaden their experience by a planned program of job rotation. They are also stimulated to develop their own skills by all of the means mentioned earlier in this discussion. Many of these executives eventually decide to accept positions in other firms for a variety of reasons. But the companies with training programs attract a steady stream of able young men, and seem to experience relatively little difficulty in keeping their executive positions properly staffed.

Whether or not the total supply of potential executives will ever fully meet the needs of American industry is still a matter of question. But the signs are encouraging that the problem is receiving increasing attention in more and more progressive companies. As individual sales executives become aware of ways in which they can increase their own opportunities for promotion, the number and quality of potential top management executives should increase steadily over the next few years.

48. HOW ADEPT ARE YOU IN SPOTTING FIVE TRAITS IN YOUNG POTENTIAL MANAGERS? *

by J.O. Vance †

The deciding factor in a company's desire to expand into new markets or new lines, or its ability to maintain a normal growth, often is the organization's reserve of promotable sales talent.

Most managements recognize the benefits of promotion from within. They also recognize that salesmen's volume performance alone is not the best indication of internal potential management talent. It is our experience that promotable candidates rate high in these areas.

Interest in Management

All salesmen at one time or another probably aspire to management positions. To some men this ambition is born of the lone desire for increased personal stature. To other salesmen promotional opportunities mean an opportunity to develop management techniques and assist in formulating company growth patterns. The latter are usually recognizable through their

* Reprinted from *Sales Management*, © February 1, 1954, pp. 72–4.
† McKinsey & Company.

interest in management techniques. These salesmen realize that they must equip themselves with knowledge to assume increased responsibilities.

A salesman actively working toward a management position will respond to discussions of management techniques in several ways. He is often interested in the "why" of management decisions, and frequently checks his own logic to see if he would have arrived at the same decision. He likes to know the work and techniques behind sales forecasts, quotas, territory definitions, incentive compensation, and sales training.

Secondly, he may evidence interest in management techniques through trial application of them in his own territory. An excellent example of this was exhibited several years ago by a salesman for a national distributor of food products. This particular salesman planned his territorial operations as if it were a sales district. Sales effort was allocated by customer groups and by areas. Customer potentials were classified by product lines and careful records were kept relating sales expense to volume. Records of competitive activity were maintained and estimates of the company's share of the market by product line were easily prepared. Today this man is a successful sales supervisor. Acceptance of management responsibility was easy because of his previous study and use of management techniques.

Business Judgment

Sound judgment is one of the primary attributes of successful management. A candidate must demonstrate the intelligence and judgment to formulate correct decisions. Salesmen differ less in degree of intelligence and quality of judgment than in their willingness to use it. Employment testing procedures usually will ensure that members of the sales team have adequate basic intelligence.

Intelligence and judgment in sales situations is highly dependent on getting all the facts. A decision may be reasonable in view of the facts at hand, only to be shown false in the light of further knowledge.

A promising promotion candidate demonstrates a tendency to get needed facts and to formulate rational rather than emotional or intuitive decisions. This type of salesman usually handles many of the routine problems of delivery, changed specifications, and credit that other men take to the manager. His decisions are soon respected by other men and you will find them "checking to see what Jim did," and using his decisions as precedents.

The salesman with the ability to collect and analyze facts in reaching decisions will probably not be accused of being unable to make up his mind. While his decisions are not "snap" judgments, he understands that judgment is a process of selection—that at a certain point a choice is necessary to reach a conclusion.

Since judgment grows through practice, the salesman who demonstrates ability early will continue to improve through experience.

Healthy Ambition

The salesman who seeks management responsibility must be ambitious, in a way that promotes both personal progress *and* long-range company interests. The promotion candidate with this healthy ambition wants executive responsibilities for deeper reasons than increased income and prestige.

He has in addition a genuine interest in making a real contribution to his company and to the business community. His ambitions are not limited to himself, nor will they hurt his fellow salesmen; rather, they include his whole organization.

Salesmen with this outlook participate readily in discussions on company growth, new products, intensified coverage, new markets, etc. These men's personal and company growth ambitions are the realistic goals that should be those of any management group.

Planning and Organizing Ability

It is often said that the most precious commodity to any salesman is time. The salesmen who should be considered for promotion quickly learn to plan and organize their activities to make the most efficient use of every minute.

A salesman for a national manufacturer of industrial valves stands out particularly in memory for his well-planned and organized use of time. This salesman's territorial routing was excellent. His work objectives and calls were planned a week in advance. When service or special calls interrupted this schedule, adjustments were made without lost motion. Time was allocated to customer groups in accordance with their potential or as competitive activity demanded. The time spent in the sales office was reduced to a minimum. Work done on preparation of bids and sales correspondence was handled with the office by telephone calls whenever possible.

This salesman had learned the art of evaluating and ranking the functions of his job and organizing his activities to accomplish these duties. This work pattern, coupled with the ability to be forward-looking in his planning and organizing of activities, was responsible for his subsequent promotion to regional manager of his company.

Ability to Work Through People

The ease with which any executive works through people contributes substantially to his eventual success. Because of the independent nature of most salesmen's work, however, this is a difficult early characteristic to evaluate. Salesmen who are successful in gaining customer cooperation in selling situations usually rate high in this attribute. It is possible to note how a salesman works through customers in gaining shelf space, obtaining displays, and influencing engineering and specifications.

It is also important to observe the salesman's work through home office personnel. In industrial selling it is especially necessary for a salesman to obtain technical and delivery information and to work with home office engineering groups. Some men achieve considerable success over others in channeling their requests through the organization and in maintaining cooperative relationships.

Finally, the degree to which a salesman is interested in helping other personnel grow is a good indication of his ability to work through people. The best promotion candidates always seem to be willing to take time to assist a junior salesman on work with new clerical people in interpreting price bulletins or specification changes.

These five early characteristics of promotion candidates are naturally seldom found in any single salesman. In the practical sense it is necessary to recognize the greatest combination of any of these attributes in the embryo stage and assist the individual in further development. This constitutes a difficult training job that cannot be accomplished through a series of training meetings alone. Rather, it requires that management spend time in the field with the salesman to observe, analyze, and coach his work on the job.

The stability of our economy depends greatly upon our ability to sell our production capacity. This places a heavy responsibility on industry to select and train capable potential candidates for sales management.

49. TRAINING FUTURE SALES LEADERS *

by Philip Gustafson †

Today's complex market, more sophisticated customers, and the increased stress on selling are putting greater demands on the first line sales supervisor.

Different companies give him different titles—branch manager, division manager, or district manager. For simplicity here we will call him the district manager.

As one marketing vice-president puts it: "We're beginning to see that if the salesman is a key man, the sales supervisor is a key-er man."

Diversification, decentralization, technology, and changing methods of

* Copyright 1957, reprinted from the April 1957 issue of *Nation's Business,* pp. 78–84.
  † Writer.

distribution account for this estimate. Today's far-flung sales forces face new problems in relating company interest to customer interest. They have greater need for expert decisions than ever before and, in today's tougher competition, they need these decisions quickly. This means decision-making in the field, and the man on the spot is the district manager.

Recognition of his importance, though slow in coming, is now coming with a rush.

Seventy-one of 104 companies which responded to a recent American Management Association survey to learn more about current practices in regard to first-line sales supervisors said they gave these men no orientation training at all, a lack which seems unlikely to continue.

Large numbers of companies are now taking their problem to management consultants and to business associations.

So many went to the American Management Association that the AMA's Marketing Division set up a national meeting of company sales managers, expecting a registration of 200. Instead, an overflow crowd of 450 piled into town for the meeting.

"We apparently struck a nerve center," says Coleman Lee Finkel, Director of AMA's Marketing Division. "The response has been so terrific that we're setting up a whole series of training seminars throughout the country and we plan to schedule more and more meetings for this important link in sales management. This is the first time these fellows have been given any real concentrated attention.

"It's much like the situation which arose when production expanded so rapidly. Suddenly, everybody needed foremen and there were foremen training courses all over the country. Now, it's the same with the first line sales supervisor."

This new interest has led to a new appraisal of district sales supervision. Out of this has grown a considerable body of knowledge about:

The job
The man
The training that matches one to the other.

Requirements for each of these will vary according to the nature of the market, the nature of the company, and the nature of the prospects. But, regardless of these variations, most district managers and the work they do have certain things in common.

The Job

Five basic functions occur in practically every job description. They are: Recruiting and selection of salesmen; training of salesmen; supervision and control of salesmen; planning; communications. Here's a look at each one in detail:

Recruiting and Selection

The district manager recruits salesman candidates and conducts the preliminary interviewing, screening, testing, and selection. Guidance comes from headquarters in the form of tests and reference procedures, but the final approval is mostly left to the field.

This has become the generally accepted practice because it's usually a long way to headquarters and therefore difficult and costly to get candidates in for interview. Also, the need is usually for a man who knows something of local conditions. Moreover, companies feel that if a district manager is going to work with a salesman constantly he'll feel a lot closer to the man if he selects him himself.

So it's important that the district manager have skill in the selection of men, that he know how to reduce his own prejudices and follow intelligently the personnel signposts which the company has put up to guide him.

Training

In the leading marketing-minded companies, the district manager always has a part in giving new men their initial training in product knowledge, company policies, territory orientations, planning and organization of work, and sales techniques. The supervisor continuously trains both new and experienced salesmen in attitudes, skills, and interpretation of company policies. One of his chief training instruments is the sales meeting. The tendency is to localize these meetings instead of holding big sessions at headquarters.

Marketing-minded companies today are emphasizing the importance of the training function. Says John M. Wilson, vice-president of sales for National Cash Register:

With us, the training and motivating of others is perhaps the most vital function of sales management. Each salesman is first taught to cast himself in the role of his own sales manager.

He must manage his territory. He must organize, plan, and put into action the same job functions at his level as his sales manager does at a higher level. He must also market-research his product. He starts that function at the junior level when he is assigned subjects for presentation at branch meetings. When he is promoted to senior salesman, he will direct a junior salesman who is working for him. He comes early to recognize that his ultimate success depends on his ability to select and train men and to multiply his efforts by the number of men employed.

Supervision and Control

In today's selling picture, the district manager is no longer a lead salesman or working manager as he often was in the past. He is an executive whose efforts are devoted to multiplying himself many-fold—in the salesmen he supervises.

Good direction starts with good planning. A good district manager helps a salesman plan intelligent coverage of his territory, which means effective and economical allocation of his time.

"Some salesmen allocate 70 or 80 per cent of their time to prospects which produce 15 per cent of the business," says Robert Baumann of Cresap, McCormick and Paget. "The supervisor must correct this and show the salesman how to do it right.

"Then there's the matter of planning strategy with the individual customer company. 'Must we wait for the Superdooper Corporation's stubborn purchasing agent to die?' the salesman may be asking himself. 'Should we wine and dine him? Or ask the sales manager to come out and help us sell him?' You've got to give him the answer. It's tough to teach strategy to a salesman, but you can do it if you show him how to think creatively. He's an intuitive type of guy."

There is a general tendency among all of the marketing-minded leaders to provide closer supervision by decreasing the number of salesmen the district manager has to supervise. The tendency is also to buttress the district manager with field experts in the technical aspects of the product or whatever specialty may be necessary in the territories being covered.

The average salesman doesn't organize his time, marketing executives say. For one thing, he doesn't make the necessary number of appointments and this wastes hours waiting around.

"The district manager must show the salesman how to put in the maximum time with his prospect," says George Butler, of Barrington Associates. "If he shows nine men how to save two hours a day, he saves a total of eighteen hours and justifies more than double his own time."

The district manager must hold meetings constantly, not for inspiration but for demonstration. This also maintains group morale.

Where the supervisor is too remote, the salesman begins to lose interest; he sees no evidence that his reports are read or his extra efforts appreciated. Where freedom of operation sounded fine to begin with, it quickly begins to pall.

The district manager is the intermediary with management. He is management's spokesman but he is also the defender of the salesman against unreasonable quotas. He is father confessor and adviser-in-chief. One day he may be saving a marriage and the next day giving a cold, scientific analysis of some new electronics development.

Intelligent and conscientious supervision is essential despite the need for more independent action by the salesman. For example, exceptional volume does not always indicate good performance. It may mean the salesman is milking his territory instead of building it up. He may be overselling customers with limited potential or opening too many new accounts. These things take analysis and correction.

The district manager must help a man see and correct his own weaknesses. Good appraisal goes along with development, and it is up to the district manager to rate his men on their merits. In the most progressive systems, rating is directly related to compensation. Compensation is an intricate subject but one of the best ways of motivating a salesman is to pay him properly and intelligently.

The district manager is the only member of management whom the salesman sees regularly. So it's important that he be sufficiently well informed from the top to interpret company policy.

Planning

Planning enters into everything the district manager does.

Centralized planning higher up in the marketing division is providing more of a framework for him to work in. But, planning on a local level continues to be important—planning of salesmen's coverage, strategy, company quotas, sales goals and, today, even profits.

The district manager now participates in setting up quotas and sales goals. In the Ditto Company, sales supervisors even participate in working out the profit goals for the year. Each branch (smallest company division) turns in its own profit-and-loss statement. Based partly on information from the field, long-term profit objectives worked out at company headquarters are then broken down to allocate dollar volume for each branch. Then branch and division manager agree upon dollar volume by product line and an estimate of net profit for the year is reached.

Although actual territories are determined at headquarters, the district manager must help "cut to fit." He must determine the adequacy of manpower and personnel planning and answer such questions as:

How old are the men?

When will some need replacing?

Who will replace them?

He must plan the coordination of advertising campaigns, promotion, and sales for best timing to get the most out of each.

Last, but not least, he must plan his own time between office administration, on-the-job training, field sales, and the supervision of salesmen, lest he find himself in a time bind.

Communications

Every company has its own system of communications within its sales organization—manuals, brochures, bulletins, meetings, and conferences. Communications between district manager and salesmen becomes a function of good supervision. There is, however, another type of communications, in which the salesmen and their supervisor pass market information back to the top planners in the marketing division.

"With all this topside planning we're doing today in marketing, you can develop an ivory tower viewpoint," says Watson Snyder, a partner in Booz, Allen and Hamilton, management consultants. "The field men can give some wonderful clues to top planners if communications are properly set up. You can make a two-way deal out of this marketing concept.

"The sales supervisor sends in an estimate, broken down as to his territory. At headquarters, it's assembled and measured against the potential and against business conditions. The final resolution is a compromise. Marketing research makes a general survey as to the number of customers and the nature of the market; it's up to the field sales force to individualize and particularize."

"The salesman must gather word on the individual prospects," says Mr. Baumann. "We must answer the question, 'Why are we getting only 10 per cent of the customer's order?' He should have a plan to get part of the remaining 90 per cent.

"Marketing research can develop certain basic indicators. It can show that a plant making axles should be buying so and so many of our widgets each year. But it's up to the salesman to tell why it isn't. This may seem obvious but time after time in our work we develop completely convincing evidence that the salesmen are in error in calculating the customer's usage of their product.

"Certainly, the salesman is not responsible for developing detailed factual data on prospective products," Mr. Baumann admits. "But he should report on new and modified uses of the products and report back on customer suggestion. These fellows can determine the feasible quota for the individual customer and get the data for setting the goal. But you must begin at the bottom to get the data to set the goals."

"The importance of good information from the field is illustrated in the case of a widely known farm machinery company," says William E. Hill of William E. Hill & Company, management consultants. "With the step-up in the size of farm units, the farmer came to require a more advanced and complex type of machinery. The manufacturer had always provided a well engineered product line and had a good dealer distribution system. Then the company found that the dealers—and the field sales force as well—were missing the accelerated change in product requirements. Two things had to be done:

"1. The company's engineering was stepped up to meet the changes; an advanced engineering group was set up to work three to five years ahead on user requirements.

"2. The sales organization was directed to greater coverage of the end user to be sure he was sold on the new stuff, and to be sure he was finding the changes.

"This meant changing the whole set-up for supervisors—and salesmen as well—and revamping the whole information—reporting system. As a result, the company is doing very well in a difficult industry."

Not only does headquarters want information on customer reactions but it wants all possible intelligence on the competition. Information such as this:

"We lost Blank Company's order because the competition gave a 10 per cent cooperative advertising allowance. This is killing us," or,

"The competition is market-testing a new package. Looks as though it would cut into our business."

It's up to the supervisor to take the responsibility for sending samples to the home office.

The Man

Although each of the five basic parts of the district manager's job will carry different weight in different companies, today's new sophisticated customer sets one universal standard which sales direction must meet.

The days when selling was a matter of pushing or even bludgeoning the prospect into buying are gone. Business today has discovered, as Edward C. Bursk, professor of business administration at the Harvard Business School, has said, that the prospect carries a hidden resource in himself; he likes to buy provided he has a chance to trust and respect the seller. This can only happen if he feels he is being allowed to consider the proposition fairly and rationally.

This has led to what is known as low pressure selling.

"Low pressure selling requires men of high caliber," says Mr. Bursk, "and men of high caliber cannot use high pressure selling."

So the district manager must be a man of high caliber. He must also have considerable managerial skill.

"The sales supervisor must direct people in a delicate, intangible thing—how to use their minds and emotions, their whole being, in fact—to sell someone," says John Sargent of Cresap, McCormick and Paget. "They are managing people's thinking."

Arthur Dougall, of Steward, Dougall and Associates, management consultants, explains how this broad general description can be sharpened to meet an individual company's needs:

"We go into the market to find out what kind of a salesman the company needs. The market situation also determines the kind of supervision required—and the caliber and character of that supervision."

Once the need is known a long-term plan is essential.

"Start out first by looking at your organization and then decide what you are going to need in supervisors," one management consultant advises. "One approach is through use of the manning table—to see what jobs will open up. In sales, you also need a manning table to find out how many supervisors you'll need and when.

"If the manning tables are well drawn up, you'll know several months in advance when you are going to need a new supervisor. But the planning must be done on a five-year basis, at least, if the program is to be carried out effectively."

Such planning will avoid the twin headaches of having either too few promotable people—or too many.

"Many a good salesman has been ruined by being made a supervisor when he doesn't have the aptitude," says Mr. Dougall. "Such a man should remain a salesman—with appropriate rewards, of course."

On the other hand:

"A company must consider whether it's building dissatisfaction into its organization by hiring men who are all potential supervisors," says Mr. Finkel. "Some managements may not be able to advance the men fast enough to keep them happy.

"Other managements—in fast-growing companies—may feel that they can find a place for all the executives they can develop. They will want every man to be a potential supervisor."

After the needs are determined, a company needs to fill the pipeline with enough people of the right kind.

A quick way to determine what kind of people are right for an individual company is an analysis of present salesmen and supervisors. Some companies have gotten a lot of help from intelligent use of selection tests. To validate the tests, they are given to successful salesmen and to those not so successful. This enables the company to set up a grading system. If the test indicates that a man is likely to be a good career salesman, he can be advanced in direct selling.

If it shows he has aptitude for administration, several other tests are available.

Asked to number the selection methods they use for sales supervisor, the executives responding to the AMA questionnaire gave these answers:

Recommendations of the salesman's immediate superior

Multiple interviews with company sales executives

Merit rating results

Sales record

Watson Snyder lists the selection methods his company uses:

1. Examine the man's record. What has he done in selling? What has he done in the community? What is the sum total of the man's activities?

2. An evaluation of the man by people who work with him and people in a supervisory position over him.

3. Personnel tests. They're good if wisely used in conjunction with other means of evaluation.

4. Interview the man.

"Our feeling is that if certain traits are confirmed by all four methods, it's pretty certain we're correct," Mr. Snyder says.

The information resulting from these inquiries will provide a basis to appraise the man's managerial aptitudes. These aptitudes are of two basic kinds:

What He Is

Drive
Qualities of character and maturity
Planning ability (analytical)
Leadership
Initiative
Effectiveness as a personal salesman

What He Knows

Knowledge of products
Understanding of advertising and promotion
Understanding of distribution methods, trends that are taking place
Selling techniques (If he's coming from outside, it should be in a similar field.)
Knowledge of customers in the particular field
Understanding of administrative and sales control techniques

When they were asked what personal qualities they look for in a potential supervisor, the 104 sales executives answering the AMA questionnaire gave pretty much these same answers.

The Training

The big problem today is training the supervisor after he's selected. And a startlingly large number of companies have suddenly come to the realization that they just haven't been doing it.

"If you fail to train the sales supervisor correctly when he starts up the ladder," says Mr. Finkel, "you're going to have an executive who will have gaps in his management know-how all the way up the line. It'll be like a kid trying to do higher mathematics without fractions.

"This is the big jump.

"A lot of men get the bends. You can't pull him out of the water too fast; you've got to put him through a process of decompression."

As a salesman, he's had little opportunity to find how his sales supervisor works by observing the supervisor in action. It's not like learning a job in the office or factory.

It is not enough to tell a man "You're a supervisor now," and send him out to supervise. He needs training in a lot of new things. Occasionally, he has to sell and teach selling. But his most important responsibility is to multiply himself in other salesmen. A consensus of management consultants and sales executives in some of the leading companies yields this list of approved training areas:

1. *Indoctrination.* This includes:

Instruction: Providing a full understanding of the job and methods of operation—the man's responsibilities, what he does.

Teaching him the use of tools: Control reports and reports on his own and his men's performances.

Planning: He should be indoctrinated into the best use of his time and that of his men.

2. *On-the-job training.* This is the most effective.

3. *Follow-up and review* of performance on the job, including refresher meetings.

When they were asked, "What methods do you find most effective in orientation training for sales supervisors?" sales executives who already have training courses answered: Home office meetings; regional meetings; lectures; role playing; job rotation; trial runs during supervisors' vacations; university and association courses.

It is significant that when they were asked what methods they liked for "continuous training," the answers were practically the same.

Most of the leading management experts cap their lists with "guided experience"—the method by which top executives train their subordinates by means of special assignment, day-to-day work contacts, and departmental problems. Guided experience rests on two accepted precepts: that the best way to learn is by doing and that the development is most effective when it takes place under the guidance of an able and sympathetic superior.

All of these devices are methods of learning to work better with people, and business is people.

Topic Index

Name Index